VOLUME FIVE

ADVANCES IN TRANSPORT POLICY AND PLANNING

Policy Implications of Autonomous Vehicles

EUROPEAN COOPERATION IN SCIENCE & TECHNOLOGY

Funded by the Horizon 2020 Framework Programme of the European Union

This publication is based upon work from COST Action Wider Impacts and Scenario Evaluation of Autonomous and Connected Transport, supported by COST (European Cooperation in Science and Technology).
www.cost.eu

VOLUME FIVE

ADVANCES IN TRANSPORT POLICY AND PLANNING

Policy Implications of Autonomous Vehicles

Edited by

DIMITRIS MILAKIS

Institute of Transport Research, German Aerospace Center (DLR), Berlin, Germany

NIKOLAS THOMOPOULOS

Department of Tourism and Transport, School of Hospitality and Tourism Management, University of Surrey, Guildford, United Kingdom

BERT VAN WEE

Faculty of Technology, Policy and Management, Delft University of Technology, Delft, The Netherlands

ELSEVIER

ACADEMIC PRESS

An imprint of Elsevier

Academic Press is an imprint of Elsevier
50 Hampshire Street, 5th Floor, Cambridge, MA 02139, United States
525 B Street, Suite 1650, San Diego, CA 92101, United States
The Boulevard, Langford Lane, Kidlington, Oxford OX5 1GB, United Kingdom
125 London Wall, London, EC2Y 5AS, United Kingdom

First edition 2020

ISBN: 978-0-12-820191-6
ISSN: 2543-0009

For information on all Academic Press publications
visit our website at https://www.elsevier.com/books-and-journals

Publisher: Zoe Kruze
Acquisitions Editor: Sam Mahfoudh
Editorial Project Manager: Shellie Bryant
Production Project Manager: James Selvam
Cover Designer: Alan Studholme

Typeset by SPi Global, India

Contents

Contributors

Jan Anne Annema
Delft University of Technology, Faculty of Technology, Policy and Management, Delft, Netherlands

Constantinos Antoniou
Chair of Transportation Systems Engineering, Department of Civil, Geo, and Environmental Engineering, Technical University of Munich, Munich, Germany

Torkel Bjørnskau
Department of Safety, Security and Environment, Norwegian Centre for Transport Research/Institute of Transport Economics TØI, Oslo, Norway

Reanne Boersma
Transport & Planning, Faculty of Civil Engineering and Geosciences, Delft University of Technology, Delft, The Netherlands

Emmanouil Chaniotakis
MaaSLab, Energy Institute, University College London, London, United Kingdom

Scott Cohen
School of Hospitality and Tourism Management, University of Surrey, United Kingdom

Federico Costantini
Department of Law, University of Udine, Udine, Italy

Angela Curl
Department of Population Health, University of Otago Christchurch, Dunedin, New Zealand

Patrícia de Carvalho Baptista
IN+ Center for Innovation, Technology and Policy Research, Instituto Superior Técnico, University of Lisbon, Lisbon, Portugal

Tomás de J. Mateo Sanguino
Higher Technical School of Engineering, University of Huelva, Huelva, Spain

Jonas De Vos
Bartlett School of Planning, University College London, London, United Kingdom

Ebru Dogan
VEDECOM Institute, Versailles, France

Hadi Ghaderi
Department of Business Technology and Entrepreneurship, Swinburne Business School, Swinburne University of Technology, Hawthorn, VIC, Australia

Moshe Givoni
Tel Aviv University, Tel Aviv-Yafo, Israel

Marjan P. Hagenzieker
Transport & Planning, Faculty of Civil Engineering and Geosciences, Delft University of Technology, Delft, The Netherlands

Jérôme Härri
Communication Systems Department, EURECOM, Sophia-Antipolis, France

Daniël D. Heikoop
Transport & Planning, Faculty of Civil Engineering and Geosciences, Delft University of Technology, Delft, The Netherlands

Eva Heinen
Institute for Transport Studies, University of Leeds, Leeds, United Kingdom

Christos Katrakazas
Department of Transportation Planning and Engineering, National Technical University of Athens, Athens, Greece; Chair of Transportation Systems Engineering, Department of Civil, Geo, and Environmental Engineering, Technical University of Munich, Munich, Germany

Simon Kimber
School of Hospitality and Tourism Management, University of Surrey, United Kingdom

Tatiana Kováčiková
Department of International Research Projects, University of Žilina, Žilina, Slovakia

Rémy Le Boennec
VEDECOM Institute, Versailles, France

José M. Lozano Domínguez
Higher Technical School of Engineering, University of Huelva, Huelva, Spain

Giuseppe Lugano
Department of International Research Projects, University of Žilina, Žilina, Slovakia

Dimitris Milakis
Institute of Transport Research, German Aerospace Center (DLR), Berlin, Germany

Miloš N. Mladenović
Aalto University, Espoo, Finland

Santhanakrishnan Narayanan
Chair of Transportation Systems Engineering, Department of Civil, Geo, and Environmental Engineering, Technical University of Munich, Munich, Germany

J. Pablo Nuñez Velasco
Transport & Planning, Faculty of Civil Engineering and Geosciences, Delft University of Technology, Delft, The Netherlands

Daniela Paddeu
University of the West of England, Bristol, United Kingdom

Kate Pangbourne
University of Leeds, Leeds, United Kingdom

George Papastefanatos
Information Management Systems Institute (IMSI), "Athena" Research Center, Athens, Greece

Graham Parkhurst
University of the West of England, Bristol, United Kingdom

Baiba Pudāne
Department of Engineering Systems and Services, Delft University of Technology, Delft, The Netherlands

Lauren Siegel
School of Hospitality and Tourism Management, University of Surrey, United Kingdom

Patrick A. Singleton
Department of Civil and Environmental Engineering, Utah State University, Logan, UT, United States

Dominic Stead
Delft University of Technology, Delft, The Netherlands

Fabro Steibel
Institute for Technology and Society of Rio de Janeiro, Rio de Janeiro, Brazil

Athanasios Theofilatos
Transport and Urban Planning Group, School of Architecture, Building, and Civil Engineering, Loughborough University, Leicestershire, United Kingdom

Nikolas Thomopoulos
Department of Tourism and Transport, School of Hospitality and Tourism Management, University of Surrey, Guildford, United Kingdom

Bert van Wee
Faculty of Technology, Policy and Management, Delft University of Technology, Delft, The Netherlands

Preface

Dimitris Milakis[a], Nikolas Thomopoulos[b], Bert van Wee[c]
[a]Institute of Transport Research, German Aerospace Center (DLR), Berlin, Germany
[b]Department of Tourism and Transport, School of Hospitality and Tourism Management, University of Surrey, Guildford, United Kingdom
[c]Faculty of Technology, Policy and Management, Delft University of Technology, Delft, The Netherlands

1. Autonomous vehicles: From research to policy

Autonomous vehicles (AVs) constitute a contemporary key area of research and development as reflected by the significant funds currently invested globally. According to the SAE (Society of Automotive Engineers) International taxonomy, in the highest levels of vehicle automation, an automated driving system is expected to perform all dynamic tasks of driving in certain (SAE level 4) or in all conditions (SAE level 5) (SAE International, 2018). In the lower levels of vehicle automation, a human should be available to take control of the vehicle (SAE level 3) or to monitor the driving environment while one is assisted to perform the lateral or/and longitudinal motion control of the vehicle (SAE levels 1 and 2). Yet, even these standards are being revised and updated to reflect the continuous need for shared learning and adaptation based on AV trials, such as SAE-J3018™ which was originally established in 2015 and updated in late 2019 (SAE International, 2019).

Large automotive companies have been envisaging vehicle automation technology for passenger transport to be available shortly after 2020, although they have indeed revised their early optimistic predictions about having fully automated vehicles on public roads by 2020 (Walker, 2020) and are currently exploring viable business models. Moreover, the COVID-19 pandemic seem to have accelerated development and use of certain forms of vehicle automation for supporting front-line health care (e.g., by delivering medical supplies to hospitals or elderly groups) and controlling the spread of the corona virus (e.g., by disinfecting public spaces), while the discussion about a significant modal shift from airplanes (i.e., short to mid-range trips) to automated vehicles has recently intensified (Rice, 2020).

In this context, research focus has been, so far, predominantly on the development of the hardware (e.g., sensors) and software (e.g., path planning algorithms) technology associated with different levels of vehicle automation (Gandia et al., 2019), particularly since it has been established that the role of hardware has been declining in contrast to the role of software within the transport sector (Thomopoulos et al., 2015). Moreover, the perception that AVs will bring mainly a change to vehicle performance led researchers to explore primarily the short-term implications for traffic flow, road safety and fuel efficiency (Milakis et al., 2017). More recently, "softer" implications of AVs for travel behavior, accessibility, culture, digital divide, health, land use, and social equity have attracted the attention of the research community, acknowledging the possibility of longer term unanticipated (Mladenović, 2019) socio-technical changes because of this emerging mobility technology (Cohn et al., 2019; Curl and Fitt, 2019; Gelauff et al., 2019; Milakis, 2019; Milakis et al., 2018; Milakis and van Wee, 2019; Soteropoulos et al., 2019; Thomopoulos and Givoni, 2015; Whittle et al., 2019; Zhang and Guhathakurta, 2018). Several scholars argue for more active governance of smart mobility ensuring and enhancing public value (i.e., maximizing individual benefits such as access to opportunities, while ensuring inclusive distribution of such benefits and minimizing adverse impacts to the environment and public health) (Docherty et al., 2018; Lyons, 2018; Pangbourne et al., 2020). Research results in all fields indicate that both short- and long-term implications of AVs are expected to be significant, including possible adverse effects for social and environmental sustainability. Moreover, such implications could vary substantially among different countries because of differences in urban form and size of cities, transport networks, travel patterns, governance structures but also due to socio-demographic, cultural and climate factors (Rode et al., 2017).

Despite this rather clear indication and the associated high public interest, policy developments in terms of type, extent, combination and timing of policy responses in this field are still at an early stage (Cohen and Cavoli, 2019; Fraedrich et al., 2018; Milakis, 2019). This might reflect the adoption of a technology driven deployment path for AVs associated with deep uncertainty about possible implications, leaving no or limited space for policy intervention (Taeihagh and Lim, 2019) that could steer deployment of AVs toward desirable, acceptable and sustainable transition as highlighted by *WISE-ACT*[a] outputs. Consequently, planners tend to adopt a reactionary "watch and wait" approach regarding AVs integration that could risk social and environmental sustainability (Legacy et al., 2019). According to Stayton and Stilgoe (2020), even the widely used SAE International

[a]Wider Impacts and Scenario Evaluation of Autonomous and Connected Transport COST Action CA16222: https://www.wise-act.eu.

taxonomy of AV levels (SAE International, 2018) reflects a technologically-centered approach describing the extent that an autonomous driving system can replace a human task. These researchers suggest that for policymakers and the public the technical capabilities of automated vehicles are not so important themselves, as the policies needed so that such vehicles offer safer, more equitable and effective transport system.

This book volume systematically reviews policy relevant implications of AVs and the associated possible policy responses. It comprises 13 chapters discussing: (a) short-term implications of AVs for traffic flow (Chapter 1), human-automated bus systems interaction (Chapter 2), cyber-security and safety (Chapter 3), cyber-security certification and auditing (Chapter 4), non-commuting journeys (Chapter 5); (b) long-term implications of AVs for carbon dioxide (CO_2) emissions and energy (Chapter 6), health and well-being (Chapter 7), data protection (Chapter 8), ethics (Chapter 9), governance (Chapter 10); (c) implications of AVs for the maritime industry (Chapter 11) and urban deliveries (Chapter 12), and (d) overall synthesis and conclusions (Chapter 13).

The book has been initiated within the Action CA16222 of the European Cooperation in Science and Technology (COST) entitled "Wider Impacts and Scenario Evaluation of Autonomous and Connected Transport" (WISE-ACT[a]). WISE-ACT has offered a unique platform for knowledge exchange and collaboration among multiple researchers from different countries with diverse backgrounds and expertise to explore relevant policy implications of AVs and identify required policy developments at global level.

In the following section, we present an overview of the 13 book chapters included in this book volume, starting with the short-term implications of AVs (Section 2.1), followed by the long-term implications of AVs (Section 2.2), the implications of AVs for the maritime and freight industry (Section 2.3) and the overall synthesis and conclusions (Section 2.4).

2. Overview of the book chapters

2.1 Short-term implications of AVs

In the first five chapters, the focus is on the short-term implications of AVs for traffic flow (Chapter 1), human-automated bus systems interaction (Chapter 2), cyber-security and safety (Chapter 3), cyber-security certification and auditing (Chapter 4), and non-commuting journeys (Chapter 5).

Narayanan et al. (2020) (Chapter 1) identify 19 factors that influence traffic flow efficiency implications of AVs: acceleration/deceleration profile, lane changing rule, longitudinal driving behavior, presence of connectivity between AVs, desired and safe gap, vehicle type (e.g., electric and internal combustion engine), penetration rate, value of travel time, induced demand, network topology, vehicle distribution in a link, implemented optimization function, type of system (e.g., private and shared), congestion pricing scheme, dedicated lane for CAVs and AVs, intersection control method, parking management, platoon size and presence of VSL. The authors group these into four categories: (i) vehicle characteristics, (ii) travel behavior, (iii) network characteristics, and (iv) policies. The expected impacts of autonomous vehicles on the roadway capacity are found to be not at all unanimous, not only because of different assumptions with respect to these factors, but also because of differences in modeling conditions. Despite the wide range in quantitative estimates of AVs on road capacity, the authors conclude that AVs have the potential to increase the capacity of roads, and therefore reduce congestion levels and travel times. But in the initial stage of introduction, due to the low penetration rates, traffic efficiency may be lower than the capacity of the current system. And due to the lower value of time AVs will induce demand, and induced demand might offset efficiency gains. The authors argue that policy makers should enact laws to ensure connectivity between AVs to experience significant benefits, integrate CAVs with public transport to avoid mode shifts, incentivize ridesharing to reduce network load, develop suitable parking management policies to avoid empty relocations and introduce congestion pricing to curb induced demand. A major limitation of the several reviewed studies relates to the assumptions for the parameters used in the modeling systems.

Heikoop et al. (2020) (Chapter 2) explore the following questions: (1) What is known about human interaction with automated bus systems? (2) Which methodologies are being used in research regarding the interaction between humans and automated bus systems? (3) What research gaps exist? (4) Which policy implications can be derived so far? Answers to the questions are: (1) the perceived usefulness of the automated bus system did not appear to be a primary determinant for its users. Public acceptance of automated bus systems is generally positive. People appear to have a high level of trust in the automated bus system, (2) questionnaires are the most used means of method for conducting experiments in relation to user acceptance or satisfaction, and (3) an important gap in literature is the lack of objective measures used for the assessment of human interaction with automated bus systems. Another gap follows from the fact that current busses drive at relatively low speeds. Therefore, there is a lack of insights into how people would interact and experience automated bus systems when they would be driving at regular speeds. A third gap is that it is not clear if infrastructure adjustments are needed for automated busses. (4) The paper addresses several policy implications, related to, among others, control allocation—when and in what situations must humans take over control; communications with vulnerable road users, the courtesy problem and communication with other drivers, the "second vehicle problem"—AVs are not prepared and will not respond appropriately when other road users deviate from the formal rules. In addition, the general wait-and-see attitude of planners need to change into a more proactive approach from public planners and authorities when deploying AVs such as automated bus systems are implemented in real-life traffic.

Cyber-security features among the highly important challenges of AV. Katrakazas et al. (2020) (Chapter 3) focus largely on software issues linking these with safety and cyber-security. Through a review of numerous academic papers, they provide a valuable overview of road safety challenges. Their approach adopts a robotics (i.e., vehicle based data) and transport engineering (i.e., collision probability perspective). Other issues identified in the literature such as human factors are also mentioned, although as elements of these two fundamental viewpoints. Cyber-security challenges are disaggregated in physical threats, safety impacts and assessment or mitigation actions. Relevant frameworks and standards are presented, offering detailed scenarios to illustrate risks in each case. Software and hardware vulnerabilities are equally important, so they conclude by offering promising recommendations. For example, they suggest the evolution of an international collaborative directory linking cyber-security liabilities with passenger and traffic safety concerns, highlighting the value of large multi-disciplinary networks such as COST Actions, e.g., WISE-ACT. Regulating such a directory within a global framework is clearly a challenge, but could introduce significant benefits (Taeihagh and Lim, 2019). Nonetheless, a lot more AV miles need to be self-driven until such an international agreement is reached based on contemporary experience of individual development of various key AV components worldwide.

AVs need a number of sensors, access technologies and the Internet to intelligently and rapidly interact with infrastructure, people and/or cloud services in a complex and interconnected ecosystem. A large part of sensors and devices that connect to the Internet, or to each other, have neither security nor the possibility of adding it. This approach is widely known and exploited by cybercriminals, who seek harm and profit indiscriminately.

Therefore, protecting data and systems from possible external intrusions is one of the main challenges nowadays. The systematic literature review of Mateo Sanguino et al. (2020) (Chapter 4) on cyber-security shows that the risk of adding automation to vehicles has not been properly understood by car manufacturers in the past and it is a serious problem just as the insecure vehicular connectivity is being addressed nowadays. Most cars use components that are based on old hardware and software developed years ago and with basic flaws inherent to design, so errors and vulnerabilities are transferred to these new generation of vehicles. The authors state that a collaborative approach in the automotive industry may be required to overcome the investments in time, money and broader organizational changes. Cybercrime as a Service (CaaS) could generate millions in losses to the automotive industry, justifying new approaches of cyber-security applied to the automobile industry, which must be flexible and adaptive along the production chain and the lifetime of CAVs.

Kimber et al. (2020) (Chapter 5) present a state-of-the-art review (Grant and Booth, 2009) on the implications of AVs for non-commuting journeys, including those for leisure, tourism, shopping and visiting friends and relatives. The review follows the PRISMA (Preferred Reporting Items for Systematic Reviews and Meta-Analyses) guidelines to identify relevant literature and subsequently present the outcomes of a qualitative synthesis of 48 articles. The authors suggest that academic literature on AVs is skewed toward commuting journeys in the urban metropoles of the Global North. They identified four key themes in their review. First, public interest in AVs for leisure might exceed that for commuting, while user requirements could be different for leisure than commuting journeys (e.g., because of the required equipment) influencing AV design. Second, sharing might be less likely for AVs non-commuting journeys because of differences in the sociality of leisure trips (e.g., silence among strangers is accepted in commuter journeys, whereas social and recreational trips often involve multiple passengers socializing). Third, some non-commuting journeys will require a lower level of automation (e.g., level 4 AVs operating within defined routes and under specific conditions: zoos, airport shuttles, urban sightseeing routes). Fourth, non-commuting journeys by AVs could involve spatial impacts (e.g., reduced need for parking space in and around schools). The authors call for more policy attention to non-commuting journeys in the AVs context including Global South. They suggest that policy and regulation focus on preserving equity, privacy and safety for shared AVs serving leisure travel and promoting infrastructure changes needed as a response to the spatio-temporal patterns of leisure activities.

2.2 Long-term implications of AVs

In the next five chapters, the focus is on the long-term implications of AVs for carbon dioxide (CO_2) emissions and energy (Chapter 6), health and well-being (Chapter 7), data protection (Chapter 8), ethics (Chapter 9), and governance (Chapter 10).

Annema (2020) (Chapter 6) explores through a literature review the potential of highly automated vehicles (AVs) to reduce carbon dioxide (CO_2) emissions in the future. The review follows a four-step approach exploring sequentially the relationship between AVs and CO_2 emissions, the interaction between AV development and battery electric vehicles (BEV) development, and the effects of AVs on vehicle kilometers traveled (VKT). In the last step the policy implications are discussed. The results show that highly automated vehicles could decrease CO_2 emission per kilometer driven through more efficient vehicle operation, vehicle design, electrification and platooning. Yet, on-board vehicle subsystems (e.g., additional ICT equipment) would possibly limit CO_2 emission benefits. Additionally, a growth in VKT because of AVs could balance out decreases of CO_2 emissions due to more efficient vehicle operation. Therefore, the net energy and CO_2 emission balance for AVs seems, at its best, to be neutral, but is probably negative. However, the potentially accelerating role of AVs in relation to the uptake of electric vehicles could have the biggest impact on the CO_2 emissions per kilometer driven, but this accelerating role in the uptake of electric technology remains uncertain. Thus, the author suggests that policies promoting alternative vehicle propulsion systems other than fossil fuel technologies seem most effective at the moment, which is aligned with contemporary literature stressing the need for "green" energy powering EVs (Kougias et al., 2020). Additional measures such as energy taxes, AV maximum speed limits as well as policies to curb the growth of VKTs could put in place to ensure further energy and emissions related benefits as soon as the adoption of electric AVs progresses.

Singleton et al. (2020) (Chapter 7) discuss potential health and well-being implications of AVs. The authors apply a deductive approach. They first review the transportation system effects on multiple dimensions of health and well-being (i.e., safety, travel satisfaction, access to activities, physical activity, air pollution and noise) as well as possible AV effects on travel behavior. Then, they combine these insights to deduce potential positive, negative, and unknown effects of AVs on health/well-being. The authors argue that AVs could lead to more automobile travel because of possibly more and longer person trips by car (though this is still uncertain, as they note) and modal shifts away from current modes to their more attractive (but also more travel-distance-intensive, for example, because of empty trips) AV counterparts (e.g., for public transport to pooled AVs). Consequently, they suggest that AVs are likely to have overall positive impacts on some health and well-being aspects (safety, travel satisfaction, access to activities) and overall negative impacts on others (physical activity), while effects are more uncertain for other topics (urban built environments, air and noise pollution). They propose an evolving systems approach to explore the multitude of potential impacts of AVs on health and well-being and conclude with policy implications (e.g., policies limiting possible negative effects of AVs such as reduced physically active travel, increased vehicle-distances traveled and urban sprawl) and future research (i.e., research questions, methods) to further explore such impacts.

Costantini et al. (2020) (Chapter 8) present a mapping review of existing legal frameworks and regulations governing mobility data management, AV trials, as well as data generated through new mobility services (e.g., ride-hailing) in Austria, Brazil, Greece, Italy, New Zealand, Slovakia, and Switzerland to assess policy challenges of AV deployment and the deriving data management and protection implications. The review was based on a survey questionnaire distributed among experts (WISE-ACT members) in the field in each of these selected seven countries. According to the review results, most countries have adopted GDPR (General Data Protection Regulation, Regulation (EU) 2016/679), or similar type of legislation for data management and protection, yet only two out of the seven selected countries have in place some limited provisions regarding data generated through AV trials. Moreover, new mobility services (e.g., ride-hailing, e-scooter sharing) are compliant with GDPR requirements in only two out of the seven selected countries. Limited regulatory provisions have been identified for AV deployment in the freight sector. The authors conclude that data management and protection of AV data is still at a nascent stage, stressing the need for collaboration among stakeholders and countries on this topic (e.g., development of "regulatory sandboxes"). They also point to two emerging issues on data protection that will require further regulatory attention in the future: (1) the capability to "re-identify" originally anonymous data through AI or Big Data integration with those available publicly confirming that data is the currency of the 21st century and (2) the increasing autonomy of AVs and the legal status of such artificial agents.

Dogan et al. (2020) (Chapter 9) address an important topic surrounding AV, namely ethics and AV. It conducts a review of contemporary literature about AV and ethics, remaining focused on these issues and not on wider transport debates. Through a range of academic literature and relevant policy reports, they offer an outline of how existing ethical theories could be applied in AV. Consequentialist and utilitarianist, deontological, contractarianist and randomness theories are reviewed to provide essential context. This allows the authors to delve into the contrasting views regarding AV decisions in critical and forced-choice situations. However, Dogan et al. acknowledge that it is ordinary situations which would require more guidelines and policy making, rather than highly improbable and uncertain unavoidable accidents. This leads them to interesting conclusions which provide input for future policy making about this highly contentious topic.

Departing from a socio-technical systems perspective and governance cultures Mladenović et al. (2020) (Chapter 10) aim to help understand country-specific governance strategies and approaches for AVs. Based on document review, it presents a comparative analysis of AV-related policy documents in Finland, United Kingdom, and Germany, countries that promote the introduction of AVs. It focuses on the assumed roles for AVs, the identified domains and mechanisms of governance, and the assumed actors responsible for steering the development process. All three countries think that AVs should contribute to the national economic growth. In Finland, a key idea is that innovations should contribute to the long-term transition to knowledge economy. The United Kingdom and German positions AVs in the context of global leadership in technological development. Key themes for governance include liability, public experiments, and data management. Actors on which governance strategies focus are drivers (which can also be an external operator), experts and citizens. All three countries take a neutral stance toward the meaning of technology. An important conclusion is governance do not see citizens as equal partners in steering technological futures, but only as an actor that can potentially resist new technology. Another important conclusion is that all three governance approaches have an underlying premise that risks are problems to be managed, without recognizing potentially unanticipated consequences, resulting in a potential threat of techno-determinism. Consequently technological development is not based on the democratic enhancement of dialog between state and society.

2.3 Implications of AVs for the maritime and freight industry

In the next two chapters, the focus is on the implications of AVs for the maritime industry (Chapter 11) and urban deliveries (Chapter 12).

Ghaderi (2020) (Chapter 11) addresses an often neglected mode of AVs, namely autonomous shipping. Through an extensive overview of key maritime projects and by referring to the unavoidable workforce challenges regarding maritime navigation, maintenance and specialized software updates in the future, Ghaderi offers an inclusive conventional literature review. This chapter highlights the need for a collaborative culture within this large diverse sector, in addition of the need to address cyber-security and data management concerns identified also within other chapters (e.g., Chapter 8 by Costantini et al., 2020; Chapter 3 by Katrakazas et al., 2020). It achieves this by contrasting automation on sea and on land, namely at ports, where significant technological advances have been already realized during the past two decades. Servicing hazardous situations or conducting search and rescue operations could be clearly beneficial tasks fulfilled by autonomous vessels in the wider port area while significantly increasing human safety. Interestingly, this chapter concludes with a glimpse to the future linking technology adoption with market structure. Key policy recommendations include the need to focus on the co-ordination of regulations and standards internationally, while supporting workforce training to develop new skills in demand. Correlating autonomy level with industry maturity level is a further chapter contribution about this growing transport sector of high importance for global supply chains. Overall though, the challenges and opportunities faced by maritime transport resemble those faced by other transport sectors considering the adoption of AVs. A fundamental conclusion is that all stakeholders need to be taken into account when evaluating such new developments, similarly to Mladenović et al. (2020)—Chapter 10, safeguarding that appropriate mechanisms exist to compensate losers through the gains of winners.

Paddeu and Parkhurst (2020) (Chapter 12) focus on the prominent topic of urban deliveries, i.e., the freight and logistics sector, particularly first- and last-mile deliveries, which have received less attention by researchers to date. It provides an international overview of technologies such as pods and Unmanned Aerial Vehicles (UAVs), with a strong United Kingdom focus due to the high uptake of e-commerce in that country. Through a review of the roles of key stakeholders and the identification of key barriers, confirmed via United Kingdom workshops, it concludes with relevant policy recommendations such as the need for training and education of the workforce, consumers and the general public. Concerns include low co-ordination levels among stakeholders, low load factors, short-term cost increases, employment implications and urban planning issues such as sharing of public space, as well as privacy, safety and security. On the other hand, Chapter 12 offers a counter-intuitive suggestion, namely that UAVs may introduce a five-fold reduction of delivery costs despite the need for at least 15 UAVs to reach the load of a delivery van. Conclusions highlight the contemporary high uncertainty on a range of key factors due to lack of evidence and the need to test new business models within emerging regulatory frameworks among the key barriers of autonomous vehicles uptake for urban deliveries. Hence, it is pertinent to explore the wider impacts of transport automation and autonomous vehicles in a sector which has been seen among the forerunners of transport automation adoption.

2.4 Overall synthesis and conclusions

In the last chapter, van Wee et al. (2020) (Chapter 13) provide an overall synthesis and conclusions pertaining to the most important findings and policy implications of each of the chapters 1–12, and discuss future paths for policy making and research. It is concluded that (a) the policy implications of AVs suggested within each topic of this book volume are still relatively broad, (b) conceptually rich research seems to be more valuable for policy making, (c) context appears to be an important factor for the uptake, impacts, and specific system design characteristics of real world AV implementation, (d) research on the global south is not developed so far with respect to AVs, (e) AVs, shared vehicles and electric vehicles (EVs) could reinforce deployment of each other, and (f) AVs will induce wider societal implications (e.g. land use, accessibility, social exclusion, governmental expenditures, the labor market, and the environment), with more indirect effects being more difficult to understand. Regarding policy making, it is concluded that (a) more attention should be given to ethics, cyber security and data protection in the AVs era, (b) future investments in motorway networks might not be no-regret anymore, because of possible reductions in congestion and decreases in the marginal values of time due to AVs, and (c) countries that introduce AVs at a slower pace can learn a lot from the real world experiences elsewhere.

References

Annema, J.A., 2020. Policy implications of the potential carbon dioxide (CO_2) emission and energy impacts of highly automated vehicles. In: Milakis, D., Thomopoulos, N., van Wee, B. (Eds.), Policy Implications of Autonomous Vehicles. Elsevier, The Netherlands, pp. 149–162.

Cohen, T., Cavoli, C., 2019. Automated vehicles: exploring possible consequences of government (non)intervention for congestion and accessibility. Transp. Rev. 39 (1), 129–151.

Cohn, J., Ezike, R., Martin, J., Donkor, K., Ridgway, M., Balding, M., 2019. Examining the equity impacts of autonomous vehicles: a travel demand model approach. Transp. Res. Rec. 2673, 23–35.

Costantini, F., Thomopoulos, N., Steibel, F., Curl, A., Lugano, G., Kováčiková, T., 2020. Autonomous vehicles in a GDPR era: An international comparison. In: Milakis, D., Thomopoulos, N., van Wee, B. (Eds.), Policy Implications of Autonomous Vehicles. Elsevier, The Netherlands, pp. 191–213.

Curl, A., Fitt, H., 2019. Will driverless cars be good for us? Now is the time for public health to act together with urban and transport planning. J. Glob. Health 9 (2), 020303.

Docherty, I., Marsden, G., Anable, J., 2018. The governance of smart mobility. Transp. Res. A Policy Pract. 115, 114–125.

Dogan, E., Costantini, F., Le Boennec, R., 2020. Ethical issues concerning automated vehicles and their implications for transport. In: Milakis, D., Thomopoulos, N., van Wee, B. (Eds.), Policy Implications of Autonomous Vehicles. Elsevier, The Netherlands, pp. 215–233.

Fraedrich, E., Heinrichs, D., Bahamonde-Birke, F.J., Cyganski, R., 2018. Autonomous driving, the built environment and policy implications. Transp. Res. A Policy Pract. 122, 162–172.

Gandia, R.M., Antonialli, F., Cavazza, B.H., Neto, A.M., de Lima, D.A., Sugano, J.Y., Nicolai, I., Zambalde, A.L., 2019. Autonomous vehicles: scientometric and bibliometric review. Transp. Rev. 31 (1), 9–28.

Gelauff, G., Ossokina, I., Teulings, C., 2019. Spatial and welfare effects of automated driving: will cities grow, decline or both? Transp. Res. A Policy Pract. 121, 277–294.

Ghaderi, H., 2020. Wider implications of autonomous vessels for the maritime industry: mapping the unprecedented challenges. In: Milakis, D., Thomopoulos, N., van Wee, B. (Eds.), Policy Implications of Autonomous Vehicles. Elsevier, The Netherlands, pp. 263–289.

Grant, M.J., Booth, A., 2009. A typology of reviews: an analysis of 14 review types and associated methodologies. Health Inf. Libr. J. 26 (2), 91–108.

Heikoop, D.D., Nuñez Velasco, J.P., Boersma, R., Bjørnskau, T., Hagenzieker, M.P., 2020. Automated bus systems in Europe: a systematic review of passenger experience and road user interaction. In: Milakis, D., Thomopoulos, N., van Wee, B. (Eds.), Policy Implications of Autonomous Vehicles. Elsevier, The Netherlands, pp. 51–71.

Katrakazas, C., Theofilatos, A., Papastefanatos, G., Härri, J., Antoniou, C., 2020. Cyber security and its impact on CAV safety: overview, policy needs and challenges. In: Milakis, D., Thomopoulos, N., van Wee, B. (Eds.), Policy Implications of Autonomous Vehicles. Elsevier, The Netherlands, pp. 73–94.

Kimber, S., Siegel, L., Cohen, S., Thomopoulos, N., 2020. The wider use of autonomous vehicles in non-commuting journeys. In: Milakis, D., Thomopoulos, N., van Wee, B. (Eds.), Policy Implications of Autonomous Vehicles. Elsevier, The Netherlands, pp. 125–148.

Kougias, I., Nikitas, A., Thiel, C., Sándor Szabó, S., 2020. Clean energy and transport pathways for islands: a stakeholder analysis using Q method. Transp. Res. D Transp. Environ. 78, 102180.

Legacy, C., Ashmore, D., Scheurer, J., Stone, J., Curtis, C., 2019. Planning the driverless city. Transp. Rev. 39 (1), 84–102.

Lyons, G., 2018. Getting smart about urban mobility—aligning the paradigms of smart and sustainable. Transp. Res. A Policy Pract. 115, 4–14.

Mateo Sanguino, T.J.M., Domínguez, J.M.L., Baptista, P.d.C., 2020. Cybersecurity certification and auditing of automotive industry. In: Milakis, D., Thomopoulos, N., van Wee, B. (Eds.), Policy Implications of Autonomous Vehicles. Elsevier, The Netherlands, pp. 95–124.

Milakis, D., 2019. Long-term implications of automated vehicles: an introduction. Transp. Rev. 39 (1), 1–8.

Milakis, D., van Wee, B., 2019. Implications of vehicle automation for accessibility and social inclusion of people on low income, people with physical and sensory disabilities and older people. In: Antoniou, C., Efthymiou, D., Chaniotakis, M. (Eds.), Factors Affecting Emerging Transportation Systems. Modeling Adoption, Satisfaction and Mobility Patterns. Elsevier, The Netherlands.

Milakis, D., van Arem, B., van Wee, B., 2017. Policy and society related implications of automated driving: a review of literature and directions for future research. J. Intell. Transport. Syst. 21 (4), 324–348.

Milakis, D., Kroesen, M., van Wee, B., 2018. Implications of automated vehicles for accessibility and location choices: evidence from an expert-based experiment. J. Transp. Geogr. 68, 142–148.

Mladenović, M.N., 2019. How should we drive self-driving vehicles? Anticipation and collective imagination in planning mobility futures. In: Finger, M., Audouin, M. (Eds.), The Governance of Smart Transportation Systems. Springer Nature Switzerland AG, Switzerland, pp. 103–122.

Mladenović, M.N., Stead, D., Milakis, D., Pangbourne, K., Givoni, M., 2020. Governance cultures and sociotechnical imaginaries of self-driving vehicle technology: comparative analysis of Finland, UK and Germany. In: Milakis, D., Thomopoulos, N., van Wee, B. (Eds.), Policy Implications of Autonomous Vehicles. Elsevier, The Netherlands, pp. 235–262.

Narayanan, S., Chaniotakis, E., Antoniou, C., 2020. Factors affecting traffic flow efficiency implications of connected and autonomous vehicles: a review and policy recommendations. In: Milakis, D., Thomopoulos, N., van Wee, B. (Eds.), Policy Implications of Autonomous Vehicles. Elsevier, The Netherlands, pp. 1–50.

Paddeu, D., Parkhurst, G., 2020. The potential for automation to transform urban deliveries: drivers, barriers and policy priorities. In: Milakis, D., Thomopoulos, N., van Wee, B. (Eds.), Policy Implications of Autonomous Vehicles. Elsevier, The Netherlands, pp. 291–314.

Pangbourne, K., Mladenović, M.N., Stead, D., Milakis, D., 2020. Questioning mobility as a service: unanticipated implications for society and governance. Transp. Res. A Policy Pract. 131, 35–49.

Rice, S., 2020. While COVID-19 Batters the Airlines, Driverless Car Technology Marches on. Forbes.com, URL, https://www.forbes.com/sites/stephenrice1/2020/05/04/while-covid-19-batters-the-airlines-driverless-car-technology-marches-on/#4dc26323619e (Accessed 11.7.2020).

Rode, P., Floater, G., Thomopoulos, N., Docherty, J., Schwinger, P., Mahendra, A., Fang, W., 2017. Accessibility in cities: transport and urban form. In: Disrupting Mobility. Springer, Cham, pp. 239–273.

SAE International, 2018. Taxonomy and Definitions for Terms Related to Driving Automation Systems for on-Road Motor Vehicles (J3016). SAE, Warrendale, PA.

SAE International, 2019. Guidelines for Safe On-Road Testing of SAE Level 3, 4, and 5 Prototype Automated Driving Systems (ADS) (J3018_201909). Warrendale, PA.

Singleton, P.A., De Vos, J., Heinen, E., Pudāne, B., 2020. Potential health and well-being implications of autonomous vehicles. In: Milakis, D., Thomopoulos, N., van Wee, B. (Eds.), Policy Implications of Autonomous Vehicles. Elsevier, The Netherlands, pp. 163–190.

Soteropoulos, A., Berger, M., Ciari, F., 2019. Impacts of automated vehicles on travel behaviour and land use: an international review of modelling studies. Transp. Rev. 39, 29–49.

Stayton, E., Stilgoe, J., 2020. It's time to rethink levels of automation for self-driving vehicles. SSRN Electron. J. 2019 (2016), 391–397.

Taeihagh, A., Lim, H.S.M., 2019. Governing autonomous vehicles: emerging responses for safety, liability, privacy, cybersecurity, and industry risks. Transp. Rev. 39 (1), 103–128.

Thomopoulos, N., Givoni, M., 2015. The autonomous car—a blessing or a curse for the future of low carbon mobility? An exploration of likely vs. desirable outcomes. Eur. J. Futures Res. 3, 1–14.

Thomopoulos, N., Givoni, M., Rietveld, P., 2015. Transpoprt and ICT—chapter 1. In: ICT for Transport: Opportunities and Threats. Edward Elgar, Cheltenham.

van Wee, B., Milakis, D., Thomopoulos, N., 2020. Overall synthesis and conclusions. In: Milakis, D., Thomopoulos, N., van Wee, B. (Eds.), Policy Implications of Autonomous Vehicles. Elsevier, The Netherlands, pp. 315–327.

Walker, J., 2020. The Self-Driving Car Timeline – Predictions from the Top 11 Global Automakers | Emerj [WWW Document]. Emerj. URL, https://emerj.com/ai-adoption-timelines/self-driving-car-timeline-themselves-top-11-automakers/ (accessed 4.30.19).

Whittle, C., Whitmarsh, L., Hagger, P., Morgan, P., Parkhurst, G., 2019. User decision-making in transitions to electrified, autonomous, shared or reduced mobility. Transp. Res. D Transp. Environ. 71, 302–319.

Zhang, W., Guhathakurta, S., 2018. Residential location choice in the era of shared autonomous vehicles. J. Plan. Educ. Res. 1–14. https://doi.org/10.1177/0739456X18776062.

CHAPTER ONE

Factors affecting traffic flow efficiency implications of connected and autonomous vehicles: A review and policy recommendations

Santhanakrishnan Narayanan[a,*], Emmanouil Chaniotakis[b], Constantinos Antoniou[a]

[a]Chair of Transportation Systems Engineering, Department of Civil, Geo, and Environmental Engineering, Technical University of Munich, Munich, Germany
[b]MaaSLab, Energy Institute, University College London, London, United Kingdom
*Corresponding author: e-mail address: santhanakrishnan.narayanan@tum.de

Contents

Abstract

Connected and autonomous vehicles are expected to gradually enter the transport modal mix sooner or later. Academic discussions of their expected impacts are well underway, often with conflicting or wide-ranging results. In this chapter, the existing literature is reviewed and summarized, with a focus on the traffic flow efficiency impacts. The expected impacts of autonomous vehicles on the roadway capacity are found not to be unanimous, partly because this seems to depend on the specific modeling conditions. Therefore, common factors that determine whether capacity is expected to

Advances in Transport Policy and Planning, Volume 5
ISSN 2543-0009
https://doi.org/10.1016/bs.atpp.2020.02.004

increase or decrease are discovered from existing studies, along with determining the factors that influence other traffic flow efficiency-related impacts, such as traffic stability and congestion. An analysis is also performed on the vehicular requirements for autonomous vehicles to serve the mobility demand, and change in vehicle kilometers traveled (VKT) that may happen. Based on the reviewed studies, 19 factors that influence traffic flow efficiency implications of autonomous vehicles are identified and grouped into four categories, namely (i) vehicle characteristics, (ii) travel behavior, (iii) network characteristics, and (iv) policies. The chapter ends with a discussion on policy recommendations in tune with the factors identified. The discussion shows that the policy makers should enact laws to ensure connectivity between AVs to experience significant benefits, integrate CAVs with public transport to avoid mode shifts, incentivize ridesharing to reduce network load, develop suitable parking management policies to avoid empty relocations and introduce congestion pricing to curb induced demand.

Keywords: Autonomous vehicle, Connected autonomous vehicle, Shared autonomous vehicle, Traffic flow implications of (C)AV, Factors for traffic efficiency

1. Introduction

Automated vehicles are vehicles with some level of automation to assist or replace human control. The Society of Automotive Engineers (SAE) has defined different levels of automation, ranging from no automated features (Level 0) to full automation (Level 5). An automated vehicle with Level 5 automation is termed as autonomous vehicle (AV). AVs that possess the capability to communicate with each other through vehicle-to-vehicle (V2V) communication and with infrastructure through vehicle-to-infrastructure (V2I) communication are called connected autonomous vehicles (CAVs). Such systems use cooperative mechanisms (refer to Shladover et al., 2015 for information). While both CAVs and AVs are driverless vehicles and they both use information obtained from sensors, CAVs also obtain information from other vehicles and the infrastructure around (Olia et al., 2018). Thus, CAVs can enable comparatively smoother and more reliable driving experience than AVs, due to their ability to overcome sensor limitations and provide the opportunity to create an internet of vehicles (Talebpour and Mahmassani, 2016).

Many researchers conclude that widespread adoption of CAVs and AVs could lead to fewer crashes, lower vehicle emissions, higher fuel economy and improved productivity (Milakis et al., 2017). However, the consensus found in the literature on CAVs and AVs becoming a reality is primarily based on huge investments from major technology companies in developing them (e.g., Korosec, 2018; Trivedi, 2018). Many vehicle manufacturers and related industrial partners unveiled their interest in deploying autonomous vehicles in shared mobility services (e.g., BMW Group, 2016; Daimler AG, 2017; Hawkins, 2017; LeBeau, 2018; O'Kane, 2018). Further, International Association of Public Transport (2017) states that enhanced mobility and equity can be achieved by deploying autonomous vehicles in shared mobility services along with their integration with public transport systems. Hence, it can be expected that the CAVs and AVs will be initially deployed in shared mobility services. Additionally, the penetration rate of CAVs and AVs will depend on a number of factors such as the level of awareness of CAVs and AVs among the general public, consumer innovativeness, safety, trust of strangers, environmental concerns, relative advantage, subjective norms, self-efficacy, and driving-related seeking scale (Gkartzonikas and Gkritza, 2019).

Numerous research studies are lately being published regarding CAVs and AVs. The diversity of characteristics of CAVs and AVs and the uncertainty related to their deployment have led to a development of a wide range of modeling frameworks on their impacts, with different conclusions based on the assumptions of the developed modeling frameworks. Although it is not appropriate to compare the results from the studies without taking the context into account, due to the wide range of modeling frameworks and assumptions, it is considered beneficial to explore the direction of impact and the range of values that can be expected. Therefore, in this chapter, the authors summarize the findings from existing studies that are related to traffic efficiency implications of CAVs and AVs, instead of critical evaluation, and identify factors that influence the implications. The effects of the identified factors are also discussed. The review process is based on a semistructured approach which includes collection of studies from Scopus, based on three keywords (*traffic efficiency of autonomous vehicles, traffic efficiency of connected autonomous vehicles and traffic efficiency of shared autonomous vehicles*) and their screening based on relevance. Given that several authors regularly publish updated modeling procedures, only the recent studies that have been published in the last 5 years (2015–2019) are included in this review. Also, the number of studies pertaining to CAVs and AVs started exploding during this period and hence, we give emphasis to this period. Other than the papers collected from Scopus, additional papers are included from the references of the screened papers. Unless specifically mentioned as CAVs, the abbreviation 'AVs' in this study refers to autonomous vehicles without connectivity.

This chapter is structured as follows: We classify the traffic flow implications into four categories, namely capacity, traffic flow stability and safety, congestion and travel time, and vehicular requirements and VKT. Thus, in Section 2, studies pertaining to road capacity changes are presented, followed by the consolidation of studies on traffic flow stability (Section 3) and travel time impacts of CAVs and AVs (Section 4). Within these sections, the study results are described sequentially based on year and then alphabetically according to authors. Afterwards, vehicle requirements are summarized, along with a discussion on the expected change in Vehicle Kilometers Traveled (VKT) (Section 5). Then, the factors that affect traffic implications of CAVs and AVs, identified from Sections 2–5 are grouped and their effects are explained, along with exploration of related policy recommendations (Section 6). Finally, conclusions are elucidated (Section 7).

2. Road capacity changes expected to be caused by (C)AVs

It is believed that the road capacity will increase with the introduction of CAVs and AVs, since they can operate at reduced headways because of their reduced reaction time. However, the gain in road capacity depends on many factors such as the presence of connectivity between AVs, penetration rate, the type of road sections considered, policies implemented by the public authorities and the algorithms used in the vehicles. Table 1 shows a summary of road capacity related impacts identified from the reviewed studies. A brief description of all the studies examined in this section is presented in Table 4.

The pertinent literature suggests that in the case of low penetration rate for (C)AVs or operation of (C)AVs with high ride quality, the impact of (C)AVs on capacity may be insignificant or negative. For example, Le Vine et al. (2015) investigate the impacts of autonomous vehicles that are assumed to have ride quality equivalent to two types of rail systems, light rail transit (urban), and high-speed rail (inter-urban). The study shows that the intersection capacity reduced by 4% when the longitudinal acceleration/deceleration and lateral acceleration are restricted to the levels of light rail transit, and by 18%, when the restriction is to the levels of high-speed rail. From the study of Ntousakis et al. (2015), it can be concluded that a desired gap of less than 1.1 s for AVs is required to obtain a positive impact on road capacity.

Table 1 Impacts of (C)AVs on road capacity.

Study	Effect
Le Vine et al. (2015)	−4%, when acceleration/deceleration profiles of AVs are restricted to the levels of light rail transit −18%, when acceleration/deceleration profiles of AVs are restricted to the levels of high speed rail
Ntousakis et al. (2015)	(+) with increase in penetration rate and desired gap less than 1.1 s
Talebpour and Mahmassani (2016)	(+) with increase in penetration rate
Liu et al. (2017)	From 2000 veh/h at zero penetration rate to 3070 veh/h at 100% CAV penetration
Talebpour et al. (2017)	(+) with implementation of dedicated lane for AVs; penetration rate should be above 50% for a two-lane highway and above 30%, in the case of a four-lane segment in Chicago
Mena-Oreja et al. (2018)	(−) till penetration rate of 20% (+) for penetration rate above 20% +9.39% to +39.21% at 100% penetration rate
Olia et al. (2018)	2046 veh/h/lane at zero penetration rate to 6450 veh/h/lane at 100% CAV penetration For AVs, capacity improvement was very little (< 2238 veh/h/lane)
Schmitz and von Trotha (2018)	−23% with 50% penetration rate Tenfold increase at 100% penetration rate
Ye and Yamamoto (2018a)	(−) with implementation of dedicated lane for AVs and penetration rate below 30% or above 70%
Ye and Yamamoto (2018b)	(+) with increase in penetration rate
Martin-Gasulla et al. (2019)	(−) at lower penetration rates (+) at lower penetration rates when a preemption technique is implemented
Medina-Tapia and Robusté (2019)	(+) more significant in circular roads than in radial roads
Yu et al. (2019)	(+) with increase in penetration rate

Note: Studies are sorted by year and then alphabetically on authors per each category; (+) indicates increase and (−) indicates decrease; Readers are referred to Table 4 for a description of the studies included in this table.

Results from Talebpour and Mahmassani (2016) show an increase in throughput, as the penetration rate of AVs increases. In a subsequent study, Talebpour et al. (2017) concludes that the implementation of a dedicated lane is beneficial in terms of throughput only when the penetration rate is above 50% for a two-lane highway, and above 30% for a four-lane segment in Chicago. By using a mesoscopic simulation framework, Liu et al. (2017) found that the road capacity increase from 2000 veh/h at zero penetration rate of CAVs to 3070 veh/h at 100% CAV penetration.

The study of Mena-Oreja et al. (2018), for a maximum platoon length of two vehicles and a desired gap with the front vehicle of 10 m, conclude that the traffic flow increases by 9.39% when 100% of the vehicles in the scenario are autonomous, compared to a scenario wherein there are no autonomous vehicles. In the case of desired gaps of 5 and 1 m, traffic flow increases by 26.09% and 39.21%, respectively. When the penetration rate is less than 20%, traffic flow is slightly degraded, and above 20%, the flow starts improving. This effect is observed due to a higher number of aborted maneuvers at lower penetration rates, which occur due to the obstruction caused by conventional vehicles. Three major factors, safe and desired gap and maximum platoon length, are found from this study that affects the road capacity. Olia et al. (2018) conclude that if a traffic stream is filled with CAVs and conventional vehicles, an increase of lane capacity from 2046 to 6450 vehicles per hour per lane is observed, as the proportion of CAVs increase from 0% to 100%. Further, the increase is much significant in scenarios wherein the CAV penetration is above 30%. In case of traffic stream being filled with AVs and conventional vehicles, the capacity remain within a narrow range of 2046–2238 vehicles per hour per lane, regardless of market penetration. Therefore, it can be concluded that AVs have a lower capability to increase highway capacity. For example, with 80% penetration rate, the increase in capacity is around 8%. Further, the capacity is found to be not statistically sensitive to detection range (100, 150, and 200 m) of AVs.

Results from Schmitz and von Trotha (2018) show that the road capacity reduces by 23% for a scenario with 50% penetration rate for AVs, but increases by tenfold in the case of 100% AV penetration, when compared to the base scenario of 100% conventional vehicles. The study of Ye and Yamamoto (2018b) concludes that the road capacity increases with an increase in the CAV penetration rate, and the increase is gradual for scenarios with penetration rates up to 30%. Furthermore, the impact of CAV's capability in terms of ability to maintain lower headways is negligible at lower penetration rates. Since CAVs are minority in the heterogeneous flow, only the ability of the autonomous driving is realized, while the added advantage of connectivity does not play a role. But the capability of the CAVs to maintain lower headways played a major role for the increase in road capacity in scenarios with penetration rates greater than 30%. An improved capability enable a higher capacity growth rate. In a subsequent study, Ye and Yamamoto (2018a) found that the implementation of dedicated lanes for CAVs reduce the performance of the overall traffic flow throughput in scenarios wherein CAV penetration rate is less than 30% or greater than 70%. CAV penetration rate and individual CAV performance are found to be the significant factors that determine the performance of a CAV dedicated lane.

Martin-Gasulla et al. (2019) proposed an approach combining a preemption technique and allowance to use special lanes for CAVs, along with formation of constrained-length platoons. The objective is to maximize throughput gain in mixed traffic scenarios with low penetration rates for CAVs. Results from the study show a decrease in throughput as penetration rate of CAVs increases, when the proposed approach is not implemented. On the other hand, when the approach is implemented, the effect is the opposite, i.e., increase in throughput with increasing penetration rates of CAVs. The reason for this is the reduced headway, which is possible when there is an increased chance of a CAV following another CAV. The gain due to the proposed approach is reduced at higher penetration rates, i.e., the proposed strategy cannot further improve the performance of a network where majority of the vehicles are CAVs. Medina-Tapia and Robusté (2019) conclude a less requirement of road supply in the presence of CAVs and further, the supply savings are more significant in circular roads than in radial roads. Yu et al. (2019) observed that the throughput increases gradually with the increasing penetration rate of AVs, mainly because of the short reaction times of AVs.

From the above, factors that affect road capacity include penetration rate, acceleration/deceleration profile of the vehicle, presence of dedicated lane for (C)AVs, safe and desired gap, platoon size, presence of connectivity, intersection control method, and network topology.

3. Effect of connectivity and automation on traffic flow stability and safety

This section explores the effect of introducing autonomous vehicles on traffic oscillations, stop-and-go motion behavior in the network, and stability of the traffic. A few studies based on experimental tests of current lower level Adaptive Cruise Control (ACC) systems point toward inefficiency of such systems to improve traffic stability (Gunter et al., 2019; Milanés and Shladover, 2014). However, studies based on experimental tests of Cooperative ACC (CACC) conclude that CACC is efficient in dampening oscillations and providing a stable flow (Milanés and Shladover, 2014). Furthermore, several microsimulation studies of higher level CAVs and AVs conclude that they will dampen the traffic oscillations and stop-and-go motion behavior in the network, while improving the traffic stability. Summary of the traffic flow stability related impacts from the reviewed studies are presented in Table 2. Table 4 contains a brief description of all the studies examined in this section.

Talebpour and Mahmassani (2016) show that the string stability of traffic flow is improved in the presence of CAVs and AVs. Furthermore, the improvement is significant even at lower market penetration rates for CAVs. Automation is found to effectively reduce shockwave formation and propagation. Oscillation and collision thresholds are found to increase, as the platoon size of CAVs decreases or market penetration rate increases. The scatter in the fundamental diagrams increases with an increase in penetration rate of autonomous vehicles up to 50%, and thereafter, it starts decreasing. The results from Zhou et al. (2017) show a greater improvement in speed dispersion for longer safe time gaps, due to the reduction in oscillations, which is possible because of increased headways. Li et al. (2017) conclude that larger time gaps between AVs improve safety performance, and collision risk reduces as the penetration rate for AVs increases. They also conclude that a combination of ACC and a variable speed limit (VSL) can achieve better safety improvements on congested freeways than utilizing one of them.

Liu et al. (2017) prove that the critical density is slightly improved with the increase of AV proportion, from which it can be inferred that the introduction of AVs makes the traffic flow more stable. Use of different lane changing rules (PLC and ALC) has little influence but the longitudinal driving behavior is found to have profound significance. Sagir and Ukkusuri (2018) try to compare the impact of different automation levels. The results show that the Level 1 and 2 vehicles could achieve better stability, when compared to the Level 0 vehicles. Level 3 automation enables efficient traffic movement by allowing a higher rate of lane changes than the lower levels. Level 4 automation is found to have a negative impact on traffic flow, due to the transition to minimal risk condition in the road segment with unclear lane markings (between mile 1 and 1.2). In Level 5, the traffic disruptions

Table 2 Summary of traffic flow stability and safety related impacts.

Study	**Variable**	**Effect**
Talebpour and Mahmassani (2016)	String stability	(+) more prominent with connectivity
	Shockwave formation and propagation	(−)
	Oscillation and collision thresholds	(+) with decrease in platoon size of CAVs or increase in market penetration rate
	Scatter in the fundamental diagram	(+) till penetration rate of 50%
		(−) for penetration rate above 50%
Zhou et al. (2017)	Traffic oscillations	(−)
	Speed dispersion	(−) especially with longer safe time gaps
Li et al. (2017)	Traffic safety	(+) with larger time gaps between AVs and application of VSL
Liu et al. (2017)	Critical density	(+)
Sagir and Ukkusuri (2018)	Traffic disruptions and oscillations	(−)
Stern et al. (2018)	Portion of stop-and-go traffic	(−)
Ye et al. (2018)	Portion of stop-and-go traffic	(−) especially at CAV penetration rates between 40% and 50%
Li and Wagner (2019)	Traffic safety	(+) with increase in penetration rate and application of VSL
		(−) when the congestion levels are thrice to the current heavy congestion levels
Qin and Orosz (2019)	String stability	(+) with high CAV penetration rate
Zheng et al. (2019)	Portion of stop-and-go traffic	(−)

Note: Studies are sorted by year and then alphabetically on authors per each category; (+) indicates increase and (−) indicates decrease; Readers are referred to Table 4 for a description of the studies included in this table.

and oscillations are absent and the vehicles have a smoother velocity and acceleration profile. Stern et al. (2018) conclude that a single autonomous vehicle can substantially reduce stop-and-go waves produced by 20 human-controlled vehicles around it in a circular road. Furthermore, the authors state that even 5% penetration rate for AVs can produce significant positive effects, provided the AVs are intelligently controlled.

Based on experimental tests, Qin and Orosz (2019) conclude that string stability can be improved with higher penetration rate of CAVs, even in the presence of information delay. In their experiments, each follower only utilizes the information of its direct predecessor. If motion information from multiple vehicles ahead is utilized, they remark that CAVs may improve string stability even at lower penetration rates. From the study of Ye et al. (2018), one can infer that a smoother traffic flow can be achieved with increasing penetration rate of CAVs, due to a reduction in the percentage of high deceleration rate. Furthermore, a higher desired net time gap results in a better smoothing of traffic flow. With gradual penetration of CAVs, the velocity distribution gradually gets centralized around the medium branch, which indicates that the traffic flow is in a transition state between free flow and congested flow. Finally, at CAV penetration rates between 40% and 50%, the proportion of stop-and-go traffic is greatly reduced. Li and Wagner (2019) conclude that AVs improve traffic conditions, which in turn contributes to significant reduction in time to collisions. This positive impact can be further improved with the application of VSL. However, when the congestion levels are thrice to the levels of current day congestion, safety is reduced. They attribute higher density and closer time gaps between vehicles for the safety reduction. Results from Zheng et al. (2019) show that the traffic flow become more stable with an increasing number of CAVs, i.e., stop-and-go waves are dampened out. Furthermore, in the scenario where only 1 of the 20 vehicles simulated is a CAV, traffic oscillations are reduced significantly, and only a marginal improvement penetration rate, presence of connectivity, platoon size, safe and desired gap, and longitudinal driving behavior are the factors identified from literature that affect traffic stability is found thereafter (number of CAVs from 2 to 10). The study also tries to ascertain the effect of the distribution of CAVs, and it is found that the parameter does not have a significant impact on the traffic stability.

Penetration rate, presence of connectivity, platoon size, safe gap and desired gap, VSL and longitudinal driving behavior are the factors identified from literature that affect traffic stability.

4. Impacts of (C)AVs on congestion and travel time

Reduction in delays in general sections and also ramps and intersections, along with decrease in congestion levels, are believed to happen due to introduction of CAVs and AVs, although the literature shows mixed results. The believed reduction could be due to better traffic stability or improved road capacity, which in turn could be due to many factors explained in Sections 2 and 3. Table 3 shows the summary of travel time related impacts from the reviewed studies. A brief description of all the studies examined in this section is presented in Table 4.

Khondaker and Kattan (2015) attempt to evaluate the effects of VSL. The results from the study show that implementation of VSL improves the traffic flow and the total travel time reductions were around 20% for 100% CAV penetration. Safety improvements are in the range of 6%–11%, and the overall fuel consumption reduced by 5%–16%. Also, it is found out that utilizing just one objective among mobility, safety, and sustainability is sufficient to achieve improvements in all the three parameters. The reason for this could be that, in all the examined scenarios, shockwaves are reduced, leading to reduction of travel time, speed variation, and sudden changes in acceleration/deceleration, which in turn lower fuel consumption and emissions. However, for 50% CAV penetration, a multiobjective optimization is required to obtain optimal inclusive benefits in mobility, safety, and sustainability simultaneously.

Levin and Boyles (2015) simulate the impacts of including AV repositioning to avoid parking fees. The results from the study show that the increase in link capacity due to introduction of AVs is offset by additional congestion caused by the modal shift from transit to AV and additional trips generated by AV relocation. A modest decrease in average link speed is observed. Modal shift from transit to AV, caused by the possibility to avoid parking cost through relocation of AVs to home, shows that parking cost is an important factor in mode choice decision. Le Vine et al. (2015) report that the delay at a signalized intersection will increase by 5% when the acceleration and deceleration profile of autonomous vehicles is restricted to that of light rail transit, and by 36% when the restriction is to that of high-speed rail.

Correia and van Arem (2016) study the effect of replacing privately owned conventional vehicles with autonomous vehicles. In a scenario wherein parking is restricted to peripheral nodes, congestion reduces, when

Table 3 Summary of travel time related impacts.

Study	Variable	Effect
Khondaker and Kattan (2015)	Total travel time	−20% for 100% CAV penetration with VSL control
Levin and Boyles (2015)	Average link speed	(−)
Le Vine et al. (2015)	Delay at a signalized intersection	+5%, when acceleration/deceleration profiles of AVs are restricted to the levels of light rail transit
		+36%, acceleration/deceleration profiles of AVs are restricted to the levels of high-speed rail
Correia and van Arem (2016)	Congestion	Do not increase congestion substantially
Patel et al. (2016)	Total travel time	−78%
Zhou et al. (2017)	Total travel time	(−) with increase in penetration rate
Liu et al. (2017)	Congestion	(−); 50% penetration rate found to be optimal
Talebpour et al. (2017)	Congestion	(+) with implementation of dedicated lane for AVs and limiting AV movement to the dedicated lane
		(−) with implementation of dedicated lane for AVs and allowing optional use of the dedicated lane
Kutgun et al. (2018)	Congestion	(−) even with moderate adoption of CAVs
		(+) with decrease in public transport and car sharing mode share
Mattas et al. (2018)	Average speed	(−) with increasing penetration rate for AVs
		(−) at lower penetration rates for CAVs
		(+) at higher penetration rates for CAVs
Naumov et al. (2018)	Average speed	(+) initially
		(−) with induced demand after initial improvement

Table 3 Summary of travel time related impacts.—cont'd

Study	Variable	Effect
Alozi and Hamad (2019)	Average delay	-86% with 100% CAV penetration and LOS of B
	Average speed	+25% to +40%
	Total travel time	−10% to −24%
Carrese et al. (2019)	Congestion	(−) with 100% penetration for ridesharing SAV system
Chen (2019)	Average travel time	From 89.93 min in the case of pretimed signal policy to 42.48 min with intelligent signal control policy
Fiori et al. (2019)	Average travel time	(−) with presence of electric vehicles and an objective to lower energy consumption
Li and Wagner (2019)	Average travel time	(+) with increase in penetration rate and application of VSL
Martin-Gasulla et al. (2019)	Control delay	−17%
Papadoulis et al. (2019)	Average travel time	(+) during all weekdays due to long vehicle platoon formation (15+ vehicles) with a slow leader
Simoni et al. (2019)	Congestion	(−) with implementation of congestion pricing
Yu et al. (2019)	Average speed	+20 kmph with 100% penetration
		+35 kmph with 100% penetration and dedicated lane for AVs
	Average travel time	−5 min with 100% penetration
	Duration of congestion	−140 min with 100% penetration

Note: Studies are sorted by year and then alphabetically on authors per each category; (+) indicates increase and (−) indicates decrease; Readers are referred to Table 4 for a description of the studies included in this table.

compared to the scenario wherein parking is provided in city center (reduction of delay from 4.77% to 2.10%). In a scenario wherein paid parking is allowed everywhere, vehicles keep moving empty locally to avoid parking, without adding major congestion because of local movements. The authors conclude that AVs can serve more trips than the conventional vehicles. Though there will be extra travel kilometers, they do not add much congestion. In the case of reduced value of travel time, AVs can serve much more trips, without adding any congestion. In the study of Patel et al. (2016), it is observed that, in most situations, the reservation-control improves the traffic conditions, compared to the base scenario with conventional signals. But in few situations, such as a congested network with several close local road and arterial intersections, signals are more efficient, since the signals are more optimized for such locations. Also, traditional merges and diverges for on- and off-ramps outperform reservation-control. When reduced reaction times are incorporated, leading to reduced headways and increased capacity, travel times improve in both freeway and arterial networks. The authors also study the downtown network of Austin, which includes freeway, arterial, and local roads, and observe that the application of reservation-control along with consideration of reduced reaction time for AVs decrease travel time by 78%.

Zhou et al. (2017) found that the total travel time in a Freeway section in Brisbane is reduced as the penetration rate of AVs increases. This is due to smoothing of traffic oscillations with an increasing percentage of AVs. Results from Liu et al. (2017) also show a similar trend (reduction of congestion degree). Further, the study concludes that an AV proportion of 50% is optimal in terms of lowering congestion degree across the whole density spectrum. Talebpour et al. (2017) found that an application of a reserved lane, together with limiting autonomous vehicles to the reserved lane, could significantly increase congestion in highways with ramps, because of shockwave formation due to mandatory lane-changing maneuvers at ramps. However, allowing optional use of the reserved lane shows an improvement in congestion levels.

Kutgun et al. (2018) perform a qualitative analysis of the congestion effects of introducing CAVs, and the results indicate that the congestion could be reduced, even with moderate adoption of CAVs. The congestion levels get worsened, when executing the mental modeler scenarios with a decrease in the public transport and car-sharing mode share. Mattas et al. (2018) conclude that the network performance in terms of speed is reduced with the increasing penetration rate of AVs. This is because of the conservative behavior of the AVs. Similarly, CAVs are found to reduce average speed at lower penetration rates, although the average speed increases for higher penetration rates. At lower penetration rates, the probability of forming a platoon for CAVs is low, resulting in a degradation of the network performance. Naumov et al. (2018) concentrate on investigating induced demand caused by the introduction of AVs. Results from the study show that the average traffic speeds increase initially in a scenario with private AVs, reducing congestion to some extent. However, this congestion reduction results in an induced demand in terms of number of new trips and vehicle-miles traveled, which in turn lead to more congestion and greenhouse gas emissions. Another scenario, wherein ride-sharing SAV system is simulated, also shows a similar pattern, except that the initial congestion reduction is very high compared to the first scenario. The results are in line with Forresters Attractiveness Principle and prove the intrinsic link between benefits of AVs and the amount of additional demand they induce. The authors then implement a vehicle miles traveled (VMT) tax of 20 cents/mile, and the result shows a net reduction in congestion. From the above, one can conclude that the introduction of AVs may not be a solution to traffic congestion in cities without implementation of proper regulations. Benefits of AVs and pooling is achievable as intended only upon implementation of policies that regulate demand for driving.

In the study of Alozi and Hamad (2019), the impacts of CAVs are assessed in terms of average delay, average speed, and travel time. With regard to average delay, the maximum reduction in delay is 86%, and occurs in the scenario with 100% CAV penetration rate and level of service (LOS) of B. Between 20% and 70% penetration rates, the reduction in delay is less, with a maximum of 17% reduction. The average speed increases with increasing penetration of CAVs, and the increase ranges between 25% and 40%. While average delay is highly sensitive to traffic volume conditions, average speed is only slightly sensitive. Travel time also shows an increasing reduction with increasing penetration of CAVs, except in lower penetration rates. The reduction ranges between 10% and 24%. Furthermore, the reductions are more significant at low traffic volumes.

Carrese et al. (2019) perform an analysis of traffic congestion in Rome for a horizon of 2050, and conclude that the residents of Rome will experience extra congestion due to suburban relocation, except where a 100% ridesharing SAV system is implemented. In the presence of CAVs and AVs, results from Chen (2019) show that the performance of actuated and pretimed signal control are similar, and significant benefit is not achieved. However, the implementation of intelligent signal control policy enables significant reductions in average travel time and stopping time. Regarding the scenario with pretimed signal policy, the average travel time is 89.93 min, while for the intelligent signal control policy, the value is 42.48 min. Based on a comparison of energy consumption of electric vehicles and vehicles with internal combustion engines, Fiori et al. (2019) state that higher average traffic speeds result in higher energy consumption for electric vehicles. Li and Wagner (2019) conclude that the average travel time reduces with an increase in AV penetration rate, in all the scenarios with free-flow traffic, lightly congested traffic and heavily congested traffic. Application of VSL reduces the average travel time further. Martin-Gasulla et al. (2019), who propose an approach to recover potential reduction in the maximum throughput in mixed traffic scenario with low penetration rates for CAVs, conclude that the control delay can be reduced by 17% in oversaturated conditions. The observed reduction in delay with the increase in penetration rate of CAVs is mainly due to decrease in the headway between CAVs. Papadoulis et al. (2019) design five different simulation models, one for each weekday, to evaluate the impacts of CAVs. Results from the study show that the average travel time increases during all weekdays due to long vehicle platoon formation (15+ vehicles) with a slow leader. However, this result is sensitive to the assumed speed distribution of vehicles in VISSIM. At 100% penetration, the travel time do not vary across the weekdays, i.e., introduction of CAVs made the travel time almost equal across all weekdays. Thus, reliable travel times can be achieved, independent of traffic conditions.

Simoni et al. (2019) evaluate the effects of four different congestion pricing and tolling strategies. Results show that all the strategies reduced travel demand and delays, and advanced congestion pricing strategies are not necessarily more effective than traditional ones in every scenario. In the case of traditional schemes for AV-oriented and the SAV-oriented scenarios, link-based pricing performs better than distance-based pricing, in terms of delay reductions. This is because of longer AV-SAV trips being not incentivized to switch to low-quality public transport in case of distance-based pricing. However, in base scenario wherein no AV-SAV trips are present, distance-based pricing performs better. Further, dynamic marginal cost pricing performs better than the link-based pricing, with difference in congestion reduction in the order of 2% to 5% between the two schemes. Similarly, travel time-based pricing results in better congestion reduction, when compared to the distance-based scheme. It should be noted that the quality of transit services is low in Austin and the efficiency of the congestion pricing schemes could be better in places where public transport system is better.

Yu et al. (2019) found that the market penetration rate of AVs is directly proportional to the total average speed. Further, in scenario without dedicated AV lane and 100% AV penetration, average speed is around 70 km/h and the average travel time is about 600 s, which shows a good improvement over the base scenario (0% AV penetration) values of 50 km/h and 900 s. Furthermore, the duration of congestion is reduced to 190 min from 330 min. With introduction of dedicated AV lane, the total average speed improves by 15 km/h, compared to the option without dedicated lane. As the penetration rate of AVs increases, average travel time of AVs increases but that of conventional vehicles decreases. When the penetration rate of AVs is 20%, average travel time of conventional vehicles is twice that of AVs, and the difference gets reduced with increasing penetration rate of AVs. At 80% penetration rate of AVs, average travel time of both conventional vehicles and AVs becomes almost equal.

With regard to SAV specific studies, reviewed studies conclude that carsharing SAV systems can increase congestion (Alam and Habib, 2018; Zhao and Kockelman, 2018), while ridesharing SAV systems can reduce traffic (Alazzawi et al., 2018; Martinez and Viegas, 2017). However, congestion can be reduced when a carsharing SAV system is integrated with public transport (e.g., Salazar et al., 2018). Alam and Habib (2018) simulated the morning peak period and they found out that the traffic reduces in the first hour, while increasing in the next 2 h. Zhao and Kockelman (2018) conclude that the average speed will reduce, when the road network is utilized by conventional vehicles, carsharing SAVs and private CAVs. Alazzawi et al. (2018) conclude that congestion will reduce in Milan with at least 50% demand for SAV ridesharing services. Martinez and Viegas (2017) conclude that the traffic levels will reduce in Lisbon with the introduction of SAV services. Lang et al. (2018) conclude that inner city areas will experience reduction in traffic, while the suburban areas will experience an increase, the reason being the higher possibility of sharing in inner city areas, which in turn is possible because of higher demand density.

Penetration rate, presence of connectivity, acceleration/deceleration profile, implementation of dedicated lane, induced demand, method of intersection control, type of (C)AV system, vehicle type, VSL, congestion pricing, and platoon size are the factors identified from literature that affect congestion and travel time.

5. Vehicular requirements for (C)AVs to serve the mobility demand and consequent changes in VKT

Vehicle requirements are usually described in terms of vehicle replacement values, which represents the number of conventional vehicles that one autonomous vehicle can replace. In unison, the studies reviewed conclude that the vehicle requirements in the era of AVs will be lower than today. But the exact vehicle replacement value is uncertain and a range between 1.1 and 11 can be found in literature. A brief description of all the studies examined in this section is presented in Table 4. Vehicle replacement value of 5–10 is concluded by International Transport Forum (2015) for Lisbon (Portugal), when carsharing and ridesharing SAV services are introduced in the city. In this study, along SAV services, modes such as walking and subway are considered. Bösch et al. (2016) use MATSIM to simulate the impacts of carsharing SAV services in Zurich (Switzerland) and conclude a vehicle replacement value range of 4–10. An agent-based simulation system is used by Dia and Javanshour (2017) and the study shows that a vehicle replacement value range of 1.75–8.3 can be achieved at Melbourne (Australia), when 25% of travelers choose privately owned autonomous cars and the rest use SAV services. Mendes et al. (2017) develop an event-based simulation model to ascertain the vehicle replacement for light rail and found out that a 39 vehicle light rail system can be replaced by 150–500 SAVs. Fagnant and Kockelman (2018) use MATSIM to find out that the vehicle replacement value will range between 8.7 and 10.8 at Austin (Texas), when the trips are carried out using ridesharing SAV services. Using MATLAB®, when ridesharing SAV services are assumed to serve the demand, Gurumurthy and Kockelman (2018) found out that the vehicle replacement value will range between 6 and 8 for the Orlando metropolitan area in Florida. Lang et al. (2018) perform an analysis at Boston using an agent based simulation system and concluded a vehicle replacement value of 1.18. Lokhandwala and Cai (2018), who perform a comparison between conventional sharing and autonomous sharing systems using New York Taxi dataset, show a vehicle replacement value of 1.93–2.451. Moreno et al. (2018) use MATSIM to simulate the effects of SAV services in greater Munich region and their results suggest a vehicle replacement value of 2.5. For the case of private AVs, Zhang et al. (2018), conclude a 9.5% reduction in private vehicles in Atlanta Metropolitan Area for the current travel patterns, using an activity-based travel Model. This translates to a vehicle replacement value of 1.1.

Most of the studies reviewed conclude that VKT will increase as a result of introductions of (C)AVs, mainly due to the induced demand and empty trips. Harper et al. (2016) attempt to estimate the possible increase in VKT in United States as a result of (C)AV availability for the currently nondriving users, elderly users and people with travel-restrictive medical conditions, and conclude a maximum 14% increase in light-duty vehicle miles traveled. Further, an increase due to demand from nondrivers is 9%, and increase due to demand from drivers with medical conditions is 2.6%. POLARIS, an activity-based modeling and traffic simulation software, is used by Auld et al. (2017) to find out the change in VKT in Chicago metropolitan area as a result of introduction of private AVs. The study shows an increase in VKT of the range +1% to +79%, based on the different assumed penetration rates for AVs, value of travel time and change in capacity. In a subsequent study, Auld et al. (2018) show that an increase in VKT of the range +15% to +43%. Zhang et al. (2018) conclude a 13.3% increase in VKT in the Atlanta metropolitan area. Kröger et al. (2019), wherein the impact of introducing AVs on travel behavior for Germany and the United States is compared using an aspatial travel demand model, conclude an increase in VKT, in the range of +2.4% to +8.6% for Germany and +3.4% to +8.6% for United States. However, the penetration rate in Germany is higher (10% or 38%), and for United States, the value is 8% or 29%. Lower fuel costs and lack of mode alternatives in United States are the reasons suggested in the study for this difference.

Change in VKT, when SAV services are introduced, also show a similar trend, i.e., increase in VKT, as observed in several studies. For example, International Transport Forum (2015): +6% to +89%, Dia and Javanshour (2017): +10% to +29%, Jager et al. (2017): +15.80%, Kondor et al. (2018): +2%, Lang et al. (2018): +16%, and Moreno et al. (2018): +7.40%. Though increase in VKT is concluded in many studies, few studies show that VKT can be reduced in certain situations. For example, a reduction in VKT is observed when ridesharing SAV services replace the current taxi system (Lokhandwala and Cai, 2018). Also, compared to autonomous ridesharing services, conventional ridesharing services reduce VKT to a greater extent. A similar trend, i.e., reduction in VKT for ridesharing SAV services, is also seen in Bischoff et al. (2017), in which a 24-h simulation of the taxi requests in Berlin was performed using MATSIM. Thus, in terms of VKT, conventional ridesharing is better than ridesharing SAV services, which is better than carsharing SAV services. A notable exception to this trend is observed in Childress et al. (2015), wherein a reduction in VKT is seen for carsharing SAV services. The reason is the

Table 4 Description of the reviewed studies.

Study	Study type	Model/analysis framework	Remarks
Ntousakis et al. (2015)	B	Aimsun	Assessment of the impacts of ACC systems on traffic flow characteristics. Simulations are run for different penetration rates of ACC-equipped vehicles, different desired time-gap settings and different networks. The study models two scenarios, one includes a single lane 4 km stretch of road and the other includes a 4 km single lane ring road with stop-and-go waves. In the first scenario, the measured flow of the road is assumed to be equal to its capacity. An intelligent driver model (IDM) and Gipps driver model are used to simulate the vehicles. Place of study: A single lane ring road of 4 km length
Childress et al. (2015)	B	SoundCast (Seattle region's activity-based travel model)	Investigation of travel behavior impacts. Base year is 2010 and private vehicle trips are assumed to be absent. Cost of SAV service is $1.03/km and there is no road capacity increase due to automation. Modes available include SAV, transit, and walking. Place of study: Puget Sound region
International Transport Forum (2015)	B	Agent-based simulation	Scenarios were built on two SAV service types (car-sharing and ride-sharing), availability of a high-capacity public transport, penetration rates of SAVs (50% and 100%) and simulation time period (full day and peak periods). Modes available included private cars, public transport, SAVs, walking, and cycling. Access time and search time for parking spaces were not included for private vehicles. Place of study: Lisbon
Khondaker and Kattan (2015)	B, C	Vissim and VT-Micro	Analysis of the impacts of VSL. The authors formulate a multiobjective optimization function to optimize mobility, safety, and sustainability. A genetic algorithm is used to solve the formulation. The simulated roadway is divided into eight sections of 1 km length each. The demand in the roadway is assumed to be 2000 veh/h, with 80% passenger cars and 20% heavy vehicles. Using Vissim, total travel time (for mobility) and time to collision (surrogate safety measure; for safety) are calculated. A microscopic fuel consumption model (VT-Micro) is used to measure the

			environmental impact. Four scenarios other than the base scenario, wherein no VSL is implemented, are tested. In the first three scenarios, only one of the multiple objectives is optimized, while in the last scenario, all the objectives are incorporated. Further, in each scenario, two different CAV penetration rates, 50% and 100%, are tested. A VSL is triggered when there is a sudden speed drop in a particular section with respect to the successive upstream sections. An artificial bottleneck as created at the 6th section, 10 min after the beginning of the simulation, and is assumed to last for 20 min. In the middle of sections 1, 2, 3, 4, 5, and 7, dynamic speed limit control signs are placed, and the speed limit in section 6 is set to 30 kmph. Place of study: A single-lane 8 km roadway
Le Vine et al. (2015)	B	Vissim	Investigation of the implications of providing AV occupants with ride quality that is equivalent (in terms of maximum rates of longitudinal and lateral acceleration) to two types of rail systems: urban light rail transit and inter-urban high-speed rail. The effects of vehicles suspensions are not explicitly modeled. All AVs are subject to the same acceleration/deceleration constraints, while human-driver behavior is heterogeneous. Place of study: An urban arterial street network consisting of a single four-way 90 degree signalized intersection with identical single-lane approaches on all four legs
Levin and Boyles (2015)	B	Modified four-step model	Investigation of the impacts of AV repositioning to avoid parking fees. Increase in link capacity is assumed to be a function of the proportion of AVs. The mode choice between AV and transit is based on a nested logit model. Within the nest of AV, the users have the choice between parking vehicle at destination and relocating the vehicle to park it at the origin (home). A feedback between traffic assignment, trip distribution, and mode choice is implemented. Value of travel time and AV ownership is used to generate demand classes, and the simulation is done for morning peak period (62,836 trips). The value of travel time utilized in the model ranges between 1.15 and 22. Place of study: Austin downtown subnetwork

Continued

Table 4 Description of the reviewed studies.—cont'd

Study	Study type	Model/analysis framework	Remarks
Bösch et al. (2016)	B	Matsim and SAV simulation model	Analysis of fleet size required to serve different levels of demand. Travel times are calculated using Matsim. Only trips made with private cars are assumed to be replaced by SAV services and the maximum waiting time is 10 min. Place of study: Zurich
Correia and van Arem (2016)	C	Mixed Integer Programming	Investigation of the impacts of replacing private conventional vehicles with AVs. The authors formulate a model called User Optimum Privately Owned Automated Vehicles Assignment Problem (UO-POAVAP). An equilibrium approach is implemented, wherein households with similar trips should have similar transport costs. The proposed model includes mode, departure and route choice. Trips of 732 synthetic households, representing the trips of 14,640 real households, are analyzed. Place of study: Delft
Harper et al. (2016)	O	Demand wedge	Estimation of the possible increase in VKT as a result of AV availability for the currently nondriving users, elderly users and people with travel-restrictive medical conditions. Place of study: United States
Patel et al. (2016)	B	Multiclass cell transmission model	Evaluation of the impacts of reduced reaction times of CAVs, and the implementation of reservation-based controls for intersections. The reservation-based control is compared with the usage of conventional signals. Reaction time for CAVs is assumed to be 0.5 s, and the fundamental diagram is adapted according to the proportion of CAVs in each cell. Place of study: Several highly congested arterial and freeway networks in Texas
Talebpour and Mahmassani (2016)	B	Microscopic simulation	Analysis of the string stability of mixed traffic streams with varying percentages of conventional vehicles, AVs and CAVs. An acceleration framework is utilized to distinguish between CAVs and AVs. Place of study: A one-lane highway with an infinite length for stability analysis and a one-lane highway with an on-ramp located in the middle of the segment for throughput analysis.

Zhou et al. (2017)	B	Microscopic simulation	Assessment of the impacts of CAVs in improving freeway merging. Cooperative IDM is utilized for simulating AVs, while Full Velocity Difference Model (FVDM) is utilized to mimic conventional vehicles. AV penetration rates of 0%, 5%, 15%, and 25% are tested. The study also included a sensitivity analysis on the safe time gaps and five different values for safe time gaps (0.4, 0.6, 0.8, 1, and 1.2 s) are tested. Place of study: A section of a freeway in Brisbane
Auld et al. (2017)	B	POLARIS (Activity-based travel demand model)	Investigation of the impacts of CAVs on travel demand. Approximately, 10.2 million travelers living in 3.8 million households, engaging in 27.9 million trips on an average day, are simulated. Value of travel time is varied from 0% reduction to 75% reduction. The capacity increase is also varied in two ways. The capacity change is varied from a 12% increase to a 77% increase in one set of scenarios. Capacity is changed according to the CAV penetration rate in the remaining scenarios. In 100% CAV penetration scenario, it is assumed that intersections can be automated, and hence, intersection control is turned off in the model. Place of study: Chicago metropolitan area
Bischoff et al. (2017)	B	Matsim	Evaluation of potential for shared rides. An insertion-based algorithm was used to simulate SAV ride-sharing services. The algorithm was tested using real-world dataset of taxi requests in Berlin (Taxi Berlin) and a vehicle capacity between two and four was assumed. Place of study: Berlin
Dia and Javanshour (2017)	B	Agent-based simulation	Development of models for simulating SAV services and assessment of the impacts of such services. 25% of existing private car users are assumed to use private autonomous cars and the remaining 75% use SAVs. Two different scenarios, maximum waiting time of 0 and 5 min, are analyzed. Only home based trips are considered and the travel demand data is based on Victorian Integrated Survey of Travel and Activity. For parking, the private vehicles return to home and the SAVs will go to nearby waiting areas. Place of study: Melbourne

Continued

Table 4 Description of the reviewed studies.—cont'd

Study	Study type	Model/analysis framework	Remarks
Jager et al. (2017)	B	Discrete event simulation combined with a multiagent approach	Assessment of impacts of electric SAV services. A central dispatcher broadcasts customer requests and electric SAVs (lightweight two-seater vehicles) compete for the service. Customers are served based on first-come, first-serve strategy. Routing, charging and trip assignment are done dynamically and autonomously by each vehicle. Power consumption is assumed to be 15 kWh per 100 km and the battery capacity is 30 kWh. Travel time is based on a factor (1.4 in off-peak and 2.0 in peak time) applied over predictions from Google Maps. The time period of simulation is one day. Place of study: Munich
Li et al. (2017)	B	Microscopic simulation	Evaluation of the safety effects and the string stability of ACC enabled vehicles in a stop-and-go traffic situation. The study simulates the vehicles using the IDM, with a modified implementation for the ACC. The authors also examine the impact of VSL on road safety. Place of study: A 10 km segment with four lanes
Liu et al. (2017)	B	Mesoscopic simulation using an improved symmetric two-lane cellular automaton model	Comparison between two lane changing principles, Polite Lane Changing (PLC) and Aggressive Lane Changing (ALC). In the former, motion of neighboring vehicles on the adjacent lanes is not disturbed by the lane-change maneuver of the CAVs. A self-centered behavior for lane-change is assumed in the latter case. Place of study: A three-lane stretch of a freeway without on and off-ramps
Martinez and Viegas (2017)	B	Agent-based simulation	Evaluation of impacts of SAV services. Synthetic data consisting of 1,138,696 daily trips was used for the analysis. A rule-based lexicographic choice process based on socio-demographic and mobility attributes of the user was used for mode choice between walking, subway or rail, shared taxi and taxi-bus. Place of study: Lisbon
Mendes et al. (2017)	B	Event-based simulation model	Comparison of performance of SAVs with the light rail system for the forecasted demand in 2035, under the same demand patterns, route alignment, and operating speeds. The demand forecast is from the projections of New York City Department of Transportation, made during the planning for the Select Bus Service in New York City.

			Induced demand is assumed on the basis of improved connectivity. The SAV system will run on the same alignment of the rail system. Simulation time period is 2 h and the first half-hour is considered as warm-up period. Passenger arrivals are based on Monte Carlo simulation. SAV capacity is assumed to be 12 and 3 scenarios, demand-responsive service with garages located between stations, demand-responsive service with stations acting as garages and fixed-route service operating in the same way as the rail system, are simulated. Place of study: Brooklyn–Queens Connector Streetcar line (New York)
Talebpour et al. (2017)	B	Microscopic simulation	Evaluation of the effects of implementing a dedicated lane for AVs. Three scenarios are analyzed, other than the base scenario in which no dedicated lane for AVs is implemented. While AVs are required to use the reserved lane in both the first and second scenarios, they can choose any lane in the third scenario. In the first scenario, AVs are required to operate autonomously everywhere and in the second scenario, human drivers operate the AVs in regular lanes. Place of study: A two-lane highway with an on-ramp and a 3.5 mile four-lane segment in Chicago, Illinois, which is located on the I-290 and has four on-ramps and three off-ramps.
Alam and Habib (2018)	B	Vissim	Evaluation of service performance of SAVs. The simulation is run for morning peak hour (06.00–09.00) and includes 57,694 commute trips. 16,900 trips, which have both the origin and destination ends within Halifax peninsula, are assumed to be eligible for using SAVs. A Latin Hypercube (LH) sampling technique is used for calibrating driving behavior and route choice parameters. The study uses a sequential modeling framework, which includes a regional transport network model, a SAV operation model and a DTA-based microsimulation model. The trips are assumed to be carried out by conventional private vehicles, if the waiting time for the arrival of a SAV is more than a certain threshold. Four scenarios are tested by varying the fleet size (450, 900, 1800, and 3600 SAVs). Place of study: Halifax (Canada)

Continued

Table 4 Description of the reviewed studies.—cont'd

Study	Study type	Model/analysis framework	Remarks
Alazzawi et al. (2018)	B	Sumo	Assessment of the impact of SAV services on urban mobility. SAV service is simulated by including a custom TraCI module to SUMO, thereby considering the effects of traffic queues and spillback. The model framework can simulate a conventional vehicle only scenario, SAV only scenario and a scenario wherein both vehicles are present. Four different data sources were used in this study: OpenStreetMap for street maps of Milan, mobile phone usage data from Telecom Italia Big Data Challenge 2014 for predicting time dependent OD matrix, traffic count data from Agenzia Mobilitá Ambiente Territorio for calibration and travel time data from Google Maps to evaluate the classical simulations against real-world data. For simulation, Milan is spatially segmented into 100 × 100 grid areas, each of size 235 m × 235 m. Private cars are assumed to have an average occupancy of 1.3 passengers, while SAVs have a maximum capacity of six passengers. Empty SAVs are rerouted to areas of high mobility demand and a matching approach based on stable marriage algorithm for unequal sets is used to pair passengers to SAVs. Simulation is split into two parts, a warm-up phase and a deployment phase. Place of study: Milan
Fagnant and Kockelman (2018)	B	Matsim	Evaluation of impacts of SAV services. This study builds on Fagnant and Kockelman (2014), by including a Dynamic Ride-Sharing (DRS) module. 1.3% of trips (2010 trip tables) in Austin are considered for the analysis. The original model from 2014 contains SAV location and trip assignment module, SAV fleet generation module, SAV movement module and SAV relocation module. Maximum waiting time is assumed to be 10 min. A non-DRS scenario, a DRS scenario and a mixed scenario are simulated. Scenario analysis is also carried out by increasing the 1.3% demand by factors of 2 and 5. Texas statewide dataset is used to simulate day-to-day variations in travel demand. Trips with travel distance more than 50 miles are not included, and Golden Section Search optimization procedure (Shao and Chang, 2008) is used to run a series of simulations. Operating costs of \$0.31 and \$0.16/km are used. Place of study: Austin

Gurumurthy and Kockelman (2018)	B	Custom framework	Assessment of dynamic ride-sharing potential for SAV services. Mobile data obtained from AirSage for a period of 30 consecutive days is used in this study. One hour aggregated mobile data is disaggregated to 1 min time-steps by randomizing the trip departure times in the dataset for minute level and then uniformly sampling the trips. Travel times are based on shortest path travel times and TransCAD is used for the same. Around 2.8 million single occupancy vehicle trips are simulated. The simulation framework consists of three blocks: SAV allocation, SAV update and waitlist management. Maximum vehicle occupancy is assumed to be 4. Different values of maximum delay (5–30 min in increments of 5 min) are simulated. Place of study: Orlando metropolitan area
Kondor et al. (2018)	O	Data-driven methodology	Estimation of commuter parking needs. The study used mobile phone network logs to estimate home and work locations for a sample of over 1 million commuters. Travel times were calculated based on average travel times between a set of road intersections, which was provided by the Land Transport Authority. Average travel time between 7 a.m. and 8 a.m. for home to work and between 4 p.m. and 5 p.m. for work to home were used. Four scenarios, conventional private cars with private parking, conventional private cars with shared parking, conventional shared vehicles and SAV services, were tested and different values, were tried out for the maximum distance allowed between destination and parking spot (up to 1.5 km). Place of study: Singapore
Kutgun et al. (2018)	O	Mental Modeler (fuzzy cognitive map of a freeway congestion)	Qualitative analysis of the congestion effects of introducing CAVs. The utilized fuzzy cognitive map consists of 15 elements (nodes) and 32 connections (vectors). Mental Modeler, a participatory modeling tool for fuzzy cognitive map, is used to simulate the system dynamics and to evaluate the impact of CAVs on traffic congestion. Two scenarios, high CAV adoption and moderate CAV adoption, are simulated, other than the base scenario, which assumes the existence of only conventional vehicles. Place of study: NA/NA

Continued

Table 4 Description of the reviewed studies.—cont'd

Study	Study type	Model/analysis framework	Remarks
Lang et al. (2018)	A, B	Conjoint analysis and Agent-based simulation	Exploration of impact of autonomous vehicles on urban mobility. The study included a survey of 2400 individuals (a representative sample across gender, age, location, and income) and the choice of modes for the survey were bus/subway, commuter rail, taxi/ride-hailing, personal vehicle, autonomous personal vehicle, autonomous taxi, autonomous shared taxi, autonomous minibus. For the analysis, the survey data was grouped into mass transit, personal car and mobility-on-demand. A simulation was conducted using the survey results for the year 2030. The simulation included 2 million daily passenger vehicle trips (from INRIX and City of Boston) and 10,000 commercial vehicle trips (from INRIX and UPS). Based on SAV share, vehicle throughput is increased by 6.3%. The simulation included modeling of each vehicle's behavior and vehicle-to-vehicle interaction. Place of study: Boston
Lokhandwala and Cai (2018)	B	Agent-based simulation	Analysis of impacts, when users switch from traditional taxis to SAVs. New York city taxi data from 2014 (07/05/2014) is used and the morning peak from 7:00 a.m. to 3:00 p.m. and the evening peak from 5:00 p.m. to midnight is considered for the analysis. Vehicle capacity is assumed to be 4 and maximum waiting time is assumed to be 5 min. Beyond 5 min, the user exits the system unserved. Minimum deviation for ride-sharing is 100 m and maximum is 10 km. Deviation tolerance is assumed to follow a triangular distribution with mean as 0.5 and minimum and maximum values as 0 and 1. Scenario analysis is carried out by varying fleet size (3000, 4000, 5000, 5500, 6000, 7000, and 8000) and percentage of users willing to share rides (0%, 25%, 50%, 75%, and 100%). Place of study: New York Taxi dataset
Makridis et al. (2018)	O	Field experiment	Investigation of the hypothesis that ACC based vehicles have a slower reaction time than their human counterparts. The study is performed with a lead car followed by a follower car. The lead car is human-controlled, while the follower car is either human or ACC controlled. The desired speed is varied from 40 to 70 kmph in increments of 10 kmph. Highly accurate positioning measurements are taken to verify the reaction times. Place of study: JRC 1.15 km track

Mattas et al. (2018)	B	Aimsun	Exploration of the influence of CAVs and AVs on traffic flow and emissions. Traffic data from the morning peak hour is considered. Conventional cars are simulated using the default Gipps model. AVs are simulated to follow the Gipps model for latitudinal control, and longitudinal control, ACC as described by Shladover et al. (2012) is used. In the case of consecutive CAVs, the authors model the longitudinal driving behavior with a CACC controller. The study assumes that the reaction time of CAVs and AVs (0.3 s) are lower than manual cars (0.8 s). Place of study: Antwerp Ring Road
Mena-Oreja et al. (2018)	B	PERMIT simulator along with SUMO and its platooning extension Plexe	Modeling of impact of automation on road capacity. A maximum platoon length of 2 vehicles and a desired gap with the front vehicle of 10, 5, and 1 m were assumed. A safe gap of 1.25 times the desired gap was used during the platooning maneuvers. Place of study: A 10 km ring road with 2 lanes
Moreno et al. (2018)	A, B	Matsim	Estimation of the impact of SAVs on average trip duration and VMT/VKT. A two step selection process for mode choice was implemented. In the first step, the available modes included auto, public transport (metro, tram, and bus), bicycling, and walking. In the second step, auto users had the choice to choose between private conventional vehicle and SAV. The probability to select SAV was based on a logit model estimated from a stated preference survey. The stated preference survey included responses from 106 individuals. Ten different substitution rates, which represents the number of SAVs that replace 10 private conventional vehicles, were tested and the values tested range from 1-for-10 to 10-for-10. Place of study: Greater Munich area
Naumov et al. (2018)	O	Dynamic differential equation model of travel demand	Investigation of the induced demand caused by the introduction of AVs. The utilized differential-equation model can capture the causal relationships between travel costs, demand for driving, travel speeds, and environmental impacts. Two scenarios, one with private AVs and another with ridesharing SAV system which can carry a maximum of two passengers, are simulated. The authors also test a vehicle Miles Traveled (VMT) tax of 20 cents/mile. Place of study: NA/NA

Continued

Table 4 Description of the reviewed studies.—cont'd

Study	Study type	Model/analysis framework	Remarks
Olia et al. (2018)	B	Paramics	Analysis of the impact of mixed traffic on road capacity. A headway of 1 s is assumed for normal autonomous vehicles. When a connected autonomous vehicle follows another connected autonomous vehicle, a headway of 0.5 s is assumed and in other cases, a value of 1 s is used. Place of study: A 20 km highway segment with two lanes and an on-ramp
Sagir and Ukkusuri (2018)	B	Vissim	Comparison of the impacts of different automation levels. The highway segment from mile 1 to mile 1.2 has unclear lane markings. Level 0, which represents exclusive human driving, is modeled with an IDM. Level 1, in which adaptive cruise control is added, is modeled with an Enhanced IDM. Level 2 vehicles with lane-keeping assist functionality are modeled using a third order auto-regressive time series. Lane changing functionality is automated in Level 3 by using the Minimizing Overall Braking Induced by Lane Changes (MOBIL) algorithm. Automated control system for operational design is used for simulating Level 4 vehicles, and Level 4 vehicles' operational design domain is assumed to be any roadway with clear lane markings. Level 5 vehicles use a complete automation architecture. Homogeneous traffic consisting of only AVs is assumed. The traffic on the highway and on-ramp is 800 veh/hr/lane and 300 veh/hr/lane, respectively. Place of study: A 1.5 mile straight two-lane highway with a single-lane on-ramp joining the highway at the 0.3 mile
Salazar et al. (2018)	C	Multicommodity network flow (mesoscopic) optimization model	Study of models and coordination policies for integrated PT-SAV system. Electric SAVs are coupled with public transport system, i.e., customer routes are optimized by accounting for both SAV and public transportation services. The goal is to maximize social welfare. Road capacity has been reduced to account for other vehicles in the road network and a scaling factor (varied between 0 and 10%) is used for the same. Travel requests are assumed to be time invariant and a simple threshold model, consistent with classical traffic flow theory, is used for estimating travel time.

			Customer and vehicle routes are represented as fractional flows. Stochastic nature of the customer arrival process and the residual traffic in the network are not considered. Only car-sharing is assumed for SAV service and the customers are assumed to set routes by themselves, using navigation apps. The study assumes perfect SAV service market, i.e., the transportation prices are set by the market equilibrium. The value of travel time is assumed to be $24.40/h and operational cost for SAV service (without consideration of electricity) is assumed to be $0.30/mile. The data used for analysis is New York Taxi data (53, 932 taxi trips carried out on 01/03/2012 between 6 p.m. and 8 p.m.). A pricing and tolling scheme to achieve social optimum is also designed and tested. Place of study: Manhattan
Schmitz and von Trotha (2018)	B	Microscopic simulation	Evaluation of impacts of AVs on road capacity. The highway consists of five lanes with two lanes turning left and one to the right, and the intersection is controlled by a traffic light. Three scenarios, 100% conventional vehicles, 50/50 split of conventional vehicles and AVs, and 100% AVs, are analyzed and only traffic within two central lane is considered. Place of study: A major intersection in highway B3 in Frankfurt am Main
Shen et al. (2018)	B	AnyLogic	The study analyses the effects of introducing SAV services for first-mile connectivity (connection to MRT stations), during morning peak hours (06:00–09:00). The data used in this study is smart card data, corresponding to trips done in August 2013. SAVs are assumed to replace 11 low-demand buses (10% of the demand) and the remaining 16 buses (90% of the demand) continue to serve. Idle SAVs are sent to the parking lot of Tampines MRT station. Maximum waiting time is assumed to be 10 min, the vehicle capacity is 4 and bus dwell time is 30 s. The first hour of simulation (06:00–07:00) is considered as warm-up period and the next 2 h are used for analysis. The cost of service is assumed to be S$1/km. Detour ratio is used to calculate discount for ride-sharing trips. Scenario analysis include different fleet sizes (10–35) and two extreme sharing settings (no one willing to share ride and everyone willing to share). Place of study: Tampines area (Singapore)

Continued

Table 4 Description of the reviewed studies.—cont'd

Study	Study type	Model/analysis framework	Remarks
Stern et al. (2018)	O	Field experiment	Analysis of the ability of intelligently controlled CAVs to dampen stop-and-go waves created due to human driving behavior. Field experiments are conducted using 360 degree camera and an Onboard Diagnostics II (OBD-II) scanner. Two different strategies to control the velocity of an AV are tested in a single-lane circular track traversed by 22 vehicles. In the first strategy, a fixed average velocity based on observations is used, while a proportional-integral (PI) controller with saturation is used in the second strategy. Place of study: A single-lane circular track with a radius of 41.4 meters
Ye and Yamamoto (2018b)	B	Two-lane cellular automaton model	Analysis of the impacts of mixed traffic consisting of conventional vehicles and CAVs. Human drivers are assumed to have a reaction time of 1 s and for CAVs, reaction time is neglected. Conventional vehicles and CAVs were randomly distributed on the road segment. Place of study: A 10 km two-lane road segment
Ye and Yamamoto (2018a)	B	Cellular automaton model	Investigation of the impacts of implementing dedicated lanes. The mixed traffic consisting of both conventional vehicles and CAVs is modeled at a microscopic level and the results are presented at a macroscopic level. Three different values of desired net time gap in the adaptive cruise control process of CAVs, which determines the headway between the vehicles, are tested. The tested values are 0.5, 0.8, and 1.1 s. Place of study: A three-lane highway
Ye et al. (2018)	B	Two-lane cellular automaton model with heterogeneous flow model	Evaluation of the impacts of mixed traffic consisting of conventional vehicles and CAVs. A reaction time of 1 s is assumed for human drivers and for CAVs, the reaction time is neglected. Place of study: A 10 km two-lane road segment
Zhang et al. (2018)	B	Activity-based travel Model	Examination of the potential changes in residential location choice because of SAV services. In this study, a residential location choice model (developed using 2011 Atlanta Travel Survey and Zillow home sales data) is integrated with the SAV simulation model of Zhang and Guhathakurta (2017). Future home location choices

			are simulated based on current home location and real estate patterns. The demand in the region is assumed to be served by SAVs. Multinomial logit model is used for residential location choice. Trip departure time distribution is from 2011 ARC travel survey, and the link level travel speeds are fetched from the travel demand model of Atlanta Regional Commission. Cost for SAV service is assumed to be $0.12/km, and a scenario analysis is conducted based on reduction in in-vehicle travel time cost (25%–100% reduction). Place of study: Atlanta Metropolitan Area
Zhao and Kockelman (2018)	B	Modified four step model	Evaluation of the impacts of autonomous vehicles. In this study, the gravity model in a tradition four-step model for destination choice was replaced with a multinomial logit model. Nested multinomial logit model for mode choice was replaced with a simple multinomial logit model. Parameters were assumed based on the original model and the National Cooperative Highway Research Program's (NCHRP) Report 716. Four modes, conventional car, private autonomous vehicle, SAV and Bus, were included for analysis, and feedback between assignment step and destination choice model was implemented. Truck trip tables were directly added to the assignment step. The value of travel time for autonomous vehicles was assumed to be half of the conventional vehicles. The analysis was done for a weekday morning peak demand in 2020. The operating costs of conventional car, private autonomous vehicle and SAV were assumed to be $0.12/km, $0.25/km, and $0.62/km, respectively. Place of study: Austin
Alozi and Hamad (2019)	B	Vissim	Assessment of the impacts of CAVs on a freeway segment connecting the two cities of Dubai and Sharjah. The freeway has three interchanges. Totally 99 scenarios are simulated by varying traffic volumes and penetration rates (0%–100% in steps of 10%). Impacts are assessed in terms of average delay, average speed and travel time. Place of study: A 7 km freeway segment of Sheikh Mohammad Bin Zayed road (E311) in Dubai

Continued

Table 4 Description of the reviewed studies.—cont'd

Study	Study type	Model/analysis framework	Remarks
Carrese et al. (2019)	A, B	Emme	Analysis of traffic congestion in Rome for a horizon of 2050. The study includes a stated preference survey completed by 201 randomly selected residents, the results of which are used to estimate behavioral models and calibrate the traffic simulation model. The respondents live inside the Grande Raccordo Anulare (GRA), which is a toll-free, ring-shaped, 68.2 km long highway, encircling the city. Induced demand is not considered and no change in road capacity is assumed. The network is assumed to be filled by conventional vehicles, private and ridesharing SAVs. The penetration rate for AVs (including private and shared) is assumed to be 50%, and four scenarios are simulated by varying the penetration rates for ridesharing SAV services. No ridesharing service is introduced in the first scenario, while in the second scenario, a penetration rate of 6% is assumed for ridesharing SAV services. In the third and fourth scenarios, the penetration rates are 24% and 100%, respectively. Place of study: Rome
Chen (2019)	B	DynaTAIWAN	Evaluation of the impacts of (C)AVs. The study investigates three different signal control policies, pretimed signal control, actuated signal control, and intelligent intersection control. The network comprises of 27 traffic zones, 132 nodes and 363 links, and includes urban streets, freeways and expressways. Three demand levels are simulated, namely low (94,980 vehicles), medium (140,900 vehicles), and high (203,500 vehicles). Place of study: Subnetwork of Kaohsiung city
Kröger et al. (2019)	B	Aspatial travel demand model	Comparison of the impacts of introducing private AVs on travel behavior. Two 2035 scenarios, a trend scenario and an extreme scenario, are analyzed. A vehicle technology diffusion model is combined with an aspatial travel demand model. Place of study: Germany and United States
Li and Wagner (2019)	B	SUMO	Investigation of the impacts of AVs on travel time. Traffic data used in the study is from New Zealand Transportation Agency, collected during early 2012. Erdmann lane changing model is used. The simulation is run for three traffic scenarios, varying from free-flowing to heavily congested traffic. Penetration rate is incremented from 0% to 100% in steps of 10%. Additionally, the authors analyze the effect of VSL, using a rule based algorithm. Place of study: Auckland Motorway SH16

Martin-Gasulla et al. (2019)	B	Vissim	Proposal of an approach combining a preemption technique and allowance to use specified lanes, along with formation of constrained-length platoons, for CAVs to maximize throughput gain at low penetration rates for CAVs. The preemption technique involves allowing CAVs to use an exclusive extra lane at intersections. The traffic light for the extra-lane is preempted for a certain amount of time to allow the platooned CAVs to pass through, when the green phase allotted to the conflicting approach is terminated. The parameters are calibrated using the observed behavior of CAVs in the driving tests conducted as part of the European Funded Project CoEXist. A total demand of 1300 veh/h is assumed. Place of study: A two-lane intersection entry
Medina-Tapia and Robusté (2019)	C	Mathematical model (continuous, two-dimensional, total-cost function)	Macroscopic analysis of a mixed traffic system consisting of CAVs and conventional vehicles. The authors state that the results are applicable to any city with radio-centric structure (e.g., Paris, Milan, Moscow, Canberra, Chengdu and Santiago de Chile). The circular city consists of nine zones, a central business district, four internal zones and four external zones, and two types of primary roads, arterial and freeway. Dedicated lanes are apportioned for CAVs that allow the formation of platoons. A static assignment model was used to solve a system optimum (SO) traffic assignment in a continuous space. Place of study: A circular city with 405,000 private trips per hour
Papadoulis et al. (2019)	B	Vissim	Evaluation of the safety impact of CAVs on motorways. The authors develop a decision-making CAV control algorithm in C++, connect the same to Vissim using its External Driver Model API and create 5 different simulation models, one for each weekday. The models are calibrated and validated using data from inductive loop detectors and traffic measurements collected by a vehicle instrumented by Loughborough University. The traffic condition on the motorway is noncongested. The car-following time-gap is assumed to be 0.6 s. Five different scenarios with CAV penetration levels of 0%, 25%, 50%, 75%, and 100% are simulated. Place of study: A motorway corridor within M1 in England

Continued

Table 4 Description of the reviewed studies.—cont'd

Study	Study type	Model/analysis framework	Remarks
Simoni et al. (2019)	B	Matsim	Evaluation of the effects of different congestion pricing and tolling strategies. A sample of 5% of the total population (45,000 agents) in the study are simulated. Two different future scenarios, AV- and SAV-oriented, are analyzed. In the SAV-oriented scenario, one vehicle is available for every 10 agents. The maximum flow allowed in a link depends on the proportion of autonomous vehicles in the link. Pricing strategies evaluated are divided into two categories, namely traditional and advanced schemes. Traditional schemes include a link-based (charging on most congested links during peak hour) and a distance-based toll, while advanced schemes include a time-varying link-based toll (dynamic marginal cost pricing scheme at link level) and a travel time-based charge that depends on network conditions. Place of study: Austin. Place of study: Austin
Yu et al. (2019)	B	Aimsun	Analysis of the impact of implementing dedicated AV lanes. The behaviors of conventional vehicles and AVs are differentiated through reaction time, desired speed, and car-following models. A random reaction time is assigned for the conventional vehicles, from an uniform distribution with a range of 1.1–1.4 s. For the AVs, the reaction time is assumed to be insignificant. The conventional vehicles desired speed is set between 99 and 121 km/h and a desired speed of 110 km/h is set for AVs. For modeling conventional vehicle car following, behavior models mimicking human behavior are used, while for the AVs, a control logic model is used. Place of study: A 10.2 km highway with three main lanes and on/off-ramps, with each ramp consisting of one lane
Zheng et al. (2019)	B	Simulation based on stochastic Lagrangian dynamics	Investigation of the capability of CAVs to mitigate stop-and-go waves. Seven scenarios are tested using 20 vehicles, with varying levels of CAV penetration (5% to 50%; 1–10 vehicles). Place of study: A 260 m long single lane circular road

Study type: A—Studies based on surveys; B—Simulation based studies; C—Optimization programming; O—Others.
Note: Studies are sorted by year and then alphabetically by authors.

shift of users to other modes of transport because of comparatively high cost of SAV service ($1.03/km). In case of an integrated PT-SAV system, wherein the SAV system replaces the public transport in low demand areas, Shen et al. (2018) conclude that VKT decreases.

From the above, factors that influence vehicle requirements and VKT are type of (C)AV system, mode shift and penetration rate, and induced demand. Possible other factors identified from Sections 2–4 which can also influence vehicle requirements and VKT include value of travel time, network topology, congestion pricing, and parking management.

6. Factors identified and related policy recommendations

Based on the analysis from Sections 2–5, 19 different factors have been identified, which influence traffic flow efficiency implications of (C)AVs. They are acceleration/deceleration profile, lane changing rule, longitudinal driving behavior, presence of connectivity between AVs, desired and safe gap, vehicle type (e.g., electric and internal combustion engine), penetration rate, value of travel time, induced demand, network topology, vehicle distribution in a link, implemented optimization function, type of system (e.g., private and shared), congestion pricing scheme, dedicated lane for CAVs and AVs, intersection control method, parking management, platoon size and presence of VSL. These factors are grouped into four categories, namely (i) vehicle characteristics, (ii) travel behavior, (iii) network characteristics, and (iv) policies, as shown in Fig. 1.

As the name implies, the first group focuses on how the characteristics of the (C)AVs will influence the traffic conditions. The factors attributed to this group examine the properties of individual vehicles. The next group determines the effect of travel behavior of the people, containing the factors penetration rate and value of travel time. The third group contains the factors network topology, vehicle distribution and optimization function. This group analyses the effect that the underlying road and vehicle networks and the utilized network management functions have on traffic. The final group includes the effects of various policies such as VSL, CAV platoon size, parking management, intersection control, dedicated lane for (C)AVs, congestion pricing and the type of (C)AV system. This group assesses how various policy related decisions affect the impacts of (C)AVs on traffic. In Sections 6.1–6.4, the individual factors are explained together with their effect.

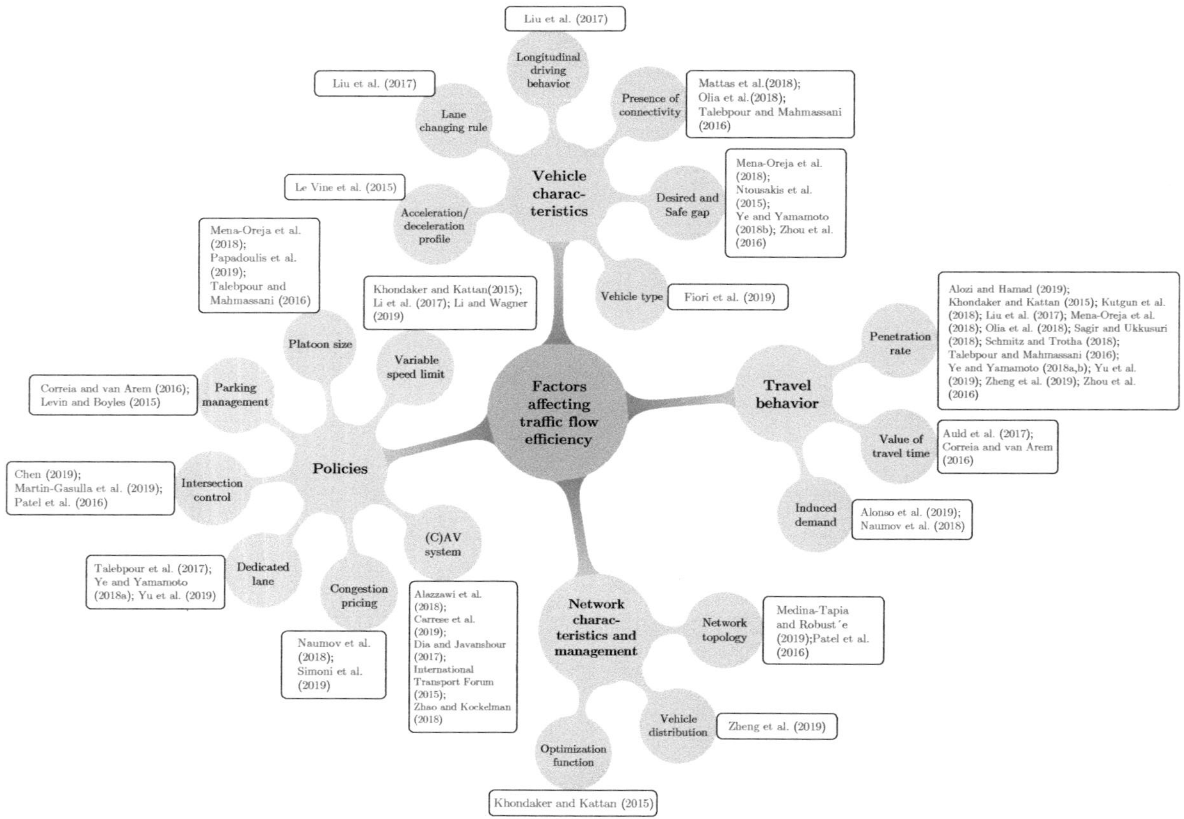

Fig. 1 Classification of factors influencing traffic flow efficiency and indicative references.

6.1 Vehicle characteristics

Looking at the group vehicle characteristics, the first factor is the acceleration/deceleration profile. If (C)AVs are allowed to have a more gentle acceleration/deceleration profile, there will be a negative impact on road capacity, because of the restriction on the dynamics of the vehicles (Le Vine et al., 2015). Policy makers and service providers have to understand that a gentle acceleration/deceleration profile will improve comfort and thereby may increase demand, but on the other hand can lead to drop in road capacity.

While there is no significant change in effect between using different lane changing behaviors such as polite and aggressive lane changing, longitudinal driving behavior is found to play a major role (Liu et al., 2017). Presence of connectivity between AVs (i.e., CAVs) significantly improves the less probable positive impacts of AVs (Mattas et al., 2018; Olia et al., 2018; Shladover, 2018; Talebpour and Mahmassani, 2016). The conservative behavior of AVs and their inability to predict the neighboring vehicles' movement during lane changing manoeuvers are the reasons for their lower ability to cause positive impacts. Therefore, policy makers have to motivate and support development of CAVs, rather than AVs. However, there can be other issues such as acceptance from different manufacturers and service providers.

On the one hand, higher desired and safe gaps are found to improve traffic stability (smoothing of traffic flow and decrease in speed dispersion due to decrease in oscillation) and safety (Li et al., 2017; Ye et al., 2018; Zhou et al., 2017), while on the other hand, they reduce road capacity improvements (Mena-Oreja et al., 2018). Especially at penetration rates above 30%, lower desired and safe gaps can substantially improve road capacity (Ye and Yamamoto, 2018b). While AVs are required to have a desired gap of less than 1.1 s for a positive impact on road capacity (Ntousakis et al., 2015), current vehicles with ACC are found to have a reaction time of around 1.1 s and the desired gap values are larger than those of conventional vehicles (Makridis et al., 2018). However, this cannot be generalized to all AV systems. Current ACC systems are designed with a focus on enhancing driver comfort and passengers' safety. This focus may change in advanced AVs in future, wherein there may be a focus also on facilitating traffic flows. Hence, further research works are needed to ascertain an optimal gap, maintaining a balance between safety, stability, and road capacity improvements. Finally, energy efficiency is positively related to lower speeds for electric vehicles, while for vehicles with internal combustion engines, lower and higher speeds relate to higher energy consumption (Fiori et al., 2019). Thus, policy makers should understand that application of electric vehicles with a motivation to attain environmental sustainability will require driving in lower speeds and hence, lower average travel times will be a result.

It should be remembered that existing simulation models (including microsimulation) do not have the capability to capture vehicle dynamics in a realistic way, for more accurate assessment of the vehicle dynamics impact on traffic flow (Ciuffo et al., 2018; Fadhloun et al., 2015; Makridis et al., 2019). Hence, policy makers should be careful, when making decisions based on the results from simulation studies. Field trials can complement the simulation studies, and decisions based on both field trials and simulation studies are expected to be better.

6.2 Travel behavior

Going over to the group travel behavior, the first factor concerns the penetration rate of CAVs and AVs. Studies concerning CAVs indicate that the road capacity will increase with an increase in CAV penetration rate, although some authors conclude that the increase will be more significant after a threshold (e.g., 20%—Mena-Oreja et al., 2018 and 30%—Olia et al., 2018; Ye and Yamamoto, 2018b). Furthermore, oscillations are found to decrease and traffic flow is found to become more stable with an increase in CAV penetration rate. Concerning AVs, the results are partly not unanimous. While Yu et al. (2019) conclude a gradual increase in capacity as the AV penetration rate increases, Schmitz and von Trotha (2018) conclude that the capacity decreases at 50% penetration rate, but increases at 100% penetration rate. Olia et al. (2018) conclude that the increase in road capacity because of AVs is only marginal. It should be noted that the results of Yu et al. (2019) are based on the application of dedicated lanes for AVs.

Results related to the impacts of change in value of travel time are also partly not unanimous. On the one hand, Correia and van Arem (2016) conclude that there will be an increase in travel due decrease in value of travel time, without adding congestion. On the other hand, Auld et al. (2017) conclude that there will be an increase in travel due to decrease in value of travel time, which results in more congestion. Furthermore, although CAVs can cause positive impacts, they also can produce induced demand (Alonso et al., 2019; Naumov et al., 2018).

Policy makers have to understand that there may be a reduction in traffic efficiency during the initials stages of (C)AV deployment, due to lower penetration rates. Furthermore, although (C)AVs can reduce the value of travel time, there will eventually be an increase in travel. Therefore, the positive impacts of CAVs may not be sufficient enough to result in a better network performance. Policy makers have to prepare for the initial reduction in efficiency and the later increase in travel.

6.3 Network characteristics

Focusing on network characteristics, with regard to network topology, Medina-Tapia and Robusté (2019) conclude that CAVs will improve road capacity more so for circular than for radial roads. Although the reason is not explicitly stated in the study, one can infer that the network topology affects the impacts of (C)AVs on traffic. Furthermore, Patel et al. (2016) show that the type of intersection control to be deployed for optimum results depends on the network characteristics. For example, they show that a reservation-based control performs better than conventional signals in general. However, in a congested network with several close local road and arterial intersections, conventional signals are found to be more efficient. Therefore, policy makers shall understand that the impact of (C)AVs on one city cannot be completely generalized for the other. Care should be taken when considering the impacts on other cities for a decision related to (C)AVs in their cities.

Distribution of AVs in a stream of vehicles is found to be insignificant in the study of Zheng et al. (2019). Their study is based on a single lane circular road consisting of 20 vehicles. However, we believe that distribution of (C)AVs within a link will have a significant effect on the traffic flow efficiency, especially at lower penetration rates.

Regarding the optimization function used to control overall vehicle movement, which falls under network management, Khondaker and Kattan (2015) show that optimizing just one objective function among mobility, safety, and sustainability is sufficient to achieve improvements in all three, when CAV penetration rate is 100%. However, when CAV penetration rate is 50%, a multiobjective optimization is required to obtain optimal inclusive benefits in mobility, safety, and sustainability simultaneously. This again shows that the policy makers have to carefully streamline the growth of (C)AVs during the initial stages.

6.4 Policies

Finally, in the policies group, studies pertaining to the factor type of (C)AV system show the same general tendencies, albeit with different results in terms of values. Generally, higher penetration rate for ride-sharing SAV service is indicated to reduce congestion (Alazzawi et al., 2018; Carrese et al., 2019; Martinez and Viegas, 2017), especially in inner city areas (Lang et al., 2018), together with reduction in VKT (Lokhandwala and Cai, 2018; Bischoff et al., 2017). SAV services replacing PT in low demand areas can also result in reduction in VKT (Shen et al., 2018). From the above, policy makers should understand that the most preferable (C)AV system is a ride-sharing SAV system. Furthermore, the SAV system should be integrated with PT, replacing PT in low demand areas. Narayanan et al. (2020) also suggest the same, supporting the deployment of (C)AVs in integrated shared mobility services, with an emphasis on ridesharing. Additionally, the policy makers have to remember that improved traffic conditions can lead to induced demand, as in Naumov et al. (2018). Congestion pricing can be implemented to curb such negative implications, since it is found to provide positive results (e.g., Naumov et al., 2018; Simoni et al., 2019).

Implementation of dedicated lanes for (C)AVs seems to lead to positive impacts, only when the penetration rate is above a threshold (e.g., 30%—Talebpour et al., 2017; Ye and Yamamoto, 2018a). At lower penetration levels, introducing dedicated lanes for AVs may result in higher travel times for conventional vehicles (Yu et al., 2019). Thus, as far as traffic implications are concerned, policy makers may avoid implementing dedicated lanes for (C)AVs, until they attain a substantial penetration rate. However, if conflicts between (C)AVs and conventional vehicles are to be avoided, dedicated lanes may be a solution.

Concerning intersection control, an intelligent signal control policy or a reservation based control enables better positive results (Chen, 2019; Patel et al., 2016). However, conventional signals perform better than reservation based controls in situations such as a congested network with several close local road and arterial intersections (Patel et al., 2016). At lower penetrations levels of AVs, application of a preemption technique (Martin-Gasulla et al., 2019) at intersections shows a positive impact. From these, the policy makers should understand that the conventional signals are still efficient for certain areas, while in the rest of the areas, advanced intersection control systems may be required.

Relocation capability of (C)AVs to avoid parking costs can result in additional trips and modal shifts from PT (Levin and Boyles, 2015), which can lead to additional congestion. However, without consideration for modal shifts, congestion effects will be lower, as in Correia and van Arem (2016). Thus, without proper parking policy in place, policy makers should understand that introduction of (C)AVs in certain cities could result in larger relocation trips to avoid parking cost. Congestion levels could become worse, when there is also a modal shift from PT (Kutgun et al., 2018).

Under mixed traffic conditions, where CAVs and conventional vehicles coexist, conventional vehicles may interfere with the platooning of CAVs. Hence, platoon size is a significant factor in determining the traffic flow implications of CAVs. Platooning, in general, is found to have positive impact, especially when the penetration rate of CAVs is above 20% (Mena-Oreja et al., 2018). This is because of the shorter distance between the vehicles driving inside a platoon. However, very long platoons can have negative impacts, because of higher probability for aborted maneuvers (Mena-Oreja et al., 2018), slow leader (Papadoulis et al., 2019), or instability due to leader's sudden break (Talebpour and Mahmassani, 2016). The policy makers should understand that the impacts of platooning depends on the penetration rate of CAVs and the traffic characteristics of a city. Finally, implementation of VSL has a positive impact on safety (Li et al., 2017; Li and Wagner, 2019), traffic flow (Khondaker and Kattan, 2015; Li and Wagner, 2019) and travel time reduction (Khondaker and Kattan, 2015; Li and Wagner, 2019). Hence, policy makers should make effective use of VSL.

7. Conclusions

Technology is a double-edged sword and automation is no exception. Although results pertaining to AVs are mixed, CAVs are concluded to be effective in producing positive traffic impacts. Therefore, policy makers should enact laws to emphasize connectivity between AVs. However, they have to remember that the positive benefits of CAVs may be absent at lower penetration rates. Furthermore, improved traffic conditions due to CAVs will lead to additional demand, and eventually, congestion will creep in again. In order to get out of this vicious cycle, strong policy regulations are needed. Three such policies identified from the literature include: application of (C)AVs in SAV services for last mile connectivity, incentivizing ridesharing, and implementation of congestion pricing schemes. When there is sufficient demand, it should be noted that public transportation is more efficient than other modes in terms of vehicle occupancy and reduction in congestion. Hence, in such situations, SAV services should complement public transport. Further, although ridesharing SAV services could significantly reduce traffic levels, improved traffic conditions again would result in increased traffic levels. Hence, congestion pricing is a necessity to curb development of additional traffic.

Since the traffic flow implications of (C)AVs depend on several city characteristics such as network topology and people behavior, policy makers should understand that a solution implemented in another city cannot be directly used in their cities, without adaptations. The policy makers should be aware of the factors that can influence the traffic implications of (C)AVs. Some of the factors that affect road capacity improvements, traffic stability and other traffic-related parameters, identified from the reviewed studies, include acceleration/deceleration profile, lane changing rule, longitudinal driving behavior, presence of connectivity between AVs, desired and safe gap, vehicle type (e.g., electric and internal combustion engine), penetration rate, value of travel time, induced demand, network topology, vehicle distribution in a link, implemented optimization function, type of system (e.g., private and shared), congestion pricing scheme, dedicated lane for (C)AVs, intersection control method, parking management, platoon size and presence of VSL. These factors are grouped into four categories, namely (i) vehicle characteristics, (ii) travel behavior, (iii) network characteristics, and (iv) policies.

Electric vehicles are being supported by the governments, with an objective to reduce emissions. However, in order to attain power efficiency, policy makers should understand that the electric vehicles may have to be driven at lower speeds, which can cause increase in average travel times. Without proper policy in place for parking management in the era of (C)AVs, policy makers should realize that relocation trips of (C)AVs, to avoid parking costs, could cause significant traffic issues. Although advanced intersection control systems may be beneficial in several areas, conventional signals will still be efficient in certain areas. Policy makers should avoid implementation of dedicated lanes for (C)AVs, until there is a penetration rate of at least 30%.

Regarding research gaps, one of the major limitations of the several reviewed studies relates to the assumptions for the parameters used in the modeling systems. Though there are increasing test beds and pilot projects for testing the AVs, excepting few like (Martin-Gasulla et al., 2019), studies are seldom seen using parameters based on the results from those tests. Given that the assumed parameters may be less realistic compared to those values obtained from the test beds, more studies are needed wherein the parameters for the modeling systems are calibrated based on the values from real world field experiments and test beds. Policy makers must depend more on studies, in which field trials complement the simulation studies.

Acknowledgments

This research has been supported by European Union's Horizon 2020 research and innovation program under grant agreement No. 815069 [project MOMENTUM (Modelling Emerging Transport Solutions for Urban Mobility)] and Horizon 2020 Framework COST (European Cooperation in Science and Technology) program [WISE–ACT project CA16222]. We would like to express our sincere gratitude to the three anonymous reviewers and the editor, who helped to improve our manuscript substantially. We also want to thank Nikita Makarov (TUM) for helping out with paper editing.

References

Alam, M.J., Habib, M.A., 2018. Investigation of the impacts of shared autonomous vehicle operation in Halifax, Canada using a dynamic traffic microsimulation model. Procedia Comput. Sci. 130, 496–503. https://doi.org/10.1016/j.procs.2018.04.066.

Alazzawi, S., Hummel, M., Kordt, P., Sickenberger, T., Wieseotte, C., Wohak, O., 2018. Simulating the impact of shared, autonomous vehicles on urban mobility—a case study of Milan. In: SUMO 2018—Simulating Autonomous and Intermodal Transport Systems, vol. 2, pp. 94–110. https://easychair.org/publications/download/28wc.

Alonso, M., Ciuffo, B., Ardente, F., Aurambout, J.-P., Baldini, G., Braun, R., Christidis, P., Christodoulou, A., Duboz, A., Felici, S., Rey, J., Georgakaki, A., Gkoumas, K., Grosso, M., Portela, M., Julea, A., Krause, J., Martens, B., Mathieux, F., Vandecasteele, I., 2019. The Future of Road Transport: Implications of Automated, Connected, Low-Carbon and Shared Mobility. Publications Office of the European Union, Luxembourg. http://publications.jrc.ec.europa.eu/repository/bitstream/JRC116644/fr-future-road-transport-online.pdf.

Alozi, A., Hamad, K., 2019. Quantifying impacts of connected and autonomous vehicles on traffic operation using micro-simulation in Dubai, UAE. In: Proceedings of the 5th International Conference on Vehicle Technology and Intelligent Transport Systems, SCITEPRESS—Science and Technology Publications, pp. 528–535.

Auld, J., Sokolov, V., Stephens, T.S., 2017. Analysis of the effects of connected-automated vehicle technologies on travel demand. Transp. Res. Record J. Transp. Res. Board 2625 (1), 1–8. https://doi.org/10.3141/2625-01.

Auld, J., Verbas, O., Javanmardi, M., Rousseau, A., 2018. Impact of privately-owned level 4 CAV technologies on travel demand and energy. Procedia Comput. Sci. 130, 914–919. https://doi.org/10.1016/j.procs.2018.04.089.

Bischoff, J., Maciejewski, M., Nagel, K., 2017. City-wide shared taxis: a simulation study in Berlin. In: 2017 IEEE 20th International Conference on Intelligent Transportation Systems (ITSC), Piscataway, NJ, IEEE, pp. 275–280.

BMW Group, 2016. BMW Group, Intel and Mobileye team up to bring fully autonomous driving to streets by 2021. https://www.press.bmwgroup.com/global/article/detail/T0261586EN/bmw-group-intel-and-mobileye-team-up-to-bring-fully-autonomous-driving-to-streets-by-2021?language=en.

Bösch, P.M., Ciari, F., Axhausen, K.W., 2016. Autonomous vehicle fleet sizes required to serve different levels of demand. Transp. Res. Rec. J. Transp. Res. Board 2542 (1), 111–119. https://doi.org/10.3141/2542-13.

Carrese, S., Nigro, M., Patella, S.M., Toniolo, E., 2019. A preliminary study of the potential impact of autonomous vehicles on residential location in Rome. Res. Transp. Econ. 75, 55–61. https://doi.org/10.1016/j.retrec.2019.02.005.

Chen, L.-W., 2019. Evaluation of traffic network performance under autonomous vehicles with intelligent signal control policies. In: Zhao, Y. (Ed.), Advances in Smart Vehicular Technology, Transportation, Communication and Applications. Smart Innovation, Systems, and Technologies, vol. 128. Springer, Cham, Switzerland, pp. 352–359.

Childress, S., Nichols, B., Charlton, B., Coe, S., 2015. Using an activity-based model to explore the potential impacts of automated vehicles. Transp. Res. Rec. J. Transp. Res. Board 2493 (1), 99–106. https://doi.org/10.3141/2493-11.

Ciuffo, B., Makridis, M., Toledo, T., Fontaras, G., 2018. Capability of current car-following models to reproduce vehicle free-flow acceleration dynamics. IEEE Trans. Intell. Transp. Syst. 19 (11), 3594–3603. https://doi.org/10.1109/TITS.2018.2866271.

Correia, G.H.d.A., van Arem, B., 2016. Solving the user optimum privately owned automated vehicles assignment problem (UO-POAVAP): a model to explore the impacts of self-driving vehicles on urban mobility. Transp. Res. B Methodol. 87, 64–88. https://doi.org/10.1016/j.trb.2016.03.002.

Daimler, A.G., 2017. Daimler and Uber join forces to bring more self-driving vehicles on the road. https://media.daimler.com/marsMediaSite/en/instance/ko/Daimler-and-Uber-join-forces-to-bring-more-self-driving-vehicles-on-the-road.xhtml?oid=15453638.

Dia, H., Javanshour, F., 2017. Autonomous shared mobility-on-demand: Melbourne pilot simulation study. Transp. Res. Procedia 22, 285–296. https://doi.org/10.1016/j.trpro.2017.03.035.

Fadhloun, K., Rakha, H., Loulizi, A., Abdelkefi, A., 2015. Vehicle dynamics model for estimating typical vehicle accelerations. Transp. Res. Record J. Transp. Res. Board 2491 (1), 61–71. https://doi.org/10.3141/2491-07.

Fagnant, D.J., Kockelman, K.M., 2014. The travel and environmental implications of shared autonomous vehicles, using agent-based model scenarios. Transp. Res. C Emerging Technol. 40, 1–13. https://doi.org/10.1016/j.trc.2013.12.001.

Fagnant, D.J., Kockelman, K.M., 2018. Dynamic ride-sharing and fleet sizing for a system of shared autonomous vehicles in Austin, Texas. Transportation 45 (1), 143–158. https://doi.org/10.1007/s11116-016-9729-z.

Fiori, C., Arcidiacono, V., Fontaras, G., Makridis, M., Mattas, K., Marzano, V., Thiel, C., Ciuffo, B., 2019. The effect of electrified mobility on the relationship between traffic conditions and energy consumption. Transp. Res. D Transp. Environ. 67, 275–290. https://doi.org/10.1016/j.trd.2018.11.018.

Gkartzonikas, C., Gkritza, K., 2019. What have we learned? A review of stated preference and choice studies on autonomous vehicles. Transp. Res. C Emerging Technol. 98, 323–337. https://doi.org/10.1016/j.trc.2018.12.003.

Gunter, G., Sprinkle, J., Seibold, B., Piccoli, B., Wang, Y., Gloudemans, D., Stern, R., Work, D., Monache, M. L. D., Bhadani, R., Bunting, M., Lysecky, R., 2019. String stability of commercial adaptive cruise control vehicles. In: Ramachandran, G.S., Ortiz, J. (Eds.), ICCPS '19 The Association for Computing Machinery, New York, NY, pp. 328–329.

Gurumurthy, K.M., Kockelman, K.M., 2018. Analyzing the dynamic ride-sharing potential for shared autonomous vehicle fleets using cellphone data from Orlando, Florida. Comput. Environ. Urban. Syst. 71, 177–185. https://doi.org/10.1016/j.compenvurbsys.2018.05.008.

Harper, C.D., Hendrickson, C.T., Mangones, S., Samaras, C., 2016. Estimating potential increases in travel with autonomous vehicles for the non-driving, elderly and people with travel-restrictive medical conditions. Transp. Res. C Emerging Technol. 72, 1–9. https://doi.org/10.1016/j.trc.2016.09.003.

Hawkins, A. J., 2017. GM says it will launch a robot taxi service in 2019. The Verge. https://www.theverge.com/2017/11/30/16720776/gm-cruise-self-driving-taxi-launch-2019.

International Association of Public Transport, 2017. Autonomous vehicles: a potential game changer for urban mobility. International Association of Public Transport. https://www.uitp.org/sites/default/files/cck-focus-papers-files/PolicyBrief_Autonomous_Vehicles_LQ_20160116.pdf.

International Transport Forum, 2015. Urban mobility system upgrade: how shared self-driving cars could change city traffic. OECD Publishing, Paris. https://ideas.repec.org/p/oec/itfaac/6-en.html.

Jager, B., Agua, F. M. M., Lienkamp, M., 2017. Agent-based simulation of a shared, autonomous and electric on-demand mobility solution. In: 2017 IEEE 20th International Conference on Intelligent Transportation Systems (ITSC), Piscataway, NJ, IEEE, pp. 250–255.

Khondaker, B., Kattan, L., 2015. Variable speed limit: a microscopic analysis in a connected vehicle environment. Transp. Res. C Emerging Technol. 58, 146–159. https://doi.org/10.1016/j.trc.2015.07.014.

Kondor, D., Zhang, H., Tachet, R., Santi, P., Ratti, C., 2018. Estimating savings in parking demand using shared vehicles for home-work commuting. IEEE Trans. Intell. Transp. Syst. 20 (8), 1–10. https://doi.org/10.1109/TITS.2018.2869085.

Korosec, K., 2018. Ford plans to spend $4 billion on autonomous vehicles by 2023. https://techcrunch.com/2018/07/24/ford-plans-to-spend-4-billion-on-autonomous-vehicles-by-2023/.

Kröger, L., Kuhnimhof, T., Trommer, S., 2019. Does context matter? A comparative study modelling autonomous vehicle impact on travel behaviour for Germany and the USA. Transp. Res. A Policy Pract. 122, 146–161. https://doi.org/10.1016/j.tra.2018.03.033.

Kutgun, H., Du Pont, V., Janzen, H., 2018. Effects of future connected autonomous vehicles on freeway congestion using fuzzy cognitive mapping. In: Kocaoglu, D.F., Anderson, T.R., PICMET, (Eds.), Managing Technological Entrepreneurship: The Engine for Economic Growth, IEEE, Piscataway, NJ, pp. 1–7.

Lang, N. S. L., Ruessmann, M., Collie, B. E., Wegscheider, A. K., Moavenzadeh, J., Loane, M., 2018. Reshaping urban mobility with autonomous vehicles: lessons from the city of Boston. World Economic Forum. http://www3.weforum.org/docs/WEF_Reshaping_Urban_Mobility_with_Autonomous_Vehicles_2018.pdf.

Le Vine, S., Zolfaghari, A., Polak, J., 2015. Autonomous cars: the tension between occupant experience and intersection capacity. Transp. Res. C Emerging Technol. 52, 1–14. https://doi.org/10.1016/j.trc.2015.01.002.

LeBeau, P., 2018. Waymo starts commercial ride-share service. https://www.cnbc.com/2018/12/05/waymo-starts-commercial-ride-share-service.html.

Levin, M.W., Boyles, S.D., 2015. Effects of autonomous vehicle ownership on trip, mode, and route choice. Transp. Res. Record J. Transp. Res. Board 2493 (1), 29–38. https://doi.org/10.3141/2493-04.

Li, D., Wagner, P., 2019. Impacts of gradual automated vehicle penetration on motorway operation: a comprehensive evaluation. Eur. Transp. Res. Rev. 11 (1), 1–10. https://doi.org/10.1186/s12544-019-0375-3.

Li, Y., Li, Z., Wang, H., Wang, W., Xing, L., 2017. Evaluating the safety impact of adaptive cruise control in traffic oscillations on freeways. Accid. Anal. Prev. 104, 137–145. https://doi.org/10.1016/j.aap.2017.04.025.

Liu, Y., Guo, J., Taplin, J., Wang, Y., 2017. Characteristic analysis of mixed traffic flow of regular and autonomous vehicles using cellular automata. J. Adv. Transp. 2017 (1705), 1–10. https://doi.org/10.1155/2017/8142074.

Lokhandwala, M., Cai, H., 2018. Dynamic ride sharing using traditional taxis and shared autonomous taxis: a case study of NYC. Transp. Res. C Emerging Technol. 97, 45–60. https://doi.org/10.1016/j.trc.2018.10.007.

Makridis, M., Mattas, K., Borio, D., Giuliani, R., Ciuffo, B., 2018. Estimating reaction time in adaptive cruise control system. In: 2018 IEEE Intelligent Vehicles Symposium (IV 2018), IEEE, Piscataway, NJ, pp. 1312–1317.

Makridis, M., Fontaras, G., Ciuffo, B., Mattas, K., 2019. MFC free-flow model: introducing vehicle dynamics in microsimulation. Transp. Res. Record J. Transp. Res. Board 2673 (4), 762–777. https://doi.org/10.1177/0361198119838515.

Martin-Gasulla, M., Sukennik, P., Lohmiller, J., 2019. Investigation of the impact on throughput of connected autonomous vehicles with headway based on the leading vehicle type. Transp. Res. Record J. Transp. Res. Board 2673 (5), 617–626. https://doi.org/10.1177/0361198119839989.

Martinez, L.M., Viegas, J.M., 2017. Assessing the impacts of deploying a shared self-driving urban mobility system: an agent-based model applied to the city of Lisbon, Portugal. Int. J. Transp. Sci. Technol. 6 (1), 13–27. https://doi.org/10.1016/j.ijtst.2017.05.005.

Mattas, K., Makridis, M., Hallac, P., Raposo, M.A., Thiel, C., Toledo, T., Ciuffo, B., 2018. Simulating deployment of connectivity and automation on the Antwerp ring road. IET Intell. Transp. Syst. 12 (9), 1036–1044. https://doi.org/10.1049/iet-its.2018.5287.

Medina-Tapia, M., Robusté, F., 2019. Implementation of connected and autonomous vehicles in cities could have neutral effects on the total travel time costs: modeling and analysis for a circular city. Sustainability 11 (2), 482. https://doi.org/10.3390/su11020482.

Mena-Oreja, J., Gozalvez, J., Sepulcre, M., 2018. Effect of the configuration of platooning maneuvers on the traffic flow under mixed traffic scenarios. In: Altintas, O. (Ed.), 2018 IEEE Vehicular Networking Conference (VNC), IEEE, Piscataway, NJ, pp. 1–4.

Mendes, L.M., Bennàssar, M.R., Chow, J.Y.J., 2017. Comparison of light rail streetcar against shared autonomous vehicle fleet for Brooklyn-Queens connector in New York City. Transp. Res. Record J. Transp. Res. Board 2650 (1), 142–151. https://doi.org/10.3141/2650-17.

Milakis, D., van Arem, B., van Wee, B., 2017. Policy and society related implications of automated driving: a review of literature and directions for future research. J. Intell. Transp. Syst. 21 (4), 324–348. https://doi.org/10.1080/15472450.2017.1291351.

Milanés, V., Shladover, S.E., 2014. Modeling cooperative and autonomous adaptive cruise control dynamic responses using experimental data. Transp. Res. C Emerging Technol. 48, 285–300. https://doi.org/10.1016/j.trc.2014.09.001.

Moreno, A.T., Michalski, A., Llorca, C., Moeckel, R., 2018. Shared autonomous vehicles effect on vehicle-Km traveled and average trip duration. J. Adv. Transp. 2018 (1), 1–10. https://doi.org/10.1155/2018/8969353.

Narayanan, S., Chaniotakis, E., Antoniou, C., 2020. Shared autonomous vehicle services: a comprehensive review. Transp. Res. C Emerging Technol. 111, 255–293. https://doi.org/10.1016/j.trc.2019.12.008. http://www.sciencedirect.com/science/article/pii/S0968090X19303493.

Naumov, S., Keith, D., Fine, C., 2018. The impact of autonomous vehicles on demand for driving: is pooling the solution to avoiding traffic gridlock? In: Record of the 36th International Conference of the System Dynamics Society. https://www.industrystudiesconference.org/conference/papers/download/136.

Ntousakis, I.A., Nikolos, I.K., Papageorgiou, M., 2015. On microscopic modelling of adaptive cruise control systems. Transp. Res. Procedia 6, 111–127. https://doi.org/10.1016/j.trpro.2015.03.010.

O'Kane, S., 2018. Former Google self-driving Wiz will help Volkswagen and Hyundai build fully autonomous cars, The Verge. https://www.theverge.com/2018/1/4/16846526/aurora-chris-urmson-volkswagen-hyundai-self-driving-cars.

Olia, A., Razavi, S., Abdulhai, B., Abdelgawad, H., 2018. Traffic capacity implications of automated vehicles mixed with regular vehicles. J. Intell. Transp. Syst. 22 (3), 244–262. https://doi.org/10.1080/15472450.2017.1404680.

Papadoulis, A., Quddus, M., Imprialou, M., 2019. Evaluating the safety impact of connected and autonomous vehicles on motorways. Accid. Anal. Prev. 124, 12–22. https://doi.org/10.1016/j.aap.2018.12.019.

Patel, R., Levin, M.W., Boyles, S.D., 2016. Effects of autonomous vehicle behavior on arterial and freeway networks. Transp. Res. Record J. Transp. Res. Board 2561 (1), 9–17. https://doi.org/10.3141/2561-02.

Qin, W.B., Orosz, G., 2019. Experimental validation of string stability for connected vehicles subject to information delay. IEEE Trans. Control Syst. Technol. 1–15. https://doi.org/10.1109/TCST.2019.2900609; https://ieeexplore.ieee.org/document/8685673.

Sagir, F., Ukkusuri, S.V., 2018. Mobility impacts of autonomous vehicle systems. In: The 21st IEEE International Conference on Intelligent Transportation Systems, pp. 485–490.

Salazar, M., Rossi, F., Schiffer, M., Onder, C.H., Pavone, M., 2018. On the interaction between autonomous mobility-on-demand and the public transportation systems. In: proc_IEEE_ITSC. Maui, HI. https://arxiv.org/pdf/1804.11278.

Schmitz, K., von Trotha, D., 2018. Capacity effect of autonomous vehicles. Arthur D. Little GmbH. https://www.adlittle.com/sites/default/files/viewpoints/adl_study_capacity_impact_autonomous_driving_study_extract_1.pdf.

Shao, R., Chang, L., 2008. A new maximum power point tracking method for photovoltaic arrays using golden section search algorithm. In: 2008 Canadian Conference on Electrical and Computer Engineering, IEEE, pp. 000619–000622.

Shen, Y., Zhang, H., Zhao, J., 2018. Integrating shared autonomous vehicle in public transportation system: a supply-side simulation of the first-mile service in Singapore. Transp. Res. A Policy Pract. 113, 125–136. https://doi.org/10.1016/j.tra.2018.04.004.

Shladover, S.E., 2018. Connected and automated vehicle systems: introduction and overview. J. Intell. Transp. Syst. 22 (3), 190–200. https://doi.org/10.1080/15472450.2017.1336053.

Shladover, S.E., Su, D., Lu, X.-Y., 2012. Impacts of cooperative adaptive cruise control on freeway traffic flow. Transp. Res. Record J. Transp. Res. Board 2324 (1), 63–70. https://doi.org/10.3141/2324-08.

Shladover, S.E., Nowakowski, C., Lu, X.-Y., Ferlis, R., 2015. Cooperative adaptive cruise control. Transp. Res. Record J. Transp. Res. Board 2489 (1), 145–152. https://doi.org/10.3141/2489-17.

Simoni, M.D., Kockelman, K.M., Gurumurthy, K.M., Bischoff, J., 2019. Congestion pricing in a world of self-driving vehicles: an analysis of different strategies in alternative future scenarios. Transp. Res. C Emerging Technol. 98, 167–185. https://doi.org/10.1016/j.trc.2018.11.002.

Stern, R.E., Cui, S., Delle Monache, M.L., Bhadani, R., Bunting, M., Churchill, M., Hamilton, N., Haulcy, R., Pohlmann, H., Wu, F., Piccoli, B., Seibold, B., Sprinkle, J., Work, D.B., 2018. Dissipation of stop-and-go waves via control of autonomous vehicles: field experiments. Transp. Res. C Emerging Technol. 89, 205–221. https://doi.org/10.1016/j.trc.2018.02.005.

Talebpour, A., Mahmassani, H.S., 2016. Influence of connected and autonomous vehicles on traffic flow stability and throughput. Transp. Res. C Emerging Technol. 71, 143–163. https://doi.org/10.1016/j.trc.2016.07.007.

Talebpour, A., Mahmassani, H.S., Elfar, A., 2017. Investigating the effects of reserved lanes for autonomous vehicles on congestion and travel time reliability. Transp. Res. Record J. Transp. Res. Board 2622 (1), 1–12. https://doi.org/10.3141/2622-01.

Trivedi, A., 2018. Honda and Toyota are piling billions of dollars into autonomous cars. https://www.bloomberg.com/opinion/articles/2018-10-04/japan-s-carmakers-throw-money-at-the-future-of-driving.

Ye, L., Yamamoto, T., 2018a. Impact of dedicated lanes for connected and autonomous vehicle on traffic flow throughput. Physica A 512, 588–597. https://doi.org/10.1016/j.physa.2018.08.083.

Ye, L., Yamamoto, T., 2018b. Modeling connected and autonomous vehicles in heterogeneous traffic flow. Physica A 490, 269–277. https://doi.org/10.1016/j.physa.2017.08.015.

Ye, L., Yamamoto, T., Morikawa, T., 2018. Heterogeneous traffic flow dynamics under various penetration rates of connected and autonomous vehicle. In: The 21st IEEE International Conference on Intelligent Transportation Systems, pp. 555–559.

Yu, H., Tak, S., Park, M., Yeo, H., 2019. Impact of autonomous-vehicle-only lanes in mixed traffic conditions. Transp. Res. Record J. Transp. Res. Board 18 (6). https://doi.org/10.1177/0361198119847475036119811984747.

Zhang, W., Guhathakurta, S., 2017. Parking spaces in the age of shared autonomous vehicles: how much parking will we need and where? Transp. Res. Record J. Transp. Res. Board 2651 (1), 80–91. https://doi.org/10.3141/2651-09.

Zhang, W., Guhathakurta, S., Khalil, E.B., 2018. The impact of private autonomous vehicles on vehicle ownership and unoccupied VMT generation. Transp. Res. C Emerging Technol. 90, 156–165. https://doi.org/10.1016/j.trc.2018.03.005. http://www.sciencedirect.com/science/article/pii/S0968090X18303188.

Zhao, Y., Kockelman, K.M., 2018. Anticipating the regional impacts of connected and automated vehicle travel in Austin, Texas. J. Urban Plan. Dev. 144 (4), 04018032. https://doi.org/10.1061/(ASCE)UP.1943-5444.0000463.

Zheng, F., Lu, L., Li, R., Liu, X., Tang, Y., 2019. Traffic oscillation using stochastic Lagrangian dynamics: simulation and mitigation via control of autonomous vehicles. Transp. Res. Record J. Transp. Res. Board 229 (1178). https://doi.org/10.1177/0361198119844455036119811984445.

Zhou, M., Qu, X., Jin, S., 2017. On the impact of cooperative autonomous vehicles in improving freeway merging: a modified intelligent driver model-based approach. IEEE Trans. Intell. Transp. Syst. 18, 1422–1428. https://doi.org/10.1109/TITS.2016.2606492.

CHAPTER TWO

Automated bus systems in Europe: A systematic review of passenger experience and road user interaction

Daniël D. Heikoop[a,*], J. Pablo Nuñez Velasco[a], Reanne Boersma[a], Torkel Bjørnskau[b], Marjan P. Hagenzieker[a]

[a]Transport & Planning, Faculty of Civil Engineering and Geosciences, Delft University of Technology, Delft, The Netherlands

[b]Department of Safety, Security and Environment, Norwegian Centre for Transport Research/Institute of Transport Economics TØI, Oslo, Norway

[*]Corresponding author: e-mail address: d.d.heikoop@tudelft.nl

Contents

Abstract

Automated driving systems promise a tremendous amount of benefits. Especially when applied in the domain of public transport, economic and passenger advantages are thought to be manifold. As technology rapidly advances, and projects involving automated buses appear throughout the world, investigating how its users and surrounding road traffic interact with these novel technologies need to advance with a similar pace. However, up to now, a reliable and up-to-date overview of performed, running, and planned projects is lacking. Moreover, little is known about human interaction with automated bus systems, and what is known is not always reported. By means of a systematic review, an overview of the current state-of-the-art knowledge on the interaction between automated bus systems and its interactors is presented. Results of these

Advances in Transport Policy and Planning, Volume 5
ISSN 2543-0009
https://doi.org/10.1016/bs.atpp.2020.02.001

studies are described and discussed, and implications are being made regarding future policies to be applied in this domain to safeguard safe interaction with automated bus systems.

Keywords: Automated bus systems, Systematic review, Projects inventory, Passenger experience, Road user interaction, Policy implications

1. Introduction

From one vehicle showing its state-of-the-art technologies, to worldwide collaborations using a variety of vehicles differing in autonomy, location, and purpose, automated driving systems are becoming increasingly intelligent and commonplace. The benefits of automated driving systems are deemed plentiful, ranging from economic to environmental, such as reduced fuel consumption and carbon emission, and from personal to temporal benefits, such as having the freedom to read emails on your way to work and improved traffic flow. Public transport is generally regarded as one of the more suitable candidates to benefit from automating certain driving tasks (Shladover et al., 2016), hence this particular domain is receiving increasingly more attention from researchers, developers, and stakeholders alike. As a result, projects involving automated public transport systems are appearing with accelerating pace, and keeping up to date about their current developments is becoming increasingly cumbersome. A comprehensive overview of all these projects would provide valuable insights for researchers regarding what has been done in the past, and what is currently ongoing or planned in the domain of automated driving systems. Overviews like this do exist, but are not always (kept) up-to-date and often lack the detailed information needed for research purposes. For instance, the Bloomberg.org Group created an interactive map on current and planned projects involving autonomous vehicles (Bloomberg.org Group, 2018), and Connected and Automated Driving Europe's website gives an overview of European projects in the field of automated road transport (Connected and Automated Driving Europe, 2019), but these are not exhaustive and detailed information is often not provided. When narrowing down to automated bus systems, finding an exhaustive and up-to-date overview of completed, running, and planning projects becomes even more challenging. From a technological, energy efficiency, and legality perspective, a recent overview article investigated predominantly European completed and ongoing automated bus projects (Ainsalu et al., 2018). Although being exhaustive in their respective perspective, this overview does not provide an insight into the human perspective and their interaction with automated bus systems.

In terms of human interaction with automated driving systems in general, several issues have been raised several decades ago already, while still remaining relevant up to this day (see, e.g., Kyriakidis et al., 2019; Saffarian et al., 2012; Stanton and Marsden, 1996). Regarding the human interaction with automated bus systems, although being different in nature due to their subject, the issues are more or less as old and remain as relevant today as those in automated driving systems in general (see, e.g., Martens et al., 2008; Nordhoff et al., 2018; Warren and Kunczynski, 2000). It is therefore important to keep an even pace with technology, and, if we want to have the consumer (keep) using promising novel technology, maintain an up-to-date knowledge base of how humans (prefer to) interact with such technologies as automated bus systems.

In this chapter, we will seek answers to the following four research questions: (1) What is known about human interaction with automated bus systems? (2) Which methodologies are being used in research regarding the interaction between humans and automated bus systems? (3) What research gaps exist? and (4) which policy implications can be derived so far?

The chapter aims to answer these questions by performing a systematic review on the topic of automated bus systems and the interaction with its (direct or indirect) users. This will be done by starting off with a broad approach to ensure an as all-encompassing cover as possible, and then narrowing down by applying a series of pre-determined filtering steps. The results of this systematic review will consequently be interpreted and represented in a thematic overview. Ultimately, the implications of these results will be discussed, and policy recommendations will be suggested.

2. Method

The systematic review was performed by following a series of steps allowed for an objective analysis of the current literature. Fig. 1 displays the series of steps taken in this systematic review.

As a first step, a Scopus search was performed on April 26, 2019. In Scopus, one can search in academic literature for specific words. One can narrow down the search by limiting their search field, for instance to title, abstract, and/or keyword only, to a specific domain like business, or to specific volumes or authors. In this systematic review, the search was limited to

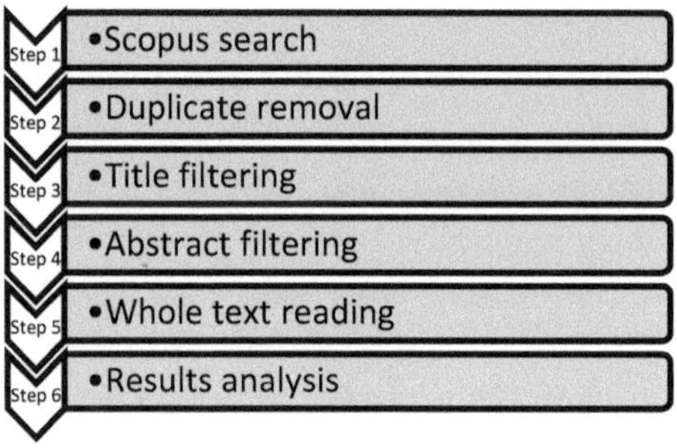

Fig. 1 Approach of the systematic review performed in this study.

Table 1 Search terms for the Scopus systematic review.

Domain	Automation	Subject
Bus(es)	Automated	Vulnerable road user(s)
Shuttle(s)	Autonomous	Cyclist(s)
Pod(s)	Driverless	Pedestrian(s)
Road transport system(s)	Self-driving	Passenger(s)
Personal rapid transit		User(s)
Transit network(s)		Public
People mover(s)		VRU(s)

title, abstract, and keyword only, but no other restrictions were applied. The systematic review queries were divided into three parts, namely domain, automation, and subject. In order to ensure an all-encompassing search, a broad scope was taken, meaning that several synonyms of the domain, the term "automation," and the subject were taken into account in the search. Determining appropriate search domains was done by investigating the titles and subjects of known literature in this domain. Regarding the domain of automated bus systems, this resulted in seven synonyms (see Table 1). For the "automation" term, four synonyms were used, and seven different subjects were determined. Also the plural versions of the terms were used, as it was noted during a piloting trial of the queries this otherwise would leave out valuable results. With these terms combined, a query was formed and submitted into the Scopus search field. An example of such a query would then be:

TITLE-ABS-KEY (cyclist OR cyclists) AND TITLE-ABS-KEY (autonomous AND (bus OR buses))

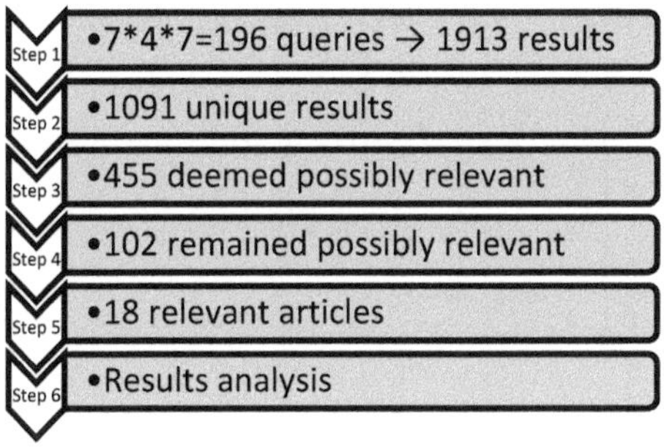

Fig. 2 Intermediate results per step of the systematic review.

This entailed a total of $7 \times 4 \times 7 = 196$ search queries, which provided 1913 results (Fig. 2). After filtering for duplicates as the second step in the systematic review, 1091 unique results were left. The third step in the process was an initial filtering procedure in which the titles of all unique articles were read, and selected or discarded based on whether it featured a user-automated bus interaction scope. This step entailed among others discarding results that were clearly technology-oriented, and involved automated systems other than buses, such as trains, while keeping titles that were either deemed relevant in any way, or found to have (an ambiguous) potential to be relevant. As a result, 455 articles were deemed relevant for this systematic review based on their title. Of the remaining articles, as a fourth step, their abstracts were read, to further filter out ultimately irrelevant articles.

With this step, 102 articles remained. Where there were any disputable (in terms of relevance) articles left, as a final step, the full article was read in order to determine its relevance, which ultimately lead to a total of 18 articles that were deemed relevant for this systematic review. Note, however, that of 5 articles out of the 102 their full papers could not be read, as they were not retrievable. It is nevertheless likely that, in line with the rest of the filtering procedure, these articles will have been irrelevant to this study as well. The relevant articles were consequently used for the analysis of this research and are presented in Section 3 (Table 2).

3. Results

3.1 Descriptive results of the systematic review

The first and most obvious result of the systematic review is that published research on this topic is still sparse. The 196 queries delivered little over a thousand results, which translates into less than 6 hits per query.

Table 2 Overview of the scientific literature that present empirical research on the interaction between automated buses and its users and/or interactors.

Author(s)	Year	Project	Location (type)	Length	Bus type	Speed	Steward	Service type	Method	No ppts	Ppt type	Categories			Measures		
Alessandrini et al.	2011	CityMobil	Verdun Square, La Rochelle, France (restricted access)	?	Many	?	Yes	Demo	Questionnaire	256	Users[a]	Acceptance	Quality of service		Importance ranking	Performance rating	
Boersma et al.	2018	STAD	Appelscha, The Netherlands (separate cycle lane)	2.5 km	EZ10	15 km/h[b]	Yes	Pilot	Questionnaire and observations	20 and 50	Users and VRUs[c]	*Undisclosed*			*Undisclosed*		
Distler et al.	2018	–	Lyon, France (public road with a.o. pedestrians)	15 min	Navya	20 km/h	Yes	Experiment	Questionnaire and observations	14	Users	Pre- and post-immersion	Automated vehicles		UTAUT[d]	CTAM[e]	
Eden et al.	2017	Smart Shuttle	Sion, Switzerland (public road with a.o. pedestrians)	1.5 km	Navya	20 km/h	Yes	Pilot	Interviews and observations	?	Users and VRUs	Attitudes and opinions	Interactions		Descriptive	Notes	Videos photos
Eden et al.	2017	Smart Shuttle	Sion, Switzerland (public road with a.o. pedestrians)	1.5 km	Navya	20 km/h	Yes	Pilot	Interviews and observations	17	Users	Attitudes and opinions			Descriptive		
Kim et al.	2017	–	Seoul National University Campus, Seoul, South Korea (campus)	4.5 km	?[f]	?	Yes	Regular service	Questionnaire	10	Users	Quality of service			Reliability	Accessibility	Safety
															Comfort	Convenience	Price
Madigan et al.	2016	CityMobil2	La Rochelle, France and Lausanne, Switzerland (public roads with a.o. pedestrians)	1.71 km and 1.585 km	? and EZ10	12 km/h[g]	Yes	Pilot	Questionnaire	349	Public[h] (users)	Performance expectancy	Behavioral intention		Adapted UTAUT		
												Social influence	Effort expectancy				
Madigan et al.	2017	CityMobil2	Trikala, Greece (public roads with a.o. pedestrians)	2.5 km	?	13 km/h	Yes	Demo	Questionnaire	315	Public (users)	Performance expectancy	Behavioral intention	Hedonic motivation	Adapted UTAUT		
												Social influence	Effort expectancy	Facilitating			

Merat et al.	2018	CityMobil2	La Rochelle, France, Lausanne, Switzerland, and Trikala, Greece (public roads with a.o. pedestrians)	2.6 km, ? and ?	?, EZ10 and ?	10 km/h	Yes[i]	Demo	Questionnaire	664	VRUs	Safety and priority	Type and mode of communication		Designated questions		
Moták et al.	2017	–	Estaing Hospital, Clermont-Ferrand, France (?)	?	?	?	?	?	Questionnaire	31[j]	Users	Intentions of re-use			Extensions	TAM[k]	TPB[l]
															Values		
Nordhoff et al.	2018	–	EUREF office campus, Berlin-Schöneberg, Germany (campus)	0.7 km	Olli	8 (avg) –10 (max) km/h	Yes	Regular service	Questionnaire	384	Users	Quality of service	Acceptance	Attitude[m]	Designated questions	Van der Laan	UTAUT
Oliveira et al.	2018	UK Autodrive	Urban Development Lab, Coventry, UK (fitted warehouse)	?	RDM	?	No	Experiment	Questionnaire	20	Users	Trust	Usability	Workload	SUS[n]	ATT[o]	NASA-TLX[p]
Portouli et al.	2017	CityMobil2	Trikala, Greece (public roads with a.o. pedestrians)	2.4 km	?	?	Yes	Demo	Questionnaire	200 and 498[q]	Users and public	Satisfaction	Safety and security	Usability	Designated questions		
												Intention of use and pay	Attractiveness	Attitudes and opinions			
Rehrl and Zankl	2018	Digibus	Koppl, Austria (public roads)	2.8 km	Navya	16 km/h[r]	Yes	Pilot and demo	Questionnaire	294	Users	Test purpose	Prior knowledge and experience	Driving pleasure	Designated questions		
												Safety	Usability				
Salonen	2018	CityMobil2	Vantaa, Finland (segregated lane [with tunnel])	0.95 km	EZ10	13 km/h	Yes	Demo	Questionnaire	197	Users	Emergency management	Safety	Security	Designated questions		

Continued

Table 2 Overview of the scientific literature that present empirical research on the interaction between automated buses and its users and/or interactors.—Cont'd

Author(s)	Year	Project	Location (type)	Length	Bus type	Speed	Steward	Service type	Method	No ppts	Ppt type	Categories			Measures		
Salonen and Haavisto	2019	–	Otaniemi, Espoo, Finland (campus)	0.7 km	EZ10	12 km/h	Yes	Pilot	Interview	44	Users	Attitude Affection	Imminent reactions	Social factors	TIB[s]	Descriptive	
Straub and Schaefer	2019	ARIBO	US Army installation, USA (army base (including roadways and sidewalks))	?	?	?	Yes	Simulation and pilot and regular service	Experiment and observation and video data and observation	24 and 20 and 86 and 91 and 3	Users and VRUs and road users[t]	Responsibility	Communication	Safety	Low-risk and high-risk	Descriptive	Videos
Wintersberger et al.	2018	–	Bavaria, Germany (public roads with a.o. pedestrians)	1 km	EZ10	?	Yes	Regular service	Interview	12[u]	Users	Opinion Trust	Usability Intention of use	Attitude	TAM2	Descriptive	

[a]Defined as those actively using/having used the bus.
[b]The max speed of the EZ10 was 40 km/h. Due to legal reasons, the max speed for this pilot was set at 15 km/h.
[c]Vulnerable road users; defined as those actively interacting with the bus from outside the bus.
[d]Unified theory of acceptance and use of technology.
[e]Car technology acceptance model.
[f]Technically, this was a taxi.
[g]The maximum speed of both vehicles was 45 km/h, but in reality not achieved.
[h]Defined as those not actively using/having used the bus, but at most merely having seen the bus.
[i]Not mentioned in-text, but deduced based on similar research.
[j]Total amount of participants in this research was over 500, but those were only used for study 1. Study 2 had 108 participants; wave 2 of study 2, the relevant part of the study for the systematic review, had 54 participants; only 80 and 31, respectively, were used in the analysis.
[k]Technology acceptance model.
[l]Theory of planned behavior.
[m]Among which were performance expectancy and effort expectancy (see Madigan et al., 2016, 2017).
[n]System usability scale.
[o]Advanced transport telematics survey.
[p]NASA task load index.
[q]519 Participants of which 21 indicated no knowledge of the autonomous mini bus.
[r]The max speed of the Navya was 45 km/h. Due to legal reasons, the max speed for this pilot was set at 20 km/h. Due to safety reasons, the max speed for this pilot was set at 16 km/h.
[s]Theory of interpersonal behavior.
[t]Defined as those actively interacting with the bus from outside the bus, who do not fall under the definition of VRUs.
[u]24, But only results of 12 described in this paper.
?, Unknown

Of those hits, a mere 1.6% were eventually found relevant to this study. Table 2 shows the details of the 18 articles that were relevant for this study. What is interesting, is that none but one (Alessandrini et al., 2011) predates 2016, which clearly indicates the relative novelty of this type of technology. Moreover, the 2011 CityMobil demonstration was a showcase placed at a relatively small market square, at which the first type of such vehicles from several different partners and manufacturers were shown, also demonstrating a range of different technologies, such as platooning and advanced (instead of the now fairly common adaptive) cruise control (ACC). This thus does not yet compare with the more recent projects which were predominantly aimed for (eventual) continuous use. Furthermore, CityMobil's successor, CityMobil2, appears to be the most prolific project in terms of scientific outreach, providing 5 of the 18 articles for this analysis.

In terms of geographic spread, it can be seen that the largest proportion of reported experiments on the interaction with automated bus systems are found in Europe, with only two articles being from outside of Europe: South Korea, and the USA (Kim et al., 2017; Straub and Schaefer, 2019). The South Korean article also reports the longest distance over which the automated bus system drove, namely 4.5 km, where the average reported distance among all articles is 1.9 km (13 articles reporting 14 distances). It should be noted, however, that this vehicle in the South Korean pilot had taxi characteristics (see also Table 2, footnote f). Furthermore, its speed was not mentioned in their paper. Assumedly, this was higher than average in Table 2, hence making it possible to drive longer distances than other vehicles listed in this paper who had more bus-like characteristics.

Navya and EZ10 are the two most prominent bus types reported in the articles, albeit noteworthy that eight of the articles did not provide any or all details of the bus types used. It is also worth noting that the buses' speed is equally underreported: in eight instances, no speeds were reported. Of particular interest is that some articles reported that the buses' maximum speed is (much) higher than that used in their pilots and/or demos. Due to legal and/or safety issues, the vehicle operators significantly reduced the maximum speed of the buses, to ensure a safe research or demonstration environment (see, e.g., Boersma et al., 2018; Madigan et al., 2016; Rehrl and Zankl, 2018). Moreover, for safety reasons, all but one (excluding those not reporting) had a safety driver/operator/steward on board of the automated bus system at all times. The one without a steward on board is that reported by Oliveira et al. (2018). Their experiment was performed under strictly secured circumstances, for instance without surrounding traffic and in a simulated city inside a laboratory. Direct communication with the research team was at all times possible, and an emergency stop button was inside the automated bus system.

As the technology behind automated bus systems is still fairly new, most of these systems are still being tested or demonstrated. This can also be seen in our results. Only 4 articles refer to (some sort of) regular service of their automated bus systems, whereas the other 13 are either demonstrations, pilots or experiments. The only article in which we were unable to explicitly identify the automated bus system's service type is that of Moták et al. (2017). As their main topic of investigation was the development of a model of acceptance, and they used an existing and already running automated bus system, elaborating on the details of that bus system may not have been their priority. They were also the only ones that did not elaborate on the trajectory length, bus type and speed, and steward presence.

The section that answers our second research question inventoried each research's methodology. Almost exclusively, the experiments performed in the articles were questionnaire-based. The works of Salonen and Haavisto (2019) and Wintersberger et al. (2018) were the only two not indicating having made use of a questionnaire. Instead, they took a (semi-structured) interview approach—which nevertheless somewhat resembles a questionnaire, but has the distinctive difference of having descriptive results, rather than ratings or rankings, which are common in questionnaires. Note that the two articles mentioned above were not the only two making use of descriptive measures. Five other articles indicated other methods, namely, observations (Boersma et al., 2018; Distler et al., 2018; Eden et al., 2017a,b) and an experimental setting and video analysis (Straub and Schaefer, 2019).

The number of participants was generally high but varied substantially between each study. The 18 articles together indicated performing 24 (sub)studies, for which only one article (Eden et al., 2017a) did not mention the number of participants recruited. The average amount of participants was 156 ($SD = 184$). The least amount of participants was 3, for sub-study 4 of Straub and Schaefer (2019), in which observations were made for the "second vehicle problem," meaning a situation where another driver who crosses the traffic behaves irregularly (i.e., against the rules of the road) or unexpectedly around the automated bus system, which eventually leads to a harmonica effect to the vehicles behind the automated bus system. The highest number of participants was 664 (Merat et al., 2018), which were recruited simultaneously in the three cities of La Rochelle, Lausanne, and Trikala, for a questionnaire-based experiment. Conducting experiments based on questionnaires usually allows for recruiting high amounts of participants. Seeing that the majority of the experiments performed in these articles are based on questionnaires, this would explain the high average amount of participants.

The nature of the participants were usually people who (just or recently) used the automated bus system. Four articles (Boersma et al., 2018; Eden et al., 2017a; Merat et al., 2018; Straub and Schaefer, 2019) indicated having conducted their research with vulnerable road users (or VRUs; i.e., pedestrians or cyclists; those who interacted with the automated bus system from *outside* of the automated bus system).

The main topic of interest of the articles was to investigate the users' acceptance of or attitude toward the automated bus systems. One of two commonly used measures to assess the users' level of acceptance of technology was the UTAUT (unified theory of acceptance and use of technology; Venkatesh et al., 2003) model, or a variation thereof (see, e.g., Madigan et al., 2016, 2017). The other is the technology acceptance model (TAM; Davis, 1986). A relatively large portion appeared to have specifically designed their questionnaire to fit their topic of interest. Five articles (Merat et al., 2018; Nordhoff et al., 2018; Portouli et al., 2017; Rehrl and Zankl, 2018; Salonen, 2018) have been found to not (only) use predesigned established questionnaires, but to also prefer aimed questions for their specific purpose. Another five articles (Eden et al., 2017a,b; Salonen and Haavisto, 2019; Straub and Schaefer, 2019; Wintersberger et al., 2018) used descriptions of their observations or interviews to make assessments of their topics of interest.

3.2 What is known about human experience and interaction with automated bus systems?

In essence, how much pleasure an automated bus system gives to its user predicts how much it will be used (Madigan et al., 2017; Moták et al., 2017; Nordhoff et al., 2016). Specifically, how an automated bus system performs, as well as how easy it is to use, are two of the main factors for (future) users (e.g., Alessandrini et al., 2011; Madigan et al., 2016; Nordhoff et al., 2018). But, interestingly, this finding is countered by Moták et al. (2017)'s results, who found ease of use to be the only *in*significant variable. Another interesting result is the impact of media and peer pressure on the public attitude toward the automated bus systems (e.g., Eden et al., 2017b; Madigan et al., 2017; Moták et al., 2017). News reports (for instance on autonomous vehicle crashes) as well as the beliefs of family and friends thus also weigh heavily on people's willingness to use an automated bus system.

Noteworthy is, supported by most of the literature selected in this study, although being relevant, the perceived usefulness of the automated bus system did not appear to be a primary determinant for its users. Following this, public acceptance of automated bus systems is generally positive (Portouli et al., 2017; Rehrl and Zankl, 2018; Salonen and Haavisto, 2019), but is influenced over time by its (reliable, consistent, or disappointing, etc.) performance (e.g., Boersma et al., 2018; Distler et al., 2018; Moták et al., 2017). Also, people appear to have a high level of trust in the automated bus system (either with a safety driver on board, e.g., Salonen and Haavisto, 2019; Straub and Schaefer, 2019, or without, e.g., Oliveira et al., 2018), although being dependent on the demographics of the user pool (Salonen and Haavisto, 2019; Wintersberger et al., 2018).

A steward on board was generally found to be important for information distribution to its users (e.g., Boersma et al., 2018), but also the surrounding traffic (Eden et al., 2017a), and the feeling of safety (Distler et al., 2018; Eden et al., 2017b; Rehrl and Zankl, 2018). This feeling of safety is generally considered to be one of people's main concerns regarding the automated bus system (e.g., Alessandrini et al., 2011; Portouli et al., 2017; Rehrl and Zankl, 2018). This concern is usually well caught, as it is usually perceived to be high (e.g., Eden et al., 2017b; Portouli et al., 2017; Salonen, 2018). Higher concerns remain about the automated bus systems' security (Distler et al., 2018; Oliveira et al., 2018; Salonen, 2018).

Interestingly, the results of Nordhoff et al. (2018) suggest that supervision from a control room rather than from inside the automated bus system is preferred, which seems out of balance with the other studies. This may be related to whether or not the automated bus system has an on-board information display which depicts its current status (see, e.g., Oliveira et al., 2018).

Communication from the automated bus system was found to be important (e.g., Boersma et al., 2018; Eden et al., 2017a; Kim et al., 2017). In terms of expectancy, for instance regarding priority, people need assurance about the automated bus systems' intent, which could also be provided by (the absence of) lane markings (Merat et al., 2018). Notifying its users and surrounding traffic about its speed and general behavior improves user acceptance (Boersma et al., 2018).

In general, people appear to be positive toward the implementation of (future) automated bus systems (e.g., Alessandrini et al., 2011; Distler et al., 2018; Eden et al., 2017b). Nevertheless, people generally appeared to have problems with the low speed of the automated bus systems. Cyclists had difficulty determining whether they should overtake (Boersma et al., 2018), while users found it ineffective (e.g., Distler et al., 2018; Kim et al., 2017; Nordhoff et al., 2018). What is more, quite often users found that the automated bus systems need some tweaking to improve smooth driving (e.g., Boersma et al., 2018; Eden et al., 2017b; Kim et al., 2017).

As a final result, specific adaptations for targeted groups appears not to be necessary for the development of automated bus systems. A one-size-fits-all approach is likely to be successful (Madigan et al., 2016, 2017; Nordhoff et al., 2018). As an exception, however, one finding that did provide a significant difference was the users' sense of in-vehicle security, where men rated it higher than women (Salonen, 2018).

4. Discussion and conclusions

With the systematic review presented in this chapter, we aimed to answer four research questions. The first questioned our current knowledge about human interaction with automated bus systems. From the scientific literature that we were able to find, a relatively small number of published articles have been found to be relevant for this study. Those that were relevant (18 articles in total), had some consensual findings as well as some conflicting results.

Consensual findings were the overall accepting attitude of the public toward the (implementation of) automated bus systems, as well as importance of the opinions of others (such as the media) for using them. This accepting nature of the public may be explained by the infrastructure of the transportation area automated bus systems are commonly aimed to be implemented in, namely the "last mile," which is commonly known as a caveat of the transportation area (see, e.g., Boyer et al., 2009). Furthermore, it was found that the automated bus systems' low speed was the most common factor that received a negative connotation. This is known to be due to people's concern about the time they have to spend traveling, which they prefer to be as low as possible (Hensher et al., 2003).

In terms of methodology (our second research question), it can be seen that questionnaires are the most used means of method for conducting experiments in relation to user acceptance or satisfaction. Established questionnaires, such as the technology acceptance model (TAM; Davis, 1986), or the unified theory of acceptance and use of technology

(UTAUT; Venkatesh et al., 2003) are frequently used. More objective measures have only been applied in a few studies (e.g., mental workload measured through, for example, heart rate variability; Shakouri et al., 2018). Also, behavioral observation, for instance by means of video registrations, has so far not been applied in many studies. The reason might be that this is a high-workload technique, requiring skilled analysts as well as a lot of time. However, there are pilots currently running where such methods have been adopted (Bjørnskau et al., 2019).

The relative lack of objective measures used for the assessment of human interaction with automated bus systems is consequently a research gap worth mentioning, answering our third research question. Another research gap is related to the low speed of the automated bus systems presented in these 18 articles. Either for legal- or safety-issues, speeds were low (max. 20 km/h), and therefore it remains to be seen how people would interact and experience automated bus systems when they would be driving at regular speeds (i.e., 50, 80, or perhaps even over 100 km/h when implemented on highways). Especially when combining several automated bus systems into platoons driving on highways, high speeds are beneficial to, among others, aerodynamic drag (see, e.g., Tsugawa, 2010); henceforth, the eventual increase of speed for these systems should be pursued.

Furthermore, most current projects involving automated buses use existing infrastructure, and risky situations have been found to occur when ordinary road users overtake the slow driving buses (Bjørnskau et al., 2019). The question then is whether infrastructural adjustments are needed (e.g., additional markings or cycle tracks), or whether under certain conditions a shared-space approach would be preferable (e.g., related to speed, position on the road; Vissers et al., 2016). The final research question, regarding policy implications, will be discussed below.

The performance of this systematic review proved to be a challenging endeavor, as it appeared that the research domain of human interaction with automated bus systems is still a niche area. Not much is known about this yet, and even less has been reported. By means of backward engineering—recalling search terms of relevant articles, and using those as search queries, to aim to be as all-encompassing as possible—another issue was elicited which is unfortunately not uncommon in the scientific domain, namely the issue of construct proliferation. This is a phenomenon where two or more different names are (mistakenly or deliberately) being coined for the same construct (see, e.g., Shaffer et al., 2016). In this systematic review, the majority of the false positives were due to this issue, as it was known that automated bus systems had at least six other domain names, and three other names for it being automated (see Table 1, left column). Because also domain names were used which are commonly used in a different domain (such as "automated people mover" which is commonly used in the airport domain), the majority of the results involved, for instance, airport rail/metro automated people movers on a guided track. More specifically, this entailed a larger domain, known as "automated guideway transit," which are driverless vehicles automatically guided along a guideway (Kittelson, and Associates, Inc., Parsons Brinckerhoff, KFH Group, Inc., Texam A&M Transportation Institute, and Arup, 2013), and include domains such as "group rapid transit," "people mover systems," "automated people movers," and "personal rapid transit." Since our domain of interest was automated bus systems *without* a guideway, the results gathered from these search queries were, apart from those proliferated, irrelevant for our study.

Other popular domains gathered by this systematic review are the technology-oriented, as well as the future-oriented domains, which either predominantly or completely focus on the technical aspects of creating, designing, and/or deploying current automated bus systems, or planning, philosophizing, and/or debating future automated bus systems. Within these articles, subjects such as users, passengers, or other vulnerable road users could be taken into account, but the interaction between topic and subject was not the focus of those articles.

A final portion of irrelevant articles within the results of the search queries involved articles that were not on empirical research, but presented, for instance, a report of a demonstration or planned projects and activities.

4.1 Limitations

Although the utmost care has been taken to be all-encompassing during the systematic review, certain existing empirical articles on automated bus systems interaction with humans may have been excluded from this analysis. Future studies could reproduce this systematic review with other focused search queries to encompass those missed out on in this study. A broader approach could be taken by, for instance, including other search terms or consulting search engines that include gray literature, although caution should be taken there in relation to the degree of freedom of these systems with respect to the interaction with its users and surrounding traffic.

During the filtering procedure, a cautious approach has been taken, to avoid mistakenly discarding a relevant article. Albeit unlikely, due to the cautious approach taken, as this was a manual process, mistakes could have been made. A replication study could be performed to acquire a form of inter-rater reliability.

5. Policy implications

The introduction of AVs as part of a transport system accentuates policy implications at different levels. At a general level there is the issue about how to introduce AVs in the transport system; should it be in the form of shared, public transport systems, as private automated cars and/or as self-driving taxis (Nenseth et al., 2019).

In this chapter we have focused on the research and the findings regarding automated bus systems. Although research results are still sparse and many questions remain, there are numerous pilots going on in cities all over the world, mostly operated by some public transport authority.[a] Simultaneously there is a rapid development of self-driving cars intended for the traditional individual car market, either for shared or private use, in the form of automated taxis (Waymo, Uber, etc.) and more or less self-driving traditional individual car use. Thus there is an ongoing race between the car/taxi industry (Volvo, Tesla, Waymo, Uber, etc.) and public transport companies about implementing automated transport services. Both real-life experience of cheaper and more flexible taxi solutions (Uber/Lyft in San Francisco) and model simulations reveal that promoting cheaper individual (i.e., private) transport solutions in the cities will increase traffic volumes. Furthermore, simulations and experiments reveal that such a development may lead to urban sprawl because living outside cities becomes more attractive with cheap and flexible transport (Milakis et al., 2018). Such developments are contrary to the widespread aims of achieving more sustainable and liveable cities. Thus it is vital that public authorities take the necessary steps to regulate the introduction of automated transport in cities in the form of shared transport solutions limiting traffic growth.

The ambition of many transport companies is to deploy automated buses in mixed traffic, and it is important to gain insight into how other road users respond. When AVs are introduced in mixed traffic, Straub and Schaefer (2019) timely point to the need for policy making at more detailed levels, i.e., about actual operations in the streets. Given the conservative and defensive driving style of the automated buses, the buses stop abruptly for any obstacle registered by the bus sensors, providing discomfort to the passengers. Some

[a] Preliminary results from the ongoing Autobus project show around 120 fairly well documented automated bus projects in 18 European countries that have been executed so far, and many more—less well documented—are being planned (Hagenzieker et al., 2020).

researchers predict that over time other road users, interacting with the bus, will be aware of this and take advantage of the bus' defensive driving style, and deny the bus the right of way in all situations. This will in turn severely reduce the buses' accessibility and eventually make it impossible for the buses to be able to operate in mixed traffic (Millard-Ball, 2018). It is therefore paramount to study empirically how normal road users respond and interact with the automated buses. Some studies are currently under way and will provide valuable insights into such issues, like the Norwegian Autobus project where normal road users' interaction with automated buses are observed over time (Bjørnskau et al., 2019).

Straub and Schaefer (2019) identify a number of policy issues that need to be addressed to successfully integrate AVs in real-life traffic: (1) Control allocation—when and in what situations must humans take over control; (2) communications with vulnerable road users—AVs follow the formal rules but are so far not able to communicate and negotiate in informal ways, which is an essential part of normal traffic. Thus, AVs can be unpredictable and create dangerous situations, precisely because they adhere 100% to the formal rules (Bjørnskau et al., 2019; Rothengatter, 1991). (3) The courtesy problem and communication with other drivers—other drivers may deviate from normal behavior when interacting with AVs, which may lead to dangerous situations. (4) The "second vehicle problem"—AVs are not prepared and will not respond appropriately when other road users deviate from the formal rules. The automated minibuses that have been in operation so far are all programmed to stop for any object close to the vehicle, resulting in numerous abrupt stops providing discomfort for the passengers. Straub and Schaefer (2019) emphasize the need to take social interaction into considerations when introducing AVs in real-life traffic and they suggest to consider AV-to-human communication guidelines, better communication/signaling systems, the role and operation of AV sensor systems and more vigorous enforcement of existing rules.

According to Milakis (2019), referring to Legacy et al. (2019), public sector planners have by and large adopted a "watch and wait" approach to the introduction of AVs, leaving the initiative very much to the providers of AV transport services. And policy-makers seem to conceive AVs more as a threat than as an opportunity (Taeihagh and Lim, 2019). Such a conservative approach is risky with respect to the general policy needs; i.e., how to introduce AVs in a way consistent with the goals of sustainable and livable cities. In some respects one may say that the introduction of automated transport accentuates an old issue—how to avoid queues and crowds in and out of the cities during rush hour. Already nearly 60 years ago, Downs (1962) pointed out that expanding road capacity was not the way to do it; it will quickly be filled up by more cars. To follow-up, making individual transport cheaper and more flexible will lead to more transport. In other words, the solution is to reduce the need for transport and smarter, shared transport. It can be achieved with shared autonomous vehicles. Thus, maybe the introduction of AVs will wake up public authorities to realize the necessity of regulating car driving in and out of our cities.

A more proactive approach from public planners and authorities may also be called for when deploying AVs such as automated bus systems in real-life traffic, following the arguments presented by Straub and Schaefer (2019), Millard-Ball (2018) and Bjørnskau et al. (2019). As shown in the overview presented above, most pilots only allow buses to travel at very low speeds, and the buses are programmed to drive extremely defensively. By the very slow speeds they deviate from normal road user behavior which may produce risky situations and which make them unattractive as a transport means. Hence, as pointed out by Straub and Schaefer (2019), there is a need for policy to make such AV transport systems more realistic in order to be considered a useful and relevant transport means integrated in the transport network, and in order to avoid risky situations in real-life traffic.

Acknowledgments

This systematic review was carried out in the context of the AUTOBUS project funded by the Norwegian research council NFR, the Norwegian Public Roads Administration, Ruter, Kolumbus and Buskerud country (NFR project 28338).

References

Ainsalu, J., Arffman, V., Bellone, M., Ellner, M., Haapamäki, T., Haavisto, N., …, Åman, M., 2018. State of the art of automated buses. Sustainability 10, 1–34. https://doi.org/10.3390/su10093118.

Alessandrini, A., Holguin, C., Parent, M., 2011. Advanced transport systems showcased in La Rochelle. In: Proceedings of the 14th International IEEE Conference on Intelligent Transportation Systems, pp. 896–900, October 5–7, Washington, DC, USA.

Bjørnskau, T., De Ceunynck, T., Fyhri, A., Pelssers, B., Hagenzieker, M., Ivina, D., Johansson, O., and Laureshyn, A., Cyclists interacting with self-driving buses—hypotheses and empirical findings in real traffic. In: International Cycling Safety Conference, Brisbane, Australia, 18–20 November 2019.

Bloomberg.org Group, 2018. Initiative on Cities and Autonomous Vehicles. Retrieved April 30, 2019, from, https://avsincities.bloomberg.org/global-atlas/.

Boersma, R., van Arem, B., Rieck, F., 2018. Application of driverless electric automated shuttles for public transport in villages: the case of appelscha. World Electr. Veh. J. 9, 1–7. https://doi.org/10.3390/wevj9010015.

Boyer, K.K., Prud'homme, A.M., Chung, W., 2009. The last mile challenge: evaluating effects of customer density and delivery window patterns. J. Bus. Logist. 30, 185–201.
Connected and Automated Driving Europe, 2019. Research. Retrieved April 30, 2019 from https://connectedautomateddriving.eu/cad-knowledge-base/.
Davis, F.D., 1986. A Technology Acceptance Model for Empirically Testing New End-User Information Systems: Theory and Results. Doctoral dissertation, Sloan School of Management, Massachusetts Institute of Technology.
Distler, V., Lallemand, C., Bellet, T., 2018. Acceptability and acceptance of autonomous mobility on demand: the impact of an immersive experience. In: Proceedings of the 2018 CHI Conference on Human Factors in Computing Systems, pp. 1–10. April 21–26, Montreal, QC, Canada, https://doi.org/10.1145/31773574.3174186.
Downs, A., 1962. The law of peak-hour expressway congestion. Traffic Q. 16 (3), 393–409.
Eden, G., Nanchen, B., Ramseyer, R., Evéquoz, F., 2017a. On the road with an autonomous passenger shuttle: integration in public spaces. In: CHI'17 Extended Abstracts. https://doi.org/10.1145/3027063.3053126. May 6–11, Denver, CO, USA.
Eden, G., Nanchen, B., Ramseyer, R., Evéquoz, F., 2017b. Expectation and experience: passenger acceptance of autonomous public transportation vehicles. In: Bernhaupt, R., Dalvi, G., Joshi, A., Balkrishan, D., O'Neill, J., Winckler, M. (Eds.), Human-Computer Interaction—INTERACT 2017. Lecture Notes in Computer Science, vol. 10516. Springer, Cham, pp. 360–363. https://doi.org/10.1007/978-3-319-68059-0_30.
Hagenzieker, M., Boersma, R., Nunez Velasco, P., Ozturker, M., Zubin, I., Heikoop, D., 2020. Automated buses in Europe: An inventory of pilots (version 0.5) Delft University of Technology. https://www.researchgate.net/publication/339271299_Automated_Buses_in_Europe_An_Inventory_of_Pilots_version_05. The Netherlands.
Hensher, D.A., Stopher, P., Bullock, P., 2003. Service quality—developing a service quality index (SQI) in the provision of commercial bus contracts. Transp. Res. A 37, 499–517. https://doi.org/10.1016/S0965-8564(02)00075-7.
Kim, S.-W., Gwon, G.-P., Hur, W.-S., Hyeon, D., Kim, D.-Y., …, Seo, S.-W., 2017. Autonomous campus mobility services using driverless taxi. IEEE Trans. Intell. Transp. Syst. 18, 3513–3526. https://doi.org/10.1109/TITS.2017.2739127.
Kittelson & Associates, Inc., Parsons Brinckerhoff, KFH Group, Inc., Texam A&M Transportation Institute, & Arup, 2013. Chapter 11: glossary and symbols. In: Transit Capacity and Quality of Service Manual. Transit Cooperative Highway Research Program (TCRP) Report 165, third ed. Transportation Research Board, Washington, pp. 11–52. ISBN 978-0-309-28344-1.
Kyriakidis, M., De Winter, J.C.F., Stanton, N.A., Bellet, T., Van Arem, B., Brookhuis, K., …, Happee, R., 2019. A human factors perspective on automated driving. Theor. Issues Ergon. Sci. 3, 223–249. https://doi.org/10.1080/1463922X.2017.1293187.
Legacy, C., Ashmore, D., Scheurer, J., Stone, J., Curtis, C., 2019. Planning the driverless city. Transp. Rev. 39, 84–102.
Madigan, R., Louw, T., Dziennus, M., Graindorge, T., Ortega, E., …, Merat, N., 2016. Acceptance of automated road transport systems (ARTS): an adaptation of the UTAUT model. Transp. Res. Procedia 14, 2217–2226. https://doi.org/10.1016/j.trpro.2016.05.237.
Madigan, R., Louw, T., Wilbrink, M., Schieben, A., Merat, N., 2017. What influences the decision to use automated public transport? Using UTAUT to understand public acceptance of automated road transport systems. Transp. Res. F 50, 55–64. https://doi.org/10.1016/j.trf.2017.07.007.
Martens, M., Pauwelussen, J., Schieben, A., Flemisch, F., Merat, N., Jamson, H., Caci, R., 2008. Human Factors' Aspects in Automated and Semi-Automatic Transport Systems: State of the Art. Deliverable No. D3.2.1, DG Research.

Merat, N., Louw, T., Madigan, R., Wilbrink, M., Schieben, A., 2018. What externally presented information do VRUs require when interacting with fully automated road transport systems in shared space? Accid. Anal. Prev. 118, 244–252. https://doi.org/10.1016/j.aap.2018.03.018.

Milakis, D., 2019. Long-term implications of automated vehicles: an introduction. Transp. Rev. 39 (1), 1–8. https://doi.org/10.1080/01441647.2019.1545286.

Milakis, D., Kroesen, M., van Wee, B., 2018. Implications of automated vehicles for accessibility and location choices: evidence from an expert-based experiment. J. Transp. Geogr. 68, 142–148.

Millard-Ball, A., 2018. Pedestrians, autonomous vehicles and cities. J. Plan. Educ. Res. 38, 6–12.

Moták, L., Neuville, E., Chambres, P., Marmoiton, F., Monéger, F., … , Izaute, M., 2017. Antecedent variables of intentions to use an autonomous shuttle: moving beyond TAM and TPB? Rev. Eur. Appl. Psychol. 67, 269–278. https://doi.org/10.1016/j.erap.2017.06.001.

Nenseth, V., Ciccone, A., Buus Christensen, N., 2019. Societal Consequences of Automated Vehicles—Norwegian Scenarios. Institute of Transport Economics, Oslo. Report 1700/2019, https://www.toi.no/publikasjoner/samfunnsmessige-konsekvenser-av-automatiserte-kjoretoy-norske-scenarioer-article35555-8.html.

Nordhoff, S., van Arem, B., Happee, R., 2016. A conceptual model to explain, predict, and improve user acceptance of driverless vehicles. Transp. Res. Rec. J. Transp. Res. Board 2602, 60–67. https://doi.org/10.3141/2602-08.

Nordhoff, S., De Winter, J.C.F., Madigan, R., Merat, N., Van Arem, B., Happee, R., 2018. User acceptance of automated shuttles in Berlin-Schöneberg: a questionnaire study. Transport. Res. F: Traffic Psychol. Behav. 58, 843–854. https://doi.org/10.1016/j.trf.2018.06.024.

Oliveira, L., Luton, J., Iyer, S., Burns, C., Mouzakitis, A., … , Birrell, S., 2018. Evaluating how interfaces influence the user interaction with fully autonomous vehicles. In: Automotive UI '18: 10th International ACM Conference on Automotive User Interfaces and Interactive Vehicular Applications, Toronto, Canada, September 23–25. https://doi.org/10.1145/3239060.3239065.

Portouli, E., Karaseitanidis, G., Lytrivis, P., Amditis, A., Raptis, O., Karaberi, C., 2017. Public attitudes towards autonomous mini buses operating in real conditions in a Hellenic City. In: 2017 IEEE Intelligent Vehicles Symposium (IV), June 11–14, Redondo Beach, CA, USA.

Rehrl, K., Zankl, C., 2018. Digibus©: results from the first self-driving shuttle trial on a public road in Austria. Eur. Transp. Res. Rev. 10, 1–11. https://doi.org/10.1186/s12544-018-0326-4.

Rothengatter, T., 1991. Normative behaviour is unattractive if it is abnormal: relationships between norms, attitudes and traffic law. In: Paper Presented at the International Road Safety Symposium, 1990, Copenhagen, Denmark.

Saffarian, M., De Winter, J.C.F., Happee, R., 2012. Automated driving: human-factors issues and design solutions. In: Proceedings of the Human Factors and Ergonomics Society 56th Annual Meeting, pp. 2296–2300. https://doi.org/10.1177/1071181312561483.

Salonen, A.O., 2018. Passenger's subjective traffic safety, in-vehicle security and emergency management in the driverless shuttle bus in Finland. Transp. Policy 61, 106–110. https://doi.org/10.1016/j.tranpol.2017.10.011.

Salonen, A.O., Haavisto, N., 2019. Towards autonomous transportation. Passengers' experiences, perceptions and feelings in a driverless shuttle bus in Finland. Sustainability 11, 1–19. https://doi.org/10.3390/su11030588.

Shaffer, J.A., DeGeest, D., Li, A., 2016. Tackling the problem of construct proliferation: a guide to assessing the discriminant validity of conceptually related constructs. Organ. Res. Methods 19, 80–110. https://doi.org/10.1177/1094428115598239.

Shakouri, M., Ikuma, L.H., Aghazadeh, F., Nahmens, I., 2018. Analysis of the sensitivity of heart rate variability and subjective workload measures in a driving simulator: the case of highway work zones. Int. J. Ind. Econ. 66, 136–145. https://doi.org/10.1016/j.ergon.2018.02.015.

Shladover, S.E., Lu, X.-Y., Song, B., Dickey, S., Nowakowski, C., Howell, A., …, Nelson, D., 2016. Demonstration of Automated Heavy-Duty Vehicles (California PATH Research Report, UCB-ITS-PRR-2005-23). Institute of Transportation Studies, University of California, Berkeley, CA.

Stanton, N.A., Marsden, P., 1996. From fly-by-wire to drive-by-wire: safety implications of automation in vehicles. Saf. Sci. 24, 35–49. https://doi.org/10.1016/S0925-7535(96)00067-7.

Straub, E.R., Schaefer, K.E., 2019. It takes two to tango: automated vehicles and human beings doing the dance of driving—four social considerations for policy. Transp. Res. A 122, 173–183. https://doi.org/10.1016/j.tra.2018.03.005.

Taeihagh, A., Lim, H.S.M., 2019. Governing autonomous vehicles: emerging responses for safety, liability, privacy, cybersecurity, and industry risks. Transp. Rev. 39 (1), 103–128.

Tsugawa, S., 2010. Automated driving systems: common ground of automobiles and robots. Int. J. Humanoid Rob. 8, 1–12. https://doi.org/10.1142/S0219843611002319.

Venkatesh, V., Morris, M.G., Davis, G.B., Davis, F.D., 2003. User acceptance of information technology: toward a unified view. MIS Q. 27, 425–478.

Vissers, L., Van der Kint, S., Van Schagen, I., Hagenzieker, M., 2016. Safe interaction Between Cyclists, Pedestrians and Autonomous Vehicles. What Do We Know and What Do We Need to Know?. R-2016-16, SWOV Institute for Road Safety Research, The Hague, The Netherlands.

Warren, R., Kunczynski, Y., 2000. Planning criteria for automated people movers: defining the issues. J. Urban Plann. Dev. 126, 166–188.

Wintersberger, P., Frison, A.-K., Riener, A., 2018. Man vs. machine: comparing a fully automated bus shuttle with a manually driven group taxi in a field study. In: AutomotiveUI '18 Adjunct. https://doi.org/10.1145/3239092.3265969, September 23–25, Toronto, ON, Canada.

CHAPTER THREE

Cyber security and its impact on CAV safety: Overview, policy needs and challenges

Christos Katrakazas[a,e,*], Athanasios Theofilatos[b], George Papastefanatos[c], Jérôme Härri[d], Constantinos Antoniou[e]

[a]Department of Transportation Planning and Engineering, National Technical University of Athens, Athens, Greece
[b]Transport and Urban Planning Group, School of Architecture, Building, and Civil Engineering, Loughborough University, Leicestershire, United Kingdom
[c]Information Management Systems Institute (IMSI), "Athena" Research Center, Athens, Greece
[d]Communication Systems Department, EURECOM, Sophia-Antipolis, France
[e]Chair of Transportation Systems Engineering, Department of Civil, Geo, and Environmental Engineering, Technical University of Munich, Munich, Germany
*Corresponding author: e-mail address: ckatrakazas@mail.ntua.gr

Contents

Abstract

Connected and Autonomous Vehicles (CAVs) will progressively change the functionality of current transportation systems, promising enhanced safety for all traffic participants. Furthermore, there is a palpable connection between road safety and cyber security breaches, as malicious software could lead to unexpected behavior of CAVs triggering collisions and causing fatalities and injuries. Therefore, policymakers and stakeholders need to take into account knowledge from both CAV safety and cyber security experts, in order to develop the essential regulations. This chapter attempts to link the two domains by reviewing recent approaches with regards to risk assessment for CAVs and cyber security, the impacts of cyber security on road safety and the corresponding challenges. With regards to collision risk assessment, approaches concerning road safety and robotics are mainly reviewed to keep a concise viewpoint on the cybersecurity problem. The main outcomes of this review were that current solutions are solely

ISSN 2543-0009
https://doi.org/10.1016/bs.atpp.2020.05.001

concerned either with collisions and casualties or with the prevention of cyber-attacks with regards to both hardware and software issues. Consequently, there is still not a reported strong correlation between cyber security breaches and the potential decrease in road safety levels. This should be the focus of policymakers in the near future, so as to develop an holistic policy framework coupling safety and cyber security which will assure a safe and efficient incorporation of CAVs in future transportation systems.

Keywords: Connected and autonomous vehicles, Road safety, Cyber security, Review, Policy

1. Introduction

Autonomous, automated or self-driving vehicles are gradually becoming a reality, envisioned to transform the current transportation systems worldwide. Among several advantages promised by industry and academia, safety is one of the cornerstones of connected and automated driving, promising to save tens of thousands of lives per year on a global scale. This will be achieved by removing the human and behavioral element from the task of driving; a factor responsible for almost 95% of crashes according to Singh (2015). A key underpinning factor for ensuring safe transportation from origin to destination is the software and the communication network infrastructure, which will facilitate, plan, decide, actuate and control the motion of the vehicle (Schuelke-Leech et al., 2019; Song et al., 2019; Suo and Sarma, 2019; van Wyk et al., 2020). A potential failure or breach of such software can compromise the safety levels for automated vehicles with regards to their passengers, as well as other traffic participants and the general public. With the ever-growing number of cyber-attacks on vehicles nowadays, due to the increase in communication and electronic modules in today's automobiles (Liem et al., 2019), a future fully automated transportation system must be fully protected against threats of such nature. As a result, cyber-security and risk management have also become a core element of designing Connected and Autonomous Vehicles (CAVs). The main scope of cyber-security risk handling is to limit the cyber-physical effects of security breaches or software/sensor/network failures and ensure safety and privacy for users of a digital or communication network (Eskandarian, 2012; Sabaliauskaite et al., 2019; Sheehan et al., 2018; Vivek et al., 2019).

Safe CAV-human interactions which can lead to a significant reduction of casualties, crashes or generic passenger discomfort, make road safety and cyber security inter-connected in terms of CAV research (Sabaliauskaite et al., 2019; van Wyk et al., 2020). However, the heterogeneous characteristics of communication and electronic systems of CAVs, the diverse nature of cyber-attacks as well as the need for security and safety systems to be operating in a real-time, time- and response-critical fashion, hinder the development of a consolidating policy framework, mapping the implications of cyber security attacks on road safety of CAVs (Booth et al., 2019; Cui et al., 2019; Jahan et al., 2019; Sztipanovits et al., 2019).

Thus, the aim of this chapter is to: (i) summarize current knowledge and review existing approaches binding cyber security and road safety, outline the potential effects of different security risks on safety aspects of CAVs, (ii) summarize current challenges and (iii) make suggestions for policy makers to mitigate effects of CAV cyber security breaches on the safety of road users. The presented overview, as well as the policy-oriented discussions in the chapter, aim to provide researchers and policy makers the necessary guidelines for enhancing safety and security of CAVs and enhance public confidence in a fully automated transportation environment.

With regards to the methodology followed in this review, a systematic search was conducted in popular scientific databases (i.e., Scopus, Google Scholar, TRID and IEEEXplore) using specific terms and Boolean operators that are described in Table 1 along with the retrieved papers. The papers that were retrieved from the search, were initially screened with regards to their title and abstract, and then by reading the full manuscript. Considered studies were the ones that were published after 2010 until July 2019, written in English and published in prestigious peer-reviewed journals and conference proceedings. Furthermore, priority was given to papers that quantify the effects of CAV cyber-security on traffic safety, as well as describe mitigation actions on vehicular cyber-security issues. In order to also introduce the most prominent problems of CAV Safety, road safety and robotics papers were also included in the review. It should be mentioned here that within road safety and robotic-related CAV papers, human factors were not considered, so as to retain the review task manageable and relevant to the main target audience of this book chapter. As the impacts of cyber-security on road safety problems, was not explicitly described in a sufficient number of papers, views of the authors of this chapter are also included in the sections of policy recommendations and potential impacts of specific cyber-security problems on collisions or injuries are also expressed.

Table 1 Keywords, screened and included papers per topic considered in this chapter.

Topic	Keywords	Results	Screened papers	Included papers
CAVs & Road Safety	"road safety" AND "connected vehicles" OR "connected and autonomous vehicles" OR "CAV"	862	41	22
Cybersecurity Threats or Failures for CAVs	"cyber-security" OR "cybersecurity" AND "autonomous vehicles" OR "connected and autonomous vehicles" OR "driverless car" OR "automated vehicles" AND "threats" OR "failures"	423	37	8
Cybersecurity impact on CAV safety	"cyber-security" OR "cybersecurity" AND "autonomous vehicles" OR "connected and autonomous vehicles" OR "driverless car" OR "automated vehicles" AND "safety impact" OR "impact on safety"	13	13	6
Cybersecurity assessment and mitigation actions	"cyber-security" OR "cybersecurity" AND "autonomous vehicles" OR "connected and autonomous vehicles" OR "driverless car" OR "automated vehicles" AND "assessment actions" OR "mitigation" OR "mitigation actions"	111	26	3

2. Safety and CAVs

Safety is the basis of advantages promised by the automotive and research communities along with enhanced traffic flow and improved user experience (e.g., development of new infotainment services), when CAVs become a part of everyday commuting. This section provides an overview of approaches concerned with the safe motion of CAVs in traffic and more specifically the inter-relationship between vehicles.

The "core" of on-road planning modules for a CAV system is algorithmically described within its software (Katrakazas et al., 2015). More specifically, tasks related to safety are part of maneuver planning which dictates the behavior that a CAV should have within traffic, and is part of the motion planning module, i.e., the module that finds a suitable path for the vehicle to follow, identifies the optimal behavior and designs the trajectory to be traced. Typically, there are two main domains investigating aspects of safety with regards to CAVs; (a) the computer science/robotics perspective and (b) the transportation engineering perspective.

In the former perspective (i.e., robotics), vehicles are treated as isolated entities and collision risk assessment is heavily based on a combination of motion prediction (i.e., the prediction of how traffic participants in the vicinity of a CAV are going to behave in the near future) with risk evaluation based on colliding trajectories (Aoude et al., 2013) and typical surrogate safety measures (Ward et al., 2014b). The robotics perspective usually employs data obtained from the state-of-the-art in vehicle sensing, e.g., laser scanners, cameras, radars, ultrasonic sensors and vehicle communications, to perform the tasks of motion prediction and risk assessment (Lefèvre et al., 2014). However, in the majority of the approaches, it fails to take into account the context of the traffic environment. More specifically, although high resolution sensors are utilized and trajectories can efficiently be predicted in the near future, approaches are lacking the human reasoning of driving actions and the perception of the traffic environment in terms of signs, signals and prioritization of "right-of-way." Toward that goal, context-aware models have emerged in recent years, so as to include aspects of the traffic environment within the decision-making task of CAVs. Mutual interactions between road users and traffic rules are taken into account in (Gindele et al., 2013; Lawitzky et al., 2013; Lefèvre, 2012; Ward et al., 2014a), while visibility conditions, occlusions and uncertainty in sensing and augmenting other traffic participants maneuvers is considered in (Taş and Stiller, 2018; Yu et al., 2019). Context-aware models, are based on principles of dynamic probabilistic inference and are developed using corresponding techniques, such as Dynamic Bayesian Networks (DBNs) (Lefèvre et al., 2012; Schulz et al., 2018; Ward et al., 2014a) and Partially Observable Markov Decision Processes (POMDP) (Bandyopadhyay et al., 2012; Brechtel et al., 2014). Such models could in principle imitate human-like reasoning behind CAV safety-critical decisions; however to-date they require a large number of variables to formulate rules of the road and take into account mutual dependencies between drivers. Consequently require a large amount of data to infer joint and conditional probabilities required by the models.

The transportation engineering perspective is based on the principle that the probability of a collision occurring on a specific road segment can be efficiently predicted in a short temporal horizon using real-time traffic dynamics (Abdel-Aty et al., 2005; Hossain et al., 2019). An essential element for employing such traffic network collision prediction schemes is the comparison and contrasting of prevailing traffic conditions prior to collisions, with the prevailing conditions during normal traffic operations (using a matched case control approach). In most cases, data from inductive loop detectors, microwave vehicle detection systems, Automatic Vehicle Identification (AVI), cameras or Bluetooth detectors are obtained from traffic authorities and aggregated in 5-min intervals to remove noise in the data (Hossain et al., 2019). This aggregation, intuitively, leads to a longer temporal horizon for safety predictions, meaning that if 5-min data are utilized to develop collision prediction classifiers, these safety predictions are going to be concerned with a future 5-min time interval. Furthermore, pre-collision and normal operation data often lead to highly imbalanced datasets (i.e., datasets where one class is highly over-represented) and often suffer from erroneous crash time reporting due to the dependence of crash reports on the corresponding police authority.

As CAV-related collisions and corresponding data are not yet widely available, traffic microsimulation is employed in order to formulate "realistic" conditions of mixed traffic environments including both typical vehicles and CAVs. In recent studies (e.g., Papadoulis et al., 2019; Virdi et al., 2019) traffic microsimulation software is utilized in order to imitate the behavior of CAVs in traffic, and the Surrogate Safety Assessment Model (SSAM; Gettman et al., 2008) is utilized to extract traffic conflicts and evaluate the safety impact of CAVs in terms of "dangerous" vehicle interactions, conflicts and collisions. It is clear that the transportation engineering perspective offers a more "high-level" and wider prediction level, but lacks in terms of data aggregation, data imbalance and erroneous time reporting.

The combination of the two perspectives could potentially enhance the safety offered by CAVs, but this is yet to be heavily researched. To the best of our knowledge, the only study that combines robotics and transportation engineering aspects of road safety for CAV risk assessment is the one by Katrakazas et al. (2019). In that study, network-level collision information provides an extra information layer in typical interaction-aware models developed in robotics, and it was found that vehicle-level collision prediction is enhanced by up to 10%.

The consideration of vulnerable road users such as pedestrians, cyclists and motorcyclists in CAV safety assessment is currently performed mainly in the robotics perspective (e.g., Camara et al., 2018; Fox et al., 2018; Millard-Ball, 2018) by formulating game-theoretical problems regarding the CAV-human interactions (Millard-Ball, 2018; Rakha et al., 2013) or by utilizing social scientific models (Bera et al., 2018; Cunningham et al., 2019; Hancock et al., 2019; Merat et al., 2018). Nevertheless, such human factor based approaches, are also considered from the transportation engineering perspective, especially with regards to pedestrians (Hudson et al., 2019; Nuñez Velasco et al., 2019; Ritchie et al., 2019; Woodman et al., 2019). Hence, it is assumed that the human factor perspective is evident in both the robotics and the transportation engineering perspective and does not form a third perspective with regards to CAV safety. However, there is still a lack on a benchmarked communication protocol between CAVs and human road users which could lead to confusion between traffic participants.

To summarize, current approaches in safety of CAVs are split between robotics and transportation engineering or in more perspective, vehicle-level assessment and network-level assessment. In robotics, highly disaggregated data are utilized, but context is not massively taken into account, and when it is, complex models hinder the real-time effectiveness of risk assessment. On the other hand, transportation engineering modules exploit aggregated data but lack in perceiving non-motorized road users and lead to imbalanced datasets. Finally, human-CAV interactions rely on game-theoretic or social sciences formulations, without being fully able to imitate current negotiations between vehicles and pedestrians or cyclists.

3. Cyber-security and CAVs

CAVs are nowadays complex IT systems, an integral part of Internet of Things (IoT) ecosystem which consists of different networking and information software and hardware components. These components communicate with each other as well as external sources for the support of core autonomous driving operations and infotainment services offered to drivers and passengers. For example, software components in a CAV (usually integrated into the Engine Control Unit—ECU or the Transmission Control Units—TCU) may be responsible for the control of power, the engine, the chassis (lane assistance) and the body (e.g., locks) of the vehicle, as well as for the communication with external networks (Global Positioning System—GPS, telco operators, edge computing, vehicle to vehicle—V2V-communication), for infotainment services (video streaming, gaming, etc.) as well as for vehicle online monitoring, diagnostics and reporting to car manufacturers.

As information and networking technologies related to CAV mature, multiple threats and risks emerge and concern the security of the systems as well as the privacy of the information collected and exchanged between humans and vehicles, or between vehicles and vehicles. The information and communication systems between vehicles and network infrastructure have the potential to be remotely attacked and accessed by malicious users. Usually exploiting system vulnerabilities or failures in the operation of the systems, such actions can pose a considerable threat to the vast socioeconomic benefits promised by CAVs (Sheehan et al., 2018).

Cyber-security refers to a set of technologies employed in CAV, which can be used to protect the integrity of networks, software and data from attack, damage or unauthorized access. Such techniques can be used to identify, prevent or mitigate a threat in the normal operation of the vehicle's systems. In the next sections, the major threats related to the cyber security of CAVs are presented.

3.1 Threats and failures

According to the level of automation, different threats and failures can occur and can determine the severity of the impact on safety. For example, in vehicles offering basic driving assistance support, the driver has full control over the vehicle's movement and the software may provide alerts and warnings when driver fails to exercise control (e.g., break or steering warning; Jiménez et al., 2012). A failure or a malicious external control of the warning module can be potentially harmful, but it is still the driver's responsibility to react and control the vehicle (Perrine et al., 2019). On the contrary, in a fully automated scenario, driver's intervention is minimized and software can control lateral and longitudinal movement in all use cases. A threat or failure on the operation of the steering module can have severe impact on the safety of the passengers (Schoitsch et al., 2012).

Furthermore, threats do not necessarily apply to the autonomous elements of a CAV, but also to its connectivity with the network infrastructure (e.g., a cloud or edge infrastructure), which is essential for the communication of the vehicle with other vehicles and transport systems. Loss of communication, due to Denial of Service (DoS) attacks or network failures can also result in major threats for the safety of the passengers, especially for critical applications, that require low-latency access to the network (Weimerskirch and Dominic, 2018).

The ENISA report (European Union Agency for Network and Information Security (ENISA), 2017) provides a taxonomy of the various threats that can affect the security and resiliency of a CAV. According to the report the following threats are identified based on the software module of the vehicle affected:

"*Physical threats,* such as fault injection, glitching, access to Hardware ports: This threat may typically consist in tampering with the ECUs or TCUs (to recover keys or access physical debug interfaces); using the device electro-magnetic emanations or power usage to leak information (side-channel); use light, power or other means to alter the device behavior and ultimately gain access to protected data (glitch, fault injection).

Unintentional software failures and malfunctions: It mainly involves threats in the consistency and proper functioning of the software systems in a CAV, such as administration errors in back-end information services or errors and leakage of data intended for diagnostic purposes. It may also involve erroneous use or administration of devices and systems, use of information from unreliable sources, unintentional change of data in an information system or finally inadequate design, maintenance and deployment of software modules in CAVs. The presence of software bugs is a basis for potential exploitable vulnerabilities. Most of the software assets deployed in a CAV can be potentially affected by such threats.

Communication Loss and Outages: The most common threat relates to the Network outage, either due to network failures or bad coverage. Especially in the early stages of 5G networks, coverage will be limited to certain locations, and applications that are latency-critical will probably suffer from bad connectivity or blind spots in the road networks. For example, a network outage may result in a denial of service for sensitive operations, such as over-the-air fixes for critical bugs or vulnerabilities. More generally, any design relying too much on connectivity exposes the vehicle to potential issues in case of outages. Vehicles should be designed to offer a usable degraded mode of operation in case of outage.

Sensitive Data Loss or Leakage: Information exchanged by CAVs are managed in private cloud environments, operated either by telco providers or vehicle manufacturers. Common threats related to the governance of the data collected in CAVs include the loss of sensitive data (e.g., GPS locations, International Mobile Subscriber Identities - IMSIs or other user identifiers) due to attacks or crashes when stored by third-party cloud service providers. Sensitive data may be lost or compromised due to physical damages in cases of a traffic crash or theft or even unencrypted private or sensitive data (such as payment information, driving habits, etc.) may be leaked when the vehicle is sold to another user.

Interception/Hacking and Phishing: Usually, these types of threats involve the man-in-the-middle/ session hijacking. A large set of infotainment applications in CAVs means that, given a poor protection of the session, e.g., application communicate over unencrypted 4G / 5G or WIFI networks, there are many incentives for an attacker to impersonate a distant user, e.g., phishing the identity of a CAV or a user in the app store may lead to financial abuse; impersonating backend systems may help the attacker in downloading a rogue firmware on the vehicle; impersonating another vehicle on a V2V session may trigger dangerous behaviors, etc.

Malicious Activity/Abuse: Finally, the malicious activity or abuse of a software operating in a CAV may result in the Denial of service (DoS) or manipulation of the hardware and software modules. A DoS can result in a form of network outage (e.g., loss of network connectivity) but also provoke faults on an ECU via a malicious payload. The potential impact of such an attack may lead to unexpected behaviors. For example, changing the firmware of a component, or otherwise altering its configuration data, a malicious user can take the control of an ECU or the control of a vehicle by sending driving-related commands (steering, braking, etc.). A malicious user may also try to change the identity of the vehicle, i.e., the way it communicates with the other vehicles or back end systems in order to perform fraud in toll systems, or for criminal purposes. It is true that the integration of infotainment and mobile ecosystems may cause an increase of potential malicious software introduced by the user. Malicious software may provide a first step for attackers in a multi-step attack, to get in driving systems via the infotainment subnetwork. Malicious software may also be a first step to gain access to professional systems (e.g., garages or backend), thus potentially gaining a privileged access on a large set of vehicles. Since, most ECUs offer linux-based or android-based OS that means that attackers may recycle well-known attack paths."

Nevertheless, apart from software breaches, the hardware part of CAVs (e.g., sensors and ECUs) could also become vulnerable in cyber-attacks.[a]

[a] Relevant hardware issues are reviewed in another chapter of this book, so interested readers may also check this chapter out.

A detailed review on sensors and vehicle parts affected is given in (Luo et al., 2019), where it is outlined that the most vulnerable sensors are the localizing ones (i.e., cameras and radars), the wireless communications and the navigational systems.

In general, according to recent reviews on cybersecurity and its impact on connected and autonomous vehicles (Harish and Amutha, 2019; Takahashi, 2018), attacks and breaches can be divided into:

"Local or inside the vehicle, which include breaches of:

- In-vehicle protocols
- CAN bus
- Local Interconnect Network (LIN)

Remote, which include attacks on

- Communications between the back-end systems and vehicles
  - Car Navigation systems
  - Car telematics
  - Remote Control Services
  - Breaches of V2X communications
- Back-end systems breaching
  - DoS attacks
  - Cross virtual machines side channeling"

For more information on the technical details of the attacks, as well as the corresponding countermeasures the reader is prompted to the aforementioned reviews.

3.2 Impact on safety

Clearly, there is a plethora of cyber security-related threats and failures, which could jeopardize the well-being of CAV passengers as well as the general safety level of various road users. This section will discuss scenarios and the potential impacts of cyber-security breaches on road safety.

Each module of CAV functionality relies on an uninterrupted flow of data originating from communication between vehicles or infrastructure, as well as the variety of on-board sensors. If malignant or tampered data enter the dataflow of CAV communication systems, the planning modules will be compromised. For example, if an intruder hacks the localization module of a CAV, unnecessary evasive maneuvers for "fake" obstacles might arise (i.e., false positives), causing massive collisions between vehicles. Furthermore, unreliable communication between automated vehicles and traffic control authorities might lead to erroneous cooperation and coordination of traffic flow, thus leading to collision-prone traffic dynamics and triggering risky maneuvering (Schoitsch et al., 2012). The strong connection between cyber security threats and the physical impact on safety is pointed out in Ferdowsi et al. (2018). Authors stated that CAV security should not be independently designed, but rather in conjunction with the control module, so as to overcome potential threats and breaches in data streams coming from sensors or communication protocols. In Lefèvre et al. (2013), the concept of "missed intervention" is presented, denoting scenarios of a breached cyber security system, which triggers the safety module to fall silent during a safety-critical event and consequently leads to a collision and potential injuries. Lefèvre et al. demonstrated that if the "silent period" is shorter than 2 s, safe functionality is ensured according to the SAE J2735 protocol, and simple rules on security lead to major safety enhancements in terms of road safety at a road intersection. Based on the work of Lefèvre et al. (2013), Xin et al. (2019), provided the first microsimulation framework for quantifying the impact of V2X privacy issues on traffic conflicts. The main drawback is that the study area was limited to only one intersection, and it was found that such "silent periods" could increase the total number of conflicts up to 8.5% when the speed ranges between 30 and 35 mph, and up to 38% between 10 and 15 mph in urban areas. Furthermore, Li et al. (2018) evaluated the rear-end collision potential of vehicles under slight cyber-attacks (attacks in which the CAVs data are randomly deviated, such that only a 1% fluctuation of communicated data, will result in significant data alterations). Li et al. concluded that attacks on positions are more dangerous than attack on speed information, and that attacks on multiple vehicle may result in more severe injuries during collisions. Similarly, Wang et al. (2019) quantified the effect of malicious information propagation on traffic flow and more specifically the effect of providing underestimated speeds, overestimated speeds and constant acceleration messages throughout platooned traffic. It was concluded that malicious information, radically influences traffic flow and thus leads to irregularities in traffic behavior (e.g., unexpected lane changes and overtaking, or disallowed maneuvering) as well as a number of collisions due to abrupt speed changes.

The aforementioned examples, demonstrate the increased interest of the research community to quantify the effects of cyber security breaches on road safety during recent times. Certainly, there is vast amount of research on cyber security for vehicular networks (Hasrouny et al., 2019), or solely on security of automated vehicles (Makarova et al., 2018). Research has realized the critical impact that cyber security is going to have on the safety of autonomous vehicles (Hicks, 2018), Still, progress has to be made in order for road safety impacts to become an integral part of cyber security and advanced automation research.

3.3 Assessment and mitigations actions

Several questions arise. For instance, how do we identify a threat and assess its impact on safety, and what are the mitigation actions CAV manufactures employ for minimizing the risk or the damage of a potential threat? How can we ensure that systems are resilient against unintentional/accidental failures and especially against those who wish to take control of them maliciously? Most well-known techniques used in IT security sector are also employed in CAV ecosystems. These techniques can be either applied posteriori of a threat occurrence to assess and limit its impact or proactively during the design phase of the CAV software and hardware to reduce the possibility of a threat. In McCarthy et al. (2014), a threat assessment model for modern vehicles is presented; the model categorizes threats along several dimensions, such as the type of an attack, the access method of the attack or failure, the module in the CAV which is affected, the casualty and financial severity. A similar approach is presented in Weimerskirch and Dominic (2018), in which each threat consists of a threat agent (attacker), one or more system components that could be attacked (attack surfaces) and one or more attack models for each component. A threat matrix is built which assesses each threat along the aforementioned dimensions.

Although the proper assessment of a threat is crucial upon occurrence, cyber security standards and practices enforce Security-by-design approaches. Threat scenarios are simulated such that vulnerabilities are identified, and their impact is assessed before the deployment of a new module in the CAV. Specific focus should be given to the fact that CAVs are nowadays complex software ecosystems incorporating different components and systems from multiple software and hardware manufacturers. Different security standards during the development and integration phase should be enforced and use-case scenarios should be exhaustively performed to eliminate risks. Software and hardware manufacturers should, as a first step, adhere to regulation related to IT security and privacy (e.g., General Data Protection Regulation—GDPR in the European Union- EU) and car manufacturers should be held liable for threats and damages due to other actors under their control, such as garages; still, liability can only be measured by the compliance to a shared standards and processes.

Traditional security techniques which must be adopted by all software systems deployed in a CAV, include encryption of communication, layering of messages, gateways and proxies for controlling information access and strong authentication for all users (not only CAV owners, but also engineers or business analysts) who may have access to the CAV data. On top of this, manufacturers should use virtualization and edge-based solutions to separate safety-critical functions from non-safety-critical.

Finally, a most promising direction for cyber security is the prediction of a threat through the continuous monitoring and analysis of diagnostics and other types of data collected and exchanged in a CAV. In this respect, machine learning and AI techniques could be used for anomalies detection such as abnormal behavior of a software module, failures and potential vulnerabilities before these occur. The detection could be followed by an alerting mechanism or even actions that eventually prevent the attack. An example related to communication network failures is predictive mobility; CAVs could be notified on network failures by other CAVs and select the best route based on the quality of the telco network, such that connectivity with external information systems is guaranteed during the route.

The transition to extremely high bandwidths of the 5G data networks, combined with the flexibility and the power of cloud and edge-computing may provide the foundation for leveraging machine learning to secure CAVs, giving them the computing power to detect threats and react in milliseconds. Moreover, as highlighted in Sharma and Kaushik (2019) current security modules utilize expensive cryptographic overheads which face problems in handling large volumes of messages and hence disrupt the critical latency of a CAV communication system.

4. Policy implications and challenges

The prominent association between road safety and cyber security, as presented in the previous sections, needs to be taken into account from policymakers, so as to accelerate the integration of CAVs in traffic. Table 2 presents an overview of key CAV cybersecurity problems and the corresponding impacts on road safety, as well as solutions that are being proposed by the authors and recent literature.

The impact of cyber-attacks and malicious information was highlighted in Milakis et al. (2017), stating the long-promised safety impacts of CAVs will be seriously compromised by cyber security breaches, and hence a

Table 2 Overview of reported CAV security problems along with their impact on road safety and proposed mitigation actions.

<table>
<tr><th>CAV security problem</th><th>Reported impact on safety</th><th>Proposed mitigation actions</th></tr>
<tr><td>Unreliable Communication (Schoitsch et al., 2012)</td><td>Lack of cooperation and coordination of traffic flow collision-prone traffic dynamics</td><td>• Categorization of threats with regards to their impact (McCarthy et al., 2014; Weimerskirch and Dominic, 2018)</td></tr>
<tr><td>Lack of consideration between vehicle control and cybersecurity modules (Ferdowsi et al., 2018)</td><td>Sensor malfunction unsafe headways</td><td>• Software and Hardware adherence to IT Security and Privacy Regulations</td></tr>
<tr><td>Breach of safety systems (Lefèvre et al., 2013)</td><td>Collisions and injuries</td><td rowspan="3">• Encryption of Communication, Message Layering, Gateways and Proxies for information control
• Exploitation of 5G technologies for cheaper cryptographic overheads (Sharma and Kaushik, 2019)</td></tr>
<tr><td>V2X Privacy issues (Xin et al., 2019)</td><td>Traffic conflicts</td></tr>
<tr><td>Malicious information on speeds and positions in platoons</td><td>Collisions with larger severity (especially if location information is tampered)</td></tr>
<tr><td>Malicious information on traffic flow (Wang et al., 2019)</td><td>Irregularities in traffic behaviors and collisions</td><td>• Threat Prediction through the continuous monitoring and analysis of diagnostics using data collected and exchanged in a CAV</td></tr>
</table>

better comprehension of different types of attacks and their impacts on safety is needed for future research and policy.

In order to accomplish that goal, an essential step is the categorization of cyber security attacks or breaches and the quantification of the effects on safety. As discussed in Section 3.2 traffic micro simulation can become a useful tool in quantifying the effect of security breaches on safety, and provide a large amount of data examples. These data examples could then be used by policymakers to draft regulatory answers to questions such as *How much time is needed to address a specific cyber-attack before it becomes safety-critical?* or *How should CAV passengers be protected from serious injuries in case of a specific cyber-attack?*

Recent studies resembling the work of automotive industries, have a focus on identifying the number of miles needed for CAVs to become reliable (e.g., Kalra and S.M.P., 2016). It is suggested that policymakers should focus not only on "collision-free" miles, but also on regulating the time or miles needed for a human driver to take control in terms of safety-critical cyber-attacks. Furthermore, guidelines should be issued concerning the level of confidence regarding the communication between vehicles in comparison to on-board sensors and potential thresholds for safe termination of the vehicle's trip. To that end, the emerging question is whether existing infrastructure should be expanded to host "security-breached" vehicles or these could be accommodated in the hard shoulder. Answering such questions could be assisted through a detailed coupling and ranking of cyber security threats with crash potential or injury levels in order to understand the effect of cyber-risk as well as the most efficient mitigation actions toward them. The association between cyber security dangers and traffic collision risk should also be specified in terms of road type (e.g., motorways, urban arterials, rural roads, built-in areas), traffic congestion levels and weather and visibility conditions (Bailey et al., 2018). Moreover, a distinction should be made between breaches in infrastructure-related communication (e.g., Perrine et al., 2019) and vehicle-level issues (e.g., Tbatou et al., 2017). The disruption of the urban environment and potential cyber-security breaches should also be taken into account as described in a thorough review of the topic from Faisal et al. (2019). In terms of data and evidence needed in order to support regulatory actions according to cyber security and road safety assessment, (since a large portion of the data would include surveillance of road users and traffic participants), ethical and privacy issues need to be addressed (Amelung-Herzongerath et al., 2015).

The SAEJ3061 standard on cyber security needs to be expanded for CAV functionality in terms of both system-level and local attacks. A critical example as mentioned in Koopman and Wagner (2017) is this of the blind trust between CAVs in a communication network; if a communication is established between two vehicles, and is encrypted according to a standard, then how fast and efficiently can one compromised vehicle be recognized? Furthermore, as the threats concerning CAVs and safety might originate from various locations, an international regulatory framework should be established to obtain a dedicated database of threats and the corresponding solutions. Moreover, a directory of liabilities according to the type of cyber security breach and the corresponding effect on safety of passengers and traffic and cooperative system between policymakers, stakeholders and the automotive industry should also be established. The ISO 26262 automotive-specific functional safety standard will also need to obtain an updated version with regards to its qualitative risk score (ASIL) for cyber-risk as long as CAVs enter public roads (Sheehan et al., 2018). To-date, several cyber security governing bodies exist around the world, however a global and cooperative liability and cyber security strategy in terms of road safety are yet to be globally and cooperatively regulated (Taeihagh and Lim, 2019).

Finally, according to McCluskey (2017), the average annual cost of cyber-crimes for UK transportation companies was £2.4 million. This cost is expected to be much higher in the era of automated driving, and hence, an efficient balance needs to be regulated in terms of cost of countermeasures to specific attacks and according to the casualty/injury/damage potential of the potential attack. This would require cooperation between traffic authorities governing road infrastructure for CAVs and vehicle manufacturing companies, which will install the necessary software and hardware for the mitigation of security breaches.

Summarizing the aforementioned sections and indications throughout the literature, countermeasures for specific types of attack exist as shown in Cui et al. (2019). What is missing throughout the literature and among policy makers is a clear link between the safety effects of these breaches, as well as implications on the severity or mitigation of potential collisions, if these attacks go through. Therefore, future policies should focus on three levels:

- Level 1: Explicitly linking cyber-attacks with collisions in terms of results. For example, if a breach is made on the car's navigational system, how severe would be an accident during a worst case scenario?
- Level 2: Standardization of procedures for ensuring mitigation of injuries and counter-gaining control of the vehicle for every combination of cyber-attack and road safety result. This could include the updating of data communication standards (e.g., SAEJ3061) but also a standardization of requirements for the motion planning algorithms within CAVs in terms of sensor or communication failure.
- Level 3: Societal and infrastructural considerations as a last safety net, in terms of cyber-security and road safety. This could include education of the society in order to promptly understand if the vehicle is compromised in order to regain human control, or policies to establish dedicated administration-provided communication networks for additional security between communicating vehicles.

5. Conclusions

Connected and Autonomous Vehicles (CAVs) aim to change the status-quo of current transportation reality. Their most outstanding advantage is the improved safety levels due to removal of human features during the driving task. In order to achieve that, however, CAVs not only need to assess risk in terms of road safety, but also take into account potential cyber security breaches which could eventually threaten the well-being of their occupants and the entirety of the traffic environment in their vicinity.

Both in terms of corresponding research and policy regulations, a holistic approach is yet to be realized. Solutions offered in the automotive and transportation research community are distinct between computer scientists, road safety experts and communication professionals. Individual solutions tackling either issues on collisions and casualties or cyber-attack countermeasures exist, however there is limited research to confirm the strong correlation between cyber security breaches and the potential decrease in road safety levels.

Policymakers and corresponding stakeholders need to bridge this explicit gap by formulating regulations that bring together the domains of road safety and cyber-security, exploiting the implications that a profusion of security attacks could have on road crashes and casualties and ensuring the efficient incorporation of CAVs in current traffic infrastructure. Emphasis should be given on the identification and documentation of the safety-related results of cyber security violations, the liability of actions, the time needed for safe countermeasures as well as the cost efficiency of those countermeasures. Finally, an international benchmarked regulatory framework could assist in assuring transferable and validated policies, regardless of the operational environment of CAVs worldwide.

Acknowledgments

The inception and writing-up of this book chapter was supported by the WISE-ACT COST Action CA16222. EURECOM acknowledges the support of its industrial members, namely, Orange, SAP, BMW Group, IABG, and Symantec.

References

Abdel-Aty, M., Pande, A., Hsia, L.Y., Abdalla, F., 2005. The potential for real-time traffic crash prediction. ITE J. 75, 69–75.

Amelung-Herzongerath, H., Troullinou, P., Thomopoulos, N., 2015. Reversing the order: towards a philosophically informed debate on ICT for transport. In: Thomopoulos, N., Givoni, M., Rietveld, P. (Eds.), ICT for Transport: Opportunities and Threats. Edward Elgar, Cheltenham, Glos., UK, pp. 205–225.

Aoude, G., Luders, B.D., Joseph, J.M., Roy, N., How, J.P., 2013. Probabilistically safe motion planning to avoid dynamic obstacles with uncertain motion patterns. Auton. Robot. 35, 51–76.

Bailey, D., Cefkin, M., Cotten, S., Crowston, K., Erickson, I., Kassens-Noor, E., Kennedy, J., King, J.L., Madill, H., Nickerson, J., Pentland, B.T., Rayhawk, K., Shortridge, A., Stilgoe, J., Straub, E., Wilson, M., Weinfeld, A., 2018. Connected and autonomous vehicles in society: an agenda for social and policy research. In: Collaboration With the MSU Institute for Public Policy and Social Research and the MSU School of Planning, Design and Construction and National Science Foundation Re.

Bandyopadhyay, T., Won, K.S., Frazzoli, E., Hsu, D., 2012. Intention-aware motion planning. In: Proc. of the 10th Workshop on the Algorithmic Foundations of Robotics, pp. 475–491.

Bera, A., Randhavane, T., Wang, A., Manocha, D., Kubin, E., Gray, K., 2018. Classifying group emotions for socially-aware autonomous vehicle navigation. In: IEEE Comput. Soc. Conf. Comput. Vis. Pattern Recognit. Work. 2018-June, pp. 1152–1160.

Booth, L., Norman, R., Pettigrew, S., 2019. The potential implications of autonomous vehicles for active transport. J. Transp. Health 15, 100623.

Brechtel, S., Gindele, T., Dillmann, R., 2014. Probabilistic decision-making under uncertainty for autonomous driving using continuous POMDPs. In: 2014 IEEE 17th International Conference on Intelligent Transportation Systems (ITSC). Qingdao, China, pp. 392–399.

Camara, F., Romano, R., Markkula, G., Madigan, R., Merat, N., Fox, C., 2018. Empirical game theory of pedestrian interaction for autonomous vehicles. Proc. Meas. Behav. 2018, 6–8.

Cui, J., Liew, L.S., Sabaliauskaite, G., Zhou, F., 2019. A review on safety failures, security attacks, and available countermeasures for autonomous vehicles. Ad Hoc Netw. 90, 101823.

Cunningham, A.G., Galceran, E., Mehta, D., Ferrer, G., Eustice, R.M., Olson, E., 2019. Control Strategies for Advanced Driver Assistance Systems and Autonomous Driving Functions. Springer International Publishing.

Eskandarian, A., 2012. Handbook of Intelligent Vehicles. Springer London, London.

European Union Agency for Network and Information Security (ENISA), 2017. Cyber security and resilience of smart cars. In: Good Practices and Recommendations. ENISA, 2017-02-1.

Faisal, A., Yigitcanlar, T., Kamruzzaman, M., Currie, G., 2019. Understanding autonomous vehicles: a systematic literature review on capability, impact, planning and policy. J. Transp. Land Use 12, 45–72.

Ferdowsi, A., Ali, S., Saad, W., Mandayam, N.B., 2018. Cyber-physical security and safety of autonomous connected vehicles: optimal control meets multi-armed bandit learning. IEEE Trans. Commun. 67, 1–30.

Fox, C., Camara, F., Markkula, G., Romano, R., Madigan, R., Merat, N., 2018. When Should the Chicken Cross the Road?: Game Theory for Autonomous Vehicle—Human Interactions. To be confirmed. Leeds, ISO, p. 690.

Gettman, D., Pu, L., Sayed, T., Shelby, S.G., 2008. Surrogate Safety Assessment Model and Validation: Final Report FHWA-HRT-08-051.

Gindele, T., Brechtel, S., Dillmann, R., 2013. Learning context sensitive behavior models from observations for predicting traffic situations. In: 16th Int. IEEE Conf. Intell. Transp. Syst. (ITSC 2013) 1764–1771.

Hancock, P.A., Nourbakhsh, I., Stewart, J., 2019. On the future of transportation in an era of automated and autonomous vehicles. Proc. Natl. Acad. Sci. 116, 7684–7691.

Harish, K.V., Amutha, B., 2019. Lecture Notes in Electrical Engineering: ICCCE 2018.

Hasrouny, H., Samhat, A.E., Bassil, C., Laouiti, A., 2019. Misbehavior detection and efficient revocation within VANET. J. Inf. Secur. Appl. 46, 193–209.

Hicks, D.J., 2018. The safety of autonomous vehicles. IEEE Technol. Soc. Mag. 37, 62–69.
Hossain, M., Abdel-Aty, M., Quddus, M.A., Muromachi, Y., Sadeek, S.N., 2019. Real-time crash prediction models: state-of-the-art, design pathways and ubiquitous requirements. Accid. Anal. Prev. 124, 66–84.
Hudson, C.R., Deb, S., Carruth, D.W., Mcginley, J., Frey, D., 2019. Pedestrian Perception of Autonomous Vehicles With External Interacting Features. Springer International Publishing.
Jahan, F., Sun, W., Niyaz, Q., Alam, M., 2019. Security modeling of autonomous systems: a survey. ACM Comput. Surv. 52, 91.
Jiménez, F., Naranjo, J.E., Gómez, O., 2012. Autonomous manoeuvring systems for collision avoidance on single carriageway roads. Sensors (Basel) 12, 16498–16521.
Kalra, N., S.M.P., 2016. Driving to safety: how many miles of driving would it take to 22 demonstrate autonomous vehicle reliability? Transp. Res. A 94 (23), 182–193.
Katrakazas, C., Quddus, M., Chen, W.-H., Deka, L., 2015. Real-time motion planning methods for autonomous on-road driving: state-of-the-art and future research directions. Transp. Res. C 60, 416–442.
Katrakazas, C., Quddus, M., Chen, W.H., 2019. A new integrated collision risk assessment methodology for autonomous vehicles. Accid. Anal. Prev. 127, 61–79.
Koopman, P., Wagner, M., 2017. Autonomous Vehicle Safety: An Interdisciplinary Challenge | Philip Koopman | Pulse | LinkedIn. Ieeexplore.Ieee.Org pp. 90–96.
Lawitzky, A., Althoff, D., Passenberg, C.F., Tanzmeister, G., Wollherr, D., Buss, M., 2013. Interactive scene prediction for automotive. In: Lawitzky, A., Althoff, D., Passenberg, C.F., Tanzmeister, G., Wollherr, D., Buss, M. (Eds.), Interactive Scene Prediction for Automotive Applications. IEEE Intelligent Vehicles Symposium, Proceedings, pp. 1028–1033.
Lefèvre, S., 2012. Risk Estimation at Road Intersections for Connected Vehicle Safety Applications.
Lefèvre, S., Laugier, C., Ibañez-guzmán, J., 2012. Evaluating risk at road intersections by detecting conflicting intentions. In: 2012 IEEE/RSJ International Conference on Intelligent Robots and Systems. Vilamoura, Algarve, Portugal, pp. 4841–4846.
Lefèvre, S., Petit, J., Bajcsy, R., Laugier, C., Kargl, F., 2013. Impact of V2X privacy strategies on intersection collision avoidance systems. In: IEEE Veh. Netw. Conf. VNC, pp. 71–78.
Lefèvre, S., Vasquez, D., Laugier, C., 2014. A survey on motion prediction and risk assessment for intelligent vehicles. ROBOMECH J. 1, 1–14.
Li, Y., Tu, Y., Fan, Q., Dong, C., Wang, W., 2018. Influence of cyber-attacks on longitudinal safety of connected and automated vehicles. Accid. Anal. Prev. 121, 148–156.
Liem, C., Murdock, D., Williams, A., Soukup, M., 2019. Highly available, self-defending, and malicious fault-tolerant systems for automotive cybersecurity. In: 2019 IEEE 19th Int. Conf. Softw. Qual. Reliab. Secur. Companion, pp. 24–27.
Luo, Q., Cao, Y., Liu, J., Benslimane, A., 2019. Localization and navigation in autonomous driving: threats and countermeasures. IEEE Wirel. Commun. 26, 38–45.
Makarova, I., Mukhametdinov, E., Tsybunov, E., 2018. Management of the reliability of intelligent vehicles as a method to improve traffic safety. Transp. Res. Procedia 36, 465–471.
McCarthy, C., Harnett, K., Carter, A., 2014. Characterization of Potential Security Threats in Modern Automobiles. Nhtsa.
Mccluskey, B., 2017. Connected cars ß the security challenge [connected cars cyber security]. Eng. Technol. 12, 54–57.
Merat, N., Louw, T., Madigan, R., Wilbrink, M., Schieben, A., 2018. What externally presented information do VRUs require when interacting with fully automated road transport systems in shared space? Accid. Anal. Prev. 118, 244–252.

Milakis, D., Van Arem, B., Van Wee, B., 2017. Policy and society related implications of automated driving: a review of literature and directions for future research. J. Intell. Transp. Syst. Technol. Plann. Oper. 21, 324–348.
Millard-Ball, A., 2018. Pedestrians, autonomous vehicles, and cities. J. Plan. Educ. Res. 38, 6–12.
Nuñez Velasco, J.P., Farah, H., van Arem, B., Hagenzieker, M.P., 2019. Studying pedestrians' crossing behavior when interacting with automated vehicles using virtual reality. Transport. Res. F: Traffic Psychol. Behav. 66, 1–14.
Papadoulis, A., Quddus, M., Imprialou, M., 2019. Evaluating the safety impact of connected and autonomous vehicles on motorways. Accid. Anal. Prev. 124, 12–22.
Perrine, K.A., Levin, M.W., Yahia, C.N., Duell, M., Boyles, S.D., 2019. Implications of traffic signal cybersecurity on potential deliberate traffic disruptions. Transp. Res. A Policy Pract. 120, 58–70.
Rakha, H., Zohdy, I.S., Kamalanathsharma, R.K., 2013. Agent-Based Game Theory Modeling for Driveless Vehicles at Intersections. Univ. Transp. Cent., Mid-Atlantic.
Ritchie, O.T., Watson, D.G., Griffiths, N., Misyak, J., Chater, N., Xu, Z., Mouzakitis, A., 2019. How should autonomous vehicles overtake other drivers? Transport. Res. F: Traffic Psychol. Behav. 66, 406–418.
Sabaliauskaite, G., Liew, L.S., Zhou, F., 2019. AVES—Automated Vehicle Safety and Security Analysis Framework, pp. 1–8.
Schoitsch, E., Schmittner, C., Ma, Z., 2012. The need for safety and cyber-security co-engineering and standardization for highly automated automotive vehicles. In: Advanced Microsystems for Automotive Applications 2015, Lecture Notes in Mobility. Springer, pp. 251–261.
Schuelke-Leech, B.A., Jordan, S.R., Barry, B., 2019. Regulating autonomy: an assessment of policy language for highly automated vehicles. Rev. Policy Res. 36, 547–579.
Schulz, J., Hubmann, C., Lochner, J., Burschka, D., 2018. Interaction-aware probabilistic behavior prediction in urban environments. In: IEEE Int. Conf. Intell. Robot. Syst, pp. 3999–4006.
Sharma, S., Kaushik, B., 2019. A survey on internet of vehicles: applications, security issues & solutions. Veh. Commun. 20, 100182.
Sheehan, B., Murphy, F., Mullins, M., Ryan, C., 2018. Connected and autonomous vehicles: a cyber-risk classification framework. Transp. Res. A Policy Pract. 124, 523–536.
Singh, S., 2015. Critical Reasons for Crashes Investigated in the National Motor Vehicle Crash Causation Survey. Natl. Highw. Traffic Saf. Adm., pp. 1–2
Song, H.M., Woo, J., Kim, H.K., 2019. In-vehicle network intrusion detection using deep convolutional neural network. Veh. Commun. 21, 100198.
Suo, D., Sarma, S.E., 2019. A test-driven approach for security designs of automated vehicles. In: 2019 IEEE Intell. Veh. Symp, pp. 26–32.
Sztipanovits, J., Koutsoukos, X., Karsai, G., Sastry, S., Tomlin, C., Damm, W., Fränzle, M., Rieger, J., Pretschner, A., Köster, F., 2019. Science of design for societal-scale cyber-physical systems: challenges and opportunities. Cyber-Phys. Syst. 5, 145–172.
Taeihagh, A., Lim, H.S.M., 2019. Governing autonomous vehicles: emerging responses for safety, liability, privacy, cybersecurity, and industry risks. Transplant. Rev. 39, 103–128.
Takahashi, J., 2018. An overview of cyber security for connected vehicles. IEICE Trans. Inf. Syst. E101D, 2561–2575.
Taş, Ö.Ş., Stiller, C., 2018. Limited visibility and uncertainty aware motion planning for automated driving. In: IEEE Intell. Veh. Symp. Proc. 2018-June, pp. 1171–1178.
Tbatou, S., Ramrami, A., Tabii, Y., 2017. Security of communications in connected cars modeling and safety assessment. In: Proc. 2nd Int. Conf. Big Data, Cloud Appl.—BDCA'17, pp. 1–7.

van Wyk, F., Khojandi, A., Masoud, N., 2020. A path towards understanding factors affecting crash severity in autonomous vehicles using current naturalistic driving data. In: Bi, Y., Bhatia, R., Kapoor, S. (Eds.), Intelligent Systems and Applications. Springer International Publishing, Cham, pp. 106–120.

Virdi, N., Grzybowska, H., Waller, S.T., Dixit, V., 2019. A safety assessment of mixed fleets with connected and autonomous vehicles using the surrogate safety assessment module. Accid. Anal. Prev. 131, 95–111.

Vivek, S., Yanni, D., Yunker, P.J., Silverberg, J.L., 2019. Cyberphysical risks of hacked internet-connected vehicles. Phys. Rev. E 100, 12316.

Wang, P., Yu, G., Wu, X., Wang, Y., He, X., 2019. Spreading patterns of malicious information on single-lane platooned traffic in a connected environment. Comput. Aided Civ. Inf. Eng. 34, 248–265.

Ward, J., Agamennoni, G., Worrall, S., Nebot, E., 2014a. Vehicle collision probability calculation for general traffic scenarios under uncertainty. In: IEEE Intelligent Vehicles Symposium, Proceedings. Dearborn, Michigan, USA, pp. 986–992.

Ward, J., Worrall, S., Agamennoni, G., Nebot, E., 2014b. The warrigal dataset: multi-vehicle trajectories and V2V communications. IEEE Intell. Transp. Syst. Mag. 6, 109–117.

Weimerskirch, A., Dominic, D., 2018. Assessing Risk: Identifying and Analyzing Cybersecurity Threats to Automated Vehicles, pp. 1–10.

Woodman, R., Lu, K., Higgins, M.D., Brewerton, S., Jennings, P.A., Birrell, S., 2019. Gap acceptance study of pedestrians crossing between platooning autonomous vehicles in a virtual environment. Transport. Res. F: Traffic Psychol. Behav. 67, 1–14.

Xin, W., Moonam, H.M., Petit, J., Whyte, W., 2019. Towards a balance between privacy and safety: microsimulation framework for assessing silence-based pseudonym-change schemes. Transp. Res. Rec. 2673, 71–84.

Yu, M.Y., Vasudevan, R., Johnson-Roberson, M., 2019. Occlusion-aware risk assessment for autonomous driving in urban environments. IEEE Robot. Autom. Lett. 4, 2235–2241.

CHAPTER FOUR

Cybersecurity certification and auditing of automotive industry

Tomás de J. Mateo Sanguino[a,*], José M. Lozano Domínguez[a], Patrícia de Carvalho Baptista[b]
[a]Higher Technical School of Engineering, University of Huelva, Huelva, Spain
[b]IN+ Center for Innovation, Technology and Policy Research, Instituto Superior Técnico, University of Lisbon, Lisbon, Portugal
*Corresponding author: e-mail address: tomas.mateo@diesia.uhu.es

Contents

Abstract

Technological advances in the automotive industry provide enormous advantages for drivers and passengers by improving the vehicle's operation and capabilities (e.g., self-driving aid systems or shared services applied to transit or to personal transport). Such is the case of autonomous vehicles (AVs) which has the potential to completely change the transport paradigm in the future. The deployment of such concept typically involves a diverse number of sensors, access technologies and the Internet to intelligently and rapidly interact with infrastructure, people and/or cloud services in a complex and interconnected ecosystem.

A large part of sensors and devices that connect to the Internet—or to each other—have no security nor the possibility of adding it. This approach is widely known and exploited by cybercriminals, who seek harm and profit indiscriminately. In this sense, connected vehicles increase their vulnerability as they are "networks over wheels," that are likely to become a reality in the road network in a near future. Therefore, protecting

Advances in Transport Policy and Planning, Volume 5
ISSN 2543-0009
https://doi.org/10.1016/bs.atpp.2020.01.002

data and systems from possible external intrusions is one of the main challenges nowadays, whose threats evolve and change further every year. So, cybersecurity should be considered as an investment by companies and not as an expense, especially taking into account additional factors to personal security such as the damage to reputation or trust when a data breach is suffered.

Around this context, a systematic literature review enabled understanding that certifications and audits based on standards and regulations developed in cybersecurity for CAVs is an increasing field. From 1989 to 2018, the contribution in literature of cybersecurity in vehicles represents 7.16% of the total publications, while those related to vehicle audit and certification represent 0.24%. Also, greater activity on this topic has been observed in the last decade compared to the first years, coinciding with the inclusion of several technological systems in vehicles. A higher contribution from universities (63.50%) is found as opposed to private companies (22.28%) and other research centers (14.20%), mainly based in North America and Europe (38.49% and 35.84%).

In face of the future challenges on cybersecurity in the automotive industry, a collaborative approach may be required to overcome the investments in time, money and broader organizational changes. The reality is that cybercrime as a service (CaaS) could generate millions in losses to the automotive industry, justifying new approaches of cybersecurity applied to the automobile industry, which must be flexible and adaptive along the production chain and the lifetime of CAVs.

Keywords: Auditing and certification, Cybercrime as a service, Connected autonomous vehicles, Security

Abbreviations

ADAS advanced driver assistance system
AV autonomous vehicle
CaaS cybercrime as a service
CAL Cybersecurity Assurance Level
CAN communication area network
CAV connected and autonomous vehicle
DoS denial of service
DOT Department of Transportation
DSRC Dedicated Short-Range Communication
EC European Commission
ECU electronic control unit
EVITA E-safety vehicle intrusion protected applications
FAVP Federal Automated Vehicle Policy
IDS intrusion detection system
IC integrated circuit
ICIT International Transportation Innovation Center
IOTA Internet of Things Application
IPS intrusion protection system
IT information technology
ISO International Organization for Standardization
LTE long term evolution

MaaS	mobility as a service
MITM	Man-in-the-Middle
MLIT	Ministry of Land, Infrastructure, Transport and Tourism
NHTSA	National Highway Traffic Safety Administration
OAA	Open Automotive Alliance
OEM	original equipment manufacturer
OTA	over-the-air
PASTA	Portable Automotive Security Testbed with Adaptability
RSU	road side units
SAE	Society of Automotive Engineers
SIoT	social IoT
SIoV	social Internet of vehicles
V2I	vehicle-to-infrastructure
V2V	vehicle-to-vehicle
V2X	vehicle-to-everything
Wi-Fi	wireless fidelity
WiMAX	Worldwide Interoperability for Microwave Access

1. Introduction

Connected and autonomous vehicles (CAVs) have started to become a reality in our lives with a significant rise over the last years, with investments for development increasing from \$15M in 2016 up to expect \$380M by 2021 according to various surveys (Everis, 2015; Greenough, 2016). Technological advances in automobiles offer users enormous advantages by improving their operation and capabilities, which have significantly evolved from the basic vehicle dynamic stabilization from the 1980s toward much smarter options currently deployed. Some technological milestones in this regard have been the early functions of the e-Call system developed in 1996, the remote diagnosis capability introduced in 2001, a network access device used for vehicle health reporting and turn-by-turn navigation in 2003, the only-data telematics used by Continental and the 4G/LTE communication with WiFi hotspot access included by Audi, Volvo or General Motors from 2014 (British Columbia FIPA, 2015).

Connectivity within cars is not completely new as sensors, telemetry and even performance data have been extensively exploited by automakers in the last decade. Currently, advancements in wireless communication technologies, sensor fusion, imaging, big data and analytics are creating new business opportunities for automotive manufacturers. This includes a wide range of applications such as warning information and comfort systems, advanced driver-assistance systems (ADAS) and automated driving. To this end, a modern vehicle in, 2015 (e.g., Ford GT) had in average more than 30 microprocessors, 50 sensors, 6 communication area networks (CANs), 10 million lines of code and 3000 different signals, delivering the equivalent of 100 GB/h of data to implement various critical functions like navigation, park assistance, adaptive cruise control, night vision, lane departure, collision mitigation and avoidance, low-speed and high-speed automated driving, eco-maneuvering and cooperative maneuvering, among others (Frost and Sullivan, 2017).

Wireless connectivity to the Internet and the ubiquity of smartphones are opening the way for connected cars, considered as the next step toward autonomous driving. The integration of the Internet into CAVs is expected not only to enhance the human cognitive abilities (e.g., improve safety and reduce road congestion), but to change the car ownership model by creating new services that result in a better travel experience for users (e.g., access content through built-in communication modules or other devices such as smartphones). As an example, technological giants such as Apple or Google have entered the automotive industry to develop self-driven vehicles with investments in the order of $10 billion (Shakeel, 2016).

Consequently, the higher the vehicle complexity as its functionalities increases, the higher the technical challenges of the embedded systems. This is especially true as vehicular connections are becoming common in such way that the hardware and software security is getting more compromised and vulnerable to hackers. Traditional cybersecurity strategies inherited from classic data networks are not enough to safeguard CAVs since they must protect people in addition to technology (e.g., data privacy or personal data leak). All the security breaches of a vehicle and its associated personal devices can be easily addressed. Nevertheless, this is being done slowly by manufacturers or not being done at all. The main reasons behind this are the lack of knowledge (i.e., car makers are new into handling hardware/software security threats) and the lack of adaptability (i.e., hardware, software and services are mainly designed to fulfill their functionality). The consequence is that more and more safety-critical functions rely on systems whose correct behavior cannot be guaranteed by traditional approaches (Heckemann et al., 2011). As a result, millions of cars are being recalled because of the vulnerabilities and risks for the personal safety of drivers and passengers. In addition, no less important is the negative social impact of the vehicle issues into the manufacturers' economy and image deterioration by widely spread attention in the media (ENISA, 2016).

1.1 Aims and objective

The current scenario of investment and development described above translates into numerous technical reports and manuscripts published in leading scientific journals and conferences. When referring to cybersecurity, the primary research includes a very rich literature mostly oriented to security threats and attacks, but there is hardly mention in the bibliography to the cybersecurity certification and auditing of the automotive industry. The main reason is that CAVs stand for an emerging multi-player market characterized by rapid advancements and innovations of the related technologies. Following this, cybersecurity has not been sufficiently addressed in any of the previous automotive standards such as ISO 26262, which has not laid the foundations for the harmonized development of this sector. So for example, SAE J3061 was recently published in 2016 as the first cybersecurity standard for the automotive industry (Schmittner et al., 2016).

Moreover, the secondary research found in the literature does not always emphasize on the historical evolution, does not cover statistical profiles, neither conducts bibliometric studies with a broad perspective of the context over time (i.e., most surveys are frequently limited to specific aspects and/or contemporary technologies). For this reason, the research question this paper aimed to examine was: which is the past, current and future interest on autonomous vehicles (AVs) cybersecurity? To accomplish that, three main objectives were established:

(1) To situate the industrial and scientific progress through the examination of who, when and about what has been made the research on AVs cybersecurity, especially focused on certification and auditing aspects.

(2) To conduct a systematic review on the literature along time comparing the most productive countries and organizations on AVs cybersecurity given the low number of available papers.

(3) To review what future cybersecurity threats lead to more compromised and vulnerable vehicles, putting the focus primarily on the CaaS within the automotive sector.

In order to highlight the contributions of this manuscript, Fig. 1 shows the scope of this work. To this end, the review paper is structured as follows. The following section describes the recent attention attracted from governments, academics and industry around AVs cybersecurity. Afterward, a summary table about the certification and auditing approaches present in the automotive industry is performed. Next section provides a contextual bibliographic analysis around AVs cybersecurity. Finally, the paper presents the future concerns and issues on AVs cybersecurity to reach the conclusions.

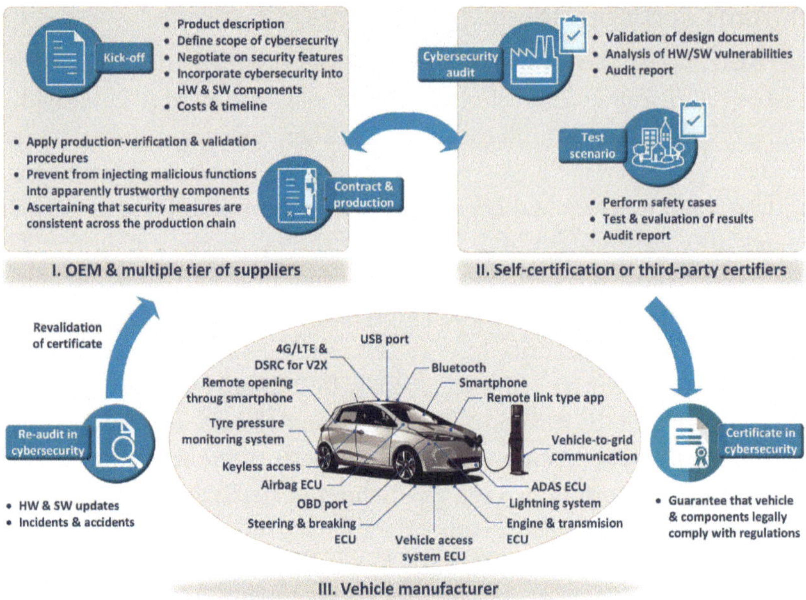

Fig. 1 Three steps toward cybersecurity certification and auditing of the automotive industry.

2. State of the art

The purpose of this section is to present the current state of the regulatory standards in the cybersecurity area that can be applied to CAVs, to assess what international groups are developing standards in combination with certifying bodies, as well as to identify what tools are being used for cybersecurity auditing. In order to analyze the current state of the art, a bibliometric analysis from scientific databases was conducted. Given the low number of papers published in this field, the search criteria was extended to identify other technical documents from generic databases and bibliographic sources. This search provided many technical documents available on regulatory agencies and standards around cybersecurity certification and auditing of CAVs. These manuscripts have been analyzed and presented in this section, which is organized into policy and planning, certifying bodies and companies, and audit techniques.

2.1 Policy and planning

Cyberattacks on the automotive industry are becoming more and more frequent as CAVs are increasing their presence on public roads. Such are the examples suffered by Jeep (Miller and Valasek, 2015), Volkswagen group (Garcia et al., 2016) and BMW (Keen Security Lab, 2018). These attacks can be carried out with the aim of controlling vehicles or discrediting a target company, affecting their sales and therefore generating a serious social impact. All without taking into account the personal damage to individuals (Chattopadhyay and Lam, 2018).

In order to provide safety and security in vehicles, the International Organization for Standardization (ISO) established the ISO 26262 standard in 2011. The purpose of this standard was to protect against attacks on critical vehicle systems with increasing technical complexity, such as the different electronic control units (ECU). Currently, ECUs support almost all the vehicle functionalities, being critical points in safety and security. ISO 26262 provides a life cycle for the vehicle security covering various phases ranging from management, development, production, operation and service to decommissioning. It also offers a safety-oriented analysis called Automotive Safety Integrity Level (ASIL), which classifies the situation severity level among four risk levels (ISO, 2018). In order to facilitate the understanding of ISO 26262, the Society of Automotive Engineers (SAE) established a guide with recommendations on design of cybersecurity systems through the SAE J3601™ standard. To this end, J3601™ defines a structured process to ensure that cybersecurity is included during the life cycle of a product consisting of: (a) concept phase; (b) product development (i.e., software, hardware and system); and (c) production, operation and service. This controlled process is intended to reduce the probability of carrying out a successful attack. Moreover, it tries to offer a clear way on how to react to a threatening scene (Boran et al., 2016). In addition, SAE J3601™ harmonizes keywords to define cyber-physical systems, attacks and threats among others, as well as clarifies the difference between accident or failure vs a malicious attack. On the other hand, it recommends that each developed product should be analyzed with a series of cybersecurity tools and verified to be reasonably free of vulnerabilities (SAE International, 2016).

ISO and SAE are also currently developing a new standard aimed at extending the cybersecurity of road vehicles, called ISO/SAE 21434, which is intended to be published by 2020 (Barber, 2018). This standard is being developed to face cybersecurity based on: (i) risk management through assessment and analysis of threats and vulnerabilities; (ii) definition of security requirements during the concept phase; (iii) validation of security measures implemented in hardware and software in compliance with established security requirements; (iv) production, operation and maintenance via cybersecurity monitoring and incident response;

(v) management of documentation, configuration, changes and security information. Finally, the standard will include a Cybersecurity Assurance Level (CAL) as an annex, which will allow prioritizing some development tasks over others according to a security level set (Hunjan, 2018). Unlike previous standards, ISO/IEC 20243 aims to provide a set of specific guidelines, requirements and recommendations to ensure the integrity of the hardware and software provided by a manufacturer. Therefore, ISO/IEC 20243 is established to reduce the risk due to threats related with malicious tainted and counterfeit products. To this end, this standard introduces the concept of product integrity through the Open Trusted Technology Provider Framework™ (O-TTPF) to assure that a product is as described and no original equipment manufacturer (OEM) or supplier has been able to alter it along the different stages: (a) product development/engineering; (b) secure development/engineering; and (c) secure supply chain (ISO/IEC, 2018).

Apart from that, in addition to the international standards, there are organizations distributed by geographical zones responsible for establishing cybersecurity regulations and recommendations in their areas of action. These include the Federal Automated Vehicle Policy 3.0 (FAVP) of the Department of Transportation (DOT) of the USA. It offers an intermodal approach to the autonomous driving systems (ADS) policy, which is oriented to all land transport systems (e.g., cars, trucks or motorcycles). FAVP has recently published a document entitled "Preparing for the Future of Transportation: Automated Vehicles 3.0" which collects a set of initiatives to promote the development, regulation and scope around automated vehicles (DOT, 2018). In this sense, there is a collaboration between USA and Canada to self-certify vehicles by manufacturers (Transport Canada, 2019). For this, the carmakers must follow the good practices proposed by the National Highway Traffic Safety Administration (NHTSA) of USA (NHTSA, 2016). In addition to these regulations, Canada has proposed a framework especially focused on user data privacy and cybersecurity (Policy and Planning Support Committee, 2019), while USA is developing a federal law for cybersecurity in AVs to obligate manufacturers or importers to include a cybersecurity policy indicating how AVs will detect and respond to cyberattacks before being sold (Senate of the United States, 2017). On the other side, the Ministry of Land, Infrastructure, Transport and Tourism (MLIT) of Japan has been working to disseminate the culture around AVs and involve people in their progress. The actions are performed as a set of experiments carried out by the Intelligent Transport System and Automatic Driving Informal Working Group and by the Automatically Commanded Steering Function Informal Working Group (MLIT, 2017). In the same way, the European Union has proposed the European Commission (EC) to carry out a pilot of communications between vehicles and infrastructures for road safety (EC, 2018a,b), according to the guidelines proposed in the certificate and security policy for automated vehicles approved by European Union Agency for Network and Information Security (ENISA, 2016). Finally, the United Nations Economic Commission for Europe (UNECE) has prepared a technical report addressing the main cyber threats and vulnerabilities identified in vehicles. In this document, UNECE proposes a set of guidelines to improve the cybersecurity policy on Europe's roads and mitigate these risks in CAVs (United Nations, 2019a). Furthermore, UNECE is working on a legal framework to treat how certified vehicles are affected by software updates that may be carried by manufacturers. This framework proposes that carmakers should indicate to UNECE or national governments when and how affect the software updates to the car certificates previously granted. If any certificate is altered, the manufacturer must initiate a process with an authorized entity to extend or generate a new certification that reflects the change produced (United Nations, 2019b).

2.2 Certifying bodies and companies

Due to the cyber threats experienced by the automotive industry, governments in different countries are urging car manufacturers to certify or homologate their CAVs to comply with regulations, in an attempt to increase consumers' confidence in the new products being developed. Certificates in cybersecurity may range from personal certificates for engineers to corporate certificates about the operation of the entire vehicle system (i.e., hardware and software). The type of certificate required currently depends on the geographical area. In USA and Canada, vehicle manufacturers are responsible for certifying that their vehicles comply with current regulations without the need for third parties that confirm it, which is called self-certification (Taiber and Zhang, 2019). This regulation also authorizes the US government to check vehicles for compliance, especially when a non-compliance or high safety risk is detected (NHTS, 2017). In contrast, industry must certify or homologate vehicles in Europe and China before they can be used on the public road. In these countries, vehicles must undergo a series of virtual and physicals test in closed circuits and public roads to achieve a valid certification, which is granted when vehicles are not a risk to other road users (Taiber and Zhang, 2019). An example of mandatory certification is the e-mark, for which third parties guarantee that a vehicle—and all its components—legally comply with the relevant EU/ECE regulations to be freely sold in the EU. In the revision made in, 2018, new security aspects such as the need to use secure features to access in-vehicle diagnostic systems (e.g., HTTPS, SSL/TLS or private keys) are required to obtain this certificate (EC, 2018a,b). An example of certifying body for the e-mark label is SGS (SGS, 2016). There are also other bodies that evaluate and certify novel concepts such as TÜD SÜD, which offers a platform called OpenGenesis specialized in artificial intelligence (AI) and machine learning of AVs (TÜV SÜD, 2018).

In relation to the certifications based on the standards described in the previous section, several certifying bodies can be found. For this purpose, CERTX has a test and certification program for autonomous vehicles, which allows to develop safer products that are better accepted by the markets. This company can test and certify vehicles in accordance with ISO 26262, ISO 21448 and ISO 21434, as well as offering personal certificates for automotive workers on the ISO 26262 and ISO 21448 standards (CERTX, 2019). Another certification body is the consortium formed by Ernest & Young, GIGATRONIK and Code White, who allows obtaining certifications in accordance with the established regulations described in ISO 26262 and ISO 27001 for AVs and cybersecurity in AVs, respectively (Ernest and Young, 2016). Complementarily, other companies such as DEKRA offer other related certifications for CAVs in compliance with the last security requirements and standards (DEKRA, 2018). These certifications deal with wireless technologies (e.g., Bluetooth SIG, NFC, WiFi or LoRa), mobile technologies and electromagnetic compatibility (e.g., e-Mark or TCB in USA). Moreover, Bureau Veritas has added a cybersecurity certification in its portfolio of services offered to vehicle manufactures based on ISO 27001 (Bureau Veritas, 2016). Finally, the Open Group consortium—formed by more than 600 institutions such as IBM, Oracle, Intel, Nissan, NASA, Carnegie Mellon University and Boston University, among others—is responsible for verifying and certifying that OEMs and multiple tier suppliers provide identical components to those described in their datasheets according to ISO/IEC 20243 (The Open Group, 2016).

Despite the advancement experienced regarding the cybersecurity certification of CAVs, there is still a large gap to overcome. In this sense, there are some national agencies asking for more progress and defining strategies to

Table 1 Certifying bodies in cybersecurity standards for connected and autonomous vehicles.

Organization	Enterprise certifications for vehicle manufacturers	Personal certifications for engineers	Additional certifications in other related technologies	Bibliographic references
SGS	e-mark (Europe)	None	None	SGS (2016)
TÜD SÜD	e-mark (Europe)	None	AI and machine learning in AVs	TÜD SÜD (2018)
CERTX	ISO 26262, ISO 21448 and ISO 21434	ISO 26262 & ISO 21448	None	CERTX (2019)
Ernest & Young, GIGATRONIK, Code White	ISO 26262 and ISO 27001	None	None	Ernst and Young (2016)
DEKRA	e-mark (Europe), TCB (USA), FCB (Canada), e-Call	None	Bluetooth SIG, ULE Alliance, Mirrolink, NFC, AllJoyn, LoRa, AirFuel and Sigfox	DEKRA (2018)
Bureau Veritas	ISO 2701	None	None	Bureau Veritas (2016)
The Open Group consortium	ISO/IEC 20243	None	None	The Open Group (2016)

test and certify new vehicle characteristics with the aim of reducing the risk of attacks. These currently include digital vehicle inspection and dynamic driving tasks, among others (DOT, 2018; EC, 2018a,b). In brief, Table 1 summarizes the various certifying bodies mentioned above.

2.3 Audit techniques

Before receiving a cybersecurity certificate from a certifying body such as those mentioned above for carmakers, the vehicle systems must be audited. This process consists in analyzing that the vehicle production has complied with the standard indications as well as that vehicles do not present reasonable vulnerabilities. To conduct an audit focused on vehicle cybersecurity,

J3061™ recommends dividing the procedure into two main aspects: (*a*) threat analysis, risk assessment and vulnerability analysis; and (*b*) penetration testing methods (Boran et al., 2016).

Among the possible tools for threat analysis, risk assessment and vulnerability analysis, Microsoft's STRIDE stands out. This tool models and identifies different threats a system can support and categorizes them according to the type (e.g., spoofing, tampering, repudiation, information disclosure, DOS and privilege elevation). To this end, STRIDE evaluates the design of a system in order to know the type of attack that it may suffer based on the data flow. This tool is currently still used as part of the Microsoft Secure Development Lifecycle (SDL) (Shevchenko et al., 2018). Another tool more focused on preventing unauthorized access to a vehicle network is called E-safety vehicle intrusion protected applications (EVITA). EVITA is a tool aimed at designing, verifying and prototyping a network architecture in vehicles with the goal of protecting vehicle-to-vehicle (V2V) and vehicle-to-infrastructure (V2I) communications (Henniger et al., 2009). In this sense, the tool HEAVENS is a proposal to facilitate the inclusion of cybersecurity requirements for electrical/electronic systems in vehicles. This tool has adopted the Microsoft's STRIDE approach by describing the possible effects of attacks that may be suffered. This tool allows identifying security vulnerabilities and expose the possible impacts that may generate for the manufacturer (e.g., financial damages, safety, operational, privacy, etc.). However, it does not aim to provide countermeasures or security mechanisms to prevent attacks from these vulnerabilities (The HEAVENS Consortium, 2016). Finally, a very useful tool when an audit is required to quantify the risk of possible cyberattacks against vehicles is the attack graph and/or attack tree. This technique makes it possible to know —from the vehicle design and/or architecture— the possible cyberattacks that a vehicle may suffer as well as estimate the risk that exists for its system (Karray et al., 2018). Some examples of applications to build attack trees or graphs are Visio, Mindmup or OmniGraffle (Gardiner, 2018).

In relation to the penetration tests, a platform for auditing CAN devices (CANSPY) highlights. This tool enables to act as a Man-in-the-Middle (MITM) entity to partially simulate ECUs and block, forward or modify frames on the fly both locally and remotely via Ethernet (Lebrun and Demay, 2016). In the same line, Toyota has introduced an open-source tool called Portable Automotive Security Testbed with Adaptability (PASTA). This tool makes it possible to research, develop and evaluate technologies related with the vehicle cybersecurity. To this end, PASTA utilizes ECUs that can be connected to other ECUs through the CAN bus and a simulator

Table 2 Tools to audit cybersecurity features in connected and autonomous vehicles.

Name	Type of audit	Methodology	Technique	Target	Year
STRIDE	Threat and vulnerability analysis, risk assessment	Noninvasive	–	Vehicle architecture	2002
EVITA	Threat and vulnerability analysis, risk assessment	Noninvasive	–	Vehicle architecture	2008
Peach	Penetration testing	Invasive	Fuzz test	CAN bus	2013
HEAVENS	Threat and vulnerability analysis, risk assessment	Noninvasive	–	Vehicle architecture	2016
CANSPY	Penetration testing	Invasive	Monitoring and injection	CAN bus	2016
PASTA	Penetration testing	Invasive	Monitoring	CAN bus	2018
Can Fuzzer	Penetration testing	Invasive	Fuzz test	CAN bus	2018
Attacks tree	Threat and vulnerability analysis, risk assessment	Noninvasive	–	Vehicle architecture	–

of vehicles that obtains the car model characteristics by means of CAN messages received by the ECUs. In this way, if a vehicle is being attacked by means of messages injected into the CAN bus, this tool allows to know whether the vehicle is being attacked by analyzing those messages and visualizing the anomalous values (Toyama et al., 2018). Another technique used to detect unauthorized inputs to the system is the so-called Fuzz tests, outstanding those tools designed exclusively to analyze automotive systems such as Peach (Bayer et al., 2015) and CAN fuzzer (Fowler et al., 2018). Both tools consist in systematically sending random data over the CAN bus and then monitoring the system response. If a fault is detected, it is recorded and the system is restarted. At the end of the test, a file is generated indicating which system entries induced an error and can potentially cause an attacker to access the system. As a result, the vehicle manufacturer is responsible for taking corrective actions to solve the vulnerabilities (Fowler et al., 2018). As a summary, Table 2 lists the main features of the tools used for vehicle auditing described in the manuscript.

3. Bibliographic analysis

A comprehensive and systematic bibliometric analysis was conducted considering the online abstract and indexing service provided by Scopus® from Elsevier. The reason for its choice—vs others such as the IEEE Xplore® digital library, Google Scholar, ResearchGate, ArXiv or DBLP—is that Scopus® is considered the world's largest scientific database. Furthermore, Scopus® is available for free and has also been used in many previous bibliometric analysis (Heradio et al., 2016; Lozano Domínguez and Mateo Sanguino, 2019; Mateo Sanguino, 2017; Van Wee and Banister, 2016). The search range considered in the study was focused on the period from 1989 to 2018 (i.e., all literature found) and performed with the following structure: TITLE-ABS-KEY ("*term_1*" OR "*term_2*" OR "*term_n*" AND "*term_i*" [...] AND NOT "*term_j*" [...]) AND (EXCLUDE (PUBYEAR, 2019)). The publications were gathered to compare complete annual periods (therefore 2019 was discarded), filtered to avoid the misuse of terms belonging to other disciplines (i.e., acronyms with various meaning) and then processed using spreadsheets to sort the results. Accordingly, the publications in Scopus® were evaluated considering the following factors: number of manuscripts per year, source type, keywords, country and affiliation of the authors. As a summary, Table 3 describes the keywords included and excluded for the search of terms in the Scopus® database following the aforementioned structure.

3.1 Study on the evolution of cybersecurity in AVs

The sample analyzed in this work included 2238 manuscripts within the category of "connected & autonomous vehicles," 768 for "V2X communication," 235 for "cybersecurity in AVs," and 8 for "certification & auditing in AVs." These values were plotted in Fig. 2 along with the most significant technological milestones around CAVs. In brief, they were the first data telematics system used in a car (2007), the approval of the ISO 26262 standard (2011), the first deployment of 4G/LTE in cars by Audi and General Motors (2014), the formation of the Open Automotive Alliance (OAA) to bring the Android platform to cars (2014), the announcement of Tesla, Google and Apple to develop their own autonomous cars (2015), the publication of the SAE J3061 recommendation (2016), and the first US automaker to deploy Dedicated Short-Range Communication (DSRC) in vehicles (2017).

Table 3 Keywords used for the search of terms in the Scopus database.

Search term	Keywords included (OR/AND)	Keywords excluded (AND NOT/ EXCLUDE)	Manuscripts found	Relative production	Citations received	Citations per paper
Connected or autonomous vehicle	Connected vehicle, autonomous car	Robot*, roving, inspection, ocean, *water, subm*, defense, military*, avionics, air*, 2019	2238	68.48%	12,455	5.56
Vehicle-to-everything communication	V2X	Robot, indexing, 2019	788	24.11%	2696	3.42
Cybersecurity in AVs	Cyber-security, vehicle, automotive, car	Drone, aer*, air*, robotic, ship, truck, smart grid, critical infrastructure, education, 2019	234	7.16%	591	2.52
Certification and auditing in AVs	Hardware, software, certification, automotive, security	Operating system domain, 2019	8	0.24%	56	7

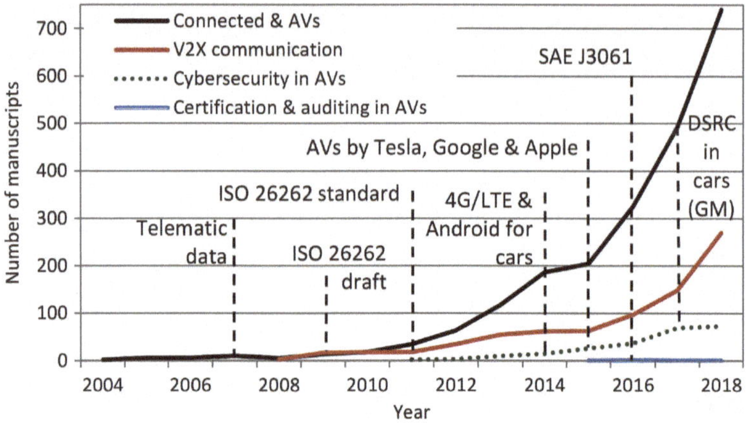

Fig. 2 Bibliographic evolution of the main concerns about security in connected and autonomous vehicles.

The above-mentioned analysis resulted in a scientific production with 64.8% of papers published on "connected & autonomous vehicles," 24.11% of papers on "V2X communication," 7.16% about "cybersecurity in AVs" and 0.24% on "certification and auditing in AVs" (see Table 3). The survey showed that the greatest weight of the research was around the "connected and autonomous vehicles," presenting a timid activity around the first years of publication (1989–2008) and a stronger activity in the last decade (2008–2018). The latter corresponds to a major period of expansion correlated with the evolution of the other subcategories. A comparison of the research fields in this time frame determined an outstanding correlation between "connected & AVs" and "V2X communication" ($r^2=0.976$, $P\ll0.01$), "connected & AVs" and "cybersecurity in AVs" ($r^2=0.988$, $P\ll0.01$), and "V2X communication" and "cybersecurity in AVs" ($r^2=0.894$, $P\ll0.01$). As the main result, this study suggests that the cybersecurity threats and vulnerabilities are significantly related with the communication technologies, and consequently with the CAVs. Note that this study could not consider the category of "certification & auditing in AVs" given the low number of papers published only recently.

An analysis on the publications per territory specifically focused on the cybersecurity in AVs (see Fig. 3) shows a significant activity mainly in North America (38.49%) and Europe (35.84%) followed by Asia (19.91%) and South America, Africa & Oceania to a lesser extent (5.75%). Additionally, a study on the most productive countries and their relationship was conducted.

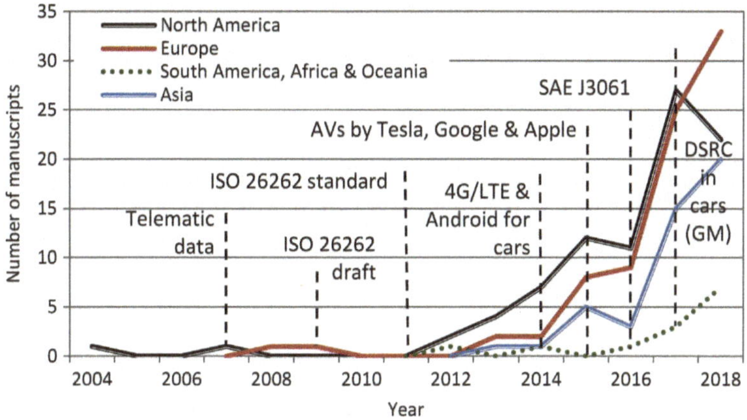

Fig. 3 Bibliographic evolution of the contributions per territory on cybersecurity in AVs.

Fig. 4 Cooperation between countries based on the publication co-authorship from 2004 to 2018.

To this end, VOSviewer was chosen as the software tool for creating, visualizing and exploring maps based on network data (Van Eck and Waltman, 2014). The results are summarized in Table 4 and Fig. 4 for which thesaurus files and the Lin-Log clustering technique were used to filter inconsistencies over a total of 38 countries. The results suggest that the USA has been the most productive country considering the first year of publication (2004), number of manuscripts (33.6%), strength in the co-authorship with other researchers (25), number of collaborations with other countries (12) and total citations received (54.69%). A contextual analysis on the average publishing year revealed how the global scientific production is being displaced. Particularly, the USA, UK, Austria, Japan and South Korea contributed their research more in 2016, while China, Germany, India, France and Singapore contributed more through research in 2017. In the same way, Canada, Poland and Tunisia

Table 4 Most productive countries from 2004 to 2018 on cybersecurity in AVs.

RP	Country	MP	MP (%)	CA	IC	CR	CR (%)	Avg. Pub. Year
1	USA	84	33.6	25	12	361	54.69	2016
2	UK	27	10.8	6	4	88	13.33	2016
3	China	20	8.0	13	13	30	4.54	2017
4	Germany	15	6.0	15	6	18	2.72	2017
5	Austria	11	4.4	5	5	51	7.72	2016
6	India	10	4.0	8	4	7	1.06	2017
7	Japan	8	3.2	6	2	10	0.90	2016
8	France	8	3.2	11	9	6	1.51	2017
9	Singapore	7	2.8	4	2	11	1.66	2017
10	S. Korea	7	2.8	3	3	6	0.90	2016

CA, co-authorship strength with other researchers; *CR*, citations received; *IC*, international collaborations; *MP*, manuscripts published; *RP*, ranking position.

contributed more in 2018. A bibliographic analysis on the correlation between the contributions of the different countries encountered a significant relationship in the research carried out between North America and Europe ($r^2=0.895$ and $P \ll 0.01$) as well as a good correlation between South America, Africa and Oceania and Asia ($r^2=0.667$ and $P<0.05$). This confirms the tradition and close cooperation between these different territories from 2004 to 2018.

An analysis on the scientific contribution of the organizations on cybersecurity in AVs encountered that universities carried out a more weighted and constant research than the other organizations (see Fig. 5). This study shows the leadership of universities (63.50%) over private corporations (22.28%) and research institutions (14.20%). An analysis on the bibliographic correlation encountered a significant relationship in the research carried out from 2004 to 2018, which confirms the close cooperation between the different organizations ($r^2=0.944$ and $P \ll 0.01$ for "Universities" vs "Institutions," $r^2=0.906$ and $P \ll 0.01$ for "Universities" vs "Corporations," and $r^2=0.952$ and $P \ll 0.01$ for "Institutions" vs "Corporations"). In this sense, the most productive organizations are summarized in Table 5, where the top of universities, institutions and corporations are shown.

An analysis on the source type of the publications on cybersecurity in AVs (see Fig. 6) shows a major contribution through conferences

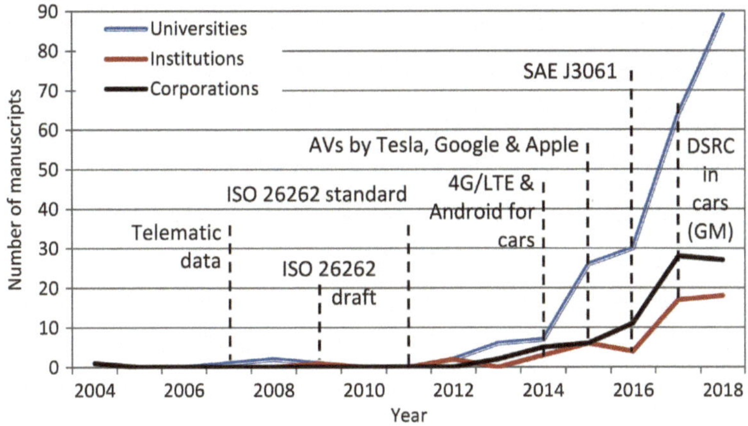

Fig. 5 Bibliographic evolution of the contributions per organization on cybersecurity in AVs.

Table 5 Most productive organizations about cybersecurity in AVs from 2004 to 2018.

RP	Organization	Country	CL	MP	MP (%)	NC	CR	CR (%)
1	AVL List GmbH	Austria	C	8	3.40	9	25	4.23
2	Alpine Electronics, Inc.	Japan	C	7	2.15	1	18	3.04
3	Coventry University	UK	U	7	2.15	3	8	1.35
4	Technische Universitat Graz	Austria	U	7	2.15	8	25	4.23
5	HORIBA MIRA Ltd.	UK	C	7	2.15	1	14	2.36
6	University of California, Berkeley	USA	U	5	2.12	4	111	18.78
7	The University of Warwick	UK	U	4	1.70	4	0	0.00
8	Institute for Infocomm Research	Singapore	I	3	1.27	5	4	0.67
9	Florida International University	USA	U	3	1.27	2	13	2.19
10	Jinan University	China	U	3	1.27	7	6	1.01

CL, university (U), institution (I) or corporation (C); *CR*, citations received; *MP*, manuscripts published; *NC*, collaborations with other organizations; *RP*, ranking position.

(82.31%) followed by journals (15.52%) and books (2.16%). The study confirms a good trend between the different sources, which suggests that a rapid and strong growth in conferences is also reflected in scientific journals and textbooks. The study on the document type found a total of 19 open access

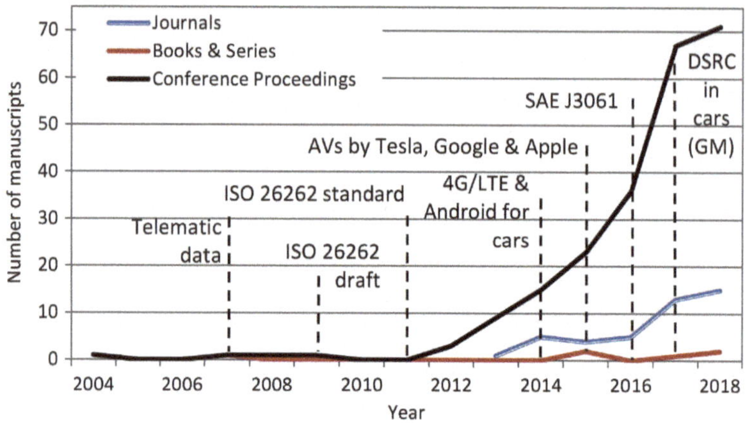

Fig. 6 Bibliographic evolution of the contributions per type of source on cybersecurity in AVs.

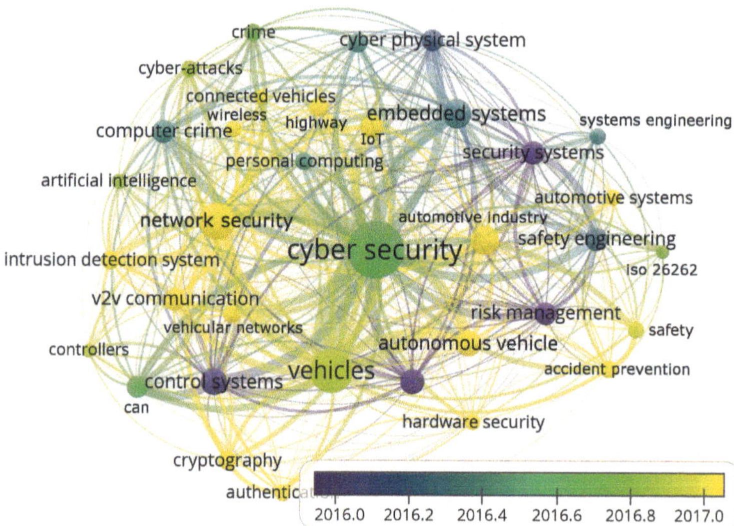

Fig. 7 Co-occurrence of the keywords in publications on cybersecurity in AVs.

manuscripts (8.12%), as well as 28 reviews and surveys (11.97%) over a total of 234 manuscripts. These results reflect the weight of primary research vs secondary research.

An in-depth comparative analysis on the co-occurrence of the keywords between the publications on "cybersecurity in AVs" vs "certification & auditing in AVs" is shown in Figs. 7 and 8. The frequency in which the terms appear allows us to assess the weight of research in these fields.

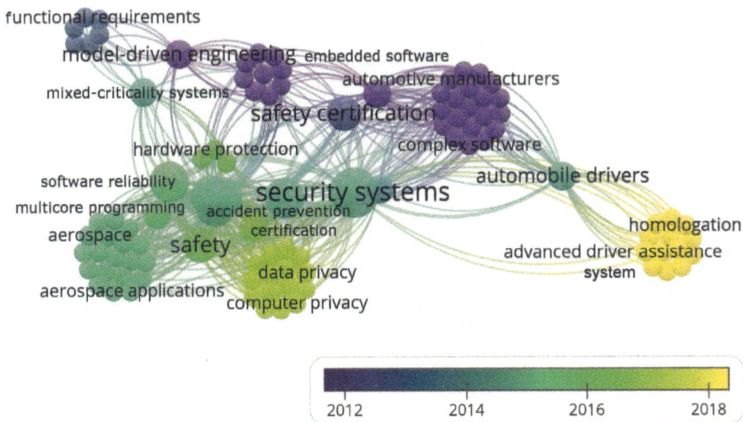

Fig. 8 Co-occurrence of the keywords in publications on certification and auditing in AVs.

The network visualization in Fig. 7 corresponds to the 40 most popular terms over a total of 1666 keywords indexed by both authors and publishers within 234 manuscripts. Accordingly, the number of documents in which some representative keywords related to this survey appear resulted as follows: "cybersecurity" (147), "vehicles" (83), "network security" (59), "automotive industry" (38), "embedded systems" (38), "control systems" (31), "autonomous vehicle" (30) and "data security" (28), among others. Moreover, the network visualization in Fig. 8 corresponds to the 40 most popular terms within 8 manuscripts. Accordingly, the number of documents in which some representative keywords related to this survey appear resulted as follows: "security systems" (6), "safety certification" (6), "accident prevention" (4), "embedded systems" (4), "safety engineering" (4), "software reliability" (4), "systems engineering" (4) and "automobile drivers" (2), among others. In this sense, the comparative analysis considering the evolution along time encountered the following results. On the one hand, research on cybersecurity in AVs was mainly displaced from control systems, security systems, data security and risk management in 2016 to network security, intrusion detection systems, autonomous vehicle, V2V communication and Internet of things in 2018. On the other hand, the research on certification and auditing in AVs was mainly focused on cost engineering, safety certification, adaptive software, data fusion in 2012, while the distributed embedded systems, collaborative systems, condition monitoring, advanced driver assistance systems (ADAS) and homologation were the key terms in research during 2017 and 2018, respectively.

4. Discussion on challenges and future trends

CAVs can bring numerous benefits ranging from improved energy and transport system efficiency. Although a very restrictive regulation could slow down their development and real-world deployment, it is necessary to provide a legal framework—looking for balance—that prevents safety and security from being sacrificed by commercial interests. The reality is that there is a danger of presenting vehicles with attractive functionalities before thinking about all their implications (e.g., hacking of traffic sign detection and recognition). The risk of adding automation to vehicles has not been properly understood by car manufacturers in the past and it is a serious problem just as the insecure vehicular connectivity is being addressed nowadays. The fact is that most cars use components based on old hardware and software developed years ago and with basic flaws inherent to design, so errors and vulnerabilities are transferred to these new generation of vehicles. Therefore, considering the average lifetime of a modern vehicle (i.e., 11 years for the EU according to the European Automobile Manufacturers' Association), car manufacturers should assume the obligation to make, maintain, guarantee and legally agree—with consumers—cyber resilience systems against attacks (e.g., a 0-day exploit). This would require new work and intervention approaches based on re-audit and re-certification processes to face situations in which, for instance, a line of code is modified producing essentially a new vehicle as a result of a software update (Gowling, 2017).

Cyberattacks targeting vehicles and automotive systems are a reality in recent years, which is likely to increase with CAVs gaining relevance, with the certainty that absolute security does not exist. Hackers always find new ways to violate systems, highlighting that current practices are weak and insufficient. So for instance, a typical programmer incurs between 10 and 30 errors per 1000 lines of code according to studies, resulting in a significant number of cybersecurity vulnerabilities (Jansen, 2018). The most common tests only detect those breaches easier to find and hackers know it. They have motivation and time enough to test all cases, including the most atypical ones. This creates an insecurity scenario where the main concern for automakers until recently was how to minimize vulnerabilities in the vehicle architecture. This has been the game for many hobbyists, hacktivists, researchers and enthusiasts around the world who have played to manipulate the vehicle software (e.g., to upset their proper performance). Nevertheless, the manufacturers' opinion regarding professional hackers is quite different, especially if our lives depend on it. Their threats could range from disabling vehicle functions (e.g., hacking the car's brakes by simply sending an SMS to the ECUs access systems) to blocking a vehicle from starting and then demanding a payment to unlock it (i.e., ransomware). Consequently, the current concern for security is also being directed toward intruder protection solutions within the own vehicle network. Therefore, manufacturers should think about solutions similar to traditional IT networks. This may consider multi-layered approaches including firewalls, intrusion detection system/intrusion protection system (IDS/IPS) and even typical anti-viruses or cloud backups to prevent, detect and response to real-time attacks in vehicles (Automotive World, 2018).

The cause of this worrying scenario is an increasing activity around CaaS, through which criminals have changed the traditional industry landscape over the last years. The main motivation behind attackers is financial gain, corresponding their actions to cybercrime (77.40%), cyber espionage (14.50%), hacktivism (4.70%) and cyber warfare (3.40%). According to a report on the activity in the year 2017, the attention in CaaS was mainly directed to the United States (23%), Europe (19%) and China (9%) over other territories (Ernst and Young, 2018). CaaS turns out to be a lucrative business whose model is supported by a fully blown organized industry with suppliers, markets and service providers. This provision is given with the aim of facilitating the commission of cybercrimes and includes a variety of services such as account hacking programs ($12.99), password stealers ($50) or DDoS attacks ($500–1200), among others. The reality is that CaaS has become more intense, global and harmful not only for persons, but also for organizations and nations. Therefore, it is a matter of time for the attention to be directed to the automotive industry—both consumers and manufacturers—including specific car models, rental companies, corporate fleets or foreign competitors (Brown et al., 2015). In this sense, the millions in losses for carmakers could be significant, whose cost per hour of inactivity is around $22,000 besides the reputational damage (Acronis, 2018). But without a doubt, what makes CaaS the greatest threat is that perpetrators perform cybercrimes with easy access to low-cost sophisticated toolkits with impunity and few technical skills. That is, attackers no longer need to rely on their own abilities to commit cybercrimes (IBM, 2017). A wide range of exploit software is now available to help offenders design and launch over-the-air attacks in connected or autonomous vehicles (e.g., network profiling and reconnaissance, authentication and encryption cracking, MITM and DoS).

Cybersecurity has become a necessity, whose solution should be seen by automakers as a future investment that will take time, money and a broad organizational restructure. As the automotive industry has a solid history in improving personal safety in a collaborative manner, this work philosophy should be extended to the implementation of cybersecurity standards in vehicles to reduce security risk. This includes to share information to facilitate prompt responses to novel threats (e.g., intelligence on vulnerabilities and attacks) as well as to adopt the best practices already learned and faced by other fields such as in critical infrastructures, rail or aviation industries (Lanctot, 2018). This means not only to apply traditional approaches based on IT solutions around authentication, encryption and integrity, but also to integrate the certification and audit processes at appropriate intervals as a security wheel. Such solutions range from learning to negotiate on the cybersecurity features of components to ascertaining that the security measures have been consistently implemented across the entire production chain (i.e., production-verification and validation procedures). Therefore, this should be extended to product-qualification procedures for OEM and multiple tier of suppliers to incorporate the cybersecurity aspect into hardware and software, and prevent from injecting malicious functions into apparently trustworthy components—such as in the cloning of ICs—introduced in the early production stages (Goldberg, 2018). As a result, every function of a vehicle should be questioned and formally documented through a deterministic way on how they could be compromised (i.e., to perform risk and vulnerability analysis through penetration testing and forensic tools). From the automaker viewpoint, to apply this approach before reaching the supply chain has the benefit of avoiding extra costs, complexity or even weight as a result of security fixes implemented as self-protection measures during the after-sale stage (e.g., over-the-air (OTA) updates partially offered to vehicles for limited parts of the software). Designed as an auditable and certifiable mechanism, it would let automakers to gain control, transparency and trust in cybersecurity and its earlier implementation would enable a smoother transition to CAVs.

4.1 Security issues in emerging vehicular applications

Social capabilities become the next barrier on the way to develop full self-driving cars so that safety, comfort and efficiency of passengers is improved. Thereby, the steps in the next decade will comprise awareness, sensing, cooperative and synchronized driving (Cisco Systems, 2018). To this end, social IoT (SIoT) is expected to provide new high-level services by using different access technologies (e.g., Wi-Fi, LTE, WiMAX, etc.), being the exchange of information in vehicles like infotainment, traffic status, parking, routes or weather the major exponents of application (Silva and Iqbal, 2019). In this sense, some examples of social Internet of vehicles (SIoV) already operational in markets are a voice chatting system for dynamic vehicular communications (RoadSpeak), a car navigator that integrates traffic voice tweets (NaviTweet) or a mobility data sharing system based on social networks (Caravan Track) (Maglaras et al., 2016). Despite the enormous possibilities to enable a social interaction between vehicles, infrastructures and pedestrians, future works should focus on trusting social media and confronting ethical dilemmas in decision making. More significant is the need to overcome issues related to security and privacy (e.g., data leaks). That is, there is the need to provide a secure ecosystem for peer interaction through public networks where smart objects such as smartphones, vehicles and roadside units (RSUs) socialize.

Another example of new business model and service is the Internet of Things Application (IOTA), an accounting open-source technology that allows the secure and wireless exchange of information with special focus on CAVs (Popov, 2017). The IOTA Foundation and the International Transportation Innovation Center (ICIT) cooperate since, 2018 to test solutions through its own IOTA node-based service network (i.e., Tangle). To this end, Volkswagen, Bosch, Orange, Accenture and Schneider Electric have progressively joined this newfangled initiative, who was planning to kick off an IOTA bill platform in Q1 2019—called DigitalCarPass—to automatically pay for certain services such as parking or recharging electric vehicles (Dasgupta and Babu, 2019). This young technology is considered as part of the future smart car economy model, the so-called mobility as a service (MaaS) also envisioned by BMW, GM, Ford, Jaguar Land Rover, Hyperledger and IBM to form one of the world's largest consortia in crypto applications. As a result, IOTA has achieved a market capitalization of ~$800 million since 2017. Nonetheless, the lack of an intelligent contract system, the energy cost of the crypto mining process, the need for a decentralized network and some serious security issues are some of the main cons that still need to be worked out nowadays. The latter mainly concerns cryptographic weaknesses, reusability of IOTA addresses and vulnerabilities to reply attacks (Yuva and Kırbaş, 2018).

5. Conclusions

The new advances achieved in the automotive industry around CAVs allows offering users with a better experience, as well as creating new paradigms and services related to mobility and transport. This revolution is arriving to vehicles through the inclusion of sensors and of Internet-based access technologies, offering cars the capability to interact with infrastructure, people and/or services (e.g., traffic, parking and weather collaborative information). As a counterpart, this ecosystem also brings new challenges in the interaction between the road actors, being cybersecurity one of the major challenges to be overcome. Both industry and governments around the world are intensively working in cybersecurity solutions to prevent vehicles from being accessed and exploited by cybercriminals interested in benefiting or causing damage to users. To this end, different bodies such as ISO and SAE are developing standards to offer recommendations and good practices to make secure and resilient cars. With this aim, governments are requiring vehicle manufacturers to certify their vehicles through self-certificates or third parties. The latter especially uses audits to grant security certificates based on (a) threat analysis, vulnerability analysis and risk assessment; and (b) penetration testing methods. The pursue of secure and resilient cars is fundamental to provide confidence to consumer in this innovative concept of CAVs. The association of cyberattacks to CAVs may hinder consumer's acceptance and adoption of this solution, justifying the automotive industry investments on this topic from an early stage.

As a conclusion from the review of the state of the art, it can be stated that certifications and audits based on standards and regulations developed in cybersecurity for CAVs is an increasing field. This is also supported from the analysis performed on the bibliography, which goes from 1989 to 2018. In this study, it was possible to identify that the contribution of cybersecurity in vehicles represents 7.16% of the total publications, while those related to vehicle audit and certification represent 0.24%. Additionally, greater activity on this topic has been observed in the last decade compared to the first years. This increase in activity coincides with the inclusion of the telematic data systems in vehicles, the approval of the ISO and SAE standards, the Internet-based access technologies (e.g., 4G/LTE or DSRC), as well as the announcements of various companies such as Tesla, Google and Apple working on AVs. As a result of the review, it was identified that a higher number of publications was mainly authorized by universities

(63.50%) as opposed to private companies (22.28%) and other research centers (14.20%). Considering the geographic location, the activity was mainly focused on North America and Europe (38.49% and 35.84%).

Moreover, the automotive industry may be a target for cyberattacks using CaaS to exploit vulnerabilities of CAVs in the near future. Attacks could be aimed at disabling or blocking vehicle functionalities to make money after restoring the system or with the purpose of damaging the public image of companies and countries. These vulnerabilities are typically caused by programming failures or by using legacy hardware and software, which have vulnerabilities well-known by hackers. In order to avoid these security breaches, vehicle manufacturers must understand the effort to provide with cybersecurity as an investment in time and money. They should also act against threats in the form of consortia instead of isolated companies as it has been traditionally done by critical infrastructures, rail or aviation industries. Consortiums should not only include vehicle manufacturers, but also manufacturers' suppliers to ensure cybersecurity in all vehicle components and throughout the manufacturing chain. Following this way of working, an auditable and certified mechanism can be designed to increase control, transparency and trust in cybersecurity onboard CAVs along the car life, thus facilitating the transition from traditional vehicles to CAVs.

Acknowledgments

We would like to thank the action CA16222 from the European Cooperation in Science and Technology (COST) entitled "Wider Impacts and Scenario Evaluation of Autonomous and Connected Transport." Thanks are also due to the Fundação para a Ciência e Tecnologia through support from IN+ Strategic Project UID/EEA/50009/2019 and contract CEECIND/02589/2017.

References

Acronis, 2018. Technology Solutions: Friend or Foe to the Auto Industry? Technical Report pp. 1–2.

Automotive World, 2018. Special Report: How Do You Secure the Autonomous Vehicle? Technical Report pp. 1–30.

Barber, A., 2018. Status of Work in Process on ISO/SAE 21434 Automotive Cybersecurity Standard. Technical Report.

Bayer, S., Enderle, T., Kengo Oka, D., Wolf, M., 2015. Security crash test—practical security evaluations of automotive onboard IT components. In: Conference Automotive Safety & Security, pp. 125–139.

Boran, L., Ward, D., Mira, H., Czerny, B.J., 2016. Overview of recommended practice—SAE J3061™. In: Cybersecurity Guidebook for Cyber-Physical Vehicle Systems. Technical Report.

British Columbia Freedom of Information and Privacy Association (FIPA), 2015. The Connected Car: Who Is in the Driver's Seat? Technical Report.

Brown, D.A., Cooper, G., Gilvarry, I., Rajan, A., Tatourian, A., Venugopalan, R., Wheeler, D., Zhao, M., 2015. Automotive Security Best Practices. Intel Security White paper, 1–16.

Bureau Veritas, 2016. Cyber Security of Connected Vehicles. Best Practices. Technical Report.

CERTX, 2019. IEC62443 in a Nutshell by CERTX, Spin off of HEIA-FR. Technical Report.

Chattopadhyay, A., Lam, K.-Y., 2018. Autonomous vehicle: security by design. arXiv. Article ID: 1810.00545.

Cisco Systems, 2018. Cisco Visual Networking Index: Forecast and Trends, 2017–2022. Technical Report, White Paper ID 1543280537836565.

Dasgupta, K., Babu, M.R., 2019. A review on crypto-currency transactions using IOTA (Technology). In: Springer Briefs in Applied Sciences and Technology, Springer, pp. 67–81.

DEKRA, 2018. Everything for your quality and safety. In: DEKRA Services for Vehicle Manufacturers and Suppliers. Technical Report.

Department of Transportation, 2018. Preparing for the Future of Transportation: Automated Vehicles 3.0. Technical Report.

ENISA, 2016. Cyber Security and Resilience of Smart Cars—Good Practices and Recommendations. European Union Agency for Network and Information Security.

Ernst & Young, 2016. Automotive cybersecurity. In: Turning the Threats of Connected Mobility Into Secure Innovation, pp. 1–15. Technical Report.

Ernst & Young, 2018. Confronting the New-Age Cyber-Criminal: Disrupting the Web of Crime. Technical Report pp. 1–25.

European Commission, 2018a. On the road to automated mobility. In: An EU Strategy for Mobility of the Future. Technical Report.

European Commission, 2018b. Regulation of the European Parliament and of the Council on the Approval and Market Surveillance of Motor Vehicles and Their Trailers, and of Systems, Components and Separate Technical Units Intended for Such Vehicles, Amending Regulations (EC) no 715/2007 and (EC) no 595/2009 and Repealing Directive 2007/46/EC. Technical Report.

Everis, 2015. Connected Car Report. Technical Report.

Fowler, D.S., Bryans, J., Ahmed Shaikh, S., Wooderson, P., 2018. Fuzz testing for automotive cyber-security. In: 48th Annual IEEE/IFIP International Conference on Dependable Systems and Networks Workshops.

Frost & Sullivan, 2017. Vehicle-to-everything technologies for connected cars. In: DSRC and Cellular Technologies Drive Opportunities. Technical Report, D7BA-TV.

Garcia, F.D., Oswald, D., Kasper, T., Pavlidès, P., 2016. Lock it and still lose it—on the (in) security of automotive remote keyless entry system. In: Proceedings 25th of the USENIX Security Symposium.

Gardiner, B., 2018. Large-Scale Attack Trees Applied to Connected Transport Systems. In: Automotive Cybersecurity Summit & Training 2018.

Goldberg, J., 2018. Traditional IT Cyber Security vs. Automotive Cyber Security Explained. GuardKnox Executive Summary. pp. 1–2.

Gowling, W.L.G., 2017. Connected and Autonomous Vehicles: a Hacker's Delight? Technical Report pp. 1–17.

Greenough, J., 2016. The Connected Car Report: Forecasts, Competing Technologies and Leading Manufacturers. Business Insider. Technical Report.

Heckemann, K., Gesell, M., Pfister, T., et al., 2011. Safe automotive software. In: 15th International Conference on Knowledge-Based and Intelligent Information & Engineering Systems, Part IV, LNAI 6884, pp. 167–176.

Henniger, O., Ruddle, A., Seudié, H., Weyl, B., Wolf, M., Wolliger, T., 2009. Securing Vehicular On-Board IT Systems: The EVITA Project. Technical Report.
Heradio, R., De la Torre, L., Galan, D., Cabrerizo, F.J., Herrera-Viedma, E., López-Serrano, M.J., 2016. Virtual and remote labs in education: a bibliometric analysis. Comput. Educ. 18, 14–38.
Hunjan, H., 2018. ISO/SAE 21434 Automotive Cybersecurity Engineering. Technical Report.
IBM, 2017. Ransomware Response Guide—IBM Incident Response Services. Technical Report pp. 1–20.
International Organization for Standardization, 2018. ISO 26262 Road Vehicles—Functional Safety. Technical Report.
International Organization for Standardization/International Electrotechnical Commission, 2018. ISO/IEC 20243: Information Technology—Open Trusted Technology Provider™ Standard (O-TTPS)—Mitigating Maliciously Tainted and Counterfeit Products. .
Jansen, P., 2018. The TIOBE Quality Indicator—A Pragmatic Way of Measuring Code Quality. TIOBE, pp. 1–16. Technical Report.
Karray, K., Danger, J.L., Guilley, S., Elaabid, M.A., 2018. Attack tree construction and its application to the connected vehicle. In: Koç, Ç.K. (Ed.), Cyber-Physical System Security. Springer, Cham, Switzerland, pp. 175–190.
Keen Security Lab, 2018. Experimental Security Assessment of BMW Cars: A Summary Report. Technical Report.
Lanctot, R., 2018. Argus helps automakers answer the global call for automotive cybersecurity regulation. In: Automotive Multimedia and Communications. , pp. 1–25.
Lebrun, A., Demay, J.-C., 2016. CANSPY a Platform for Auditing CAN Devices. Technical Report.
Lozano Domínguez, J.M., Mateo Sanguino, T.J., 2019. Review on V2X, I2X, and P2X communications and their applications: a comprehensive analysis over time. Sensors 19 (12), 1–29Article ID: 2756.
Maglaras, L.A., Al-Bayatti, A.H., He, Y., Wagner, I., Janicke, H., 2016. Social internet of vehicles for smart cities. J. Sens. Actuator Netw. 5 (3), 1–22.
Mateo Sanguino, T.J., 2017. 50 years of rovers for planetary exploration: a retrospective review for future directions. Robot. Auton. Syst. 94, 172–185.
Miller, C., Valasek, C., 2015. Remote Exploitation of an Unaltered Passenger Vehicle. Technical Report.
Ministry of Land, Infrastructure, Transport and Tourism, 2017. White Paper on Land, Infrastructure, Transport and Tourism in Japan. Technical Report pp. 355–358.
National Highway Traffic Safety Administration, 2016. Cybersecurity Best Practices for Modern Vehicles. Technical Report.
National Highway Traffic Safety Administration, 2017. Understanding NHTSA's Regulatory Tools. Technical Report.
Policy and Planning Support Committee (PPSC) Working Group on Automated and Connected Vehicles, 2019. Automated and Connected Vehicles Policy Framework for Canada. Technical Report.
Popov, S., 2017. The Tangle. White Paper, .pp. 1–28. Available at https://static.coinpaprika.com/storage/cdn/whitepapers/165497.pdf.
SAE International, 2016. J3061 Cybersecurity Guidebook for Cyber-Physical Vehicles Systems. Technical Report.
Schmittner, C., Ma, Z., Reyes, C., et al., 2016. Using SAE J3061 for automotive security requirement engineering. In: International Conference on Computer Safety, Reliability, and Security, pp. 157–170.

Senate of the United States, 2017. H.R. 3388—Self Drive Act, 115th Congress. Technical Report.
SGS, 2016. Minimum Requirements for Manufacturer Documentation and the Preparation of Test Specimens. Technical Report.
Shakeel, I., 2016. Connected Cars: A Big Question Mark Towards Privacy. Infosec ResourcesTechnical Report.
Shevchenko, N., Chick, T.A., O'Riordan, P., Scanlon, T.P., Woody, C., 2018. Threat Modeling: A Summary of Available Methods. Software Engineering Institute, Carnegie Mellon University. Technical Report.
Silva, R., Iqbal, R., 2019. Ethical implications of social internet of vehicles systems. IEEE Internet Things J. 6 (1), 517–531.
Taiber, J., Zhang, L., 2019. International Alliance for Mobility Testing and Standardization (IAMTS). Technical Report.
The HEAVENS Consortium, 2016. Derivable D2 Security Models. Technical Report.
The Open Group, 2016. The open trusted technology provider™ standard for product integrity and supply chain security. In: A New ISO/IEC Standard and Accreditation Program for Product Integrity and Supply Chain Integrity. Technical Report.
Toyama, T., Yoshida, T., Oguma, H., Matsumoto, T., 2018. PASTA: Portable Automotive Security Testbed with Adaptability. Technical Report.
Transport Canada, 2019. Canada's Safety Framework for Automated and Connected Vehicles. Technical Report.
TÜD SÜD, 2018. Genesis, New Platform for Assessment and Certification of AI for Autonomous Driving. Technical Report.
United Nations, 2019a. Proposal for Recommendation on Cyber Security. Document ID: ECE/TRANS/WP.29/GRVA/2019/2. Technical Report.
United Nations, 2019b. Draft Recommendation on Software Updates of the Task Force on Cyber Security and Over-the-Air Issue. Document ID: ECE/TRANS/WP.29/GRVA/2019/3. Technical Report.
Van Eck, N.J., Waltman, L., 2014. Visualizing bibliometric networks. In: Measuring Scholarly Impact: Methods and Practice. Springer, pp. 285–320.
Van Wee, B., Banister, D., 2016. How to write a literature review paper? Transp. Rev. 36 (2), 278–288.
Yuva, N., Kırbaş, I., 2018. Directed acyclic graph based on crypto currency application example: IOTA. In: International Conference on Data Science and Applications, pp. 92–99.

Further reading

The Open Group, 2019. Standard Open Group Membership. Full Membership List—All Categories. Technical Report.

CHAPTER FIVE

The wider use of autonomous vehicles in non-commuting journeys

Simon Kimber[a,*], Lauren Siegel[a], Scott Cohen[a], Nikolas Thomopoulos[b]

[a]School of Hospitality and Tourism Management, University of Surrey, United Kingdom
[b]Department of Tourism and Transport, School of Hospitality and Tourism Management, University of Surrey, Guildford, United Kingdom
*Corresponding author: e-mail address: s.kimber@surrey.ac.uk

Contents

Abstract

Non-commuting journeys, which include social and recreational journeys, make up a substantial proportion of household travel and these journeys are mostly taken by car. Autonomous vehicle (AV) deployment has the potential to dramatically transform the way people work and travel, as well as reshape leisure travel patterns. Yet, the wider societal implications of AVs beyond commuting, such as travel for leisure and tourism, have received minimal academic attention. This state-of-the-art review follows PRISMA guidelines and addresses this gap through a qualitative synthesis of 48 articles that focuses on the influence of AV use on non-commuting journeys, including those for leisure, tourism, shopping and visiting friends and relatives. Key findings identified in this review include interest in AVs for leisure exceeding that for commuting, sharing being less likely when AVs are used for leisure, non-recognition that some non-commuting journeys will require a lower level of automation and that the spatial impacts of AVs for non-commuting journeys, like commuting journeys, are a

Advances in Transport Policy and Planning, Volume 5
ISSN 2543-0009
https://doi.org/10.1016/bs.atpp.2020.02.003

double-edged sword. The chapter concludes that non-commuting journeys will be the some of the earliest ways for which AVs will be adopted and provides a number of policy recommendations to help address this transition.

Keywords: Autonomous vehicles, Non-commuting, Leisure, Recreation, Tourism, Sharing

1. Introduction

Commuting journeys constitute the primary focus of the majority of research within the transport field (Pudāne et al., 2019; Singleton, 2018; Woldeamanuel and Nguyen, 2018). This is unsurprising given the volume of regular commuting journeys undertaken daily worldwide. Yet, 32% of journeys in the UK are non-commuting journeys (DFT, 2017). Such journeys include social and recreational journeys, such as for leisure, shopping, school-runs and other journey purposes.

Autonomous vehicles (AVs), like any new technological development, offer ample opportunities to improve existing mobility systems, but equally, their introduction could potentially exacerbate current transport challenges (Milakis et al., 2017; Thomopoulos and Givoni, 2015) depending on their deployment. New mobility services, including AVs, open up novel opportunities regarding the use of travel time. Scholars have previously argued about the productive use of travel time, resulting in a different valuation of the value of travel time (VoTT), where in activities beyond work can have positive utility (Lothlorien and Mokhtarian, 2001; Malokin et al., 2019). Despite the plethora of ways that travel time may potentially be used more productively in AVs, and indications that leisure and tourism journeys may constitute their earliest form of adoption (Cohen and Hopkins, 2019), the wider societal implications of AVs beyond commuting, such as travel for leisure and tourism, have received minimal attention in academic literature.

Through a state-of-the-art review of AV research—based on the Grant and Booth (2009) definition of state-of-the-art[a]—which follows the PRISMA guidelines, this chapter therefore focuses on how AVs may influence non-commuting journeys. Non-commuting journeys are taken here to include those for social and recreational purposes such as for leisure, tourism, shopping or for visiting friends and relatives. Despite the lack of accurate monitoring of such journeys worldwide, it is assumed in this chapter that such journeys constitute between a quarter and a third of overall journeys.

[a] State-of-the-art here is based on the Grant and Booth (2009) typology of review articles, which is primarily contrasted with the systematic review.

2. Background

Unsurprisingly, overcoming technological challenges surrounding AV deployment dominates multidisciplinary debates among academics and practitioners. Gandia et al. (2019) have reviewed AV-relevant literature, finding that outputs by engineering, computer science, transportation, and automation control systems scholars dominate the AV literature. Along the same lines, Cavoli et al. (2017) found in their review of AV literature, that a mere six percent of the total literature on AVs was categorized as social science research. While this may be partially attributable to the early stages and high technological requirements of AV deployment; Yun et al. (2016) and Gandia et al. (2019), as well as networks of experts (e.g., WISE-ACT2[b]) point out that it will become increasingly important to consider the wider impact of AVs, particularly their social and business aspects.

Furthermore, urban mobility and urban areas have been at the core of testing innovative AV applications (Canitez et al., 2018; Hopkins and Schwanen, 2018). Most studies to date have primarily focused on urban mobility in the Global North (Cohen and Hopkins, 2019), and while research such as by Jain et al. (2016) have considered autonomous transport solutions in India, such research is an exception on the whole. This urban-centric focus on the Global North within the AV literature is likely to be due to a number of complex factors, including the concentration of large key players with significant capital as well as the technological infrastructure available in such locations.

A further key issue highlighted in the literature in relation to the deployment of AVs is vehicle and ride sharing, which is encompassed within the term Shared Autonomous Vehicles (SAVs). Sharing is largely held to be a fundamental and desirable element of AV deployment, particularly from a policy making perspective. This is largely based on the suggestion that a shared fleet of AVs, i.e., TaxiBots, may serve the needs of a city such as Lisbon only with 10% of the current fleet size (OECD ITF, 2015). Trust and acceptance of sharing options such as taxi services, will be a decisive factor regarding AV adoption, with early literature showing that the younger population segments would be the early adopters of such applications (Haboucha et al., 2017; Tussyadiah et al., 2017). Research suggests that the highest proportion of demand for AV use, as well as the strongest

[b] Wider impacts and scenario evaluation of autonomous and connected transport: www.wise-act.eu.

potential business case, is likely to be by younger generations in central or downtown metropolitan areas (Moreno et al., 2018; Nazari et al., 2018; Webb et al., 2019).

Within the limited body of literature on social perspectives of AV use, the vast majority of literature focuses thus far overwhelmingly on commuting, and in particular how AVs might change commuting patterns (Moreno et al., 2018; Nazari et al., 2018). In addition to the habitual nature of commuting for large numbers of people, this focus can be seen as, in part, as a product of the disciplinary backgrounds (largely from transport engineering, geographical and behavioral science) that influence many of those conducting research within the transport and AV fields (Preston, 2016). A significant proportion of transport literature is focused on the use and value of travel time, which is in turn linked with the monetary value which travelers place on time spent in transit. Consequently, it is not surprising that much of the data and data sets used as the basis for predicting public attitudes to AVs and SAVs (Singleton, 2018; Webb et al., 2019) have come from commuting and travel survey research.

However, this narrow focus on commuting is an aspect of transport research that has been challenged over the years. Law (1999) has critiqued the literature for its emphasis on the journey to work and its neglect of the many other trips that constitute essential parts of daily life. Grieco and Urry (2011: 1) also comment that there has not been enough "insertion of the social" into analyzing travel and transport, while Cresswell (2006) similarly argues that all types of mobility and travel should be the focus of research. Equally, this narrow focus can also be observed within AV literature, and, just as the attention of transport literature has focused on work trips and commuting, Kellerman (2018) highlights that much of the limited existing body of social literature on potential AV use is also focused on commuting and day-time urban mobilities. Yet, travel statistics from a range of countries suggest that contrary to what academic studies imply, commuting is not the main purpose of most trips, and therefore the focus of AV research needs broadening to incorporate social and recreational journeys beyond commuting. To illustrate this argument, Department for Transport (DFT, 2017) evidence shows that over 25% of all trips taken in England in 2016 were for leisure purposes (visiting friends and relatives [VFR], sports, holidays and daytrips), and that this figure rises to 32% if walking is considered a leisure activity. Likewise, in the United States, social and recreational journeys accounted for nearly 60% of household travel in 2009 (NTHS, 2009).

A further noteworthy point is the link between travel mode and journey purpose. In England, for example, while over half (58%) of English surface rail journeys are for business or commuting purposes, when it comes to car journeys, more journeys are carried out for shopping than for commuting (DFT, 2014). Similarly, in the United States, the greatest growth in travel has been unrelated to work and it has been noted that peak congestion around attractions and leisure spots can be worse than congestion in city centers at rush hour (Federal Highways Administration, 2005). Many new mobility services, such as e-scooters (Anderson-Hall et al., 2019; Mathew et al., 2019; Orr et al., 2019), are also used for non-commuting purposes, thus it stands to reason that the introduction of AVs will lead to AV use for non-commuting purposes as well (c.f. Cohen and Hopkins, 2019).

In summary, this state-of-the-art (Grant and Booth, 2009) review is motivated by the concern that academic literature on AVs is skewed toward commuting journeys in the urban metropoles of the Global North. This chapter seeks to challenge this bias by considering the future wider implications of AVs in non-commuting journeys. This is an important knowledge gap within AV literature, with few sources explicitly considering the non-commuting potential impacts of future AV use. Apart from Tussyadiah et al. (2017) consideration of the travel possibilities of robo-taxis and Cohen and Hopkins' work (2019) on the possibilities of AVs in urban tourism, there has been little wider consideration of how AVs might change individual lives and societies beyond the confines of the daily work commute. From going to an out of town shopping mall or shopping village, to taking pets on a family day out, to city breaks and touring holidays, there are many unanswered questions regarding how people are likely to use AVs. This gap in knowledge also has major policy implications, both in terms of the business models required for non-commuting AV use, but also for regional and national tourism boards and destination management organizations (DMOs). Given the increasing number of AV deployment schemes, there is an urgent need to consider the policy implications of non-commuting AV use.

3. Methods

Conducting a literature review has its own challenges given the diverse types and aims of reviews (Van Wee and Banister, 2016). As an alternative, Pearman (1988) and Banister and Hickman (2013) have also suggested scenario based exploratory studies in such cases. However, this is considered as a more restrictive approach, so in this case, a state-of-the-art review (Grant and Booth, 2009) has been selected as being more appropriate for this context as it can provide a balanced overview of the benefits and costs based on evidence-based suggestions founded in relevant literature. The aim of this chapter is to carry out a state-of-the-art review (Grant and Booth, 2009) on non-commuting AV journeys following the PRISMA guidelines (Liberati et al., 2009; Moher et al., 2009). As explained by Moher et al. (2009): "*PRISMA is an evidence-based minimum set of items for reporting in systematic reviews and meta-analyses.*"[c] Use of the PRISMA flow diagram which highlights the identification, screening, eligibility and inclusion criteria of the reports that fall under the scope of a review, acts as a useful guide for authors, reviewers and editors (Selçuk, 2019). Despite the lack of consensus about the term "state-of-the-art," other than that such reviews "*consider more current matters*" (Higgins and Green, 2011, p. 32), Grant and Booth (2009, p. 95) stress the contribution of such type of reviews is in offering *new* perspectives on "*current matters.*" Therefore, this chapter adopts Kellerman's (2018) perspective that AV research has to consider the wider implications of AVs for non-commuting journeys.

As this review follows the PRISMA protocol (Moher et al., 2009), it adheres to a standard procedure that utilizes a PICO framework from the research question or topic statement (Shamseer et al., 2015). Table 1 outlines the PICO framework adopted for this review in terms of population, intervention, control and outcome. The inclusion criteria for this study were sources that discussed autonomous vehicles and discussions of non-/commuting journeys.

Table 1 PICO framework (population, intervention, control and outcome) utilized in this review.

Population	Traveling non-commuters/non-commuting travelers
Intervention	The use of autonomous vehicles
Control	Use of non-autonomous vehicles
Outcome	Travel behavior

[c] Find out more information about PRISMA here: http://prisma-statement.org/.

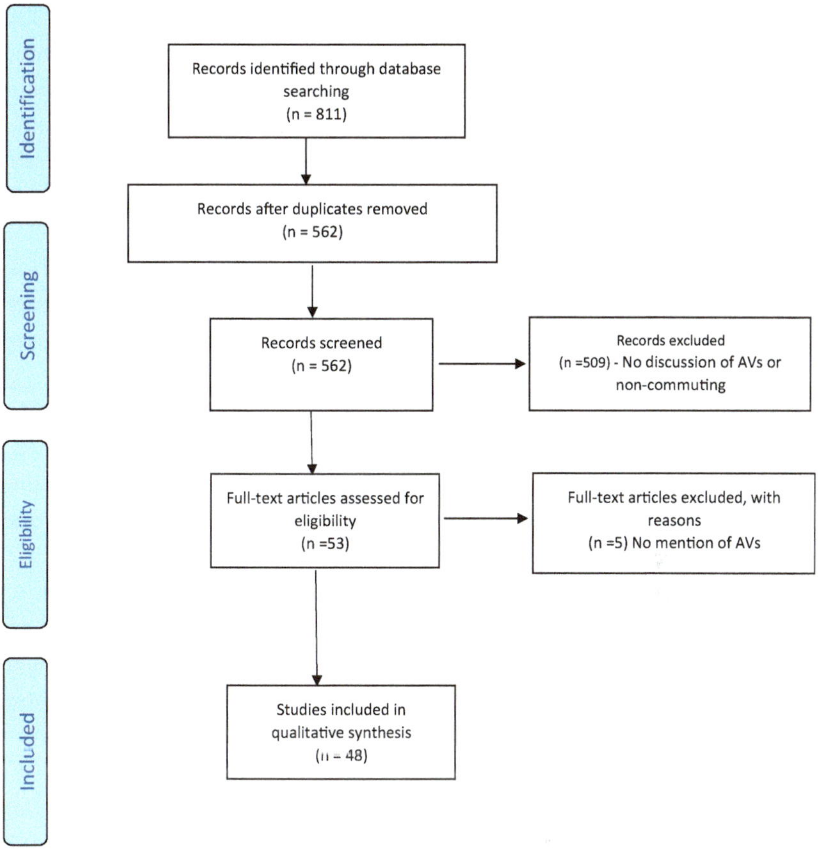

Fig. 1 Reviewed papers by year.

The research for this review was carried out from February until June 2019. No time parameters were applied as restrictions, although naturally the bulk of AV literature has emerged within the last decade (Fig. 1). Similar AV reviews conducted at the same time have considered a single database, such as Web of Science (WoS) (e.g., Cavazza et al., 2017; Gandia et al., 2019) or Scopus (e.g., Cavoli et al., 2017). However, it has been identified that WoS is set up in a manner which at times under-represents social sciences research in favor of physical and natural sciences (Mongeon and Paul-Hus, 2016). Consequently, this chapter attempts to address such shortcomings by identifying peer-reviewed sources through at least three databases, following the example of other similar academic reviews (e.g., Barros et al., 2019; Milakis et al., 2017). Literature for this review was based on searches carried out on Scopus, Web of Science (WoS), and

Transport Research International Documentation (TRID) databases, considering only peer-reviewed journal articles, book chapters, and conference proceedings. Other sources of information such as industry and governmental paper and non-reviewed articles (i.e., gray literature) were excluded on the grounds of keeping the number of articles reviewed manageable and valuing peer review as an important factor in such a controversial field as AV deployment. However, in contrast to the decision by Milakis et al. (2017) to include Google Scholar as a third search database, Google Scholar was not used due to accuracy concerns highlighted in previous research (Jacsó, 2005) and the challenges of conducting systematic analysis based on Google Scholar (Harzing and Alakangas, 2016).

The search terms used in this state-of-the-art review (Table 2) were generated from the PICO framework (Table 1). In terms of analysis scope, the sources were searched on the selected databases as three separate searches, and the results were combined together, using the bibliographic management software program Zotero. Out of the PICO framework, four search concepts were developed (Table 2) following the PRESS 2015 guidelines (McGowan et al., 2016). These guidelines were used to ensure that sufficient PICO elements had been included, and that the search elements were neither too narrow nor too broad. Because multiple definitions are used in the field of AVs (Gandia et al., 2019), this study used multiple keywords in a manner similar to previous AV reviews (e.g., Cavazza et al., 2017; Cavoli et al., 2017; Gandia et al., 2019; Milakis et al., 2017). Using Cavoli et al. (2017) and Gandia et al. (2019) as a starting point, the most common words and phrases used to refer to AVs were identified and tested for relevancy on the three bibliographic databases. The various keywords

Table 2 Search terms and strategy used in this state-of-the-art review: #1 AND #2 AND #3 AND #4.

No.	Concept	Terms
1	Autonomy	"Autonomous" OR "driverless" OR "automated" OR "selfdriving" OR "self-driving" OR "smart" OR "intelligent"
2	Vehicle	"Car" OR "vehicle" OR "automobile"
3	Non-commuting	"Commut*" OR "-commuting" OR "non-commuting" OR "non_work"
4	Trip	"Travel" OR "trip" OR "journey" OR "tour*"

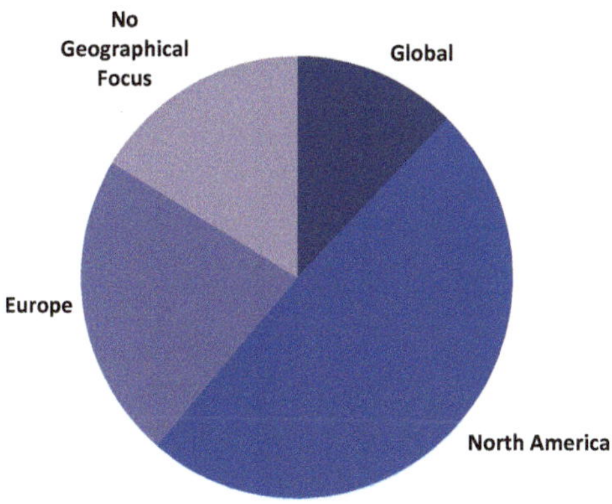

Fig. 2 PRISMA flow diagram. *Moher, D., et al., 2009. Preferred reporting items for systematic reviews and meta-analyses: the PRISMA statement. Ann. Intern. Med. Am. Coll. Physicians 151 (4), 264–269.*

were linked with the Boolean operator "OR," while the four search concepts were linked with the Boolean Operator "AND."

Searches on the three databases yielded 811 results with publication dates ranging from 1990 to 2019, with the vast majority published within the last decade (Fig. 1). In line with PRISMA procedures (Liberati et al., 2009; Moher et al., 2009), the four-phase flow PRISMA diagram was used to guide and structure this state-of-the-art review process (Fig. 2). After duplicate articles were removed, the 562 remaining articles were screened based on the pre-defined inclusion criteria. The search strategy generated many returns of articles discussing mass transit systems, smart highways and transportation demand systems, and these were excluded so that only articles discussing autonomous vehicles and commuting (or non-commuting) were considered for full text assessment. The focus of this search was on all types of vehicles, i.e., not only on cars, but not on transport systems, e.g., mass transit. The study team was aware that the search terms used resulted in the exclusion of a few key sources (e.g., Cohen and Hopkins, 2019; LaMondia et al., 2016; Nikitas et al., 2017; Thomopoulos and Givoni, 2015); however, these sources were incorporated into discussions of the findings in Section 5. Of the 53 full text articles assessed, a further five were excluded because on full text examination they were found not to discuss AV journeys, but instead discussed non-related aspects of autonomous technology and vehicle technology. The remaining 48 articles were subjected to individual in-depth analysis by the study team members, where the contents of each source were systematically analyzed based on a relevant matrix to identify the key themes arising from this literature review. Twenty percent of the articles were cross-reviewed by at least two members of the study team to ensure consistency and accuracy, aiming to eliminate any reviewer or background bias (Barros et al., 2019).

4. Findings

The following sections present and discuss the key insights emerging from the 48 sources fully reviewed. Table 3 offers an overview of these sources, including their geographical focus and their key findings. None of the sources reviewed focused specifically on non-commuting journeys. Only 10 (21%) included non-commuting (i.e., leisure or recreational

Table 3 Overview of the 48 fully reviewed sources.

	First author	Year	Geographical focus	Applicable findings
	Ashkrof	2019	Netherlands	Trust in AVs is most significant component for adoption; usage is perceived to be more favorable for long-distance leisure trips
Addresses leisure	Haboucha	2017	Israel & North America	Younger and older populations are underrepresented in AV research
	Howard	2014	Berkeley, California, USA	General public more likely to use AVs, before standardization, five trips or less per year for recreation
	Kornhauser	2013	New Jersey, USA	Creation of an ATN could eliminate the need to own a traditional vehicle
	Laidlaw	2017	Toronto, Canada	More interest in potential entertainment and recreation uses for AVs than for shopping and errands
	Lavasani	2017	Miami, USA	Willingness to pay for AVs depends on household type and length of commute
	Lavieri	2019	Dallas, USA	Riders are more open to sharing in leisure activities than commuting; leisure segment is more fruitful for further exploration

Table 3 Overview of the 48 fully reviewed sources.—cont'd

	First author	Year	Geographical focus	Applicable findings
	Moreno	2018	Munich, Germany	AVs may not solve traffic congestion—if SAVs make transport cheaper then demand will increase
	Nazari	2018	Washington State, USA	SAVs have potential to change future urban mobility, but in the near future mixed human-autonomous driving will dominate
	Pudane	2018	Netherlands	Introduction of AVs may alter demand of activities throughout the day; more options for emerging mobile businesses and deliveries
	Galanis	2014	Global	AVs will positively contribute to society—reduce air pollution, traffic congestion, etc.
	Assanis	2018	USA	Coordination of CAVs can virtually eliminate all stand-still traffic conditions
	Azimi	2015	NA	Intersection management systems will allow CAVs to communicate with one another toward improved traffic flow
	Bailey	2018	Singapore	Considers activities during AV use and proposes safety concerns would limit spectrum of activities
Does not address leisure	Basar	2017	USA	Considers new tolling schemes in the context of future mobile technologies
	Brown	2018	New York, USA	Potential for on-demand aviation to become future autonomous air taxi service and competitive with current car ridesharing services
	Buehler	2018	USA	Future AVs will lure people away from public transportation with highest uses in urban areas

Continued

Table 3 Overview of the 48 fully reviewed sources.—cont'd

First author	Year	Geographical focus	Applicable findings
Burghout	2015	Stockholm, Sweden	SAVs could reduce private cars by 95%
Carrese	2019	Rome, Italy	AVs may cause residents to relocate outside of cities because of changed perceptions of the value of travel time
de Looff	2018	Netherlands	Develops new insights on activities conducted while traveling in AVs
Folsom	2017	NA	Ultra-light vehicles could form the bedrock of future urban mobility system
Homem de Almeida Correia	2019	Netherlands	Traveling alone is preferred over sharing, potentially resulting in more traffic and longer journeys
Jäger	2017	Munich, Germany	Implementation of robo-taxis in large cities would result in 30% less cars on the road
JahedulAlam	2018	Halifax, Canada	Suggests SAVs can reduce rush hour traffic but consideration is needed to reduce empty trips just after rush hour
Jain	2016	Ahmedabad & Bangalore, India	Rapid urbanization will lessen environmental ramifications; increased CAP use could reduce road space needed
Ji	2017	NA	Evaluates cost-effectiveness of using traditional vehicles versus AVs
Johnston	2000	NA	Smart highways can improve conditions for future drivers
Kang	2018	Virginia, USA	Possibility of reduced parking needs but alternatively more empty vehicles; AVs could aid those with limited driving capabilities
Large	2017	NA	Vehicle redesign is explored to enable effective AV experience

Table 3 Overview of the 48 fully reviewed sources.—cont'd

	First author	Year	Geographical focus	Applicable findings
	Liu	2018	NA	Self-parking AVs may reduce city center parking needs; no need to park at home means more recreational and green space; reduction in total travel costs
	Lutin	2013	NA	AVs could reduce accident rates, greater mobility for the elderly and disabled
	Malokin	2019	North Carolina, USA	AVs could change the productive nature of travel and ability to multitask will be important to AV adoption
	Mangharam	2014	USA	AVs will make travel safer
	Menon	2016	Florida, USA	Parking difficulties most likely to drive AV adoption
	Moorthy	2017	Michigan, USA	Shared AVs will provide more value and time for leisure activity and productive work
Does not address leisure	Raney	2004	Palo Alto, California, USA	Considers how varying commuting methods can be connected to workplaces and introduces idea of feeder stations
	Shaw	2019	San Francisco, USA	The ability to engage in travel-based multitasking can influence travel mode choice
	Singleton	2018	Portland, Oregon, USA	Productivity of in-vehicle activities will likely be less than currently anticipated
	Steck	2018	Germany	Passengers with longer commutes more likely to use AVs for at least part of their journeys
	Tian	2019	China	Appropriately encouraging ridesharing occupancy can reduce road congestion, peak periods, individual travel cost, etc.
	Wadud	2018	Bangladesh	In-vehicle activities may dictate design of AVs; travel time will be made more useful in AVs

Continued

Table 3 Overview of the 48 fully reviewed sources.—cont'd

First author	Year	Geographical focus	Applicable findings
Wang	2019	Puget Sound, Washington State, USA	Commuters already using public transport will be more likely to use SAVs over private AVs
Webb	2019	Brisbane, Australia	Commuters were found to be more willing to share transport than other users; users with children will be more apprehensive; AV use could eliminate traffic congestion and need for parking space
Winter	2017	Netherlands	Early adopters are more favorable to ridesharing; travel cost is less important than travel time
Woldeamanuel	2018	USA	Standardization of AVs will condition people to live further from cities
Zakharenko	2016	NA	Addresses AV parking concerns and proposes empty vehicles can park on city edge
Zhang	2018	Atlanta, USA	Suggests SAVs could significantly reduce commuting costs and commuters could relocate further from city center
Zhong	2019	USA	AVs don't seem likely to change commuting value significantly

journeys) as part of their analysis, which confirms the point made by Kellerman (2018) regarding the lack of research focus on the wider implications of AV deployment, particularly in the social sciences. The main focus of the fully reviewed papers was overwhelmingly on commuting (Table 3). However, many of the papers discussed some aspects of non-commuting journeys as part of wider discussions on potential AV use.

The geographical focus of these papers was heavily skewed toward the Global North, with North America dominating (Fig. 3). The United States and Europe are at the forefront of AV trials and testing (Canitez et al., 2018), therefore it is reasonable that 72% of the sources reviewed focused on these geographic areas. Nevertheless, it was also found that there

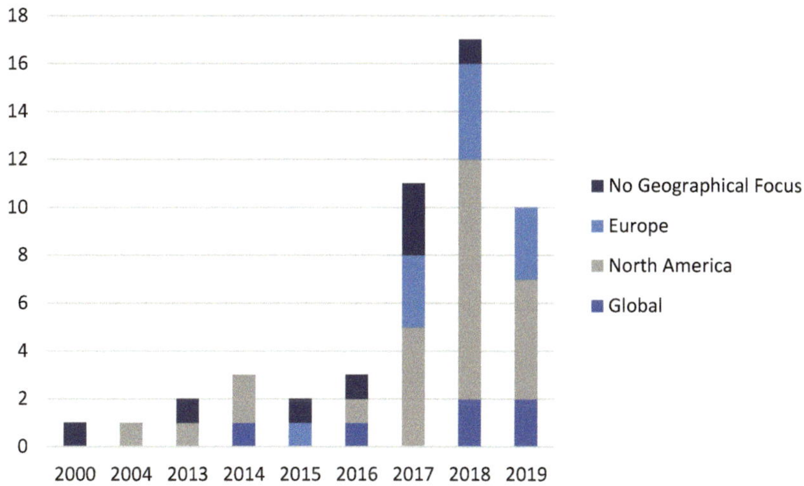

Fig. 3 Geographical focus of reviewed papers.

are distinct differences between anticipated AV use in the United States and Europe, as for example regarding private or shared use of AVs.

Four key themes arose from the review of these sources (Table 3) which are directly linked with the search concepts used in this review (Table 2), namely:

- Interest in AV for leisure exceeding commuting;
- Sharing being less likely for AV non-commuting journeys;
- Non-recognition that some non-commuting journeys will require a lower level of automation;
- That spatial impacts of AV for non-commuting journeys are a double-edged sword.

The findings of each key theme are presented and discussed in the following sub-sections.

4.1 Leisure exceeds commuting in AV interest

It is curious that only 10 of the reviewed sources mention leisure or recreation in their analysis, given that there is evidence, that in terms of travel purpose, potential AV users may be more interested in using AVs for leisure than for commuting. This suggests there is a gap between how academic studies predominantly conceive of AV use and actual public interest. Specifically, Laidlaw and Sweet (2017) observe that a significant proportion of travelers at this stage seem more interested in the potential of AVs for leisure than for commuting, more so for entertainment and recreation opportunities than for shopping and errands. Ashkrof et al. (2019) add that interest for *long-distance* leisure journeys by AV exceeds that of *short-distance* commuting journeys. The latter is reflected in the marginal value of travel time, estimated as less negative for leisure travel over commuting, and of long-distance over short-distance journeys (Ashkrof et al., 2019). This is likely due to pleasurable activities like sleeping during an AV trip being more feasible when trips are long, and users are at leisure. The use of AVs for long-distance leisure journeys would likely compete with short-haul flights, rail and coach journeys. It is alleged that AVs would allow sleeping holidaymakers to arrive to their destination after traveling overnight, barely noticing the journey time (Pudāne et al., 2019).

Some studies assume trip purpose to be commuting but go on to note that various leisure activities will be undertaken within the AV during the commute, with sleeping or watching television being popular choices (Pudāne et al., 2019; Wadud and Huda, 2018). From this it can be deduced that while the dominant academic mode of envisioning AVs may be for commuting, with the occupants either working or at leisure during the daily commute, there is also the potential for AVs used for leisure trips wherein the occupants may be working or at leisure, or a mix of both. None of the reviewed studies suggested that AV users might have sex during the journey, despite observations elsewhere that this may take place (Cohen and Hopkins, 2019).

Non-commuting journeys will have different storage requirements than commuting journeys, whether they be for recreation or shopping for instance. Although some sources have focused on AV storage requirements for commuting journeys (Singleton, 2018; Woldeamanuel and Nguyen, 2018), very few address the storage needs for non-commuting journeys (for exceptions see Haboucha et al., 2017; Malokin et al., 2019; Pudāne et al., 2019 who briefly consider this). The need to carry required equipment, ranging from travel luggage and baby seats, to pets, regular sports or holiday activities equipment (e.g., skis), and even licensed weapons carried for activities such as hunting will all impact upon user requirements and AV design. Such requirements and use of travel time open up niche business opportunities for AV developers and the need for appropriate policy frameworks for transport providers and tourism boards or destination management organizations (DMOs).

4.2 Sharing is less likely for non-commuting journeys

Sharing already features at the core of the debate surrounding AVs (c.f. Haboucha et al., 2017). Users are prepared to use SAVs if they would reduce their travel time and cost while commuting (Webb et al., 2019). Laidlaw and Sweet (2017) report that willingness to use a SAV is related to trip purpose and the current commuting mode of transport. They found that car drivers are the least likely to use SAVs overall, while 60% of public transit commuters are interested in using SAVs. This review has also found that studies of SAVs are largely emanating from European contexts, with those from the United States primarily assuming AVs will be privately owned. This cultural and contextual influence on willingness to share has important implications for sustainability, which affect both commuting and non-commuting journeys.

Some nuances emerge when sharing is considered outside of the context of commuting. For instance, Moreno et al. (2018) find that pick-up waiting time for SAV journeys will be a crucial factor if users are running errands or going to a doctor appointment. While this is not to suggest that pick-up waiting time is not also important in daily commuting, it highlights that the *irregularity* of some non-commuting journeys may make sharing less feasible, depending on how rapid and punctual shared on-demand autonomous mobility systems become.

Through a comparison between commuting and leisure journeys by using the "willingness to share" concept in the context of Dallas (USA), Lavieri and Bhat (2019) highlight the importance of privacy, in addition to the common time and cost variables used in such studies. They suggest that ride hailing services appear to be an option to promote AV ride sharing for leisure journeys, although sharing may be easier to promote within commuters. Lavieri and Bhat's (2019) findings more importantly show that respondents are more willing to share an AV for work rather than leisure, suggesting privacy and time spent in a vehicle with strangers may be more of an issue in leisure journeys. This may be explained by the predominant difference in sociality between the two trip purposes: silence among strangers is accepted in commuter journeys, whereas social and recreational trips often involve multiple passengers socializing, wherein sharing with an additional stranger may be experienced as awkward. When such AV journeys involve recreational passengers for instance consuming alcohol (Malokin et al., 2019), sharing with strangers becomes even more problematic.

While SAV use for tourism purposes such as city sightseeing seem ready for development and less problematic (Cohen and Hopkins, 2019), and *individual* passengers traveling from A to B to engage in leisure seem likely to avail themselves of SAVs, key barriers to sharing remain when non-commuting journeys are taken by more than one traveler, e.g., groups of friends or a family. AV shape and size is a vital consideration here, which should be further explored to accommodate such needs, given the importance of SAV use, as opposed to private AVs, in a desirable transport future.

4.3 Lower level of automation required?

The significance of automation level is another important theme among the reviewed sources. Despite ongoing debates about the definition of automation levels, this chapter adopts the six (0–5) SAE4[d] defined levels of automation for the purposes of this review. While the allure of highly automated AVs is partly the ability to conduct various activities while traveling (i.e., multitasking) (Kang and Miller, 2018; Malokin et al., 2019), and there is general consensus that the full potential of AVs is only realized at automation Level 4 and above, full automation (Level 5) is often assumed in discussion of the potential of AVs (e.g., Pudāne et al., 2019). Indeed, this will be necessary to commute from various homes to workplaces, allowing unlimited variations in any conditions, while allowing the users to engage in a range of work or leisure activities while on board.

Yet, within the context of non-commuting journeys the few studies that did discuss leisure have overlooked the possibility that many non-commuting journeys will be able to operate at Level 4, i.e., under limited conditions. These will often be SAV that operate within defined routes and under specific conditions, such as for instance within zoos, as airport shuttles, as transport between train stations and city centers or on urban sightseeing routes. These may decide to operate only during the day, or in good weather conditions. This lower requirement for level of automation, combined with the earlier observation that potential users seem more interested in AVs for leisure than for commuting (Laidlaw and Sweet, 2017), points to non-commuting contexts, as potentially some of the earliest adopters of AVs. This makes the neglect of non-commuting journeys within the AV literature all the more curious given the need for future policy recommendations regarding SAV adoption.

4.4 Spatial impacts as a double-edged sword

The spatial impacts of AV are noteworthy and heavily entwined for both commuting and non-commuting journeys. Most apparent is that the spatial impacts of AV will be double-edged, in the sense that they will have both positive and negative impacts. The spatial impacts of AV on commuting

[d] Society of automotive engineers https://www.nhtsa.gov/technology-innovation/automated-vehicles-safety#issue-road-self-driving.

journeys in terms of congestion, urban sprawl and parking are well-developed in the literature. As an example, microsimulations by Alam and Habib (2018) suggest that a fleet of 900 SAVs could serve 20% of total morning commute trip requests in the city of Halifax (Canada), significantly reducing congestion. Parking and congestion will be directly influenced by AV/SAV use and most sources reviewed forecast a reduction in both (Burghout et al., 2015; Tian et al., 2019; Zakharenko, 2016). Empty trips are an unavoidable concern arising, however (Moreno et al., 2018), with Zakharenko (2016) calculating the cost of empty journeys at US$0.1841 per user per km of a roundtrip empty journey. In contrast, the spatial impacts for non-commuting journeys are hardly considered, confirming the main position of this chapter.

School-run journeys provide a telling example emerging from the literature. It is suggested that like the rush of the daily commute, there will be a noticeable impact on school-run journeys due to their non-flexible daily routine (Pudāne et al., 2019; Zhang and Guhathakurta, 2018). It has furthermore been found that those drivers who chauffeur other household members are more likely to pay for an AV (Laidlaw & Sweet, 2018). Such impact varies of course according to local and national policies and arrangements linked with children traveling to school, but overall suggests that AV will play a significant role in school-run journeys. A deriving outcome will be the reduced need for parking space in and around schools, but also the increased need for drop-off and pick-up points. Little consideration has been given to the flip side of this development, e.g., the likelihood that these journeys will be taken in private AV rather than SAV, and the resultant congestion at peak hours, the contribution these developments may make to further exacerbating urban sprawl and the potential induced demand for further automobility once parents are released from the burden of school runs.

School runs are just one example of how AV deployment in non-commuting journeys may be a mixed blessing in terms of spatial impacts. The cost of urban sprawl is high, estimated at US$400 billion annually for the United States (Litman, 2015). It is therefore essential that the spatial impacts of AV on non-commuting journeys, including urban sprawl, are also brought into the view of policymakers so as to support compact city development and avoid car dependent urban planning (Rode et al., 2017).

5. Conclusion

As with any new topic of emerging interest, AVs are the focus of attention for a wide range of academics and practitioners worldwide.

Nevertheless, the bulk of available research focuses on commuting impacts of AVs, despite the fact that between one third and one quarter of journeys in developed countries are for non-commuting purposes. This state-of-the-art review (Grant and Booth, 2009) was therefore motivated by this concern, namely, that academic literature on AV is skewed toward commuting journeys in urban metropoles of the Global North as has been previously identified (Thomopoulos and Nikitas, 2019). This chapter sought to challenge this bias by considering the future wider implications of AV on non-commuting journeys, including social and recreational journeys.

Key issues that have emerged through the review of relevant literature (Table 3) are that:

- Interest in AV for leisure exceeds that for commuting;
- Sharing is less likely when AV are used for leisure;
- There is a lack of recognition in the literature that some non-commuting journeys will require a lower level of automation;
- The spatial impacts of AVs for non-commuting journeys, like commuting journeys, are a double-edged sword that will have both positive and negative effects.

Overall, only 21% of sources reviewed partially focused on the influence of AV on non-commuting journeys, with the rest ignoring non-commuting entirely, with all but three of the reviewed papers with a specific geographical focus, focusing on the Global North, indicating a significant gap to be addressed in future research. A key overall point emerging from the review is that despite the lack of attention in the academic literature, non-commuting journeys will be some of the earliest ways for which AVs will be adopted. This insight demands that more scholarly attention is paid to the manifold uses of AVs beyond commuting, especially in light of the barriers to sharing in non-commuting AV journeys, and the negative implications of this for the sustainability of the transport system (Thomopoulos and Givoni, 2015).

This state-of-the-art review has certain limitations. Relying on specific databases introduces certain types of bias associated with the Boolean terms used, which may result in the unintended omission of relevant research using different terms. Furthermore, due to the nature of this review and the focus of this book, it has not been possible to review in more depth specific aspects in the selected sources, for example, with regards to the use of travel time. These shortcomings could be the focus of future research, along with a more precise focus on impacts of AV on the tourism and leisure industries while relevant literature grows.

The most valuable outcome of this state-of-the-art review, however, is that it has allowed the identification of a range of areas in need of relevant policies, locally, nationally, and internationally. AV-related policies and investment need to focus more on non-commuting journeys, especially long-distance leisure journeys, since such journeys may be the ones first to serve potential AV users. The local culture and context also needs to be taken into account for leisure activities, since it is a decisive factor influencing the uptake of SAV. At the intersection of SAV and non-commuting journeys, policy and regulation need to be in place to preserve equity, privacy and safety among all riders in light of potential issues such as riders bringing on board leisure equipment or other personal items that may pose harm to vulnerable others (e.g., children). Additionally, policies should adapt to both the short- and long-term implications of AV deployment, such as changes in infrastructure and spatio-temporal patterns of leisure activities. Multilateral coordination about levels of automation and spatial impacts of use of AVs are essential, particularly in areas with common transport networks such as Europe. Lastly, it is indispensable to incorporate the Global South in contemporary AV policy developments due to the large levels of urban growth that are projected.

Acknowledgment

The authors would like to thank the four reviewers for the constructive comments to improve this chapter and acknowledge the support of the WISE-ACT COST Action CA16222 which contributed in the development of this book chapter through relevant activities and outputs.

References

Alam, M.J., Habib, M.A., 2018. Investigation of the impacts of shared autonomous vehicle operation in Halifax, Canada using a dynamic traffic microsimulation model. Procedia Comput. Sci. 130, 496–503, Elsevier B.V. https://doi.org/10.1016/j.procs.2018.04.066.

Anderson-Hall, K., et al., 2019. Governing micro-mobility: a nationwide assessment of electric scooter regulations. In: Transportation Research Board 98th Annual Meeting. Washington D.C.

Ashkrof, P., Homem de Almeida Correia, G., Cats, O., van Arem, B., 2019. Impact of automated vehicles on travel mode preference for different trip purposes and distances. Transp. Res. Rec. 2673 (5), 607–616. https://doi.org/10.1177/0361198119841032.

Banister, D., Hickman, R., 2013. Transport futures: thinking the unthinkable. Transp. Policy 29, 283–293.

Barros, P., Fat, L.N., Garcia, L.M., Slovic, A.D., Thomopoulos, N., de Sá, T.H., … Mindell, J.S., 2019. Social consequences and mental health outcomes of living in high-rise residential buildings and the influence of planning, urban design and architectural decisions: a systematic review. Cities 93, 263–272.

Burghout, W., Rigole, P.J., Andreasson, I., 2015. Impacts of shared autonomous taxis in a metropolitan area. In: The 94th Annual Meeting of the Transportation Research Board.
Canitez, F., Cantafio, G., Thomopoulos, N., 2018. WISE-ACT Atlas of AV Trials, WISE-ACT Workshop #1, Bratislava.
Cavazza, B.H., Gandia, R.M., Antonialli, F., Nicolaï, I., Zambalde, A.L., Sugano, J.Y., de Miranda Neto, A., 2017, September. Management and business of autonomous vehicles: a systematic integrative bibliographic review. In: 12th European Conference on Innovation and Entrepreneurship ECIE 2017, p. 141.
Cavoli, C., et al., 2017. Social and Behavioural Questions Associated with Automated Vehicles: A Literature Review. UCL Transport Institute, January.
Cohen, S.A., Hopkins, D., 2019. Autonomous vehicles and the future of urban tourism. Ann. Tour. Res. 74 (October 2018), 33–42. https://doi.org/10.1016/j.annals.2018.10.009.
Cresswell, T., 2006. On the Move: Mobility in the Modern Western World. Taylor & Francis.
DFT, 2014. Transport Statistics Great Britain 2014—Average Number of Trips (Trip Rates) and Distance Travelled by Purpose and Length-NTS0409. Accessed 13/11/2019. https://www.gov.uk/government/statistical-data-sets/nts04-purpose-of-trips.
DFT, 2017. Transport Statistics Great Britain 2017—Mode Share TSGB103-0105. Accessed 10/3/2019. https://www.gov.uk/government/statistical-data-sets/tsgb01-modal-comparisons.
Federal Highways Administration, 2005. Traffic Congestion and Reliability: Trends and Advanced Strategies for Congestion Mitigation. No FHWA-HOP-05-064. Accessed 01/12/2109. https://ops.fhwa.dot.gov/congestion_report/chapter3.htm.
Gandia, R.M., et al., 2019. Autonomous vehicles: scientometric and bibliometric review. Transp. Rev. 39 (1), 9–28, Routledge. https://doi.org/10.1080/01441647.2018.1518937.
Grant, M.J., Booth, A., 2009. A typology of reviews: an analysis of 14 review types and associated methodologies. Health Info. Libr. J. 26 (2), 91–108, Wiley Online Library.
Grieco, M., Urry, J., 2011. Mobilities: New Perspectives on Transport and Society. Ashgate Publishing, Ltd.
Haboucha, C.J., Ishaq, R., Shiftan, Y., 2017. User preferences regarding autonomous vehicles. Transp. Res. Part C Emerg. Technol. 78, 37–49. https://doi.org/10.1016/j.trc.2017.01.010.
Harzing, A.-W., Alakangas, S., 2016. Google Scholar, Scopus and the Web of Science: a longitudinal and cross-disciplinary comparison. Scientometrics 106 (2), 787–804, Springer.
Higgins, J.P.T., Green, S., 2011. Cochrane Handbook for Systematic Reviews of Interventions. John Wiley & Sons.
Hopkins, D., Schwanen, T., 2018. Automated mobility transitions: governing processes in the UK. Sustainability 10 (4), 956, MDPI. https://doi.org/10.3390/su10040956.
Jacsó, P., 2005. Google scholar: the pros and the cons. Online Inf. Rev. 29 (2), 208–214, Emerald Group Publishing Limited.
Jain, P., Bhumre, P., Jain, S., 2016. Common Automobile Program to Improve Mass Transportation. SAE Technical Paper. https://doi.org/10.4271/2016-01-0154.
Kang, D., Miller, J., 2018. Low-effort techniques for incorporating driverless vehicles in legacy regional planning models. In: Transport Research Board Annual Meeting.
Kellerman, A., 2018. Automated and Autonomous Spatial Mobilities. Edward Elgar, Cheltenham.
Laidlaw, K., Sweet, M.N., 2017. Estimating consumer demand for autonomous vehicles in the greater Toronto-Hamilton area: 2016 survey and model results. In: 97th Annual Meeting of the Transportation Research Board, Washington DC, pp. 1–26, (Retrieved on October; Vol. 9, p. 2018).
LaMondia, J.J., Fagnant, D.J., Qu, H., Barrett, J., Kockelman, K., 2016. Shifts in long-distance travel mode due to automated vehicles: statewide mode-shift simulation experiment and travel survey analysis. Transp. Res. Rec. 2566 (1), 1–11.

Lavieri, P.S., Bhat, C.R., 2019. Modeling individuals' willingness to share trips with strangers in an autonomous vehicle future. Transp. Res. A Policy Pract. 124, 242–261.
Law, R., 1999. Beyond "women and transport": towards new geographies of gender and daily mobility. Prog. Hum. Geogr. 23 (4), 567–588, Sage Publications Sage CA: Thousand Oaks, CA.
Liberati, A., et al., 2009. The PRISMA statement for reporting systematic reviews and meta-analyses of studies that evaluate health care interventions: explanation and elaboration. PLoS Med. 6 (7), e1000100, Public library of science.
Litman, T., 2015. Evaluating Public Transit Benefits and Costs. Victoria Transport Policy Institute, Victoria, BC, Canada.
Lothlorien, S.R., Mokhtarian, P.L., 2001. The positive utility of the commute: modeling ideal commute time and relative desired commute amount. Transportation 28 (2), 179–205. https://doi.org/10.1023/A:1010366321778.
Malokin, A., Circella, G., Mokhtarian, P.L., 2019. How do activities conducted while commuting influence mode choice? Using revealed preference models to inform public transportation advantage and autonomous vehicle scenarios. Transp. Res. A Policy Pract. 124 (April), 82–114. https://doi.org/10.1016/j.tra.2018.12.015.
Mathew, J.K., et al., 2019. Analysis of E-scooter trips. Institute of Transportation Engineers, ITE J. 89 (6), 44–49.
McGowan, J., et al., 2016. PRESS peer review of electronic search strategies: 2015 guideline statement. J. Clin. Epidemiol. 75, 40–46, Elsevier.
Milakis, D., Arem, B., van Wee, B., 2017. Policy and society related implications of automated driving: a review of literature and direction for future research. J. Intell. Transp. Syst. 21, 324–348.
Moher, D., et al., 2009. Preferred reporting items for systematic reviews and meta-analyses: the PRISMA statement. Ann. Intern. Med. 151 (4), 264–269, Am. Coll. Physicians.
Mongeon, P., Paul-Hus, A., 2016. The journal coverage of Web of Science and Scopus: a comparative analysis. Scientometrics 106 (1), 213–228, Springer.
Moreno, A.T., Michalski, A., Llorca, C., Moeckel, R., 2018. Shared autonomous vehicles effect on vehicle-km Traveled and average trip duration. J. Adv. Transp. 2018https://doi.org/10.1155/2018/8969353.
Nazari, F., Noruzoliaee, M., Mohammadian, A.(.K.)., 2018. Shared versus private mobility: modeling public interest in autonomous vehicles accounting for latent attitudes. Transp. Res. Part C Emerg. Technol. 97, 456–477. https://doi.org/10.1016/j.trc.2018.11.005.
Nikitas, A., Kougias, I., Alyavina, E., Njoya Tchouamou, E., 2017. How can autonomous and connected vehicles, electromobility, BRT, hyperloop, shared use mobility and mobility-as-a-service shape transport futures for the context of smart cities? Urban Sci. 1 (4), 36.
NTHS, 2009. National Household Travel Survey 2009. Federal Highway Administration. Accessed 10/3/2019. https://www.fhwa.dot.gov/policyinformation/pubs/hf/pl11028/onh2011.pdf.
OECD ITF, 2015. 'Urban Mobility System Upgrade: How Shared Self-Driving Cars Could Change City Traffic' Organisation for Economic Co-operation and Development/International Transport Forum. OECD Publishing. Accessed 1/12/2019. https://www.itf-oecd.org/sites/default/files/docs/15cpb_self-drivingcars.pdf.
Orr, B., Macarthur, J., Dill, J., 2019. The Portland E-scooter experience. In: TREC Friday Seminar Series. Available at: https://pdxscholar.library.pdx.edu/trec_seminar/163.
Pearman, A.D., 1988. Scenario construction for transport planning. Transp. Plan. Technol. 12 (1), 73–85.
Preston, V., 2016. Commuting. Oxford Bibliographies. Accessed: 1/7/2019. Available at: https://www.oxfordbibliographies.com/view/document/obo-9780199874002/obo-9780199874002-0033.xml.

Pudāne, B., et al., 2019. How will automated vehicles shape users' daily activities? Insights from focus groups with commuters in the Netherlands. Transp. Res. Part D: Transp. Environ. 71 (June 2018), 222–235, Elsevier. https://doi.org/10.1016/j.trd.2018.11.014.

Rode, P., Floater, G., Thomopoulos, N., Docherty, J., Schwinger, P., Mahendra, A., Fang, W., 2017. Accessibility in cities: transport and urban form. In: Meyer, G., Shaheen, S. (Eds.), Disrupting Mobility. Springer, Cham, pp. 239–273.

Selçuk, A.A., 2019. A guide for systematic reviews: PRISMA. Turk. Arch. Otolaryngol. 57 (1), 57.

Shamseer, L., et al., 2015. Preferred reporting items for systematic review and meta-analysis protocols (PRISMA-P) 2015: elaboration and explanation. BMJ 349, g7647, British Medical Journal Publishing Group.

Singleton, P.A., 2018. How useful is travel-based multitasking? Evidence from commuters in Portland, Oregon. Transp. Res. Rec. 2672 (50), 11–22. https://doi.org/10.1177/0361198118776151.

Thomopoulos, N., Givoni, M., 2015. The autonomous car—a blessing or a curse for the future of low carbon mobility? An exploration of likely vs. desirable outcomes. Eur. J. Futur. Res. 3 (1), 14. https://doi.org/10.1007/s40309-015-0071-z.

Thomopoulos, N., Nikitas, A., 2019. Smart urban mobility futures, editorial for special issue. Int. J. Automot. Technol. Manag. 19 (1–2), 1–9.

Tian, L.-J., Sheu, J.-B., Huang, H.-J., 2019. The morning commute problem with endogenous shared autonomous vehicle penetration and parking space constraint. Transp. Res. B Methodol. 123, 258–278, Elsevier.

Tussyadiah, I., Zach, F.J., Wang, J., 2017. In: Schegg, R., Stangl, B. (Eds.), Attitudes Toward Autonomous on Demand Mobility System: The Case of Self-Driving Taxi. Springer, Cham, pp. 755–766.

Van Wee, B., Banister, D., 2016. How to write a literature review paper? Transp. Rev. 36 (2), 278–288, Taylor & Francis.

Wadud, Z., Huda, F.Y., 2018. The potential use and usefulness of travel time in fully automated vehicles. In: Transport Research Board 97th Annual Meeting. https://trid.trb.org/.

Webb, J., Wilson, C., Kularatne, T., 2019. Will people accept shared autonomous electric vehicles? A survey before and after receipt of the costs and benefits. Econ. Anal. Policy 61, 118–135, Elsevier B.V. https://doi.org/10.1016/j.eap.2018.12.004.

Woldeamanuel, M., Nguyen, D., 2018. Perceived benefits and concerns of autonomous vehicles: an exploratory study of millennials' sentiments of an emerging market. Res. Transp. Econ. 71 (January), 44–53. https://doi.org/10.1016/j.retrec.2018.06.006, Elsevier.

Yun, J.J., et al., 2016. The relationship between technology, business model, and market in autonomous car and intelligent robot industries. Technol. Forecast. Soc. Chang. 103, 142–155.

Zakharenko, R., 2016. Self-driving cars will change cities. Reg. Sci. Urban Econ. 61 (September), 26–37, Elsevier. https://doi.org/10.1016/j.regsciurbeco.2016.09.003.

Zhang, W., Guhathakurta, S., 2018. Residential location choice in the era of shared autonomous vehicles. J. Plan. Educ. Res. 1–14. https://doi.org/10.1177/0739456X18776062.

CHAPTER SIX

Policy implications of the potential carbon dioxide (CO_2) emission and energy impacts of highly automated vehicles

Jan Anne Annema*
Delft University of Technology, Faculty of Technology, Policy and Management, Delft, Netherlands
*Corresponding author: e-mail address: j.a.annema@tudelft.nl

Contents

Abstract

This chapter explores the extent to which the adoption of highly automated vehicles (AVs) will lead to carbon dioxide (CO_2) emission reduction in the future. Additionally, policy implications are given. Based on existing literature, this chapter shows that the adoption of AVs will result in a modest improvement of CO_2 emission per kilometer traveled compared to non-autonomous vehicles in the future. Combined with the expectations that AVs will lead to a modest to, even, high growth in vehicle kilometers traveled (VKT) compared to business as usual, the net energy and CO_2 emission balance for AVs seems, at its best, to be neutral, but is probably negative. The potential accelerating role of AVs in relation to the uptake of electric vehicles might have the largest positive impacts on the CO_2 emissions per kilometer driven, but this accelerating role of AV technology in relation to the uptake of electric vehicles is uncertain. For the time being the most useful policy implication to curb road transport CO_2 emissions seems to be to continue with policies that promote the use of alternatives for fossil fuels, such as electricity.

Keywords: Automated vehicles, Environment, Carbon dioxide emission, Policy implications

ISSN 2543-0009
https://doi.org/10.1016/bs.atpp.2020.03.001

1. Introduction

In 2016 the current transport system emitted around 8.05 Gt of carbon dioxide (CO_2) worldwide, or 25% of all economic sectors (industry, buildings, other) (IEA, 2019). Recently, the IPCC (2018) estimated that human activities (for which CO_2 emission is the most important) caused approximately 1.0 °C of global warming above pre-industrial levels. Additionally, they state that global warming is *likely* to reach 1.5 °C between 2030 and 2052 if it continues to increase at the current rate. Road-based travel is responsible for the largest share of the transport CO_2 emissions at 68% (IEA, 2019). Broadly speaking, it is difficult to reduce CO_2 emission caused by transport. For example, within the European Union greenhouse gas emissions from transport (including aviation) increased by 25% between 1990 and 2017, despite efforts to reduce these emissions (EEA, 2019). New technologies such as biofuels, hydrogen and electric vehicles have penetrated the market far slower than optimists in the 1990s expected. As well as this, attaining behavioral change, whereby people would use the more environmentally friendly transport modes (public transport, bicycles, walking) rather than to cars, has turned out to be difficult. Perhaps there is hope on the technological horizon. This chapter aims to analyze whether highly automated vehicles will contribute toward reducing the CO_2 emissions of transport in the future. The questions this chapter aims to answer are: "*to what extent will the adoption of highly automated vehicles lead to CO_2 emission reduction in the future*"? And: "*what policies might be needed to steer the possible adoption of highly automated vehicles in the right direction from an environmental point of view*"?

"Highly automated" vehicles is a rather vague concept. In the scientific papers reviewed for this chapter different definitions of automated vehicles are used (implicitly or explicitly). In this chapter, broadly-based results and analysis from various papers are used which define automated vehicles as a vehicle that can navigate itself and have connectivity capabilities (vehicle-to-vehicle, vehicle-to-infrastructure and other cooperative communication networks) (definition based on Taiebat et al., 2018).

In this chapter, in Section 2, the approach used to write this chapter is given. In Section 3, the mechanisms which might affect AVs' energy use (and CO_2 emissions) per kilometer driven are explained. In Section 4, the potential energy and CO_2 emission impacts per kilometer driven of AVs are explored quantitatively. Section 5, analyses the relation between the adoption developments of AV and battery electric vehicles (BEV). In Section 6, the potential volume impacts of AVs compared to conventional vehicles are shown in order to explore the total future environmental impacts of AVs. In Section 7, the policy implications are discussed.

2. Approach

This paper is based on a review of scientific literature. A four-step approach was followed to select and review literature for this chapter:

1. The first step in the approach was to find scientific literature on the relation between highly automated vehicles and the environment. The search quickly led to two very elaborate papers on this topic. The first is by Taiebat et al. (2018) which contains a literature review of this topic using 111 recent scientific papers. It was decided not to repeat this review but, instead, to use this review paper in this chapter of the book to give state-of-the-art knowledge related to energy use and the CO_2 emission impacts of AVs per kilometer driven. The other elaborate paper found was by Gawron et al. (2018) who carried out a very extensive and high quality Life Cycle Assessment of AVs. Again, it was decided to use this paper in this chapter to show quantitatively what the potential environmental impacts of AVs might be, per kilometer driven.
2. One of the results of the analysis in step 1 was that powertrain developments (toward the uptake of BEVs) are dominant in achieving relatively high CO_2 emission reductions per kilometer driven. Therefore, in step 2, based on a brief scientific literature overview, a concise analysis was made of the interaction between AV development and BEV development. The "scopus.com" and "google scholar" search machines were used, applying the strings: "autonomous vehicles" AND "electric vehicles" (synonyms for "autonomous vehicles" and "electric vehicles" were also used in all kinds of combinations).
3. In the two previous research steps the impacts of AVs on CO_2 emission and energy use per kilometer driven were explored. Naturally, total CO_2 emission and the energy impacts of AVs are the result of the CO_2 emission factor estimates (g/km traveled) multiplied by the estimated kilometers driven (Vehicle Kilometer Traveled, VKT). In order to be able to explore total CO_2 emission and the energy impacts of AVs, in the third research step some very recent literature on VKT estimations for AVs was briefly reviewed. Only very recent papers were selected (at the time of writing this chapter—summer 2019). The studies that were selected

used different research methods, they focused on different regions and they used different assumptions.

4. Finally, based on the results of steps one to three, policy implications (if any) were discussed.

3. Energy use and CO_2 emission per kilometer driven

The CO_2 emission of road transport is the simple result of an emission factor (grams of CO_2 per kilometer driven) multiplied by the amount of kilometers driven. Broadly speaking, there is consensus in the literature studied that highly automated vehicles will decrease CO_2 emissions per kilometer driven. In an extensive literature review by Taiebat et al. (2018), they conclude that it is generally expected that AVs will improve energy efficiency and reduce CO_2 emissions per kilometer driven. Table 1 summarizes their results. They show that in scientific literature, four major mechanisms can be distinguished which affect energy use (and CO_2 emissions) per kilometer driven.

The first mechanism, vehicle operation, is, among other things, related to the notion that AV algorithms can eliminate the heterogeneity in real-time decisions which human drivers make while driving, resulting in an

Table 1 Major influencing mechanisms and their positive and negative impacts on AV fuel efficiency (Taiebat et al., 2018).

Major influencing mechanisms	Positive impacts	Negative impacts
Vehicle operation	Higher energy efficiency	Faster highway speeds
Vehicle design	• Optimal driving cycle	Additional ICT equipment needs for navigation and communication
Electrification	• Eco-routing	Aerodynamic shape alteration
Platooning	• Reduce cold starts	Higher auxiliary power requirement
	• Less idling	
	• Less speed fluctuations	
	• Powertrain downsizing	
	• Self-parking	
	Safety-enabled vehicle light-weighting	
	Vehicle right-sizing	
	Complementary electrification benefits	
	Platooning	

optimized driving cycle. AVs may drive less dynamically (aggressively) compared to human driven vehicles, with less speed fluctuations, with fewer complete stops, with less idling, and so forth. All of the examples given result in lower energy consumption per kilometer driven compared to a human driver. On the other hand, AVs might be safer in operation due to the elimination of human errors that may result when higher speeds are allowed, and which counteracts the efficiency gains just mentioned.

The second mechanism, vehicle design, is a bit more uncertain but here, the general notion is that the safety of AVs might be higher compared to conventional vehicles, resulting in opportunities to design relatively light and small AV vehicles (and thus more fuel-efficient ones). Vehicle-right-sizing (Table 1) is the idea that AV technology is capable of matching specific vehicles to specific trips. For example, if a party of people calls for a cab, a bigger and more energy-consuming autonomous cab could be sent to them by the cab fleet owner, compared to a situation where only one person calls for a cab. By doing so, fuel-efficiency gains at fleet level will be gained. However, there may be downsides to vehicle design. First, AVs need additional ICT devices which consume energy to produce, and which cost auxiliary power to use. Second, ICT devices, such as GPS antennae or LiDAR (light detection and ranging), could alter the aerodynamic shape of AV vehicles, compared to conventional vehicles, causing higher energy use per kilometer driven, especially while driving at high speeds.

The third mechanism (Table 1), complementary electrification benefits, is the idea that AV technology "*can provide a strong complement to EV technology*" (Taiebat et al. (2018, p. 11453). In Section 3, we will discuss this mechanism in depth.

Finally, the fourth mechanism, is platooning. Broadly speaking platooning is the synchronized movement of two or more AVs trailing each other closely, which reduces aerodynamic drag for the vehicles following on behind. These improved aerodynamics can result in energy savings per kilometer driven for the whole platoon, compared to the vehicles driving separately.

4. Life Cycle Assessment

Quantitatively, the net energy and CO_2 impact of AVs per kilometer driven is still uncertain with estimates that show fuel efficiency improvements per mechanism (listed in Table 1) of a few to sometimes 50%, but also deteriorations in the same order (see, for example, U.S. Energy Information Administration, 2018). Gawron et al. (2018) tried to estimate a net impact

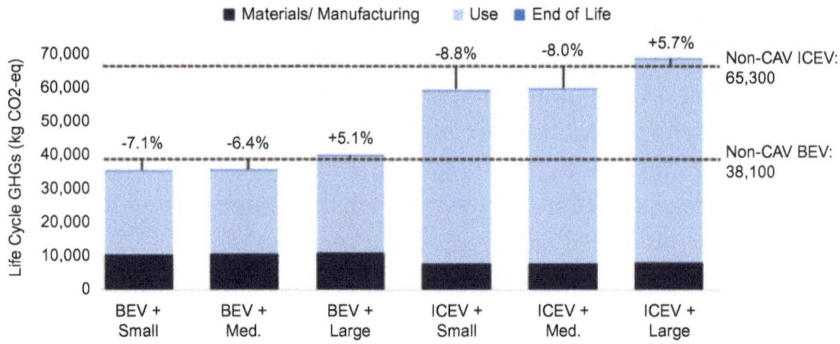

Fig. 1 Life cycle greenhouse gas emissions (GHGs) for six highly automated vehicles. (Gawron et al., 2018).

considering all of these mechanisms by carrying out a Life Cycle Assessment (LCA) of AVs. In the life cycle phases for AVs they included the production, manufacturing and assembly of the materials, the usage and end-of-life management. In Fig. 1 their results for life cycle greenhouse gases[a]tru are given for six of, what they call, AV "scenarios." In these scenarios they combined two propulsion systems with three vehicle sizes. They compared three battery electric AVs (BEV), namely small, medium and large, and three internal combustion engine AVs (ICEV), also small, medium and large with two medium sized non-automated cars, a non-autonomous electric car (lower dotted line) and a non-autonomous ICEV (top dotted line).

A few observations related to Fig. 1 can be made. The most important one is that when comparing the medium-sized, non-autonomous vehicles with the medium-sized AVs, indeed, some net life cycle CO_2 emission reduction can be observed but the impact of high automation is modest with a 6.4% decrease for BEV AVs and 8% decrease for ICEV AVs per kilometer driven. It is important to realize here that the lifetime volume driven for all of the vehicles compared is the same (a 160,000 mile lifetime). In this analysis by Gawron et al. (2018), the relatively modest positive environmental effect of AVs per kilometer driven is in accordance with the previous section: the

[a] Greenhouse gas or CO_2-equivalent emissions is nearly the same for transport as their CO_2 emissions. CO_2 is the dominant greenhouse gas emitted by transport. Other greenhouse gases such as methane (CH_4) and nitrogen dioxide (N_2O) are only emitted in small amounts by transport. Due to these relatively small amounts, they barely count in the CO_2 equivalent, despite the fact that these gases do have a far stronger warming potential compared to CO_2 and, therefore, count relatively heavily in the CO_2 equivalent because this equivalent is a weighted summation of all greenhouse gases emitted according to their warming potential. In the Netherlands, for example, the difference between CO_2 emissions and CO_2-equivalent emissions of road transport is only 1% (https://www.clo.nl/indicatoren/nl013032-emissies-naar-lucht-door-wegverkeer).

net result of an emission increase, due to on-board vehicle subsystems (e.g., more drag due to design issues, data transmission) and, on the other hand, an emission decrease, due to operational effects (e.g., eco-driving, platooning).

The second observation is that when comparing the small, medium and large AV systems there is a significant increase in life cycle CO_2 emissions from medium to large. The reason is the need for a large LiDAR and a more extensive external supporting structure for these larger vehicles which consume a relatively high amount of energy. This observation shows that safety-enabling light-weighting and right-sizing may be very important AV impacts (Table 1) for attaining emission reductions with the AV technology.

The third observation is that the powertrain development—BEV or ICEV—is dominant in achieving relatively high CO_2 emission reductions. However, this shift from ICEVs to BEVs could take place without any AV technology development. Nevertheless, the AV technology may help accelerate this shift (Gawron et al., 2018). Fig. 1 shows that this "accelerating BEV uptake" role of AV technology could be a more significant environmental impact of AV technology, compared to the idea that AV technology in itself is more energy efficient per kilometer driven, compared to non-autonomous technology. In the next section, the role of AVs in potentially accelerating the adoption of battery electric vehicles will be discussed.

5. Electrification

In the literature studied, several arguments are given as to why high automation of vehicles may accelerate a shift from ICEVs to BEVs. The perception that BEVs have a limited driving range is considered to be a major barrier for people buying a BEV (Li et al., 2017). Therefore, one type of argument (based on Brown et al., 2014) as to why AV technology could accelerate BEV uptake is that an electric AV could extend BEV driving ranges by clever route selection. For example, electric AVs can choose routes with fewer stops, which are relatively energy-efficient. Additionally, automation can optimize the driving cycles of BEVs because an algorithm can drive smoother and, thus, more energy efficiently, compared to a human driver. Another idea is that AV algorithms could maximize energy recovery when breaking, resulting in longer BEV driving ranges and even extended battery lives, compared to non-automated vehicles. Related to the potentially positive "right-sizing" impact of AVs (see Section 2), Chen et al. (2016) argue that in a shared autonomous electric fleet, trip matching can take place in order to guarantee that every trip requested (short or long) can be made without the problems associated with the battery running low. By doing so, the range anxiety barrier could be mitigated.

Another type of argument as to why AV technology could accelerate BEV uptake is that AVs might improve BEV economics. Here, the argument is that AVs might increase vehicle utilization rates (see Section 6 below), which "*will improve the economics of low running cost vehicles more than others*" (Offer, 2015, p. 28). Electric AVs are typically expected to be these "low running cost vehicles" due to their expected high utilization rate plus the cost characteristics of BEVs, namely their relatively high purchase costs and low operational costs, when compared to conventional vehicles (Mazur et al., 2018; Offer, 2015; Weiss et al., 2017). The lower operational costs of BEVs can be explained because they have a higher energy conversion efficiency compared to internal combustion engines. Fig. 2 illustrates the relative cost advantages per kilometer driven for high mileage BEVs.

AV technology can have other positive impacts on BEV usage which might also accelerate BEV adoption. Iacobucci et al. (2018, 2019) found in their modeling studies that by optimizing shared autonomous electric vehicle (SAEV) fleets, the charging costs of EVs can be significantly reduced

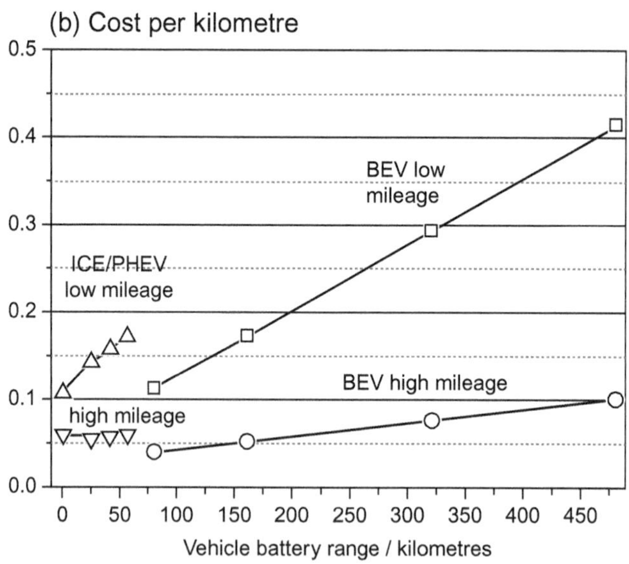

Fig. 2 Cost per kilometer ($/km) for hybrid cars (Internal Combustion Engine combined with a Plug-in Electric motor, ICE/PHEV) and for BEVs. "Low" yearly mileage of 13,216 km is compared to a vehicle utilization rate increased by 5 times to a "high" yearly mileage of 66,064 km (Offer, 2015).

compared to a non-autonomous fleet (SEV). The reason they give is that the charging costs of EVs are dependent on the variable electricity prices. Due to the automation of SEVs, the SAEV fleets can charge more easily at low electricity prices. Iacobucci et al. (2019) indicate that by using historical electricity price data from Japan, the charging costs for SAEV fleets can be reduced by 10% compared to the current charging strategy of SEVs. In the future, vehicle automation can create even more cost advantages, as it is expected that electricity prices will become more volatile (Iacobucci et al., 2018, 2019).

AV technology could even accelerate wider adoption of solar and wind power because electric AVs might be able to participate in the development of so-called vehicle-to-grid (V2G) technology (Lam et al., 2016). V2G technology entails the possibility of bidirectional electricity flows between EVs and the electricity network (Tan et al., 2016). This bi-directionality allows renewable energy to be stored in the EV when it is abundant and to be made available to the grid when the solar and wind power generation output is low. According to Römer et al. (2012), V2G enables storage of excess energy, balancing supply and demand in a flexible way and, therefore, makes the increase of the amount of renewable energy in the electricity network feasible. The idea is that AVs can be programmed to park in the right location to fully support V2G services where and when needed (and at the highest electricity price). Also, algorithms in electric AVs could efficiently deal with bidirectional flows between the vehicle and the electricity grid and the transport of passengers. Especially when large fleets of SAEVs become popular, these algorithms might create a flexible and decentralized storage facility. Anderson et al. (2016) even argue that if AVs were fully integrated, wireless V2G services could become available and make V2G technology more flexible. So, if electric AV technology allows improved V2G usage, two mechanisms can be distinguished which would promote extra environmental benefits. First, the balancing role of electric AVs supports the economics of sustainable energy sources, such as wind and solar, which might result in a higher usage of these technologies. Second, electric AV owners can receive remuneration from the grid operators when they deliver this service to the grid, which makes the electric AVs economically attractive to potential buyers and, because of this, an accelerated uptake of these electric and environmentally friendly vehicles (which use more and more sustainably-produced electricity according to the first mechanism) may take place.

It should be noted that this potential accelerating role of highly automated vehicles for the adoption of BEVs and, possibly, more wind and solar power, is dependent on the speed of development and adoption of highly automated vehicles. Right now, all over the world the deployment of policies to stimulate the sales and use of BEVs seem to have taken off. According to IEA (2018, p. 10): "*the strongest current policy signals emanate from electric car mandates in China and California, as well as the European Union's recent proposal on carbon dioxide (CO_2) emissions standards for 2030.*" If the BEV breakthrough is relatively fast in the next few decades because of deployment of these EV policies, but the high automation AV breakthrough is relatively slow, the accelerating role of AVs with regards to more environmentally friendly technologies will be modest.

6. AVs impact on vehicle kilometer traveled

The CO_2 emissions of road transport is the result of the CO_2 emission factor (g/km traveled) multiplied by the kilometers driven (Vehicle Kilometer Traveled, VKT). In a recent review of AV modeling studies (Soteropoulos et al., 2019) it has been shown that in many instances it is expected that AVs will increase vehicle kilometers traveled and reduce public transport and slow modes shares. In Table 2, some recent volume studies are presented. The general message is clear: they expect an increase in VKT after AVs have been adopted compared to a business-as-usual scenario. Altered generalized costs for AV travel compared to non-autonomous car travel, such as lower value for travel time savings and lower operating costs for AVs, partially explain this increase. Additionally, AVs may lead to extra VKT because new car trips can be made by people who are currently unable (or not allowed) to travel by car, such as disabled people, children, and people who have consumed alcoholic beverages. Finally, VKT may rise due to AV technology because empty trips are possible during which AVs are relocating to other customers, or they are looking for a parking spot, for example.

The only studies that indicate that AVs might decrease VKT assume that large shared automated vehicle fleets will arise because many people are willing to share rides (Soteropoulos et al., 2019). However, it is yet unknown whether many people are, indeed, really willing to share rides. In their study, Lavieria and Bhat (2019) identified that privacy concerns are currently discouraging individuals from using pooled ride-hailing services. They think that privacy-sensitivity may be worsened in a shared AV context because individuals may find themselves alone with a stranger in a vehicle without the presence of a professional driver, as is the case in private ride-hailing services. Their results show that potential "*users are less sensitive to the presence of*

Table 2 An overview of AV literature on the impacts of vehicle kilometers traveled (VKT).

	VKT increase	Cause of Increase	Method
Zhao and Kockelman (2018)	20%	Relatively low values of travel time; relatively competitive pricing. Both result in greater demand for longer distance travel and less transit system use. Empty-vehicle travel for self-parking.	Case study with travel demand model
Kröger et al. (2019)	2.4% or 8.6% Germany 3.4% or 8.6% USA	New automobile user groups, e.g., travelers with mobility impairments. Altered generalized costs of travel, e.g., due to a lower value of travel time savings for car travel.	Scenario analysis with demand model
Lu et al. (2018)	Roughly 30%	Unoccupied vehicle travel (routing, relocation, parking)	Agent-based modeling
Taiebat et al. (2019)	2–47% for an average household	Lower marginal cost of VKT	Microeconomic modeling
Moreno et al. (2018)	8%	Unoccupied vehicle travel (routing, relocation, parking)	Stated Preference
Harb et al. (2018)	83%	Possibility to multitask, zero occupancy rides, added convenience.	Naturalistic experiment
Kloostra and Roorda (2019)	9%	Increased demand Unoccupied vehicle travel (routing, AVs prefer highways)	Demand modeling

strangers when in a commute trip compared to a leisure-activity trip" (p.). Also, the strength of AVs' promise to make time more productive can be somewhat weakened by pooled AV ride-hailing because some sort of social interaction is perhaps required. Indeed, high income groups demonstrate high pooling aversion in all dimensions (Lavieria and Bhat, 2019).

7. Conclusion and policy implications

According to scientific literature the impact of highly automated vehicles on CO_2 emissions per kilometer driven seems modest. With this modest improvement of CO_2 emission per kilometer traveled and a modest to, even, high expected growth in VKT compared to business as usual, the net energy and CO_2 balance for AVs seems at its best neutral but is probably negative. The potentially accelerating role of AVs in relation to the uptake of electric vehicles might potentially have the biggest impact on the CO_2 emissions per kilometer driven, but this accelerating role in the uptake of electric technology is uncertain. Thus, the final picture for the environmentally friendliness of highly automated AVs compared to non-autonomous vehicle development seems not too favorable. In their review, Wadud et al. (2016) came to more or less the same conclusion. They think that at relatively low levels of automation, modest energy savings could be realized. Yet at a high level of automation (the topic of this chapter) they also identify the possibility of substantial increases in travel activities and, thus, in net energy consumption.

What are the policy implications? First, from a CO_2 emission reduction point of view, a shift from fossil-fueled internal combustion engines to electric vehicles is most effective. AV technology might accelerate this shift but to introduce specific policies to already focus on this accelerating role, seems premature right now. It seems more useful to just continue putting policies in place to promote alternative vehicle propulsion systems other than fossil fuel technologies. For example, policies such as the European CO_2 emission standards for new cars, that has already been mentioned, and all kinds of tax and/or subsidy policies to give EVs price advantages compared to fossil fuel technologies. If, in the meantime, AV adoption goes faster than expected, this technology will at least support the shift from fossil fuels to electricity. Second, when the adoption of electric AVs progresses, policies could be implemented which would result in the highest energy-efficiency possible because the electricity (even that produced by solar and wind) which the AVs will use, will also have external costs which politicians might want to internalize. Sections 3 and 4 showed that the energy use (and CO_2 emission) for electric AVs per kilometer driven are, among other things, dependent on clever eco-driving algorithms, right-sizing, potentially negative aerodynamic drag, speed, and so forth. So policies could be put in place, such as energy taxes and AV maximum speed limits, in order to introduce incentives to the market to become as fuel-efficient as possible.

Finally, there seems to be a need for policies which can curb the growth of VKTs due to AV technology, since this growth can result in a very steep increase in marginal external costs of road transport from a policy perspective. It should be noted that this chapter is about only one sort of external transport costs, namely CO_2 emission and external costs of electricity production. Compared to other external costs of a high growth in AV kilometers traveled, such as congestion, these costs might be relatively small. It therefore seems important to develop policies to internalize the external costs of AVs, such as road pricing and/or congestion pricing (for an example see Millard-Ball, 2019), from a broader perspective than solely the environmental costs. Still, perhaps some form of road-pricing for AVs might also help to manage the energy use and CO_2 emissions of AVs.

References

Anderson, J.M., Nidhi, K., Stanley, K.D., Sorensen, P., Samaras, C., Oluwatola, O.A., 2016. Autonomous Vehicle Technology: A Guide for Policymakers. RAND Corporation, Santa Monica.

Brown, A., Gonder, J., Repac, B., 2014. An Analysis of Possible Energy Impacts of Automated Vehicle. In: Road Vehicle Automation. Springer International Publishing, pp. 137–153.

Chen, T.D., Kockelman, K.M., Hanna, J.P., 2016. Operations of a shared, autonomous, electric vehicle fleet: Implications of vehicle & charging infrastructure decisions. Transp. Res. A Policy Pract. 94, 243–254. https://doi.org/10.1016/j.tra.2016.08.020.

EEA, 2019. https://www.eea.europa.eu/data-and-maps/indicators/transport-emissions-of-greenhouse-gases/transport-emissions-of-greenhouse-gases-11, site accessed.

Gawron, J.H., Keoleian, G.A., De Kleine, R.D., Wallington, T.J., Kim, H.C., 2018. Life cycle assessment of connected and automated vehicles: sensing and computing subsystem and vehicle level effects. Environ. Sci. Technol. 52 (5), 3249–3256. https://doi.org/10.1021/acs.est.7b04576.

Harb, M., Xiao, Y., Circella, G., Mokhtarian, P.L., Walker, J.L., 2018. Projecting travelers into a world of self-driving vehicles: estimating travel behavior implications via a naturalistic experiment. Transportation 45 (6), 1671 1685.

Iacobucci, R., McLellan, B., Tezuka, T., 2018. Modeling shared autonomous electric vehicles: potential for transport and power grid integration. Energy 158, 148–163. https://doi.org/10.1016/j.energy.2018.06.024.

Iacobucci, R., McLellan, B., Tezuka, T., 2019. Optimization of shared autonomous electric vehicles operations with charge scheduling and vehicle-to-grid. Transp. Res. Part Emerg. Technol. 100, 34–52. https://doi.org/10.1016/j.trc.2019.01.011.

IEA, 2018. Global EV Outlook 2018. s.l.: IEA.

IEA, 2019. CO_2 Emissions Statistics. International Energy Agency, Paris. iea.org, (site accessed 12th of May 2019).

IPCC (Intergovernmental Panel on Climate Change), 2018. Global Warming of 1.5 °C. IPCC, Switzerland. https://report.ipcc.ch/sr15/pdf/sr15_spm_final.pdf, (site accessed 15/01/2020).

Kloostra, B., Roorda, M.J., 2019. Fully autonomous vehicles: analyzing transportation network performance and operating scenarios in the greater Toronto area, Canada. Transp. Plan. Technol. 42 (2), 99–112.

Kröger, I., Kuhnimhof, T., Trommer, S., 2019. Does context matter? A comparative study modelling autonomous vehicle impact on travel behaviour for Germany and the USA. Transp. Res. Part Policy Pract. 122, 146–161.

Lam, A.Y.S., Yu, J.J.Q., Hou, Y., Li, V.O.K., 2016. Coordinated autonomous vehicle parking for vehicle-to-grid services. In: 2016 IEEE International Conference on Smart Grid Communications, SmartGridComm 2016, 3053(c), 284–289. https://doi.org/10.1109/SmartGridComm.2016.7778775.

Lavieria, P.S., Bhat, C.R., 2019. Modeling individuals' willingness to share trips with strangers in an autonomous vehicle future. Transp. Res. Part A 124, 242–261.
Li, W., Long, R., Chen, H., Geng, J., 2017. A review of factors influencing consumer intentions to adopt battery electric vehicles. Renew. Sustain. Energy Rev. 78, 318–328.
Lu, M., Taiebat, M., Xu, M., Hsu, S.-C., 2018. Multiagent Spatial Simulation of Autonomous Taxis for Urban Commute: Travel Economics and Environmental Impacts'. J. Urban Plan. Dev. 144 (4), 04018033.
Mazur, C., Offer, G.J., Contestabile, M., Brandon, N.B., 2018. Comparing the effects of vehicle automation, policy-making and changed user preferences on the uptake of electric cars and emissions from transport. Sustainability 10 (3), 1–19. https://doi.org/10.3390/su10030676.
Millard-Ball, A., 2019. The autonomous vehicle parking problem. Trans. Policy 75, 99–108.
Moreno, A.T., Michalski, A., Llorca, C., Moeckel, R., 2018. Shared autonomous vehicles effect on vehicle-km traveled and average trip duration. J. Adv. Transp. 2018, 1–10.
Offer, G.J., 2015. Automated vehicles and electrification of transport. Energ. Environ. Sci. 8 (1), 26–30. https://doi.org/10.1039/c4ee02229g.
Römer, B., Reichhart, P., Kranz, J., Picot, A., 2012. The role of smart metering and decentralized electricity storage for smart grids: the importance of positive externalities. Energy Policy 50, 486–495. https://doi.org/10.1016/j.enpol.2012.07.047.
Soteropoulos, A., Berger, M., Ciari, F., 2019. Impacts of automated vehicles on travel behavior and land use: an international review of modelling studies. Trans. Rev. 39 (1), 29–49. https://doi.org/10.1080/01441647.2018.1523253.
Taiebat, M., Brown, A.L., Safford, H.R., Qu, S., Xu, M., 2018. A Review on Energy, Environmental, and Sustainability Implications of Connected and Automated Vehicles. Environ. Sci. Technol. 52 (20), 11449–11465. https://doi.org/10.1021/acs.est.8b00127.
Taiebat, M., Stolper, S., Xu, M., 2019. Forecasting the impact of connected and automated vehicles on energy use: a microeconomic study of induced travel and energy rebound. Appl. Energy 247, 297–308.
Tan, K.M., Ramachandaramurthy, V.K., Yong, J.Y., 2016. Integration of electric vehicles in smart grid: a review on vehicle to grid technologies and optimization techniques. Renew. Sustain. Energy Rev. 53, 720–732. https://doi.org/10.1016/j.rser.2015.09.012.
U.S. Energy Information Administration, 2018. Autonomous Vehicles: Uncertainties and Energy Implications. U.S. Department of Energy Washington DC. www.eia.gov.
Wadud, Z., MacKenzie, D., Leiby, P., 2016. Help or hindrance? The travel, energy and carbon impacts of highly automated vehicles. Transp. Res. Part Policy Pract. 86, 1–18.
Weiss, J., Hledik, R., Lueken, R., Lee, T., Gorman, W., 2017. The electrification accelerator: understanding the implications of autonomous vehicles for electric utilities. Electr. J. 30 (10), 50–57. https://doi.org/10.1016/j.tej.2017.11.009.
Zhao, Y., Kockelman, K.M., 2018. Anticipating the Regional Impacts of Connected and Automated Vehicle Travel in Austin, Texas. J. Urban Plan. Dev. 144 (4), 04018032.

CHAPTER SEVEN

Potential health and well-being implications of autonomous vehicles

Patrick A. Singleton[a,*], Jonas De Vos[b], Eva Heinen[c], Baiba Pudāne[d]
[a]Department of Civil and Environmental Engineering, Utah State University, Logan, UT, United States
[b]Bartlett School of Planning, University College London, London, United Kingdom
[c]Institute for Transport Studies, University of Leeds, Leeds, United Kingdom
[d]Department of Engineering Systems and Services, Delft University of Technology, Delft, The Netherlands
[*]Corresponding author: e-mail address: patrick.singleton@usu.edu

Contents

Abstract

Transportation's effects on health and well-being are widely recognized. In the near future, autonomous vehicles (AVs) are expected to revolutionize transportation options and ways of travel. Consequently, the effect of AVs on population health and well-being is a crucial topic of interest for transportation policymaking, one that has received comparatively little attention. This chapter discusses (and anticipates) potential AV impacts on health and well-being. First, we summarize knowledge surrounding effects of transportation on physical health (traffic safety, air and noise pollution, and physical activity) and well-being (travel satisfaction, access to activities, etc.). We then discuss how AVs may affect traveler behaviors, focusing on mode shifts toward private, shared, and/or

Advances in Transport Policy and Planning, Volume 5
ISSN 2543-0009
https://doi.org/10.1016/bs.atpp.2020.02.002

pooled AVs, and how these shifts may lead to an overall increase in automobile travel, even if not necessarily in person-travel. Finally, we interpret the previous two sections to deduce potential positive, negative, and uncertain health/well-being effects of AVs. We expect benefits from improved safety, well-being, and access to opportunities; disadvantages from reduced physical activity; and uncertain impacts around land use changes and emissions. We conclude by discussing policy implications and research paths forward.

Keywords: Autonomous vehicles, Health, Well-being, Travel behavior, Safety, Access, Physical activity, Pollution, Satisfaction

1. Introduction

The transportation sector is currently undergoing a rapid transformation, in large part due to new mobility options and services made possible by technological developments. The emergence of "micro-mobility" modes, transportation network companies, mobility-as-a-service, vehicle-to-vehicle/infrastructure communications, and other changes will likely disrupt how people get around, how communities plan for future transportation needs, and how policymakers deal with (positive and negative) impacts of a complex transportation system. Adding on to these, autonomous vehicles (AVs), or self-driving cars (and trucks), if and when they become widespread in the future, may generate huge shifts in mobility patterns and behaviors. Therefore, policymakers and scholars are already actively investigating the many policy implications of ubiquitous automated driving. Much research currently addresses the impacts of AVs on vehicle ownership and use, energy consumption, and location choices, yet the area of health and well-being has received comparatively less attention, according to a recent review (Milakis et al., 2017). A possible reason for this knowledge gap is the uncertainty regarding how AVs may affect travel behavior (Soteropoulos et al., 2019), including AV ownership and use models (private, shared, and/or pooled), which have important implications for health and well-being analyses. Nevertheless, research in the area of AVs and health is increasing, with recent publications by Richland et al. (2016), Crayton and Meier (2017), and Curl et al. (2018), and even two articles (Dean et al., 2019; Sohrabi et al., 2020) available since our work on this chapter commenced in mid-2019.

In this chapter, we discuss the potential implications of AVs for health (both physical and mental health) and well-being (happiness, satisfaction, and fulfillment). Given the relative lack of empirical evidence on this topic, we employ a deductive approach rather than a systematic review of the literature. First, we review the major pathways by which the transportation system affects multiple dimensions of health and well-being. Given the importance of travel choices in these pathways, we then summarize some of the most relevant ways in which AVs may change travel behaviors. Finally, we combine these insights to deduce potential positive, negative, and unknown effects of AVs on health/well-being, leading to a discussion of policy implications and a prospective research agenda (a similar deductive approach was also used by Curl et al. (2018) and Sohrabi et al. (2020)). Although we cannot offer definitive conclusions because the exact technology and future use of AVs is still unknown, we aim to initiate a broader conversation among planners and industry leaders about potential health and well-being impacts of AVs. This is a crucial conversation for the present time, because AV use is not yet ingrained in travelers' daily lives and policies can still play a major role in helping lead the automated driving transition toward healthier outcomes.

2. How transportation influences health and well-being

Transportation is linked to various health and well-being outcomes. In recent decades, this linkage has been increasingly recognized among academics and practitioners (De Vos, 2018b; Malekafzali, 2009; van Wee and Ettema, 2016), resulting in new interdisciplinary collaborations, journals (the *Journal of Transport & Health*), and conferences (e.g., the International Conference on Transport & Health). There are various ways to discuss the health and well-being impacts of transport, although it is beyond the scope of this chapter to discuss this in detail (see, e.g., Giles-Corti et al. (2016) for a conceptualization). In this section, we first discuss relationships between transportation and physical health, followed by an overview of intersections with well-being. Our aim is not to conduct a systematic review, but rather to provide an overview of existing (systematic) reviews or, in the absence of such studies, key policy and empirical papers. We conclude by summarizing these impacts in a conceptual framework.

2.1 Physical health

The four main pathways through which travel affects physical health are the following: (i) traffic safety, (ii) air pollution, (iii) physical activity, and (iv) noise. This selection of impacts is based on the current list of the health risks of transportation acknowledged by the World Health Organization (WHO, 2019a), although we excluded climate change in our discussion. These impacts correspond with the main risk exposures listed by Giles-Corti et al. (2016).

2.1.1 Traffic injuries and deaths

Poor traffic safety has long been recognized as a detriment to individual and public health. According to the WHO, road traffic crashes are one of the top 10 causes of death worldwide and the leading cause of death for children and young adults (WHO, 2018a). Several developed countries have successfully reduced the number of deaths and relative deaths by inhabitants and distances traveled (OECD, 2019). Nevertheless, the absolute number of deaths globally due to road traffic has continued to climb in recent years, reaching 1.35 million people in 2016; however, relative to the size of the world's population, it has stabilized. Between 2013 and 2016, there were no reductions in road traffic deaths in any low-income country (WHO, 2018a).

The distributions of traffic casualties and serious injuries, as well as the risk of serious injury or death from traffic, is unequally distributed and depends on location and travel mode. Controlling for the number of inhabitants, the risk is three times higher in developing countries compared to developed countries (27.5 vs 8.3 deaths per 100,000 population) (WHO, 2018a). In the EU, the majority of traffic fatalities occur on urban (38%) or rural roads (53%); few take place on motorways (9%) (Eurostat, 2017). Globally, pedestrian and cyclists constitute a quarter of all fatalities, motorized two-wheelers comprise another quarter, and car occupants 29% (WHO, 2018a). This distribution varies by location. Most deaths in Africa are of pedestrians and cyclists, whereas in south-east Asia, deaths occur primarily for motorized two-wheelers. In Europe and the US, car occupants constitute the highest number of deaths, but non-occupants are overrepresented among deaths and serious injuries (USDOT, 2019). Driver errors cause more than 90% of traffic collisions (USDOT, 2015).

2.1.2 Air pollution

In addition to contributing to climate change, the transportation sector is responsible for a large proportion of urban air pollution, including particulate matter, CO_2, and NO_x. In the EU, transportation contributes a quarter of direct greenhouse gas emissions and a fifth of CO_2 emissions (EEA, 2018a). Although many sectors have successfully reduced their emissions in recent decades, transportation emissions are stable in the UK and EU

(DfT, 2018; EEA, 2018b). Transportation is thus not only a major contributor, but its relative contribution is growing. Road travel is estimated to be responsible for up to 30% of particulate emissions in European cities and up to 50% in OECD countries, mostly due to diesel traffic, though the exact amount varies widely between locations (WHO, 2019b). Moreover, air travel (a heavily polluting mode) continues to grow.

The WHO estimates that 4.2 million annual deaths result from exposure to ambient (outdoor) air pollution, and 91% of the global population lives in areas exceeding WHO exposure guidance levels. Health consequences of ambient air pollution include lung cancer, acute lower respiratory tract infection, stroke, ischemic heart disease, and chronic obstructive pulmonary disease (WHO, 2018b).

Differences exist in exposure to air pollution and the inhaled dose by mode of travel. Most studies report that car commuters have the highest cumulative exposure levels (Cepeda et al., 2017). However, due to the active nature of walking and cycling and resulting higher respiratory rates, active commuters have higher inhalation doses than do commuters using motorized modes.

2.1.3 Physical activity

The lack of physical activity is a major cause of morbidity and mortality (Lee et al., 2012). The WHO (2010) recommends spending at least 150 min of moderate-intensity aerobic activity—or at least 75 min of vigorous-intensity aerobic activity (or an equivalent combination)—a week. Annually, two million deaths can be attributed to a lack of physical activity. A lack of physical activity is a leading risk factor for obesity and cardiovascular disease, type 2 diabetes, and some types of cancer. Independent of the level of physical activity, sedentary behavior (total sitting and TV-viewing time) is associated with greater risks for several major chronic diseases (Patterson et al., 2018).

Levels of engagement in physical activity differ by location and socioeconomic characteristics. Globally, 25% of adults are insufficiently active (WHO, 2018c). Women are more likely to be insufficiently active than men, and a higher gross domestic product is often associated with lower physical activity levels (WHO, 2018c).

The decrease in physical activity over time has coincided with an increase in motorization, including motorized transportation. Walking, cycling, and other forms of active travel provide a sufficient level of physical activity to improve health and well-being (Chief Medical Officers, 2011). For example, a cycling level corresponding to WHO recommendations results in a 10% reduction in the risk of all-cause mortality (Kelly et al., 2014). Walking and cycling levels sharply differ between locations, and the social and spatial context has a strong influence (Heinen et al., 2010).

2.1.4 Noise

Despite receiving less attention than the previous three topics, noise is increasingly acknowledged to have negative health impacts. Noise can affect the auditory system and result in hearing loss and tinnitus. Moreover, noise (especially following long-term exposure) has additional adverse health effects resulting from psychological and physiological distress, homeostasis disturbance, and increasing allostatic load (Basner et al., 2014, in WHO, 2018d). Exposure to noise can disturb sleep, cause cardiovascular and psychophysiological effects, reduce performance, and provoke annoyance responses and changes in social behavior (WHO, 2018d).

Road traffic is the largest contributor to noise pollution in urban areas and is the most important source of noise annoyance. Over 70 million Europeans are assumed to have a day–evening–night noise level greater than 55 dB as a result of road traffic noise (EEA, 2014, 2018c). In addition, noise from air transportation can be high in specific areas. Noise levels increase with higher traffic volumes and speeds, but urban design, road surfaces, and weather conditions influence noise levels as well.

2.2 Well-being

In recent decades, interest in linkages between travel and well-being has rapidly increased (De Vos et al., 2013; Mokhtarian, 2019). In this section, we consider three main effects of transportation on mental health and well-being: (i) travel satisfaction, (ii) access to activities, and (iii) spill-over effects on the activity at the destination.

2.2.1 Travel satisfaction

Travel satisfaction refers to the emotions people experience during trips and how they evaluate these trips (De Vos and Witlox, 2017). After the development of a reliable tool to measure travel satisfaction—the satisfaction with travel scale (Ettema et al., 2011)—multiple studies (from different geographical contexts) have analyzed determinants of travel satisfaction. The chosen travel mode has an important influence on how people perceive their trips: specifically, active travel mostly results in the highest levels of travel satisfaction, while public transit (bus in particular) is perceived least positively (De Vos et al., 2016; Singleton, 2019b; Ye and Titheridge, 2017). Most studies also find a negative effect of trip duration on travel satisfaction (Higgins et al., 2018; Morris and Guerra, 2015), since long trips might be a mental and physical burden. Positive (or negative) attitudes toward the chosen travel mode positively (or negatively) impact satisfaction with the trip made (De Vos, 2018a; St-Louis et al., 2014), while traveling alone has a negative effect on satisfaction levels (De Vos, 2019; Zhu and Fan, 2018). The effects of the built environment and travel distance on travel satisfaction remain unclear so far (De Vos et al., 2016; Ye and Titheridge, 2017). Finally, satisfaction can be influenced by the activities people undertake while traveling. For public transit users, productive activities and talking to other passengers are found to positively affect satisfaction levels, while entertaining and relaxing activities seem to negatively influence travel satisfaction (Ettema et al., 2012; Lyons et al., 2007); perhaps they are done to cope with a burdensome trip. Since experiencing positive emotions can improve people's life satisfaction (by stimulating original thinking, fostering skills, liking of self and others, etc. (Lyubomirsky et al., 2005)), travel satisfaction can directly influence well-being and mental health.

2.2.2 Access to activities

Transportation also affects well-being by providing access to activities at different locations (accessibility additionally influences physical health through access to health care, healthy food, and recreational opportunities). Elements such as life satisfaction, personal growth, and realization of the best in oneself are significantly influenced by the participation in (and performance of) out-of-home activities enabled by travel (Ettema et al., 2010; Morris, 2015). Even the potential to travel (motility)—having access to transportation options (e.g., living close to public transport, owning a car) and the knowledge and skills to use them (Kaufmann et al., 2004)—can generate feelings of freedom, competence, and belonging.

Not being able to reach rewarding out-of-home activities due to limited travel options can consequently affect quality of life in a negative way (Delbosc and Currie, 2011; Lucas, 2012). Especially low-income groups and individuals with limitations on physical or cognitive functioning (e.g., older adults) might suffer from transportation disadvantage and social isolation. Travel might also restrict the execution of certain rewarding activities, as time spent traveling cannot be used for other activities (disregarding activities during travel). For instance, Stutzer and Frey (2008) found that long commute trips resulted in low levels of subjective well-being, partly due to limited time for family activities. On the other hand, examining relationships between commute duration and life satisfaction is complicated (Clark et al., 2019; Morris and Zhou, 2018), since long commutes are often linked to (financially) rewarding jobs, owning a house, and being married, which positively impact life satisfaction.

2.2.3 Spill-over effects on the activity at the destination

Not only does transportation provide access to out-of-home activities, but the performance of (and satisfaction with) that activity can be influenced by perceptions of the preceding travel episode. In fact, travel satisfaction might mainly influence life satisfaction indirectly (De Vos, 2019), i.e., through satisfaction with destination activities. Morris and Zhou (2018) associated longer commute durations with lower positive emotions at work. Friman et al. (2017) found that satisfaction with the trip to work influenced the mood directly after the commute trip but not later in the day. Studies focusing on children found active travel to be associated with a positive mood after arriving at school or during the first school lesson (Stark et al., 2018; Westman et al., 2017). In addition to satisfaction with the destination activity, travel may also affect the performance of that activity. Stress experienced during the commute can negatively affect job performance (Legrain et al., 2015); while Loong et al. (2017) found that cyclists felt most energized at work, drivers were least energized. On the other hand, travel time can also be used to mentally prepare for the activity ahead, potentially improving the performance of that activity (Jain and Lyons, 2008).

2.3 Conceptual framework

So far, we have discussed health and well-being impacts as a consequence of transportation. However, in order to fully understand the impacts of changes in transportation supply—such as the introduction of AVs—it is crucial to recognize that such changes first influence individuals' travel choices (which are also partly affected by the acceptance levels of AVs; see, e.g., Becker and Axhausen (2017) for a review on acceptance of AVs), which subsequently affect health and well-being. Handy (2014) explains how choices of travel amount, travel mode, and other dimensions (e.g., time-of-day, driving speed and style, physical and mental condition) impact individual and population health. Fig. 1 translates her discussion into a conceptual diagram and supplements it with well-being impacts. It also relates to other conceptualizations of health–transportation relationships (e.g., van Wee and Ettema, 2016).

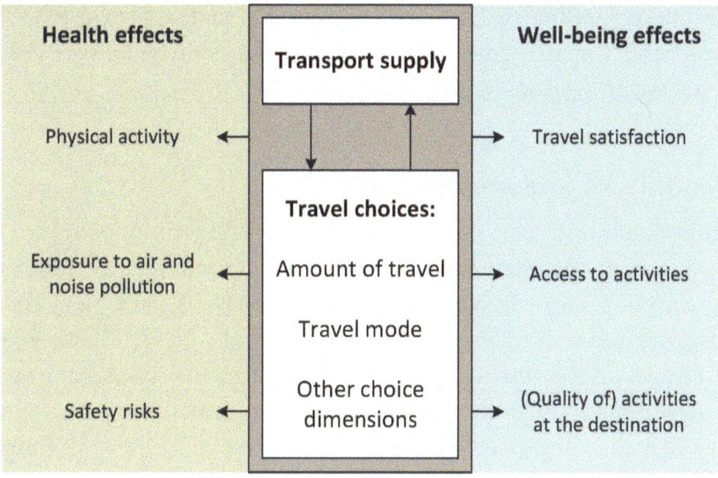

Fig. 1 Conceptual framework of individual health and well-being impacts of travel choices.

Fig. 1 demonstrates not only how the characteristics of the transportation supply (e.g., AVs) directly impact health and well-being, but also how supply interacts with demand—the various dimensions of travel choices. Therefore, these two should be examined jointly when studying AV effects on health and well-being. Although we focus on individual effects in the following sections, the population effects of AVs can be thought of as the sum of individual impacts and any higher-order influences due to aggregation (e.g., access to activities leads to land use changes, which again influences the access to activities).

3. Expected effects of autonomous vehicles on travel behavior

The major anticipated benefits of AVs are that they would make "driving" safer and reduce negative emotions (e.g., stress) often linked with navigating a car through traffic. By reducing the burdens of driving and navigating, AVs could allow travelers to use travel time for other purposes: working, reading, entertainment, or rest (Pfleging et al., 2016; Singleton, 2019a). According to Fig. 1, this change in transportation supply would influence travel choices, which would further affect individual and population health and well-being. In particular, the amount of individual travel together with travel mode choice (including the various proposed forms of AV-sharing) influences vehicle-distances traveled, which carries health and well-being impacts. These two travel behavior dimensions are discussed in the following sections.

3.1 Amount of individual travel

Literature suggests that the introduction of AVs will prompt people to travel longer distances for their daily activities (choosing further destinations and/or traveling more frequently); supporting results have been obtained from activity-based modeling studies (Auld et al., 2017; Childress et al., 2015). However, it is worth noting that these studies assume that improved travel experiences—commonly formalized as reduced values of travel time—will make people accept longer in-vehicle travel times. Although this may occur in aggregate, two individual-level considerations warrant discussion. First, new activities performed during travel could interact with other daily activities and lead to a variety of total travel time developments, including a possibility of reduced daily travel time (Mokhtarian, 2018; Pudāne et al., 2018).[a] Second, increased travel time means less time for other activities, possibly altering travelers' daily activity schedules. Changing daily routines to accommodate more travel is not easy or desired by all (Zmud et al., 2016). Alternatively, increased travel for holidays seems a more likely consequence of AVs, since that does not require systematic changes in daily activity schedules (LaMondia et al., 2016).

The other proposed source of increasing individual travel amounts comes from longer-term changes to home and/or work locations, resulting (as before) from the reductions in travel disutility. This would lead to an unwelcome effect of urban sprawl (Heinrichs, 2016; Zakharenko, 2016). However, the implications of accepting longer commute durations (and possible counter-arguments for doing so) should also be considered carefully, e.g., in the context of travelers' daily activity schedules. Furthermore, if value of time is used as the main predictor of travel behavior changes, then it should preferably be obtained from stated choice studies using a trip-making or residential location (as opposed to mode choice) context. Adopting the latter, Krueger et al. (2019) did not observe significant changes in the value of travel time.

[a] An example in Pudāne et al. (2018) shows how a traveler, who is able to rest in an AV, may eliminate a detour to home after work and go straight to an evening activity, thereby reducing the total travel time. Such activity rearrangement is fully rational and in line with microeconomic theory, given a certain activity wish list. Although such instances may occur less often than activity rearrangements that result in more travel, the possibility of less individual travel cannot be excluded *a priori*.

3.2 Travel mode choice

That AVs could lead to a higher mode share for (private) cars is just as widely expected as the potentially increasing travel distances (e.g., Soteropoulos et al., 2019). To reduce the negative effects of such modal shifts, shared and pooled AVs are often suggested as more sustainable future modes. Therefore, the question of shared AV acceptance and success has been among the top priorities in AV-research in the last few years (Haboucha et al., 2017; Krueger et al., 2016; Lavieri and Bhat, 2019; Nazari et al., 2018; Stoiber et al., 2019). Although most studies find increased acceptance of car-sharing as compared to the low present levels (Conway et al., 2018), the travelers most interested in shared AV systems are current public transit, car-sharing, or active mode users, not private car users (Haboucha et al., 2017; Krueger et al., 2016; Nazari et al., 2018). Relatedly, shared/pooled-AV acceptance is high in places where travelers are accustomed to attractive public transit options (Stoiber et al., 2019). Finally, even among current non-automated modes, car-sharing has been shown to be a weak substitute to private car travel and tends to replace public transit and bicycle modes instead (Carrone et al., 2019; Gehrke et al., 2018).

These empirical studies support an intuitive idea that travelers prefer the mode most similar to their current choice: the travel option that is the best substitute for their current ways of travel (van Wee et al., 2019). We represent this concept in Fig. 2, which shows characteristics of current and future AV modes and expected modal shifts. Even though this comparison does not include all relevant travel characteristics and is qualitative—the exact values and relative importance of attributes could magnify or reduce the impact of various characteristics—it provides a framework to discuss potential modal shifts in an AV future. Overall, we expect modal shifts toward private, shared, and pooled AV modes. However, changes in distances traveled are determined not only by the relative preferences for new AV modes, but also by the shifts away from current modes.

Although, at first glance, shared or pooled AVs could seem to be a close substitute to private cars, Fig. 2 shows that, with respect to many attributes, they resemble—and hence could substitute—current car-sharing, taxis, and, most importantly, public transit.[b] Furthermore, it can be argued that the

[b] There may be exceptions to this correspondence, as shown by the thin arrows in Fig. 2. For example, public transit passengers who currently like the ability to be productive while traveling may be attracted to the activity facilitation made possible by shared or even private AVs. In the opposite direction, current car drivers who choose to own because they value or require door-to-door service and departure time flexibility may find some value in shared or even pooled AVs, if the lower costs and multitaskability outweigh the loss of privacy and personalization.

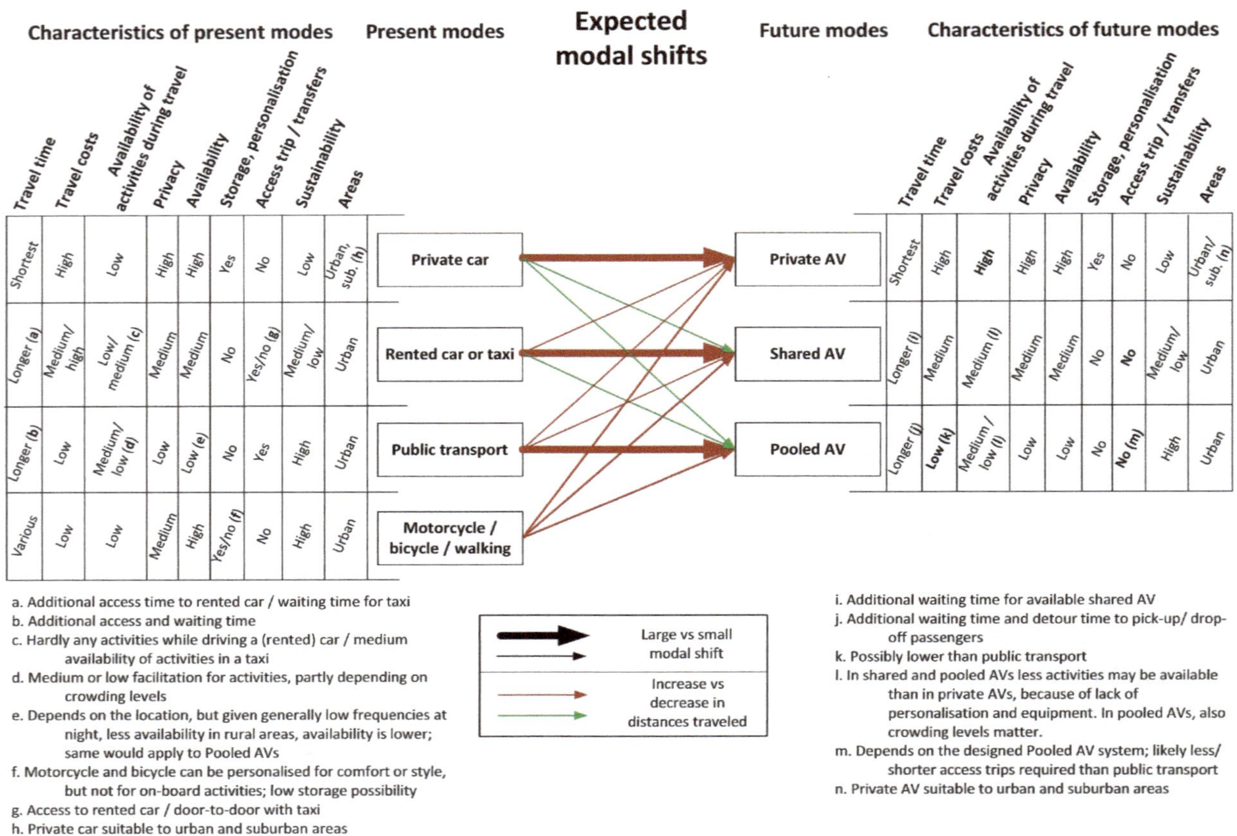

Fig. 2 Comparison of present and future transportation modes and expected modal shifts.

new AV modes improve upon their current mode "counterparts" (highlighted bold on the right side of Fig. 2). For today's private car users, private AVs offer much greater possibility to engage in new non-driving activities during travel. Shared AVs would provide present rental car and car-sharing users a comparable level of multitasking facilities, plus reduced access times and improved door-to-door and one-way services (Krueger et al., 2016). For public transit riders, pooled AVs would likely pick-up and drop-off closer to the destination and might even be cheaper than public transit thanks to the savings of driver costs (Bösch et al., 2018), especially outside of dense urban areas.[c] These benefits will likely motivate the users of the current modes to shift to the most similar automated modes. Results of Pakusch et al. (2018) empirically support these trends, although they also argue that the current modes will most likely remain popular in the near future.

The preceding discussion on the shifts from current modes to their AV "counterparts" is crucial, because we expect that this shift would result in increased vehicle use and distances traveled (the thick red arrows in Fig. 2), due to three potential reasons. First, if travelers experience the new mode as superior to the present mode, they (in aggregate) might use it more—for longer and/or more frequent travel (however, see Section 3.1 for points of caution). Ferdman (2020) even warns that corporations, who may own the future shared or pooled AV fleets, will have an interest in prolonging trips to maximize exposure to in-vehicle advertising. Second, the nature of shared/pooled AVs is such that greater vehicle-distances will be traveled to satisfy the same number of person-trips, compared to the most similar non-automated mode. Shared AVs would travel further distances to provide door-to-door travel, instead of requiring drivers to pick-up and drop-off vehicles at designated locations. The same is true for pooled AVs, which would (additionally) generate greater travel distances than public transit because they have a lower capacity/occupancy. Third, all automated modes might involve empty travel: to access the next customer for a shared AV or to share a private vehicle among household members; to perform pick-up or drop-off tasks independently (reducing some trip chaining behavior); or to access cheaper parking.

[c] Some have noted that AVs might even attract a portion of active mode users (cyclists and pedestrians) because of the much greater convenience to use AVs for short trips (e.g., it would not be necessary to look for a parking spot); however, Fig. 2 hypothesizes that this shift would not be great due to dissimilarity of active modes and AVs in other aspects.

To summarize, this section has argued that AVs may change travel choices in a way that would lead to more automobile travel, even if not necessarily to more person-travel. In particular, this increase could be most strongly determined by modal shifts away from current modes to their more attractive (but also more travel-distance-intensive) AV counterparts.

4. Potential effects of autonomous vehicles on health and well-being

We now turn our attention to outlining potential effects that AVs could have on health and well-being. It should be noted that these impacts are speculative, deduced in part from our discussions in earlier sections—about the more general health/well-being impacts of the current transportation system and how/why AVs might affect traveler behaviors within that system. Rather than conducting a systematic review ourselves, we also rely in part upon summaries of the literature identified in a recent scoping review (Dean et al., 2019). Recent work by Richland et al. (2016), Crayton and Meier (2017), Curl et al. (2018), and Sohrabi et al. (2020) is also particularly informative.

We organize this section around the central transportation—health/well-being linkages we identified earlier: safety, travel satisfaction, access to activities, physical activity, air pollution and noise. Within each topic, we discuss the variety of possible benefits and adverse effects of AVs that we and others have considered. Despite the potential varied effects, based on our exploration we suggest that AVs are likely to have overall positive impacts on some health and well-being aspects (safety, travel satisfaction, access to activities) and overall negative impacts on others (physical activity), while effects are more uncertain for other topics (urban built environments, air and noise pollution).

4.1 Overall positive effects

4.1.1 Improved safety

The most consistently cited health benefit of AVs is the reduction of injuries and deaths from traffic collisions (Dean et al., 2019; Pettigrew et al., 2018). AVs will be (ostensibly) safer than current vehicles because they will be driven by computers rather than people, thus removing the human element—the cause of the majority of traffic crashes (USDOT, 2015). The computer vision systems of fully-automated vehicles are expected to improve collision avoidance, lane keeping, and other driving tasks, while connected vehicles/infrastructure will allow for sharing vehicle trajectories and improving safety in high-crash-risk situations (e.g., queues, intersections) (Milakis et al., 2017). Crashes could be reduced by 40% or more (Fagnant and Kockelman, 2015).

Nevertheless, such safety benefits may be modest until AV penetration rates are high and AVs can operate without any human intervention; also, aggregate safety gains could be reduced if AVs lead to more car travel. Safety could actually decrease for AVs in which humans are required to monitor and take over driving under certain conditions (Strand et al., 2014). Recent fatalities involving such vehicles highlight these and other questions regarding the safety performance of AVs in challenging (low light, poor weather) conditions and in complex or unique traffic situations. Cyberattacks may also be a threat (Petit and Shladover, 2014). Finally, there are ethical and legal issues remaining to be resolved over how AVs should act in situations where a collision is unavoidable (Bonnefon et al., 2016): does the computer prioritize protecting the vehicle occupants over non-occupants (including vulnerable road users)? The way in which this issue is resolved could exacerbate existing inequalities in safety between motorized and non-motorized users. Nevertheless, we expect overall positive health benefits from improved safety.

4.1.2 Improved travel satisfaction and spill-over effects

AVs will likely improve travel experiences of "driving" that affect mental health and well-being. By removing the need to operate a vehicle when traveling alone, AVs may reduce many of the stresses associated with navigating urban traffic and congestion (Crayton and Meier, 2017; Curl et al., 2018; Dean et al., 2019; Richland et al., 2016), thus improving mental well-being and physical health. By providing opportunities to do other, more productive/rewarding things while traveling by car, AVs may also improve enjoyment and happiness with travel (and satisfaction with the destination activity). Although these well-being effects may be substantial, they should not be overestimated (Singleton, 2019a).

There could also be some negative impacts to well-being as a result of AVs. Some studies find that the increased possibility to use travel time productively creates psychological pressure to do so and may actually decrease travel satisfaction and well-being (Pudāne et al., 2019; Shaw et al., 2019). Furthermore, sharing and especially pooling AVs reduces one of its core benefits: the improved travel experience and the multitasking possibility during travel. This is also reflected in stated choice studies that find the value of travel time to be lower for shared (exclusive use) AVs than pooled AVs (e.g., Krueger et al., 2016). Finally, some people enjoy the act of driving and gain status from owning a specific vehicle; these intrinsic experiences related to driving might be diminished when (especially shared) AVs dominate (Curl et al., 2018).

4.1.3 Greater access to activities

We and others expect that AVs will likely improve access to activity opportunities, for a couple of reasons. First, distant activities—which may have been too time-consuming to reach with conventional cars—might become accessible if people do not "lose" time and can perform certain activities (e.g., working, studying, etc.) during AV travel (Meyer et al., 2017). More generally, formerly outside-the-trip activities can be brought into the trip, thereby freeing time for new or expanded out-of-trip activities (Mokhtarian, 2018; Pudāne et al., 2018). Even if travelers do not (frequently) make use of the enhanced accessibility, there is an "option-value" from having greater activity opportunities (Laird et al., 2009).

Second, AVs can increase accessibility for people with mobility limitations (Curl et al., 2018; Dean et al., 2019; Pettigrew, 2017; Richland et al., 2016). A large minority of the population cannot (easily) transport themselves to/from daily activities: young children, older adults, and people with certain physical and intellectual disabilities (Bennett et al., 2019; Pettigrew et al., 2018). By eliminating the need to rely on others for travel, AVs will likely improve access to health care, grocery stores, jobs, education, etc., for these people. These user groups are expected to be among the main drivers of increased AV travel demand (Harper et al., 2016). Improved mobility may also help people living in rural areas to access hospitals and other services. Additionally, by facilitating independent mobility and access to opportunities, including social activities and connections with family and friends, AVs may indirectly reduce social isolation, increase social inclusion/connectivity, and improve mental health and quality of life (Curl et al., 2018; Pettigrew, 2017; Richland et al., 2016).

At the same time, AVs have the potential to widen existing disparities in transportation access, depending on how they are implemented and managed and how much they cost to use. Private AV ownership models may exacerbate inequalities by increasing financial barriers to accessing driver-less mobility, especially for low-income and aging populations (Curl et al., 2018; Dean et al., 2019; Pettigrew et al., 2019). Historically-disadvantaged communities (including low income, people of color, and immigrant communities) already face financial, technological, and social barriers to accessing electric and shared mobility, issues unlikely to be addressed simply through the addition of AVs (Cohen and Shirazi, 2017). Finally, there are concerns that increasing suburban sprawl and mode shifts toward AVs may reduce funding and political support for public transportation, thus exacerbating access for transit-dependent populations (Cohen and Shirazi, 2017; Fleetwood, 2017).

4.2 Overall negative effects

4.2.1 Reduced transport-related physical activity

Due to some of the positive well-being effects anticipated (see above) and other improvements to the existing suite of transportation options (see Fig. 2), we and others expect AVs to reduce transport-related physical activity by taking some mode share away from walking, bicycling, public transit, and other forms of active transportation (Crayton and Meier, 2017; Curl et al., 2018; Milakis et al., 2017; Sohrabi et al., 2020; Soteropoulos et al., 2019). Such modal shifts away from these active modes pose a high health risk, because—as Handy (2014) notes—trips with active modes are more beneficial if they replace sedentary passive travel in a car (as opposed to being newly-generated leisure trips). Similarly, replacement of active mode trips with less active AV travel is likely more harmful for the individual (per distance traveled) than current car trips becoming longer or more frequent in AVs. Less physically-active transportation and more sitting (in AVs) is likely to increase risks of obesity and non-communicable diseases (Crayton and Meier, 2017).

Although the exact impacts are difficult to predict, AVs may offer some pathways to increase overall physical activity. Being productive in AVs may free up time for other physically-active non-travel activities, or compensating behavior may increase leisure-time physical activity, and it is possible (though not highly likely) that AVs could be equipped with exercise machines (Crayton and Meier, 2017; Curl et al., 2018). Road capacity might increase with connected AVs, and some suggest that this (plus a reduction in demand for on-street parking) might open up road space for non-motorized infrastructure (Milakis et al., 2017; Soteropoulos et al., 2019). Yet, these opportunities seem unlikely to outweigh negatives from mode shifts. Overall, we expect physical activity obtained through personal transportation to decrease.

4.3 Uncertain effects

4.3.1 Changes to urban built environments

Two main perspectives have been articulated regarding how AVs might change built environments. The "hopeful view" for health (Richland et al., 2016) is that AVs will lead to denser urban developments and reallocation of road space (Crayton and Meier, 2017; Curl et al., 2018; Dean et al., 2019; Milakis et al., 2017). In dense urban areas, land is valuable and in high demand. According to Fraedrich et al. (2019), widespread AV adoption is expected to reduce the need for parking in dense urban centers as AVs, after dropping off passengers, can drive themselves to a remote (cheaper) location to wait for their next trip (shared and pooled AVs might furthermore reduce the total number of vehicles, thus also reducing parking demands). As previously mentioned, road space may be reallocated toward transit and/or walk/bicycle infrastructure. Altogether, this may open up land for more development as well as public space, which has the opportunity to make for more attractive, walkable urban environments, thus facilitating greater physical activity. Also, people interested in using AVs might be inclined to move to cities if AVs are introduced there first.

The pessimistic view is that AVs will increase urban sprawl and lead to more land dedicated to transportation and parking (Crayton and Meier, 2017; Curl et al., 2018; Richland et al., 2016). This view presumes that the reduced disutility of travel would lead to a willingness to live further from work and therefore increased levels of urban sprawl and automobile dependence (Mokhtarian, 2018; Soteropoulos et al., 2019). However, this link is complex (see Section 3), and a recent study shows that travel disutility is not reduced in the context of residential location (Krueger et al., 2019). Nevertheless, even if AVs do not lead to increased person-travel (and thereby urban sprawl), the increases in vehicle travel (see Section 3.2) could further strain crowded and congested urban street networks, forcing more traffic onto local streets and making them less conducive for walking and cycling. At the same time, other parts of urban/suburban locations (especially those in close proximity to urban centers) may experience an influx of parked or circling (empty) AVs (Ostermeijer et al., 2019). Land area dedicated to cars would increase, thus deteriorating walkable environments, discouraging physical activity, and further exacerbating geospatial inequities in healthy travel behaviors. Because these land use and built environment changes are likely to occur over a long period of time, we are uncertain about whether they will be positive or negative, overall.

4.3.2 Air pollution and noise

Overall impacts of AVs on air pollution and noise are similarly uncertain (Crayton and Meier, 2017; Dean et al., 2019; Sohrabi et al., 2020). There are likely to be benefits since many experts expect AVs to be battery-electric powered (Pettigrew, 2017). Even without electrification, more smooth driving operations, improved navigation, and fewer cold starts (especially for shared/pooled AVs) could lower tailpipe emissions of air pollutants such as NO_x, CO, and CO_2 (Milakis et al., 2017). In the long run, heavy safety equipment may not be as necessary, thus reducing vehicle weights and emissions (Richland et al., 2016). Reduced vehicle emissions would yield public health benefits in population centers, but the overall emission (including GhG) impacts of increased electric energy demand depend upon the portfolio of energy generation methods in different regions. Areas with less renewable and more polluting electric energy sources would see less health benefits.

On the other hand, the impact of more trips and longer vehicle-distances traveled by AVs could work against some of these emissions reductions (Richland et al., 2016; Wang et al., 2018). While electric vehicle engines operate more quietly, the majority of road noise comes from tire/pavement interactions (Rochat and Reiter, 2016) that would be only modestly decreased (if at all) and potentially counteracted by increased traffic volumes and faster speeds (Sohrabi et al., 2020). The impacts of AVs on air pollution will likely depend greatly upon changes in travel demand as well as the degree to which AVs are also EVs (Crayton and Meier, 2017).

4.3.3 Other

These discussions do not include other secondary and tertiary impacts of AVs on people's lives that may have implications for health, well-being, and equity, but that may act outside of the transportation system or in transport-adjacent ways. Positively, affordable shared/pooled AVs could help economically disadvantaged households free themselves from the burden of auto ownership and spend more money on health care and healthy food. AVs could also reshape the last mile of shipping and shopping, allowing people (especially those with mobility limitations) cheaper, quicker, and easier ordering and delivery of groceries, prescriptions, and other consumer goods. Negatively, improved traffic safety may reduce organ transplant availability (Pettigrew, 2017). Replacing drivers with computers could eliminate hundreds of thousands of transportation industry jobs (Crayton and Meier, 2017; Fagnant and Kockelman, 2015; Sohrabi et al., 2020), and increased independent mobility for seniors could reduce employment in home care (Pettigrew et al., 2019). Nevertheless, Clements and Kockelman (2017) offer a comprehensive analysis of AV effects on different industries, including also job and efficiency gains in different sectors. They conclude that AVs will bring a net gain for the economy. Overall, consideration of the multitude of potential impacts of AVs on health and well-being, some of which may not be apparent today, requires an evolving systems approach.

5. Conclusions

In this chapter, we have aimed to fill a gap in the literature discussing potential health and well-being implications of AVs. Given the scarcity of empirical work on this topic, our perspectives are based on merging understanding of current transportation–health relationships with discussion on potential travel behavior changes in an AV-era. As our discussion of the positive, negative, and uncertain effects of AVs on health and well-being makes clear, there appear to be likely benefits (improved safety, satisfaction, and access) as well as disadvantages (reduced physical activity), but much about these and other impacts remains unknown. It is our hope that this chapter: (1) increases awareness of the importance of considering health/well-being impacts of AVs; (2) encourages policymakers to consider how best to facilitate health benefits and mitigate disadvantages of AVs; and (3) inspires researchers to study these relationships and impacts in more detail. Toward these latter two aims, we close this chapter by discussing potential policy implications and research programs.

5.1 Policy implications

Policy measures should try to limit the possible negative effects of AVs on health and well-being, such as reduced physically-active travel and increased vehicle-distances traveled and urban sprawl. Spatial planning policies creating compact and mixed-use neighborhoods and restricting new suburban neighborhoods located far away from city centers (i.e., urban sprawl) therefore remain important. Improved infrastructure for cyclists and pedestrians (e.g., separated bike lanes, broad sidewalks with safe crossings) could mitigate the active travel-reducing effect of AVs, especially if road space can be reallocated from automobile parking and travel lanes. Care should be taken to avoid further legal restrictions on how, where, and when pedestrians can access and cross streets, as conflicts with automatically-yielding vehicles may become a point of contention.

The types of AVs people use may have an impact on the severity of health impacts (Dean et al., 2019; Fitt et al., 2018). Private AVs could have more negative effects, such as additional and longer car trips (especially for holiday purposes) but also equity issues due to the large up-front costs. However, shared and pooled AVs may also be associated with increased distances traveled due to their lower capacity (compared to public transport), door-to-door service policy, and empty trips. Therefore, we would recommend that policymakers seeking to prioritize health and well-being should focus on provisions for active travel rather than placing high hopes on shared AVs.

Attention should also be paid to facilitating a more widespread and equitable distribution of the health and well-being benefits of AVs in the areas of safety, travel satisfaction, and access to activities. Zoning and other urban development policies should ensure that disadvantaged communities do not end up on the receiving end of large AV parking and circulation zones. Pricing or other policies could discourage AVs in places where they might compete with more healthy modes (like public transportation, walking, and bicycling in dense urban areas) and encourage AVs in more exurban and rural areas where they might improve access the most. The safety of non-occupants and vulnerable road users should be considered when developing collision avoidance and decision algorithms, as there are ethical issues involved in forced choice situations in which a collision is unavoidable (Bonnefon et al., 2016; Fleetwood, 2017; Goodall, 2017). Financial incentives and subsidies, as well as programs to develop technological skills, may be warranted to help people in poverty, older adults, or rural residents to use AVs to access healthy opportunities and experience improved independent mobility and well-being. Other policy and planning strategies for AVs (not necessarily focused on health/well-being) are described in Zmud et al. (2017).

5.2 Research agenda

The difficulty with analyzing the effects of AVs on health and well-being is that AVs are currently very niche. As a result, it is hard to measure how people will change their travel behavior and how this will affect health and well-being. Ideally, one would measure individual and/or population health outcomes or risk factors before and after the introduction of AVs, compared to a control group. While difficult to conduct, such experimental or quasi-experimental designs may start to be possible as AV technology advances and AV testbeds expand. In the meantime, various other research approaches are possible.

Stated choice experiments are a common way to study options or attributes that are rare or non-existent. Among stated choice approaches, most attention has been devoted to willingness-to-pay for AVs and choice of privately-owned vs shared/pooled AVs (Gkartzonikas and Gkritza, 2019). However, other choices—e.g., activity generation and scheduling, location choices—are also outcomes of interest. To estimate some of these effects, more stated choice experiments should be directed toward destination choice (including residential location choice, as in Krueger et al., 2019) and trip-making choice in the AV-era. Changes to daily activity schedules should also be considered (Pudāne et al., 2019).

This relates to a widely-known limitation of all stated choice studies: respondents' answers might differ from their real reaction to AVs in the future, partly because their knowledge of different types of AVs may be limited and partly because the options provided by the researchers may condition their answers. An alternative approach is to simulate AV trips in the real-world. A privately-owned self-driving vehicle could be mimicked by providing respondents a free chauffeur service for a certain period of time (see, for instance, Harb et al., 2018). Of course, the high expense associated with these types of experiments makes it difficult to obtain large sample sizes, negatively affecting representativeness. Another promising approach is to research travel behavior in locations where chauffeur-driven cars are commonplace (Wadud and Huda, 2019). As analog for shared/pooled AVs, the impacts of ride-hailing services on travel behaviors and mode shifts could be studied (e.g., Alemi et al., 2018; Clewlow and Mishra, 2017). In all cases, the presence of a human driver likely affects user trust of the service and, possibly, the availability of some activities during travel, therefore challenging the transferability of knowledge to a driver-less situation.

A different way to simulate AVs and their health/well-being effects is to develop scenarios and model the impacts. Recent tools—e.g., the Integrated Transport and Health Impact Modeling Tool, based in epidemiological evidence—can model the health impacts (due to traffic injuries, air pollution, and physical activity) of various transportation scenarios. These health impact modeling tools could conceivably be used to examine the impacts of various AV adoption or policy scenarios (Pourrahmani et al., 2020). This information would be particularly useful to gain a better understanding of the relative magnitude of the tradeoffs between the positive effects of improved safety and the negative effects of reduced physical activity. Recent studies have found that the physical activity benefits of scenarios or interventions with even modest increases in active travel far outweigh the elevated safety risks and pollution exposure (Mueller et al., 2015); although, those studies did not consider AV scenarios.

No matter what method is used, there are key research questions that could illuminate potential health and well-being impacts as AVs become more widely used. The degree to which people are willing to use (and pay for) the experiential and productivity benefits of AVs is a critical travel behavioral factor—affecting mode choices, travel amounts, and location choices—and should be further investigated. Similarly important is the value travelers assign to the privacy and personal attributes of private AVs over shared/pooled AVs, given their differing societal impacts. Across all areas, research should also pay more attention to equity considerations and the distribution of the benefits and costs of AVs.

Overall, the existing state of the knowledge suggests that the effects of AVs on health and well-being are still uncertain and require continued attention. Great benefits are expected from this innovation—such as improvements in traffic safety—but the ripples from AV introduction will likely spread beyond the most obvious gains and have more varied (and potentially negative) impacts on health and well-being. We hope that this chapter has shed light on these future possibilities and opened gateways for further research and discussion.

References

Alemi, F., Circella, G., Handy, S., Mokhtarian, P.L., 2018. What influences travelers to use Uber? Exploring the factors affecting the adoption of on-demand ride services in California. Travel Behav. Soc. 13, 88–104.

Auld, J., Sokolov, V., Stephens, T.S., 2017. Analysis of the effects of connected–automated vehicle technologies on travel demand. Transp. Res. Rec. 2625, 1–8.

Basner, M., Babisch, W., Davis, A., Brink, M., Clark, C., Janssen, S., Stansfeld, S., 2014. Auditory and nonauditory effects of noise on health. Lancet 383, 1325–1332.

Becker, F., Axhausen, K.W., 2017. Literature review on surveys investigating the acceptance of automated vehicles. Transportation 44 (6), 1293–1306.

Bennett, R., Vijaygopal, R., Kottasz, R., 2019. Willingness of people with mental health disabilities to travel in driverless vehicles. J. Transp. Health 12, 1–12.

Bonnefon, J.F., Shariff, A., Rahwan, I., 2016. The social dilemma of autonomous vehicles. Science 352, 1573–1576.

Bösch, P.M., Becker, F., Becker, H., Axhausen, K.W., 2018. Cost-based analysis of autonomous mobility services. Transp. Policy 64, 76–91.

Carrone, A.P., Hoening, V.M., Jensen, A.F., Mabit, S.E., Rich, J., 2019. Car sharing preferences and mode substitution: a stated choice experiment. In: Presented at the World Conference on Transport Research, Mumbai.

Cepeda, M., Schoufour, J., Freak-Poli, R., Koolhaas, C.M., Dhana, K., Bramer, W.M., Franco, O.H., 2017. Levels of ambient air pollution according to mode of transport: a systematic review. Lancet Public Health 2, e23–e34.

Childress, S., Nichols, B., Charlton, B., Coe, S., 2015. Using an activity-based model to explore the potential impacts of automated vehicles. Transp. Res. Rec. 2493, 99–106.
Clark, B., Chatterjee, K., Martin, A., Davis, A., 2019. How commuting affects subjective wellbeing. Transportation 1–29. https://doi.org/10.1007/s11116-019-09983-9.
Clements, L.M., Kockelman, K.M., 2017. Economic effects of automated vehicles. Transp. Res. Rec. 2606, 106–114.
Clewlow, R.R., Mishra, G.S., 2017. Disruptive transportation: the adoption, utilization, and impacts of ride-hailing in the United States. In: Research Report—UCD-ITS-RR-17-07. Institute of Transportation Studies, University of California, Davis.
Cohen, S., Shirazi, S., 2017. Can we Advance Social Equity with Shared, Autonomous and Electric Vehicles? Institute of Transportation Studies at the University of California, Davis.
Conway, M., Salon, D., King, D., 2018. Trends in taxi use and the advent of ridehailing, 1995–2017: evidence from the US National Household Travel Survey. Urban Sci. 2, 79.
Crayton, T.J., Meier, B.M., 2017. Autonomous vehicles: developing a public health research agenda to frame the future of transportation policy. J. Transp. Health 6, 245–252.
Curl, A., Fitt, H., Dionisio-McHugh, R., Ahuriri-Driscoll, A., Fletcher, A., Slaughter, H., 2018. Autonomous Vehicles and Future Urban Environments: Exploring Changing Travel Behaviours, Built Environments, and Implications for Wellbeing in an Ageing Society. National Science Challenge 11: Building Better Homes, Towns and Cities, Christchurch, NZ.
De Vos, J., 2018a. Do people travel with their preferred travel mode? Analysing the extent of travel mode dissonance and its effect on travel satisfaction. Transp. Res. A 117, 261–274.
De Vos, J., 2018b. Towards happy and healthy travelers: a research agenda. J. Transp. Health 11, 80–85.
De Vos, J., 2019. Analysing the effect of trip satisfaction on satisfaction with the leisure activity at the destination of the trip, in relationship with life satisfaction. Transportation 46, 623–645.
De Vos, J., Mokhtarian, P.L., Schwanen, T., Van Acker, V., Witlox, F., 2016. Travel mode choice and travel satisfaction: bridging the gap between decision utility and experienced utility. Transportation 43, 771–796.
De Vos, J., Schwanen, T., Van Acker, V., Witlox, F., 2013. Travel and subjective well-being: a focus on findings, methods and future research needs. Transp. Rev. 33, 421–442.
De Vos, J., Witlox, F., 2017. Travel satisfaction revisited. On the pivotal role of travel satisfaction in conceptualising a travel behaviour process. Transp. Res. A 106, 364–373.
Dean, J., Wray, A.J., Braun, L., Casello, J.M., McCallum, L., Gower, S., 2019. Holding the keys to health? A scoping study of the population health impacts of automated vehicles. BMC Public Health 19, 1258.
Delbosc, A., Currie, G., 2011. Exploring the relative influences of transport disadvantage and social exclusion on well-being. Transp. Policy 18, 555–562.
Department for Transport (DfT), 2018. Transport Statistics Great Britain. https://www.gov.uk/government/collections/transport-statistics-great-britain#about-the-transport-statistics-great-britain-data-and-reports, accessed 20 December 2018.
European Environment Agency (EEA), 2014. Noise in Europe 2014. EEA, Luxemburg.
EEA, 2018a. Greenhouse Gas Emissions From Transport. https://www.eea.europa.eu/data-and-maps/indicators/transport-emissions-of-greenhouse-gases/transport-emissions-of-greenhouse-gases-11, accessed 13 July 2019.
EEA, 2018b. Transport Emissions. https://ec.europa.eu/clima/policies/transport_en, accessed 12 September 2018.
EEA, 2018c. Environmental Noise, Briefing. https://www.eea.europa.eu/airs/2018/environment-and-health/environmental-noise, accessed 13 July 2019.

Ettema, D., Friman, M., Gärling, T., Olsson, L.E., Fujii, S., 2012. How in-vehicle activities affect work commuters' satisfaction with public transport. J. Transp. Geogr. 24, 215–222.
Ettema, D., Gärling, T., Eriksson, L., Friman, M., Olsson, L.E., Fujii, S., 2011. Satisfaction with travel and subjective well-being: development and test of a measurement tool. Transport. Res. F 14, 167–175.
Ettema, D., Gärling, T., Olsson, L.E., Friman, M., 2010. Out-of-home activities, daily travel, and subjective well-being. Transp. Res. A 44, 723–732.
Fagnant, D.J., Kockelman, K., 2015. Preparing a nation for autonomous vehicles: opportunities, barriers and policy recommendations. Transp. Res. A 77, 167–181.
Ferdman, A., 2020. Corporate ownership of automated vehicles: discussing potential negative externalities. Transp. Rev. 40, 95–113.
Fitt, H., Curl, A., Dionisio-McHugh, R., Fletcher, A., Frame, B., Ahuriri-Driscoll, A., 2018. Think Piece: Autonomous Vehicles and Future Urban Environments: Exploring Implications for Wellbeing in an Ageing Society, second ed. National Science Challenge 11: Building Better Homes, Towns and Cities, Christchurch, NZ.
Fleetwood, J., 2017. Public health, ethics, and autonomous vehicles. Am. J. Public Health 107, 532–537.
Fraedrich, E., Heinrichs, D., Bahamonde-Birke, F.J., Cyganski, R., 2019. Autonomous driving, the built environment and policy implications. Transp. Res. A 122, 162–172.
Friman, M., Olsson, L.E., Ståhl, M., Ettema, D., Gärling, T., 2017. Travel and residual emotional wellbeing. Transport. Res. F 49, 159–176.
Gehrke, S., Felix, A., Reardon, T., 2018. Fare Choices: A Survey of Ride-Hailing Passengers in Metro Boston. Metropolitan Area Planning Council, Boston.
Giles-Corti, B., Vernez-Moudon, A., Reis, R., Turrell, G., Dannenberg, A.L., Badland, H., … Owen, N., 2016. City planning and population health: a global challenge. Lancet 388, 2912–2924.
Gkartzonikas, C., Gkritza, K., 2019. What have we learned? A review of stated preference and choice studies on autonomous vehicles. Transp. Res. C 98, 323–337.
Goodall, N.J., 2017. From trolleys to risk: models for ethical autonomous driving. Am. J. Public Health 107, 496.
Haboucha, C.J., Ishaq, R., Shiftan, Y., 2017. User preferences regarding autonomous vehicles. Transp. Res. C 78, 37–49.
Handy, S., 2014. Health and travel. In: Gärling, T., Ettema, D., Friman, M. (Eds.), Handbook of Sustainable Travel. Springer, Dordrecht, pp. 199–214.
Harb, M., Xiao, Y., Circella, G., Mokhtarian, P.L., Walker, J.L., 2018. Projecting travelers into a world of self-driving vehicles: estimating travel behavior implications via a naturalistic experiment. Transportation 45, 1671–1685.
Harper, C.D., Hendrickson, C.T., Mangones, S., Samaras, C., 2016. Estimating potential increases in travel with autonomous vehicles for the non-driving, elderly and people with travel-restrictive medical conditions. Transp. Res. C 72, 1–9.
Heinen, E., van Wee, B., Maat, K., 2010. Commuting by bicycle: an overview of the literature. Transp. Rev. 30, 59–96.
Heinrichs, D., 2016. Autonomous driving and urban land use. In: Maurer, M., Gerdes, J.C., Lenz, B., Winner, H. (Eds.), Autonomous Driving: Technical, Legal and Social Aspects. Springer Nature, pp. 213–231.
Higgins, C.D., Sweet, M.N., Kanaroglou, P.S., 2018. All minutes are not equal: travel time and the effects of congestion on commute satisfaction in Canadian cities. Transportation 45, 1249–1268.
Eurostat, 2017. Transport Accident Statistics. https://ec.europa.eu/eurostat/statistics-explained/pdfscache/7375.pdf, accessed 13 July 2019.
Jain, J., Lyons, G., 2008. The gift of travel time. J. Transp. Geogr. 16, 81–89.

Kaufmann, V., Bergman, M.M., Joye, D., 2004. Motility: mobility as capital. Int. J. Urban Reg. Res. 28, 745–756.
Kelly, P., Kahlmeier, S., Götschi, T., Orsini, N., Richards, J., Roberts, N., Scarborough, P., Foster, C., 2014. Systematic review and meta-analysis of reduction in all-cause mortality from walking and cycling and shape of dose response relationship. Int. J. Behav. Nutr. Phys. Act. 11, 132.
Krueger, R., Rashidi, T.H., Dixit, V.V., 2019. Autonomous driving and residential location preferences: evidence from a stated choice survey. Transp. Res. C Emerg. Technol. 108, 255–268.
Krueger, R., Rashidi, T.H., Rose, J.M., 2016. Preferences for shared autonomous vehicles. Transp. Res. C 69, 343–355.
Laird, J., Geurs, K., Nash, C., 2009. Option and non-use values and rail project appraisal. Transp. Policy 16, 173–182.
LaMondia, J.J., Fagnant, D.J., Qu, H., Barrett, J., Kockelman, K., 2016. Shifts in long-distance travel mode due to automated vehicles: statewide mode-shift simulation experiment and travel survey analysis. Transp. Res. Rec. 2566, 1–11.
Lavieri, P.S., Bhat, C.R., 2019. Modeling individuals' willingness to share trips with strangers in an autonomous vehicle future. Transp. Res. Rec. 124, 242–261.
Lee, I.M., Shiroma, E.J., Lobelo, F., Puska, P., Blair, S.N., Katzmarzyk, P.T., 2012. Effect of physical inactivity on major non-communicable diseases worldwide: an analysis of burden of disease and life expectancy. Lancet 380, 219–229.
Legrain, A., Eluru, N., El-Geneidy, A., 2015. Am stressed, must travel: the relationship between mode choice and commuting stress. Transport. Res. F 34, 141–151.
Loong, C., van Lierop, D., El-Geneidy, A., 2017. On time and ready to go: an analysis of commuters' punctuality and energy levels at work or school. Transport. Res. F 45, 1–13.
Lucas, K., 2012. Transport and social exclusion: where are we now? Transp. Policy 20, 105–113.
Lyons, G., Jain, J., Holley, D., 2007. The use of travel time by rail passengers in Great Britain. Transp. Res. A 41, 107–120.
Lyubomirsky, S., King, L., Diener, E., 2005. The benefits of frequent positive affect: does happiness lead to success? Psychol. Bull. 131, 803–855.
Malekafzali, S., 2009. Healthy, Equitable Transportation Policy: Recommendations and Research. PolicyLink, Oakland.
Meyer, J., Becker, H., Bösch, P.M., Axhausen, K.W., 2017. Autonomous vehicles: the next jump in accessibilities? Res. Transp. Econ. 62, 80–91.
Milakis, D., Van Arem, B., Van Wee, B., 2017. Policy and society related implications of automated driving: a review of literature and directions for future research. J. Intell. Transp. Syst. 21, 324–348.
Mokhtarian, P.L., 2018. The times they are a-changin': what do the expanding uses of travel time portend for policy, planning, and life? Transp. Res. Rec. 2672, 1–11.
Mokhtarian, P.L., 2019. Subjective well-being and travel: retrospect and prospect. Transportation 46, 493–513.
Morris, E.A., 2015. Should we all just stay home? Travel, out-of-home activities, and life satisfaction. Transp. Res. A 78, 519–536.
Morris, E.A., Guerra, E., 2015. Are we there yet? Trip duration and mood during travel. Transp. Res. F 33, 38–47.
Morris, E.A., Zhou, Y., 2018. Are long commutes short on benefits? Commute duration and various manifestations of well-being. Travel Behav. Soc. 11, 101–110.
Mueller, N., Rojas-Rueda, D., Cole-Hunter, T., de Nazelle, A., Dons, E., Gerike, R., Goetschi, T., Panis, L.I., Kahlmeier, S., Nieuwenhuijsen, M., 2015. Health impact assessment of active transportation: a systematic review. Prev. Med. 76, 103–114.
Nazari, F., Noruzoliaee, M., Mohammadian, A.K., 2018. Shared versus private mobility: modeling public interest in autonomous vehicles accounting for latent attitudes. Transp. Res. C 97, 456–477.

OECD, 2019. Road Accidents. https://data.oecd.org/transport/road-accidents.htm, accessed 13 July 2019.
Chief Medical Officers, 2011. Start Active, Stay Active: A Report on Physical Activity from the Four Home Countries. Department of Health, Physical Activity, Health Improvement and Protection, London.
Ostermeijer, F., Koster, H.R., van Ommeren, J., 2019. Residential parking costs and car ownership: implications for parking policy and automated vehicles. Reg. Sci. Urban Econ. 77, 276–288.
Pakusch, C., Stevens, G., Boden, A., Bossauer, P., 2018. Unintended effects of autonomous driving: a study on mobility preferences in the future. Sustainability 10, 2404.
Patterson, R., McNamara, E., Tainio, M., de Sá, T.H., Smith, A.D., Sharp, S.J., Edwards, P., Woodcock, J., Brage, S., Wijndaele, K., 2018. Sedentary behaviour and risk of all-cause, cardiovascular and cancer mortality, and incident type 2 diabetes: a systematic review and dose response meta-analysis. Eur. J. Epidemiol. 33, 811–829.
Petit, J., Shladover, S.E., 2014. Potential cyberattacks on automated vehicles. IEEE Trans. Intell. Transp. Syst. 16, 546–556.
Pettigrew, S., 2017. Why public health should embrace the autonomous car. Aust. N. Z. J. Public Health 41, 1–3.
Pettigrew, S., Talati, Z., Norman, R., 2018. The health benefits of autonomous vehicles: public awareness and receptivity in Australia. Aust. N. Z. J. Public Health 42, 480–483.
Pettigrew, S., Cronin, S.L., Norman, R., 2019. Brief report: the unrealized potential of autonomous vehicles for an aging population. J. Aging Soc. Policy 31 (5), 486–496.
Pfleging, B., Rang, M., Broy, N., 2016. Investigating user needs for non-driving-related activities during automated driving. In: Proceedings of the 15th International Conference on Mobile and Ubiquitous Multimedia. ACM, pp. 91–99.
Pourrahmani, E., Jaller, M., Maizlish, N., Rodier, C., 2020. Health impact assessment of autonomous vehicles in San Francisco, Bay Area using the Integrated Transport and Health Impacts Model (ITHIM). In: Presented at the 99th Annual Meeting of the Transportation Research Board, Washington, DC.
Pudāne, B., Molin, E.J., Arentze, T.A., Maknoon, Y., Chorus, C.G., 2018. A time-use model for the automated vehicle-era. Transp. Res. C 93, 102–114.
Pudāne, B., Rataj, M., Molin, E.J., Mouter, N., van Cranenburgh, S., Chorus, C.G., 2019. How will automated vehicles shape users' daily activities? Insights from focus groups with commuters in the Netherlands. Transp. Res. D 71, 222–235.
Richland, J., Lee, J., Butto, E.D., 2016. Steering Autonomous Vehicle Policy: The Role of Public Health. Altarum Institute, Washington, DC.
Rochat, J.L., Reiter, D., 2016. Highway traffic noise. Acoust. Today 12, 38–47.
Shaw, F.A., Malokin, A., Mokhtarian, P.L., Circella, G., 2019. It's not all fun and games: an investigation of the reported benefits and disadvantages of conducting activities while commuting. Travel Behav. Soc. 17, 8–25.
Singleton, P.A., 2019a. Discussing the "positive utilities" of autonomous vehicles: will travelers really use their time productively? Transp. Rev. 39, 50–65.
Singleton, P.A., 2019b. Walking (and cycling) to well-being: modal and other determinants of subjective well-being during the commute. Travel Behav. Soc. 16, 249–261.
Sohrabi, S., Khreis, H., Lord, D., 2020. Autonomous vehicles and public health: a conceptual model and policy recommendation. In: Presented at the 99th Annual Meeting of the Transportation Research Board, Washington, DC. https://ceprofs.civil.tamu.edu/dlord/Papers/Sohrabi_et_al_AV_Health_TRB.pdf, accessed 1 December 2019.
Soteropoulos, A., Berger, M., Ciari, F., 2019. Impacts of automated vehicles on travel behavior and land use: an international review of modelling studies. Transp. Rev. 39, 29–49.
Stark, J., Meschik, M., Singleton, P.A., Schützhofer, B., 2018. Active school travel, attitudes and psychological well-being of children. Transp. Res. F 56, 453–465.

St-Louis, E., Manaugh, K., van Lierop, D., El-Geneidy, A., 2014. The happy commuter: a comparison of commuter satisfaction across modes. Transp. Res. F 26, 160–170.
Stoiber, T., Schubert, I., Hoerler, R., Burger, P., 2019. Will consumers prefer shared and pooled-use autonomous vehicles? A stated choice experiment with Swiss households. Transp. Res. D 71, 265–282.
Strand, N., Nilsson, J., Karlsson, I.M., Nilsson, L., 2014. Semi-automated versus highly automated driving in critical situations caused by automation failures. Transp. Res. F 27, 218–228.
Stutzer, A., Frey, B.S., 2008. Stress that doesn't pay: the commuting paradox. Scand. J. Econ. 110, 339–366.
U.S. Department of Transportation (USDOT), 2015. Critical Reasons for Crashes Investigated in the National Motor Vehicle Crash Causation Survey. USDOT, Washington.
USDOT, 2019. Traffic Facts Annual Reports Tables. https://cdan.nhtsa.gov/tsftables/tsfar.htm, accessed 1 July 2019.
van Wee, B., Ettema, D., 2016. Travel behaviour and health: a conceptual model and research agenda. J. Transp. Health 3, 240–248.
van Wee, B., van Cranenburgh, S., Maat, K., 2019. Substitutability as a spatial concept to evaluate travel alternatives. J. Transp. Geogr. 79, 102469.
Wadud, Z., Huda, F.Y., 2019. Fully automated vehicles: The use of travel time and its association with intention to use. Proc. Inst. Civ. Eng. Transp. 1–15. https://doi.org/10.1680/jtran.18.00134.
Wang, A., Stogios, C., Gai, Y., Vaughan, J., Ozonder, G., Lee, S., … Hatzopoulou, M., 2018. Automated, electric, or both? Investigating the effects of transportation and technology scenarios on metropolitan greenhouse gas emissions. Sustain. Cities Soc. 40, 524–533.
Westman, J., Olsson, L.E., Gärling, T., Friman, M., 2017. Children's travel to school: satisfaction, current mood, and cognitive performance. Transportation 44, 1365–1382.
World Health Organization (WHO), 2010. Global Recommendations on Physical Activity for Health. WHO, Geneva.
WHO, 2018a. Global Status Report on Road Safety. WHO, Geneva.
WHO, 2018b. Ambient (Outdoor) Air Quality and Health. https://www.who.int/en/news-room/fact-sheets/detail/ambient-(outdoor)-air-quality-and-health, accessed 13 July 2019.
WHO, 2018c. Physical Activity. https://www.who.int/news-room/fact-sheets/detail/physical-activity, accessed 13 July 2019.
WHO, 2018d. Environmental Noise Guidelines for the European Region. WHO, Copenhagen.
WHO, 2019a. Transport and Health Risks. https://www.who.int/sustainable-development/transport/health-risks/en/, accessed 11 November 2019.
WHO, 2019b. Air Pollution. https://www.who.int/sustainable-development/transport/health-risks/air-pollution/en/, accessed 13 July 2019.
Ye, R., Titheridge, H., 2017. Satisfaction with the commute: the role of travel mode choice, built environment and attitudes. Transp. Res. D 52 (Pt. B), 535–547.
Zakharenko, R., 2016. Self-driving cars will change cities. Reg. Sci. Urban Econ. 61, 26–37.
Zhu, J., Fan, Y., 2018. Daily travel behavior and emotional well-being: effects of trip mode, duration, purpose, and companionship. Transp. Res. A 118, 360–373.
Zmud, J., Goodin, G., Moran, M., Kalra, N., Thorn, E., 2017. Advancing Automated and Connected Vehicles: Policy and Planning Strategies for State and Local Transportation Agencies. National Cooperative Highway Research Program, Washington.
Zmud, J., Sener, I.N., Wagner, J., 2016. Self-driving vehicles: determinants of adoption and conditions of usage. Transp. Res. Rec. 2565, 57–64.

CHAPTER EIGHT

Autonomous vehicles in a GDPR era: An international comparison

Federico Costantini[a,*], Nikolas Thomopoulos[b], Fabro Steibel[c], Angela Curl[d], Giuseppe Lugano[e], Tatiana Kováčiková[e]
[a]Department of Law, University of Udine, Udine, Italy
[b]Department of Tourism and Transport, School of Hospitality and Tourism Management, University of Surrey, Guildford, United Kingdom
[c]Institute for Technology and Society of Rio de Janeiro, Rio de Janeiro, Brazil
[d]Department of Population Health, University of Otago Christchurch, Dunedin, New Zealand
[e]Department of International Research Projects, University of Žilina, Žilina, Slovakia
[*]Corresponding author: e-mail address: federico.costantini@uniud.it

Contents

Abstract

Due to the extensive amount of data generated by an autonomous vehicle (AV) and the information flowing among AVs and through surrounding infrastructure, data governance legislation poses as a significant challenge especially in the perspective of their large-scale introduction. Regulation (EU) 2016/679, which is known as GDPR and entered into force in May 2018, has been a tipping point in personal data protection even in countries outside the European Union (EU). Although the majority of EU

Advances in Transport Policy and Planning, Volume 5
ISSN 2543-0009
https://doi.org/10.1016/bs.atpp.2020.02.005

member States have already adapted their legal systems to its provisions, a few others are still on the process, and institutions and companies are challenged by the need to comply. This chapter conducts a mapping review of existing regulations in seven countries, namely Austria, Brazil, Greece, Italy, New Zealand, Slovakia and Switzerland, to assess policy challenges of AV testing and deployment focusing on the implications in terms of data protection. Potential areas of cooperation are identified, as well as evidence of divergent approaches, which are discussed in order to provide valuable suggestions for policy making at local, European and international level for AV testing and deployment.

Keywords: GDPR, Data protection, International comparison, AVs trials, Regulatory sandboxes, Living labs

1. AVs as disruptive technologies: A brief overview about transport policy challenges

Information has become more important and valuable than ever, with some stating that data might be considered as the currency of the 21st century (Floridi, 2014; Harari, 2018). Even in transport, data are equally vital as vehicles and infrastructures for the seamless operation of advanced systems and deriving business eco-systems rapidly grown around them (Costantini et al., 2019; Floridi, 2019b; Thomopoulos et al., 2015). It can be argued that as the concept of transport, originally bound to the physical displacement of passengers and freight, is turning into a more sophisticated, inclusive and incorporeal concept, the automotive industry is being transformed from hardware- to software-focused (Kováčiková et al., 2018).

Concurrently, in the attempt of addressing those emerging technologies (Rotolo et al., 2015), legal frameworks are facing equally profound transformation (Glancy, 2012; Lugano et al., 2019). Indeed, in developed countries Information and Communication Technology (ICT) has been required to protect data sources and communication since the beginning of the 21st century. Such frameworks have been also linked with advancements within the Intelligent Transport Systems (ITS) sector. The contemporary EU (European Union) regulation in ITS is underpinned by the Directive 2010/40/EU,[a] the Delegated Regulations based on it—namely Delegated

[a] Directive 2010/40/EU of the European Parliament and of the Council of July 7, 2010 on the framework for the deployment of Intelligent Transport Systems in the field of road transport and for interfaces with other modes of transport (OJ L 207, 6.8.2010, p. 1–13).

Regulation No 305/2013,[b] No 885/2013,[c] No 886/2013,[d] No 2015/962,[e] No 2017/79[f] and No 2017/1926[g]—besides the EU Regulation 2015/758[h] and two European Commission decisions.[i]

In this context, the recent global expansion of AVs[j] represents a potential disruptive innovation (Christensen and Bower, 1996; Christensen et al., 2015; Yu and Hang, 2010).[k] Indeed, as many other technologies currently being introduced and tested worldwide, such as artificial intelligence (AI), cloud computing, distributed ledger technology (DLT), AVs promise a revolutionary impact on the transport and mobility sectors (Hogan and Helfert, 2019; Hogan et al., 2019), presenting extraordinary opportunities,

[b] Namely, Commission Delegated Regulation (EU) No 305/2013 of November 26, 2012 supplementing Directive 2010/40/EU of the European Parliament and of the Council with regard to the harmonized provision for an interoperable EU-wide eCall (OJ L 91, 3.4.2013, p. 1–4).

[c] Commission Delegated Regulation (EU) No 885/2013 of May 15, 2013 supplementing ITS Directive 2010/40/EU of the European Parliament and of the Council with regard to the provision of information services for safe and secure parking places for trucks and commercial vehicles (OJ L 247, 18.9.2013, p. 1–5).

[d] Commission Delegated Regulation (EU) No 886/2013 of May 15, 2013 supplementing Directive 2010/40/EU of the European Parliament and of the Council with regard to data and procedures for the provision, where possible, of road safety-related minimum universal traffic information free of charge to users (OJ L 247, 18.9.2013, p. 6–10).

[e] Commission Delegated Regulation (EU) 2015/962 of December 18, 2014 supplementing Directive 2010/40/EU of the European Parliament and of the Council with regard to the provision of EU-wide real-time traffic information services (OJ L 157, 23.6.2015, p. 21–31).

[f] Commission Delegated Regulation (EU) 2017/79 of September 12, 2016 establishing detailed technical requirements and test procedures for the EC type-approval of motor vehicles with respect to their 112-based eCall in-vehicles systems, of 112-based eCall in-vehicle separate technical units and components and supplementing and amending Regulation (EU) 2015/758 of the European Parliament and of the Council with regard to the exemptions and applicable standards (OJ L 12, 17.1.2017, p. 44–85).

[g] Commission Delegated Regulation (EU) 2017/1926 of May 31, 2017 supplementing Directive 2010/40/EU of the European Parliament and of the Council with regard to the provision of EU-wide multimodal travel information services (OJ L 272, 21.10.2017, p. 1–13).

[h] Regulation (EU) 2015/758 of the European Parliament and of the Council of April 29, 2015 concerning type-approval requirements for the deployment of the eCall in-vehicle system based on the 112 service and amending Directive 2007/46/EC (OJ L 123, 19.5.2015, p. 77–89).

[i] Namely, Decision No 585/2014/EU of the European Parliament and of the Council of May 15, 2014 on the deployment of the interoperable EU-wide eCall service (OJ L 164, 3.6.2014, p. 6–9), and Decision (EU) 2017/2380 of the European Parliament and of the Council of December 12, 2017 amending Directive 2010/40/EU as regards the period for adopting delegated acts (OJ L 340, 20.12.2017, p. 1–3).

[j] Although no consensus exists among academics and practitioners regarding the definition of AVs, this chapter focuses on wider data management and protection issues which are intertwined with highly automated or fully automated, i.e., autonomous vehicles. Therefore, no attempt is made to define the term AV more precisely since this is beyond the scope of this chapter, but may as well be addressed within this book.

[k] In this chapter we use the concept of "disruptive technology," which is widely accepted, since others, as "emerging technologies," are debated among scholars (Rotolo et al., 2015).

as well as many concerns in different fields (urban development, transport equity, environmental sustainability, labor market, cybersecurity, data protection) as some studies recently pointed out (Alavi et al., 2018; Blyth et al., 2016; Floridi, 2019a; Ronzhyn and Wimmer 2019). As a matter of fact, an increasing number of vehicle manufacturers are already entering this market, along with multiple city authorities aiming at reaping potential benefits (Milakis et al., 2017; Thomopoulos and Givoni, 2015) and a lot of initiatives have been already adopted by the EU or are currently in progress concerning *Cooperative Intelligent Transport Systems* (or also "C-ITS") according to COM/2016/766.[l]

Since effects of disruptive technologies are uncertain, and consequences could be impossible to control potentially irreparable large-scale damages, in recent years governments are tackling disruptive technologies with a new kind of legislation, namely "regulatory sandboxes." Indeed, legal provisions are enacted specifically to create restricted environments where, under given conditions, new technologies along with relevant regulations are tested, minimizing the risk of drawbacks (Zetzsche et al., 2017). Despite that "regulatory sandboxes" could be the most suitable tool for legislators to manage uncertainty, it has to be said that such initiatives *per se* do not exclude the possibility of unexpected outcomes but certainly increase the complexity of legal frameworks, which are already challenged by others factors, such as the multiplication of legal sources brought by globalization and regionalism, as well as the risk of different treatment for the same cases brought by the fragmentation of jurisprudence. Consequently, uncertainty, which is inevitable in a complex legal system, could be increased by the introduction of "regulatory sandboxes."

This approach has been adopted by several countries also in Europe. Indeed, apart from "Living Labs" which have been introduced for mobility and IT services for a number of years already (e.g., FP-7 SUNSET),[m] new ones have emerged in Slovenia,[n] Spain[o] and the UK.[p] Such sandboxes include advanced AV proving grounds realized in Sweden[q] and Hungary[r] (Alonso Raposo and Ciuffo, 2019), while a range of other similar grounds

[l] COM/2016/766 final of November 30, 2016. *A European strategy on Cooperative Intelligent Transport Systems, a milestone toward cooperative, connected and automated mobility.*

[m] www.sunset-project.eu.

[n] http://avlivinglab.com.

[o] http://catalonialivinglab.com.

[p] https://www.smartmobility.london.

[q] http://www.astazero.com.

[r] https://zalazone.hu.

are under development. On this account it is important to underline that it is the EU suggesting the implementation of "regulatory sandboxes" in fields where AI could be deployed with unpredictable consequences, as stated in COM(2018) 237 of April 25, 2018, *Artificial Intelligence for Europe* (p. 9). Specifically, the development of testing facilities where AVs can be safely experimented is encouraged in COM(2018) 795 of December 7, 2018, *Coordinated Plan on Artificial Intelligence* (Annex, p. 8) and in the High Level Expert Group Policy *Investment Recommendations for Trustworthy AI* of June 26, 2019 (p. 27), and endorsed in many initiatives at a national level such as the one adopted by Germany (German Federal Government, *Artificial Intelligence Strategy*, November 2018).

Data governance in ITS and in particular of AVs is crucial, since information is the key not only for implementing technologies, but also for evaluating their social impact and even for establishing policies and thus legal regulation. In addition, it has to be considered that technologies are often applied in combination and in the future they will be even more deeply intertwined—for example, the implementation of DLT in ITS (Hogan and Helfert, 2019; Hogan et al., 2019)—making both their impact more disruptive and their assessment more challenging. Finally, it is important to highlight that the data relating to AVs can differ not only by nature (personal and not personal data, as elaborated in the next section) but also by content (ordinary working conditions of ITS or test results of AVs). Therefore it is necessary to shape an innovative approach that encompasses all these considerations testing them into practice.

2. Data protection and AVs: Implementing GDPR in the EU and cooperating with other countries

It is noteworthy that the aforementioned legal provisions are integrated with others about cybersecurity and data protection, such as Directive (EU) 2016/1148 "Network Information Security" (also "NIS"),[s] Regulation (EU) 2016/679 ("General Data Protection Regulation," henceforth GDPR),[t]

[s] Directive (EU) 2016/1148 of the European Parliament and of the Council of July 6, 2016 concerning measures for a high common level of security of network and information systems across the Union (OJ L 194, 19.7.2016, p. 1–30).

[t] Regulation (EU) 2016/679 of the European Parliament and of the Council of April 27, 2016 on the protection of natural persons with regard to the processing of personal data and on the free movement of such data, and repealing Directive 95/46/EC (OJ L 119, 4.5.2016, p. 1–88).

Directive (EU) 2016/680,[u] Directive (EU) 2016/681[v] and the most recent EU Regulation 2018/1807[w] concerning the free flow or non-personal data, which entered into force on May 29, 2019. Further provisions are anticipated to be enacted when EU Directive 2002/58 will be repealed by a regulation which was under discussion in 2019.[x]

GDPR is the prominent legislation regarding data protection within the EU, setting also a global standard, as it represents the backbone of the future EU digital economy. Indeed, GDPR replaces previous Data Protection Directive 95/46/EC,[y] introducing several crucial improvements (Voigt and Von Dem Bussche, 2017), rewriting former fundamental principles and complementing them with the requirement of accountability (article 5, Paragraph 2), which becomes the cornerstone of GDPR compliance. Furthermore, it imposes new obligations for the Data Controller, such as the "Data Breach" notification (articles 33 and 34) and the Data Impact Assessment (article 35), while introducing new roles as the Data Processor (article 28) and the Data Protection Officer (articles 37–39). Third, it increases the rights of the Data Subject establishing new prerogatives, including the "right to be forgotten" (article 17), which before was only declared by the notorious decision "Google Spain."[z] Lastly, it reorganizes the institutional network of European and national authorities (Chapter IV), while redesigning the criteria for assigning and assessing responsibilities in case of infringement (Chapter VII). In sum, GDPR paves the way for an advanced legal framework in personal data protection, setting an international standard concept of data governance.

[u] Directive (EU) 2016/680 of the European Parliament and of the Council of April 27, 2016 on the protection of natural persons with regard to the processing of personal data by competent authorities for the purposes of the prevention, investigation, detection or prosecution of criminal offenses or the execution of criminal penalties, and on the free movement of such data, and repealing Council Framework Decision 2008/977/JHA (OJ L 119, 4.5.2016, p. 89–131).

[v] Directive (EU) 2016/681 of the European Parliament and of the Council of April 27, 2016 on the use of passenger name record (PNR) data for the prevention, detection, investigation and prosecution of terrorist offenses and serious crime (OJ L 119, 4.5.2016, p. 132–149).

[w] Regulation (EU) 2018/1807 of the European Parliament and of the Council of November 14, 2018 on a framework for the free flow of non-personal data in the European Union (OJ L 303, 28.11.2018, p. 59–68).

[x] COM (2017) 10: Proposal for a Regulation Of The European Parliament And Of The Council concerning the respect for private life and the protection of personal data in electronic communications and repealing Directive 2002/58/EC (Regulation on Privacy and Electronic Communications), Procedure 2017/0003/COD.

[y] Directive 95/46/EC of the European Parliament and of the Council of October 24, 1995 on the protection of individuals with regard to the processing of personal data and on the free movement of such data (OJ L 281, 23.11.1995, p. 31–50).

[z] Judgment of the Court (Grand Chamber), May 13, 2014, Google Spain SL and Google Inc. v. Agencia Española de Protección de Datos (AEPD) and Mario Costeja González, Case C-131/12, ECLI:EU:C:2014:317.

Under the GDPR regulation, institutions and companies can ensure risk management and process optimization (Gellert, 2018) adopting a proactive approach toward incoming technologies, particularly about the Internet of Things and Artificial Intelligence (Pagallo et al., 2019; Wachter, 2018; Wiatrowski, 2018). Indeed, efficient data management brings together essential people, processes, and technologies to safeguard increasingly understandable, accurate, complete, reliable, secure, and discoverable data, thus protecting business assets and supporting economic growth.

Within this rapidly changing context, data collection and processing through AVs raises multiple legal issues depending on the information management framework in place, no matter if it takes place within controlled environments (e.g., proving grounds) or within public space (e.g., public roads).

In the first case, it can be observed that the main principle is confidentiality, which is applicable for any type of data. Among them, a peculiar category is represented by "personal data," which are related to identified—or identifiable—physical individuals. Despite that some rights are granted to drivers, passengers or pedestrians as "*data subjects*" (article 4(1) GDPR), in principle the ownership of such data is entitled exclusively to those who ultimately control them, and so are defined as the "*Data Processor*" (article 4(7) GDPR). According to Delegated Regulation (EU) 2015/962, "*accessibility, exchange and re-use*" of special kinds of data, specifically "static road data" (article 4), "dynamic road data" (article 5) and "traffic data" (article 6) have to be granted. Furthermore, an EU regulation defines the technological standard to be adopted for data transmission, which is currently DATEX II.[aa] The key purpose of such provisions is naturally road safety, which constitutes a primary objective nationally (e.g., Sweden, UK) or internationally (e.g., EU).

In the second case, data are crucial for AV deployment both within pub lic space and within Living Labs, since they embody precisely the purpose of such experiments. As it can be easily imagined, also due to the huge investments made to design, build and maintain vehicles, onboard devices and infrastructure, the value of respective findings achieves a strategic objective not only in terms of pure research outcomes, but also of industrial production and even of geopolitical strategic needs. On one hand, the general interest in sharing the final results of public funding may be prioritized or, at least, allowing interested parties to take an indirect advantage out of them. On the other hand, there is a legitimate expectation of a proportionate benefit by those who contribute in the early stages of such endeavors and investments.

[aa] https://datex2.eu/.

Data management and protection is unsurprisingly placed at the core of this challenge, since investors would be entitled without exceptions granting any "accessibility, exchange and re-use"—or else—to the general public or to third parties.

All of the legislation previously outlined may be suitable in addressing past or contemporary challenges, yet it is largely unknown whether it will be fit for purpose in addressing with the same efficacy the forthcoming disruptive innovations including AV deployment. Due to the increased significance of data in emerging AV value chains, the regulatory frameworks surrounding AVs and AV trials, particularly about ethical, legal and social (ELS) challenges (Thomopoulos et al., 2015), are still at an embryonic stage. Aside a handful of US states (e.g., Arizona, California, Nevada) and European countries (e.g., UK) which have already introduced the first wave of relevant regulations, most countries are still adapting to the broad requirements of GDPR or their equivalent national legislation. However, given the vast volume of data that would be generated daily by AVs, it is critical to formulate such regulations. Moreover, it is essential to foster cross-country collaboration regarding data management not only in the EU where many member states are closely interconnected, e.g., through a borderless area (Schengen area), but also internationally across countries and continents. Due to existing global supply chains of vehicle manufacturing and since vehicle manufacturers already state in their Terms and Conditions of sale that all vehicle generated data is owned by them, it is apparent that this is a field of international concern for both practitioners and policy makers.

Therefore, this chapter reviews existing data protection regulations and policies directly related to ICT, transport and AV regulations as well as policies in different countries and continents, namely Austria, Brazil, Greece, Italy, New Zealand, Slovakia and Switzerland to assess policy challenges of AV deployment and the deriving data management and protection implications. New mobility services are used as a proxy for the policy and regulatory context in an AV and GDPR era. Through this mapping review, this chapter highlights cross-country similarities and variations focusing on key implications for AVs, classified in selected categories. Ultimately, this synthesis chapter (van Wee and Banister, 2016) contributes in identifying contemporary synergies and gaps in advance of any widespread deployment of AVs globally. Through an in-depth review of contemporary practice (e.g., sandboxes) and policy informing indices (e.g., AV Readiness Index—KPMG, 2019), it offers valuable insights, particularly for policy makers in non-car manufacturing developed countries as well as for those in the Global South who are in some ways dependent on data protection regulations in the country of vehicle manufacture.

The remainder of this chapter is structured as follows: Section 3 outlines the methodology applied; Section 4 presents the findings of the expert survey conducted in the countries in focus; Section 5 discusses these findings and highlights upcoming challenges; Section 6 concludes, offering policy relevant recommendations.

3. Method

Conducting a literature review is a task with its own challenges, particularly in an emerging field of global interest (van Wee and Banister, 2016). However, conducting a literature review about an emerging topic of global interest is even more challenging due to the lack of sufficient quantity and quality of literature to review. Consequently and due to the focus of this chapter on regulatory and legal aspects, the choice has been to focus on a review of relevant local, national and international regulations.

A structured survey questionnaire with closed and open ended questions was distributed by the authors to selected WISE-ACT[ab] experts who are familiar with both the transport and regulatory challenges of AV deployment, as well as with relevant data management and protection context in their respective countries. These experts are affiliated with European research networks, national research institutes, national transport authorities, NGOs (Non-Governmental Organisations), and Universities. This mix of affiliations both in the Global South and North ensures not only a wealth of expertise, but also diverse stakeholder perspectives depending on the objectives of each expert's affiliated organization. The survey was divided in three sections:

- Data protection regulations;
- AV-related regulations;
- New mobility services regulations.

The choice of countries was based on multiple concurring criteria: review and assess AV data management and protection regulations in a range of countries of variable size across continents, with or without car manufacturing firms in their territory which are represented in WISE-ACT. The selected countries are mentioned in Table 1. Three of them (Brazil, Italy and Slovakia) have car

[ab] WISE-ACT (Wider Impacts and Scenario Evaluation of Autonomous and Connected Transport) is a COST Action consisting of more than 150 participants from 38 COST Countries, 3 International Partner Countries, as well as the Joint Research Centre (EU) (2019): https://www.cost.eu/actions/CA16222.

Table 1 Experts' survey overview of AV deployment data management and protection.

Question no.	Question	Austria	Brazil	Greece	Italy	New Zealand	Slovakia	Switzerland
2	Is GDPR (or similar) implemented in the country?	■	■	■ a	■	■	■	■
3a	Is there a legal framework in the country about managing mobility data?	■			■ a	■		■
3b	Do these mobility data legal framework(s) include provisions about AV data?	■ a		■ a				
4	Is there AV specific legislation in the country?	■		■ a				■
5a	Is AV testing allowed in the country?	■		■	■	■		■
5b	Is there any specific provision about AV testing data ownership and management?	■ a			■			
6	Is there a specifically assigned Authority/Department at national/regional/local level focusing on AV legislation and policy in the country?				■			■
7a	Is any vehicle manufacturer established in the country?		■		■	■	■	
7b	Do their vehicle sale T&Cs include a specific clause about data management?				■			
7c	Does this comply with GDPR (or similar) already?							
8a	Do new mobility services providers (e.g., Uber) operate legally in the country?	■ a	■	■		■	■	
8b	Is there any relevant legislation/case regarding new mobility services (type) data management/protection/sharing?				■	■		
8d	Have there been any relevant fines to date?			■				
9	Is any other new mobility service provider operating in the country?	■	■	■	■	■	■	■
9c	Do their service use T&Cs include a specific clause about data management?					■		
9d	Does the new mobility service comply with GDPR (or similar)?		■ a		■ a			

[a]Positive answer with special arrangements in place regarding the specific matter.
Gray highlight = positive answer.

manufacturers in their territory, including some which are foreign-based firms. New Zealand does not have a traditional vehicle industry, but has an AV developer. The selection was made after cautious consideration and the understanding that car manufacturing countries which are at the forefront of AV deployment—such as China, Germany, Japan, Sweden, the UK, the USA —already have been putting structures in place to address relevant challenges. Less attention and progress has been paid to date on the challenges of countries with diverse size, available infrastructure and stage of economic development, hence this chapters aims at covering this gap in both the literature and practice.

Therefore, a mapping review (Grant and Booth, 2009) was identified as the most appropriate method for the review in this chapter. The key objective of mapping reviews is to map out and categorize existing sources, which can then be used as the foundation for further in-depth "*reviews or primary research by identifying gaps in the […] literature*" (Grant and Booth, 2009, p. 94). A feature of this method is that it is constrained according to the determined and available time and resources, while it does not require a formal quality assessment of sources used. Eventually, it aids in identifying areas for further primary or secondary research, which is perfectly aligned with the objectives of this chapter.

4. Findings

This section presents the findings of the experts' survey, highlighting the variation identified among the selected countries regarding AV data management and protection regulations. A summary of those variations is presented in Table 1, followed by an in-depth review of the context in each country.

4.1 Austria[ac]

There are data protection provisions through national legislation, i.e., BGBl. I Nr. 165/1999 and its updated version BGBl. I Nr. 14/2019, which, however, does not specify the level of fines despite allowing claims for damages.

AV testing is permitted in the country (BGBl. II Nr. 402/2016 update BGBl. II Nr. 66/2019 "AutomatisiertesFahrenVerordnung") and mobility data are managed according to BGBl. I Nr. 38/2013 "IVS Gesetz." The national authority responsible for AV deployment is the Department for Mobility Transformation and Transport Decarbonisation within the Federal Ministry

[ac] Input provided by Klar and Vlk (2019).

for Transport, Innovation and Technology (BMVIT), while AustriaTech is the National Contact Point for Automated Mobility. Relevant regulations specify the traffic situations, road types and speed range within which AV trials and driving assistance systems may be tested. Three test use cases had been possible in 2019 after submitting an application to the BMVIT:

- Automated mini-buses;
- Motorway pilot scheme with lane-change;
- Self-driving military vehicles.

These test use cases are being reviewed. Two applications have been granted permission by 2019: the first concerning valet parking, the second a motorway assistant with automated lane keeping. The existing Code of Practice offers additional assistance to vehicle manufacturers and AV trial organizers in order to progress from system development to vehicle production. Yet, the only AV data specific provision is about the data generated by the accident recorder which every AV is required to be equipped with. Austria is unique among the set of selected countries since another paragraph is dedicated to the handling of video material which is generated during AV trials.

New mobility services such as Uber are regulated at a provincial level, e.g., in Vienna LGBl. Nr. 36/2011 (GesamteRechtsvorschriftfür Wiener Taxi-, Mietwagen- und Gästewagen-Betriebsordnung) which is based on the BGBl. Nr. 112/1996 (Update BGBl. I Nr. 153/2006) on state level (Gelegenheitsverkehrs-Gesetz).[ad]

4.2 Brazil[ae]

The first Brazilian legislation to reference data protection was issued in 1984, but only after a recent wave of regulations (including the 2011 Access to Information Act, the 2014 Internet Bill of Rights, and the 2018 General Data Protection Law) has the country achieved a strong data protection and privacy rights framework (Aleixo et al., 2019).[af] The current legislation also adopts network security as a principle, and its content relates to security practices, data pseudonymization, and privacy by design. There is no specific legal framework about managing mobility data, although the 2012 Urban Mobility Act establishes, as a priority, the use of collective transportation to cities, including collective and individual mobility, ranging from buses to taxis, and already applied to new mobility services.

[ad] The total amount of fines owed by Uber until October 2018 was ca. 680 000 EUR, e.g., https://www.ots.at/presseaussendung/OTS_20180425_OTS0187/entscheidung-des-gerichts-einstweilige-verfuegung-gegen-uber.

[ae] Input provided by Steibel and Silva (2019).

[af] https://carnegieendowment.org/programs/technology/cyber/encryption.

Brazil has no AV specific legislation, nor is AV testing specifically allowed or regulated by a specific agency. The 1997 Brazilian Traffic Code Act has no provision for the absence of a driver, which imposes challenges for AV developments in the country. Moreover, Brazil requires the approval and licensing for vehicle circulation from federal and state organizations, as well as for homologation of vehicle components according to technical standards by the National Institute of Metrology, Quality, and Technology (INMETRO) or the Brazilian Association of Technical Standards (ABNT), which introduce additional challenges for AV deployment within the country (Lima et al., 2018).

The country has a long tradition of car manufacturers, with more than 20 of them established in the county, representing a global range of industries. Uber and other similar mobility smartphone applications have operated in the country since 2014. Such transport modes have no specific legislative provisions, although they are allowed to operate, as ruled by the Federal Supreme Court. Besides Uber, several other ride-hailing, ride-sharing, bicycle and e-scooter services operate in the country. The Terms and Conditions of most smartphone applications provide generic provisions about data management and protection within the country.

4.3 Greece[ag]

The case of Greece is interesting because until 2019 it was one of only two EU countries, to have received a fine by the European Commission for not fully incorporating GDPR in their national legislation. However, some relevant regulations and provisions pre-existed and GDPR has been incorporated in national legislation since September 2019. The Personal Data legislation in Greece was under review until July 2019 pending voting at the national Parliament. So in practice the previous legislation (2472/1976—GGS A 50/10.4.1997) which incorporated the previous EU Directive (95/46/EC) applied as long as it was not against the GDPR. The highest fines imposed in relation to data management and protection (150.000 EUR) have been based on 2472/1997 and 3471/2006 and have been imposed on the four nationally operating telecommunication firms (Decisions 60/2018, 61/2018, 62/2018, 63/2018). A further 150.000 EUR fine has been imposed in 2019 on a large multi-national accounting firm for breaches in employee data management and protection.

Ministerial Decision 50308/7695 has been issued (GN 1837/2015: Terms and Conditions) to operate an urban AV bus (GGS 1837/

[ag] Input provided by Stergiadis et al. (2019).

26.08.2015) which was implemented at the Municipality of Trikala for the experimental application of AV municipal buses within CityMobil2. According to the clauses of that decision, the person in charge or Operator of this AV is perceived as a driver according to the National Driving Legislation in regards to all the administrative, penal and legal responsibilities. It is implicitly assumed that GDPR regulations need to be adhered to and a Data Impact Assessment conducted, but national legislation was not adjusted at that time to allow fine imposing powers to respective local or national authorities.

Although Greece does not have a traditional car manufacturing industry, Tesla opened a small research facility in Greece during 2019. Uber operates certain services in Athens despite some ongoing disputes. Other new mobility service providers as well as a range of ITS (Intelligent Transport Systems) firms exist, including e-scooter operations which were launched in Thessaloniki in December 2018.

4.4 Italy[ah]

In Italy the Legislative Decree "Decreto Legislativo" 196/2003 provides the pivotal legislation in the field of data protection. It is noteworthy that it encompasses not only the incorporation of GDPR, but also of current EU safeguards about privacy in electronic communications, hence data protection in mobile services. Such provisions do not include special provisions regarding AV data.

AV testing is allowed in Italy by article 1 of Law December 27, 2017, n. 205 enforced with a specific bylaw: "Decreto" February 28, 2018 ("Smart Roads" Decree). The first authorization has been issued on May 9, 2019 for AV trials in Turin and Parma. The law does not define the ownership of the data, yet it has provided a detailed list of data which have to be collected (article 12, par. 1 lett. e), and imposes to the car owner to share such data with the public authority for 12 months (article 16, par. 1 lett. b).

The Italian Ministry of Transport has established a special branch specifically devoted to monitor AV testing and developments, called "Osservatorio tecnico di supporto per le Smart Road del Ministero delle Infrastrutture e dei Trasporti." Despite the transformation of FIAT, the historic Italian automotive manufacturing brand, into FCA, no AV manufacturer operates in Italy at the time of writing. FCA has developed a web-based platform which allows customers to create a personal profile. Uber operates in Italy only with some of the services provided worldwide. Namely,

[ah] Input provided by Costantini (2019).

UberPop[ai] is not operating after some legal controversies in which the interpretation of the discipline of road circulation was debated (Legislative Decree 285/1992). There are also other mobility service operators, providing different services such as car sharing, car-pooling and bike sharing.

4.5 New Zealand[aj]

New Zealand is unique within this set of selected countries in that it does not have any explicit legal requirement for a driver to be present in a moving vehicle, meaning that there is no legal barrier to testing a fully driverless vehicles (i.e., AV). AVs could be tested on public roads provided they comply with the standard safety requirements. As in other countries, vehicle testing may take place on private land without any third party consent. There are no specific requirements for testing of AV beyond those that would apply to testing any other vehicle. The operator of the vehicle (even if not in the vehicle) must have a driver's license and those undertaking testing must have appropriate public liability and professional indemnity insurance. New Zealand's "no fault" social insurance scheme, funded through the Accident Compensation Commission (ACC) covers personal injury. The New Zealand Transport Agency (NZTA) has outlined a process for applying for testing on public roads—which includes ensuring that vehicles are compliant (or exempted from) with the Land Transport Act, for example, if they have been modified. New Zealand has an additional unique feature since AV trials for air transport (i.e., drones) are permitted in the country.

New Zealand does not have a traditional car manufacturing industry, but there is one AV company. New mobility services are operating in New Zealand including ride-sourcing and micro-mobility. There has been a claim against the privacy act regarding the sharing of information between Uber and the police (Badillo-Lopez vs Uber New Zealand, decided on March 22, 2019).

Legislation regarding data protection provided by the New Zealand "Privacy Act" of 1993 has been repealed and replaced starting from March 1, 2020 by the "Privacy Bill" of 2018. The new legal framework will provide stronger powers, mandatory reporting, new offenses and increased fines. The act is described as having EU adequacy status, facilitating data transfers from the EU to New Zealand, but does not comply entirely with GDPR.[ak]

[ai] UberPop was the brand under which in Italy Uber provided the service of connecting private drivers to passengers.

[aj] Input provided by Curl (2019).

[ak] See the Privacy Bill digest n. 2588 at https://www.parliament.nz/en/pb/bills-and-laws/bills-digests/document/52PLLaw25881/privacy-bill-2018-bills-digest-2588.

There are mandatory notification requirements for privacy breaches, less requirements on consent, complaints may be raised directly with the company[al] involved, there is no restriction of automated decision making tools, no requirement for privacy by design or privacy impact assessment. Data protection in electronic communications is provided by the "Telecommunications Information Privacy Code," which is in force in its revised version since September 28, 2017.

There are no specific provisions regarding data ownership and management for AVs, whereas the Ministry of Transport states that it will monitor and draw on international developments alongside likelihood of commercial availability of AVs.

4.6 Slovakia[am]

In Slovakia, national legislation has been adapted with the entry into force of the GDPR by the Law No. 18/2018 on Personal Data Protection (New DPA). A key actor in data protection is the Office for Personal Data Protection of the Slovak Republic,[an] an independent state authority which performs the supervision of data protection. Citizens can file a complaint to this Office and obtain a statement, which is, however, not sufficient for a decision. Such decisions are taken by the court, to which the complaint may also be filed directly. Hence, statements from the Office for Personal Data Protection are not essential for decisions on these cases. A peculiar aspect of the Slovak system is that people are not used to liability claims as in the UK or the USA. Filing such a complaint is not common and the justice system is generally perceived as slow and with non-transparent procedures.

No specific legislation on AV is available. Generally, the personal data protection legislation is applied as far as it concerns personal data. This gap will be filled in by the Smart Mobility 4-year project, funded through ESIF Structural Funds, managed by the Ministry of Transport and Construction, in collaboration with the office of the Deputy Prime Minister for Investments and Informatisation. This project will develop the legislative and regulatory framework in 2021 and implement it in 2022. Uses of AV data will be covered, including open data and sharing of data.

Four foreign car manufacturers originally from France, Germany, South Korea, UK and one domestic are established in Slovakia. New mobility service providers are also operating, e.g., Uber operates legally in Slovakia since

[al] The term used in New Zealand's legal framework is "agency."
[am] Input provided by Lugano and Kováčiková (2019).
[an] https://dataprotection.gov.sk.

May 2019, after 1 year of suspension of services due to a court decision. This decision established that Uber and any other similar service should fulfill the obligations of any other "regular taxi service" in the country. Even if classified in a different category than taxi service providers, shared mobility operators are popular. From a legislative point of view, these services fall in a "gray area" since they are presented as "community services" and no court case has been filed yet.

4.7 Switzerland[ao]

The Swiss Federal Data Protection Act (DPA) applies in this country and the Telecommunications Act 784.10 provides the legal framework regarding the management of mobility data. AV trials are permitted on public roads based on Federal Road Traffic Law (SVG) article 106, paragraph 5, however, no special arrangements are in place regarding AV data other than the DPA ones. It is noteworthy that trial authorizations require documentation or confirmation that the legal provisions governing data protection will be complied with, and that data security is assured. The authority in charge of AV trials is the Federal Office of Roads—Federal Office for Spatial Development.

New mobility services operate under local regulations which are issued at a local (Canton) level, e.g., in Lausanne Uber can operate according to the same regulations applicable for taxis and drivers.

5. Discussion and policy implications

A variety of valuable findings have been identified in the previous section, which are discussed and contrasted hereinafter. It appears that the "GDPR era" has arrived, since all selected countries (Table 1: 2)—and most EU member states—have adopted GDPR or a similar type of legislation recognizing the contemporary significance of data management and protection. Following fines by the European institutions, all EU member States plan to have the GDPR regulation incorporated in their national legislation by 2020. New Zealand on the other hand has a range of unique features, which allow that Country to introduce some type of data management legislation, but not to fully comply with GDPR requirements. Moreover, five out the seven selected countries permit some type of AV trial within their public roads, in addition to AV trials taking place at any private areas which are naturally not restricted. Nonetheless, only two (Austria and Greece) out of the

[ao] Input provided by Kyriadikis (2019).

seven selected countries (Table 1: 4) have in place some limited provisions regarding data generated through AV trials.

In contrast, new mobility services are operating in all selected countries. This includes ride-hailing services (e.g., Uber) offered either legally or through indirect channels which has imposed legal battles and fines, as well as other new mobility services such as shared e-scooter schemes. Interestingly, such new mobility services are compliant with GDPR requirements in only two out of the seven selected countries (Table 1: 9d). Therefore, new mobility services appear to be a useful proxy to be used when assessing the data management and protection compatibility of a country or location for AV deployment. The fact that new mobility services are often regulated at a local level (e.g., Austria, Italy, Switzerland, UK), whereas AV trials and data management are regulated at a national level, creates an additional layer of data governance complexity. The latter is particularly important for cross-border collaboration which is common with the EU, e.g., between Austria, Hungary and Slovenia regarding AV trials. A further striking finding is that despite the anticipated importance of AV deployment for freight transport, limited arrangements are already in place about this sector.

At a policy level, it can be argued that aside leading large countries with extensive resources and established automotive manufacturers available, there is no clear policy leadership. In spite of the adoption of GDPR or similar legislation and regulations, awareness and debates among practitioners about AV data management and protection are in their early days. Contemporary familiarization with new mobility services may be useful in raising awareness about both the wider opportunities and challenges among policy makers and the general public.

Overall, this section has highlighted that new mobility services are a contemporary trend, but still the debate surrounding AV data management and protection has not received adequate attention by academics and practitioners to date. GDPR may be perceived either as a "carrot" or as a "stick," but in either case, the focus needs to be diverted in this field too alongside other crucial aspects of AV deployment. Collaboration is essential not only between policies across countries, but also across public and private stakeholders, to shape a liveable future vision including AVs. Consequently, any AV Readiness Index (KPMG, 2019) or other similar index should provide information about data management and protection practice to offer a holistic overview to interested stakeholders.

Table 2 contains a synthesis of the findings, divided by country, concerning actors involved in data protection regulations, AV-related regulations and new mobility service regulations.

Table 2 Summary about AV data management and protection in the selected set of countries.

Country	Austria	Brazil	Greece	Italy	New Zealand	Slovakia	Switzerland
(a) Data protection regulations/ *actors* involved	Data protection provisions through national legislation	Data protection and privacy rights framework (2011 Access to Information Act, the 2014 Internet Bill of Rights, and the 2018 General Data Protection Law)	GDPR incorporated in national legislation at the end of 2019	Data protection provisions through national legislation	Data protection provisions through national legislation currently under revision (does not comply with GDPR)	Data protection provisions through national legislation/ *Office for Personal Data Protection of the Slovak Republic*	Data protection provisions through national legislation
(b) AV-related regulations/ actors involved	National regulations on AV testing/Department for Mobility Transformation and Transport Decarbonisation within the Federal Ministry for Transport, Innovation and Technology (BMVIT) and AustriaTech as the National Contact Point for Automated Mobility	No AV specific legislation	No AV national legislation	National regulations on AV testing/Ministry of Transport	Any explicit legal requirement for a driver to be present in a moving vehicle, no specific provisions regarding data ownership and management for AVs/Ministry of Transport with a monitoring role	No AV specific legislation	National regulations on AV testing/Federal Office of Roads—Federal Office for Spatial Development
(c) New mobility service regulations/ actors involved	Regulated at a provincial level	No specific regulation	No specific regulations	National legislation on road circulation (not new mobility services specific)	No specific regulations	No specific regulations	Under local regulations which are issued at a local (Canton) level

6. Conclusion and recommendations

Based on a mapping review (Grant and Booth, 2009), this chapter has managed to identify common ground and key differences regarding AV data management and protection between the seven selected countries (Table 1). By classifying a range of countries based on their size, economic development stage and whether they host a car manufacturer on their territory, this chapter offers a concise overview of the contemporary legal frameworks and regulations governing mobility data management, AV trials, as well as data generated through new mobility services.

Interestingly, countries outside the EU have already introduced regulations similar to GDPR despite some EU countries have incorporated GDPR in their national legislation in 2019–2020. Data management and protection of AV data is still at a nascent stage, which demonstrates the urgent need to inform users and divert stakeholder focus to this issue. This need is further enhanced by the inherent difficulty in distinguishing between personal and non-personal data. Anonymization is a key factor at this level, but the discussion on such a topic is beyond the scope of this chapter.

Facilitating such a development at an international level is naturally a challenge, but using established *fora* such as UNECE or the EU would certainly enhance relevant efforts. An important finding of this mapping review is undoubtedly that collaboration within and among countries is an indispensable part of the next step of AV deployment. Including the Global South in such developments would naturally constitute a key component of this process, given the rapid urbanization and motorization trends in these countries (Thomopoulos and Nikitas, 2019).

However, only limited resources have been available for this chapter, therefore it is acknowledged that a more comprehensive review is required based on a representative sample of selected countries. If this was to be conducted, then it would mean that the mapping review of this chapter has been useful in identifying a gap for further primary research. Such research could include in-depth interviews with key stakeholders, as well as with individuals directly involved in the legislative process at diverse levels, i.e., local, national, international.

Several issues remain unanswered about this issue. First, the capability to "re-identify" originally anonymous data through AI or Big Data integration with those available publicly is increasing rapidly, challenging current methods of enhancing privacy protection—such as "k-anonymity"

(Samarati and Sweeney, 1998) or forced introduction of randomness under a certain threshold of statistical population, or other measures such as "pseudo-anonymization" (article 4(5), 25 and 32 GDPR).

Furthermore, future developments in AI technologies will likely allow AVs to increase their level of autonomy (Russell and Norvig, 2016), yet the legal status of such artificial agents is still under discussion, as confirmed by The European Parliament Report with recommendations to the Commission on Civil Law Rules on Robotics (Delvaux, 2016; Floridi, 2019a). Besides the promising results in the field of "explainable AI," or "XAI" (Adadi and Berrada, 2018), there remains a lack of consensus concerning the property of the data produced by newly developed machines, especially those which can hardly be isolated and separated by the artificial "brains" in which their knowledge is embedded.

Third, the worldwide growth of "regulatory sandboxes" can be seen as an extraordinary opportunity to facilitate the deployment of AVs, yet cooperation among Living Labs is crucial in framing a common approach to AVs and a consistent transport policy. It is noteworthy that in the report "The Future of Road Transport" it is suggested to create a European Network of Living Labs in order to coordinate the efforts for ensuring viable solutions in a field, such as transport, where "*technical and social issues are strongly intertwined*" (Alonso Raposo and Ciuffo, 2019: 43). Establishing multidisciplinary networks of experts such as WISE-ACT is one of the recommended options to make good progress in this respect. The recommendation deriving from the analysis in this chapter is that this approach could help not only to nurture a common vision fostering the development of a harmonized European transport policy, but also to share information such as best practices and outcomes which have a more immediate effect and which can be used to foster public awareness about AVs.

Acknowledgments

The authors are grateful to the experts in Austria, Brazil, Greece, Italy, New Zealand, Slovakia and Switzerland for their valuable time and input completing our survey. Additionally, the authors would like to acknowledge the support provided by the WISE-ACT COST Action CA16222 which facilitated the development of this book chapter through meetings, Short Term Scientific Missions and workshops.

References

Adadi, A., Berrada, M., 2018. Peeking Inside the Black-Box: A Survey on Explainable Artificial Intelligence (XAI). vol. 6. IEEE Access, pp. 52138–52160. https://doi.org/10.1109/ACCESS.2018.2870052.

Alavi, A.H., Jiao, P., Buttlar, W.G., Lajnef, N., 2018. Internet of Things-enabled smart cities: state-of-the-art and future trends. Measurement 129, 589–606.

Aleixo, G., Guimarães Gobbato, A., Garcia de Souza, I., Langenegger, N., Lemos, R., Steibel, F., 2019. The Encryption Debate in Brazil [WWW Document]. Carnegie Endowment for International Peace. https://carnegieendowment.org/2019/05/30/encryption-debate-in-brazil-pub-79219.

Alonso Raposo, M., Ciuffo, B. (Eds.), 2019. The Future of Road Transport—Implications of Automated, Connected, Low-Carbon and Shared Mobility. Publications Office of the European Union, Luxembourg.

Blyth, P.-L., Mladenovic, M.N., Nardi, B.A., Ekbia, H.R., Su, N.M., 2016. Expanding the design horizon for self-driving vehicles: distributing benefits and burdens. IEEE Technol. Soc. Mag. 35, 44–49.

Christensen, C.M., Bower, J.L., 1996. Disruptive technologies: catching the wave. J. Prod. Innov. Manag. 1, 75–76.

Christensen, C.M., Raynor, M.E., Mcdonald, R., 2015. What is disruptive innovation? Harv. Bus. Rev. 93, 44–53.

Costantini, F., 2019. Wise-Act Report.

Costantini, F., Archetti, E., Di Ciommo, F., Ferencz, B., 2019. IoT, intelligent transport systems and MaaS (mobility as a service). In: Schweighofer, E., Kummer, F., Saarenpää, A. (Eds.), Proceedings of the 22nd International Legal Informatics Symposium IRIS 2019. Weblaw, Salzburg, pp. 245–254.

Curl, A., 2019. Wise-Act Report.

Delvaux, M., 2016. Report With Recommendations to the Commission on Civil Law Rules on Robotics (2015/2103(INL)).

Floridi, L., 2014. The 4th Revolution. How the Infosphere Is Reshaping Human Reality. Oxford University Press, Oxford.

Floridi, L., 2019a. What the near future of artificial intelligence could be. Philos. Technol. 32, 1–15. https://doi.org/10.1007/s13347-019-00345-y.

Floridi, L., 2019b. Autonomous vehicles: from whether and when to where and how. Philos. Technol. 32, 569–573.

Gellert, R., 2018. Understanding the notion of risk in the General Data Protection Regulation. Comput. Law Secur. Rev. 34, 279–288.

Glancy, D., 2012. Privacy in autonomous vehicles. Santa Clara L. Rev. 52 (4), 1171–1239.

Grant, M.J., Booth, A., 2009. A typology of reviews: an analysis of 14 review types and associated methodologies. Health Info. Libr. J. 26, 91–108. https://doi.org/10.1111/j.1471-1842.2009.00848.x.

Harari, Y.N., 2018. 21 Lessons for the 21st Century. Jonathan Cape, London.

Hogan, G., Helfert, M., 2019. Transparent Cloud Privacy: Data Provenance Expression in Blockchain. https://doi.org/10.5220/0007733404300436.

Hogan, G., Dolins, S., Senturk, I.F., Fyrogenis, I., Fu, Q., Murati, E., Costantini, F., Thomopoulos, N., 2019. Can a blockchain-based MaaS create business value? In: Decentralized 2019 Proceedings. https://doi.org/10.3390/proceedings2019028001.

Joint Research Centre (EU), 2019. https://ec.europa.eu/jrc/en/research-facility/living-labs-at-the-jrc/call-expression-interest-future-mobility-and-digital-energy-solutions.

Klar, W., Vlk, T., 2019. Wise-Act Report.

Kováčiková, T., Buzna, L.U., Pourhashem, G., Lugano, G., Cornet, Y., Lugano, N. (Eds.), 2018. Intelligent Transport Systems—From Research and Development to the Market Uptake. Springer, Cham.

KPMG, 2019. 2019 Autonomous Vehicles Readiness Index. KPMG.

Kyriadikis, M., 2019. Wise-Act Report.

Lima, D., Miranda Neto, A., Martinesco, A., Texeira da Silva, S., 2018. Automated driving systems and their insertion in the Brazilian scenario: a test track proposal. SAE Int. J. Trans. Saf. 6 (1), 39–54. https://doi.org/10.4271/09-06-01-0004.

Lugano, G., Kováčiková, T., 2019. Wise-Act Report.
Lugano, G., Hudák, M., Ivančo, M., Loveček, T., 2019. From the mind to the cloud: personal data in the age of the internet of things. In: Zhou, Y., Fischer, M.H. (Eds.), AI Love You: Developments in Human-Robot Intimate Relationships. Springer International Publishing, Cham, pp. 111–130. https://doi.org/10.1007/978-3-030-19734-6_6.
Milakis, D., Arem, B., Wee, B., 2017. Policy and society related implications of automated driving: a review of literature and directions for future research. J. Intell. Transp. Syst. 21, 324–348. https://doi.org/10.1080/15472450.2017.1291351.
Pagallo, U., Casanovas, P., Madelin, R., 2019. The middle-out approach: assessing models of legal governance in data protection, artificial intelligence, and the Web of Data. Theory Pract. Legis. 7 (1), 1–25.
Rotolo, D., Hicks, D., Martin, B.R., 2015. What is an emerging technology? Res. Policy 44 (10), 1827–1843.
Rozhyn, A., Wimmer, M.A., 2019. Literature review of ethical concerns in the use of disruptive technologies in Government 3.0. In: Berntzen, L. (Ed.), ICDS 2019: The Thirteenth International Conference on Digital Society and eGovernments. Curran Associates, Washington.
Russell, S.J., Norvig, P., 2016. Artificial Intelligence: A Modern Approach, third ed. Pearson Education Limited.
Samarati, P., Sweeney, L., 1998. Protecting Privacy When Disclosing Information: k-Anonymity and Its Enforcement Through Generalization and Suppression. Harvard.
Steibel, F., Silva, P., 2019. Wise-Act Report.
Stergiadis, A., Kefalopoulos, M., Thomopoulos, N., 2019. Wise-Act Report.
Thomopoulos, N., Givoni, M., 2015. The autonomous car—a blessing or a curse for the future of low carbon mobility? An exploration of likely vs. desirable outcomes. Eur. J. Futures Res. 3, 14. https://doi.org/10.1007/s40309-015-0071-z.
Thomopoulos, N., Nikitas, A., 2019. Smart urban mobility futures, special issue editorial. Int. J. Automot. Technol. Manag. 19 (1/2), 1–9.
Thomopoulos, N., Givoni, M., Rietveld, P., 2015. ICT for Transport: Opportunities and Threats. Edward Elgar, Cheltenham, Gloucester, UK.
Voigt, P., Von Dem Bussche, A., 2017. The EU General Data Protection Regulation (GDPR). A Practical Guide. Springer International Publishing, Cham.
Wachter, S., 2018. The GDPR and the Internet of Things: a three-step transparency model. Law Innov. Technol. 10, 266–294.
Wee, B., Banister, D., 2016. How to write a literature review paper? Transp. Rev. 36, 278–288. https://doi.org/10.1080/01441647.2015.1065456.
Wiatrowski, A., 2018. Blockchain Technology—A Threat or a Solution for Data Protection? Jusletter IT. 22 February 2018. https://jusletter-it.weblaw.ch/en/issues/2018/IRIS/blockchain-technolog_96aad6c440.html.
Yu, D., Hang, C.C., 2010. A reflective review of disruptive innovation theory. Int. J. Manag. Rev. 12, 435–452.
Zetzsche, D.A., Buckley, R.P., Barberis, J.N., Arner, D.W., 2017. Regulating a revolution: from regulatory sandboxes to smart regulation. Fordham J. Corp. Financ. Law XXIII, 31–103.

CHAPTER NINE

Ethical issues concerning automated vehicles and their implications for transport

Ebru Dogan[a,*], Federico Costantini[b], Rémy Le Boennec[a]
[a]VEDECOM Institute, Versailles, France
[b]University of Udine, Udine, Italy
[*]Corresponding author: e-mail address: ebru.dogan@vedecom.fr

Contents

Abstract

The introduction of automated vehicles (AV) in the market progresses before the stakeholders fully understand the capacity and the limitations of this complex technology. While this can be considered as a usual course of deployment of a new technology, future large-scale expansion of AV at the societal level makes public acceptance a key issue. One of the main aspects of public acceptance is the ethical concerns raised by AV. In the current chapter, we will mainly review the research on the ethical issues related to ethics-by-design of AV through its moral agency, application of different ethical theories to the decision making in critical situations, and whether ethics setting should be mandatory or personal. Our review shows that while there are several ethical frameworks proposed for AV, research on public acceptance mostly contrasts utilitarian and deontological ethics. Algorithmic implementation of the proposed frameworks, however, is yet to be done. In the second part, we will address several ethical issues relevant for the implementation of AV in transport system and policy decision making.

Keywords: Automated vehicle, Ethics, Moral dilemma, Decision making, Transport policy

ISSN 2543-0009
https://doi.org/10.1016/bs.atpp.2020.05.003

1. Introduction

The ethical aspects of automated vehicles (AV) started raising public attention when the draft version of an article on "the social dilemma of autonomous vehicles" (Bonnefon et al., 2016) was uploaded on Arxiv.[a] A year later, the "Moral Machine" project,[b] impersonating AV caught in moral dilemmas, reached more than 35 million people around the world (Awad et al., 2018). While the promises of the AV have been made on the grounds of safety, environmental impact, traffic efficiency, and economic benefits, a prerequisite for the realization of these ambitious benefits is the public acceptance and market adoption of the AV. One of the issues that occupy public acceptance is the ethical challenges posed by AV. In fact, failure to take into account public concerns about the ethical issues raised by a new technology resulted in abandoning of some technologies in the past (e.g., carbon capture system in the Netherlands, Terwel et al., 2012).

Public attention is focused especially on what sort of ethical framework is needed for decision making of AV in unavoidable accident situations. Such issues are not entirely new, as confirmed by the fact that the discussion on AV ethics revamped the famous "trolley problem," a moral experiment invented more than 50 years ago (Foot, 1967; Thomson, 1985). Research so far indicates that there is no straightforward answer to this question. Even if there were suitable solutions to moral dilemma, it is doubtful that defining an ethical framework for the decision making of AV could be sufficient to unfold the ethical issues posed by AV.

AVs can revolutionize transportation technologies and the mobility system at a higher level with important implications for the entire society, including travel behavior, social arrangements, and land use. While the ethical issues on the AV per se tackle the moral decisions and actions in critical situations, those concerning AVs as part of a transport system address a wider spectrum related to transport policy. Some of the ethical issues relevant for policy making seem to be clouded by public concerns with the ethics-by-design. Given that transport policies are usually evaluated based on efficiency and effectiveness, but not always on equity, the current chapter aims to address an important evaluation criterion.

[a] https://arxiv.org.

[b] http://moralmachine.mit.edu/.

In this chapter, we will first summarize how different ethical theories have approached the behavior of AVs in critical situations (Section 3). Next, we discuss some ethical issues relevant for the implementation of AVs in transport system (Section 4). Finally, we identify the gaps in the current literature and propose directions for future research.

2. Method

A literature review was carried out on Scopus database in March 2019. The keywords "ethics" AND "automated vehicle" OR "autonomous vehicle"—since the two are often used interchangeably, and the plural forms were entered in the search field of any kind, that is, title, abstract, content, or keyword. The initial search resulted in 2972 outcomes. The interface did not allow removal of the duplicates. After a very strict filtering through the titles, the number of entries was reduced to 139. Articles that were mainly related to human factors, law, pure technology, autonomous systems other than the AV, and machine ethics in general were excluded at this stage. Next, the abstracts of the remaining publications were reviewed, after which there were 36 publications. At the final stage, 25 of these were retained for the review (Table 1). This methodology concerns Section 3 of the current chapter. Section 4 does not provide a systematic review, unlike Section 3, partly due to the low number of resources addressing the ethical aspects of implementation of AV in transport.

3. Overview of the current discussion concerning AV in critical situations

Ethical inquiries concerning moral dilemmas involving AVs tend to swing between two opposite positions. On the one hand, the over-extension of the traditional ethical framework to the field of AVs could lead to an unjustified anthropomorphization. On the other, excluding a priori moral agency leads to a lack of substantial criterion for allocating liability. In our view, the theoretical legitimacy of values cannot be separated from the practical feasibility of the extension of moral assessment to non-human agents such as AVs.

Attributing the capacity to make decisions to AV raises three issues: (1) whether it would be legitimate to attribute agency to AVs according to the traditional understanding of it; (2) what the criteria for the righteous behavior to be implemented in AVs could be; (3) what the consequences of a

Table 1 Articles included in the literature review on the ethical challenges of AVs.

Comment	**Source**
AV is not endowed with a high-level, autonomous agency, but with a lower-level agency that requires human-machine collaboration	Nyholm (2017, 2018a,b)
AV that is designed after the principle of meaningful human control need to enable tracking and tracing	Santoni de Sio and van den Hoven (2018)
Attribution of a high-level of agency to AV leads to concerns about responsibility gap for the harms that might be caused by AV	Hevelke and Nida-Rümelin (2015)
Utilitarian approach—users prefer a utilitarian AV at the cost of self-sacrifice	Bonnefon et al. (2016), Li et al. (2016), Wintersberger et al. (2017), Awad et al. (2018), Bergmann et al. (2018), Faulhaber et al. (2019)
Utilitarian approach—people have a tendency to take the age of potential victims into account	Wintersberger et al. (2017), Awad et al. (2018), Bergmann et al. (2018)
There is a conflict between individual and collective interests manifested in unwillingness to buy a self-sacrificing AV	Bonnefon et al. (2016)
Deontological ethics—the design of AV and the automated mobility can follow preset rules, such as giving priority to human life under all circumstances or forbidding involving the innocent in AV decisions	Luetge (2017), Ethics Task Force (2018)
Contractarian ethics—the decisions of AV could follow the principle of maximin for impartiality	Contissa et al. (2017), Leben (2017)
Doctrine of necessity—intentional killing by AV could be justified as necessary defense under specific circumstances	Santoni de Sio (2017)
Doctrine of necessity—for intentional killing by AV to be necessary, it should satisfy the principle of pareto efficiency	Keeling (2018)
Chance—as AV is not a moral agent, the ethical decisions of AV should be made randomly to avoid AV being subject to human judgment	Grinbaum (2018)

Table 1 Articles included in the literature review on the ethical challenges of AVs.—cont'd

Comment	Source
Ethics settings of AV should be left to the driver as mandatory ethics settings would be against individual's autonomy and paternalistic	Loh and Loh Sombetzki (2017), Brandão, 2018
Ethics settings of AV should be mandatory as the users are not well equipped with the sufficient level of knowledge and expertise required for the task	Lin (2014)
Mandatory ethics settings (1) would avoid prisoner's dilemma and (2) are coherent with government's regulatory responsibilities	Gogoll and Müller (2017)
A hybrid approach to ethics settings of AV could ensure the implementation of traffic regulations in the AV and leave the remaining decisions to the liberty of the individual	Etzioni and Etzioni (2017)
Ordinary driving situations also require non-trivial ethical considerations, especially given that the high penetration level of AVs will have a large-scale impact	Himmelreich (2018), Goodall (2019)

wrongful conduct should be. We elaborate on the first two issues in the following sections. The third one, being related to the rules of allocation of liability for damages and entailing the solution of legal conundrums, falls out of the scope of this chapter.

3.1 Representation of automated vehicle as an artificial agent

Human drivers often engage in ethical decision making, even if they are not aware of doing so deliberately. For instance, drivers' decision to maneuver in order to avoid harm to a jay-walker has an ethical component because it could put the driver in danger, even if the odds are small (Goodall, 2016). With the AV, such decisions to regulate safe coexistence of road users become non-trivial since the AV replaces not only the low-level vehicle control functions (e.g., speed control), but also the high-level decision making functions. The latter are issues which typically involve ethics and entail the problem of formalizing such methods for decisions that affect the collectivity (Greene et al., 2016).

The attribution of full autonomy and agency to AV is debated, sometimes even contested, by the general public (Li et al., 2016). Notably, Nyholm (2017, 2018a,b) argues that the agency attributed to AV seems to be of a highly autonomous or independent type, akin to the agency of human adults in their faculties, which eventually gives rise to a responsibility gap for the harms that might be caused by the AVs (Hevelke and Nida-Rümelin, 2015). He claims that AV does not have a high-level autonomous agency and proposes a kind of agency that could be exercised by a collaborative human-machine system. In a similar vein, Santoni de Sio and van den Hoven (2018) discuss the implications of meaningful human control in the case of AV. This does not necessarily mean a direct human control on the system, but refers to a design principle that enables *tracking* of moral reasons endowed by the human agents during the design and deployment process, and *tracing* of decisions to at least one human agent in the chain of design and operation of AVs. Nonetheless, the attribution of agency raises questions concerning the definition of the criteria for the righteous behavior and expectations that moral principles should be programmed into the algorithms governing the AV so that its decisions are morally acceptable. The question, then, is what kind of ethical framework AV should be embodied with in order to handle unavoidable accidents involving harm to humans.

3.2 Ethical frameworks proposed for accident management

The majority of the existing literature on the AV ethics focuses on the imminent accident situations and the forced-choice decisions that the vehicle has to make. Since there is no ethical theory specific to the situation of the AV, most of these inquiries are the application of the existing ethical theories to the case of AV. In this section, we provide an overview of the ethical theories proposed for the decision making by AV in accident management, relevant research, and their critics. According to the most common understanding in contemporary ethics, we classify five approaches: consequentialism, deontologist ethics, contractarianism, doctrine of necessity, and a quite new proposal based on the application of randomness.

3.2.1 Consequentialist ethics

Consequentialist ethics is concerned with the outcomes of an action, regardless of the qualities of the agent, circumstances, or the nature of the action.

It covers different frameworks about the moral rightness of an action, ranging from pure egoism to pure altruism (Sinnott-Armstrong, 2019). The most commonly known form of consequentialism is traditional utilitarianism, according to which humans should pursue "*the greatest happiness for the greatest number*" (Bentham, 1988).

The work on the utilitarian decision making for AV and the media coverage mostly focus on the "trolley problem," where the AV must choose between two actions with fatal outcomes.[c] Several studies demonstrated that people were in favor of a utilitarian AV that would sacrifice its passenger for a greater good of saving higher number of lives (Bergmann et al., 2018; Bonnefon et al., 2016; Faulhaber et al., 2019; Li et al., 2016; Wintersberger et al., 2017), although the percentage was lower when drivers imagined a child or a family member in the car with them (Bonnefon et al., 2016). However, when questioned about their intention to buy, drivers expressed a strong preference for an AV which would protect its passenger at all costs, instead of a utilitarian one (Bonnefon et al., 2016). Moral Machine project extended the decision making options to include different types of road users and personal characteristics in order to come up with a comprehensive utility function (Awad et al., 2018). The findings revealed that people, particularly in western cultures, approved of an AV that would prioritize the life of young people, a common result with other research (e.g., Bergmann et al., 2018; Wintersberger et al., 2017), similar to the quality of life analysis adopted largely in economics and insurance.

Using the trolley problem as basis for the AV decision making has been criticized for philosophical methodology stating that the dilemmas were not meant to resolve moral issues. Thus, people's responses to dilemmas should not be taken literally (Dewitt et al., 2019). Besides, the sort of consequence that is considered is malleable, such as "*to minimize death toll*" (Bonnefon et al., 2016) or "*to minimize overall harm*" (Gogoll and Müller, 2017). Nevertheless, the results of the utilitarian studies are valuable for unraveling a prominent social dilemma stemming from the conflict between self-interest and public interest. While people agree on the outcome that is in the public's interest, they tend to prefer the option that serves their self-interest when they are directly involved in a situation.

[c] The analogy with the "trolley problem" has been criticized for several reasons (see Nyholm and Smids, 2016).

3.2.2 Deontological ethics

Deontological theories express the attempt to define principles in order to build a consistent system of tenets by which the agent is expected to abide. Hence, they focus on the duties, instead of the consequences of an action. These principles or duties can be different depending on the perspective adopted. The most well-known deontological philosopher is Immanuel Kant, who proposed the universal imperative to "*treat human beings as an end, not simply as a means*" (Kant, 1998).

While some authors reformulate prioritized interests as rational moral principles (e.g., "*to minimize global damage*," Goodall, 2014), others offer a detailed array of declared values, which are analytically defined and explained. A good example of the latter approach is the report released by the German Federal Government Ethics Commission for connected and automated vehicle (Luetge, 2017), where it is stated that the utmost priority in unavoidable accident situations should be given to the life of the individual, accepting damage to animals and property (Rule 1). Furthermore, it is clearly stated that it is "*prohibited to offset victims against each other*" in the case of an unavoidable accident (Rule 9), that is, the vehicle algorithms should not be programmed to prioritize life of one person against another under any circumstances. It is also stated that "*those parties involved in the generation of mobility risks must not sacrifice non-involved parties*" (Rule 9). These provisions are aligned with the original Kantian moral imperative and express the moral duty to protect other people's lives regardless of their direct involvement in mobility. This report constitutes the basis of a report by the Task Force on Ethical Aspects of Connected and Automated Driving (2018).

Defining rules for an AV to abide by irrespective of the people involved solves the challenge of putting value on human lives. However, it does not answer questions about or tell how to apply these rules in the vehicle algorithms. Additionally, the rules tend to specify well what not to do, but not what to do. Finally, defining a complete set of rules to represent an ethical system for AV would be a considerably difficult task (Goodall, 2014).

3.2.3 Contractarianism

Contractarianism claims that moral principles are established via mutual agreement among self-interested parties to solve the problem of social cooperation. According to Rawls (1971), being ignorant to their own specific conditions should prevent individuals from establishing or manipulating social rules to their own advantage and lead them to agree at a re-distribution of resources based on the "*maximin principle*," which aims to improve the situation of the worse-off person, because they might all equally be in the position of the worse-off person.

Leben (2017) suggests an application of the principle of maximin to the case of AV and its extension to the second worse-off person. He argues that people in the original position should agree on maximizing the interests of the next worse-off person because they have an equal chance of being the next person in row. Leben shows through variations of the trolley problem that a utilitarian algorithm would always choose the same action resulting in a lower disutility, while a Rawlsian algorithm would choose different actions depending on whether the protection of the passenger or the pedestrian would be the maximin. Contissa et al. (2017) argue that a Rawlsian algorithm might give counterintuitive outcomes. They propose additionally to take into account the gravity of the injuries in calculating the utility function of each party. Of course, these arguments assume that AV could estimate the survival likelihood of each individual concerned. Even if this would be technically possible, a choice made behind a veil of ignorance implies that people should accept to remain indifferent to the decision making whether they are pedestrians or passengers.

3.2.4 Legal necessity and justified killing

In response to difficulty of consensus on which ethical framework to embed in AV, Santoni de Sio (2017) proposes an ethico-legal approach of the doctrine of necessity. Accordingly, Santoni de Sio argues that the AV's intentional killing, which would normally be legally prohibited, could be justified as a necessary defense in unavoidable accident situations under very specific circumstances[d] in which the person killed would have died anyway, even though the AV had not taken the specific action that caused the killing. Keeling (2018) suggests that Santoni de Sio's explanation still would not create the consensus that it aimed among the proponents of different ethical frameworks, and presents an alternative interpretation of the doctrine of necessity based on the Pareto efficiency principle. Subsequently, for an intentional harm to be justified, there should not be an alternative distribution of harm among the affected parties in which all of the parties would be at least better-off and at least one of the affected parties should be strictly

[d] Santoni de Sio refers to Re A conjoined twins case (2001), in which the court specified three conditions in their decision permitting the intentional killing of one of the twins in order to save the other under necessity based on the medical evidence showing that one of the twins was guaranteed to die, while the other had a very high chance of living (cf. Santoni de Sio, 2017).

better-off with the allocation of intentional harm. Kleeing explains how the Pareto efficiency principle could bring about consensus about inflicting harm in at least some unavoidable accident situations. With the Pareto efficiency principle, he complements the process-oriented approach of Santoni de Sio with decision-theoretic terms.

3.2.5 Randomness and procedural justice

The last position for the ethical decision making for AV that we will cover is explored by Grinbaum (2018), according to whom randomness could be used as a tool to *avoid* moral dilemmas altogether. Grinbaum argues that machines based on artificial intelligence, including AV, are intrinsically unable to discern good or evil, thus, should not be actors of moral decisions that would subject them to the judgment of humans. Randomness could allow AV to make ethical decisions without being judged by the humans about the righteousness of their decisions. The requisite for randomness is that the user has to trust the procedures of decision making, and that this trust is more important than the need for an explanation. Accordingly, the moral decision making should be opaque, even to the developer, and this opaqueness should be evident to the user. If the user has reasons to believe that the developer has some kind of insight or a key to the backdoors of the decision making system, opacity cannot be predicated. Hence, it can be argued that randomness approaches, such as Grinbaum's, rely on procedural justice in order to create the conditions under which such randomness can operate in defining the ethical framework for AV.

3.3 Mandatory or personal ethics settings

The overview of the ethical frameworks in the previous section reveals the diversity of different approaches, as well as their benefits and drawbacks. Assuming that having an operational framework for ethical decision making for AVs were possible, who should decide the exact settings? It is not surprising to find arguments for both mandatory and personal ethics settings.

One of the main reasons in favor of personal ethics settings is that the driver is likely to bear the responsibility for the AVs moral decisions since the AV is not an autonomous agent and, thus, cannot be expected to engage in deliberation about distinguishing right from wrong in highly unpredictable situations. Another major and related argument is a critique against a sort of (moral) paternalism, which could legitimate the interference with the autonomy of individuals with the belief that this would improve their welfare. Given the uncertainty and difficulty in establishing whether the measures taken in the name of other people's own good are indeed the right ones, interfering with the user's autonomy by imposing ethics settings would not be justified (Brandão, 2018). Furthermore, it is argued that such imposition would be unfair and paternalistic since no authority can discern in advance the moral convictions of the user (Loh and Loh Sombetzki, 2017).

As a proponent of mandatory ethics settings, Lin (2014) argues that determining their vehicle's ethics settings would be too much of a burden for the users, who do not have the expertise to scrutinize the ethical code with which they would want their vehicle to be aligned. In a more thorough analysis, Gogoll and Müller (2017) state that providing the user with choices corresponding to different ethical frameworks would require analyzing and modeling every possible accident situation. This does not seem to be feasible because it is highly probable to miss a contextual variable, an unforeseen situation, or an important moral variable. Additionally, the authors make an analogy with "prisoner's dilemma."[e] More precisely, they assume that some people would be motivated by altruistic morality to begin with. If everyone confronted with an unavoidable accident tries to minimize harm to themselves, those altruists who would be willing to accept some harm reciprocally in order to minimize total harm would be crowded out. The death toll would be higher in a world where people would act selfishly and not want to sacrifice themselves compared to a world where people would cooperate and share the risk. Gogoll and Muller argue that a common ethics settings prescribed by the government would be in everybody's interest in order to avoid such social disorder. This would also be in line with government's monitoring and regulatory responsibilities.

In favor of a hybrid approach, Etzioni and Etzioni (2017) claim that the current traffic regulations already reflect the collective ethical views dictated by the society and governed by authorities, and that the ethical decisions remaining out of this general frame should be left up to the individuals.

How should the settings among which the driver should choose be produced, then? There is a consensus that the government and the policy making agencies introduce a set of principles that would maximize road safety for all, which would then be implemented by the car manufacturers. Those in favor of mandatory ethics settings see these as industry standards to be implemented for all users in the same way (Gogoll and Müller, 2017),

[e] The "prisoner's dilemma" is a well-known problem in game theory. It is meant to show the different consequences in rational decision making between cooperation and non-cooperation.

while those in favor of personal ethics settings propose to leave the choice of which principles their vehicle should conform to the driver as the primary moral agent responsible for the decision making (Brandão, 2018; Loh and Loh Sombetzki, 2017). This is aligned with the view that AV becomes a moral proxy of its user, instead of a moral agent, and thus, should reflect the user's ethical preferences (Sandberg and Bradshaw-Martin, 2013).

4. Ethical reflections on the automated vehicle in transport

While the issues related to the ethics-by-design, such as the ethical framework for the decision making of AV behavior in critical situations, has been largely addressed, little work has been carried out on the issues calling for an ethical reflection on the implementation of AV in the transport. In fact, a comprehensive literature review by Milakis et al. (2017) on the implications of AVs for transport policy demonstrates that intangible issues, such as social equity, economy, or public health, are under-researched compared to tangible issues (e.g., safety, road capacity, or travel costs). As a matter of fact, the far-reaching effects of transportation for society make ethics relevant. Very often, concepts such as fairness, justice, equity, and fair distribution of costs and benefits emerge in debates about AV and its implementation in transport. We will, thus, raise few of the ethical concerns that we consider relevant for the decision making process, while not being exhaustive.

The current debate on the integration of AVs in the transport systems is dominated by private actors with a focus on technology development and economic competitiveness, treating the users as mere "*clients*" instead of citizens who could participate in the decision making process (Alonso Raposo et al., 2019; Papa and Ferreira, 2018). Hence, not only the actual end users are treated as objects (the "*means*," in Kantian terms) instead of moral subjects (*ends*) who deserve moral considerations, but also they are reduced to a "*mere network element*" (Luetge, 2017). What would the actual place of human be in the complex technological and economic system of AV, except for being client? Will the users be free to choose to *not* delegate travel decisions without being deprived of their access to goods and services? The implementation of AV should not compromise people's autonomy and their access to exercise basic rights (EGE, 2018). Nor should it make people technology-dependent in their travel choices or use of mobility services.

On a related topic, experts and citizens express concerns about social justice, namely, whether the automated transport systems would be implemented in an equitable and inclusive manner (Declaration de Montreal, 2018; Papa and Ferreira, 2018). Epting (2019), for instance, argues that planning automated road transport mainly with the benefit of the currently mobile road users in mind may exacerbate the injustice and the challenges currently experienced by the vulnerable road user groups (e.g., people with disabilities, elderly citizens, people living in transport deserts, etc.). He, thus, proposes giving priority to the needs of vulnerable road user groups in the planning of automated road transport.

Similar concerns are articulated with respect to whether the benefits of automated transport systems would be equally accessible across all groups in a society (Declaration de Montreal, 2018; Papa and Ferreira, 2018). Vehicle automation is expected to bring about economic benefits (e.g., saved from healthcare, accident and legal costs). The models for fair distribution of these benefits accessible to all in a society are yet to be defined (EGE, 2018). Some basic decisions concern whether the benefits should be invested in new, sustainable public transport opportunities and urban design, be returned to users as transport subsidies, or remain as profit for the private actors. The answers, in fact, are tied to the challenging decisions about how individual and collective, public and private interests should be balanced.

We are aware that these ethical aspects are not fully acknowledged by the policy making processes for the non-automated transportation that we have today, either (Anciaes and Thomopoulos, 2014). The increasing public awareness about the disruptive impact of AV, however, could encourage policy makers to adopt a more transparent and inclusive process not to jeopardize public acceptance.

We have mentioned before that the transport policies were usually evaluated based on efficiency and effectiveness, but not always on equity. For instance, one may consider giving priority to the needs of vulnerable road user groups moral and socially inclusive. However, this moral reflection is likely to be clouded by efficiency factors dominating policy decisions. One way to increase the inclusion and the weigh of social costs and benefits and to give space to user expectations could be to employ a multi criteria analysis, which seems to be better adapted to the local policy decisions, despite the criticisms about subjectivity of the value judgments of the decision makers. Hence, there is clearly a trend and willingness to make informed decisions in an inclusive way in policy making.

In this regard, Van Wee and Roeser (2013) propose that the evaluation of transport policies could adopt *a context-sensitive approach*, that is, it could take into account morally relevant factors, in addition to traditional indicators of efficiency and effectiveness. Given the diversity of the morally relevant features, it is axiomatic that which feature to take into account or to give priority to, and how to resolve trade-offs become an issue. In this respect, democratic participation, that is, giving people a meaningful role in public engagement and deliberation about transport policies that have direct consequences on their quality of life, can help stakeholders comprehend the values and priorities of the people. In return, having a say in the decision making process could enhance the legitimacy of policy decisions, thereby the likelihood of public acceptance.

Roeser (2018) takes the traditional participatory approach a step further in her emotional deliberation approach to risk. By this, she defends giving people a say in the decision making process, as well as taking into account people's (moral) emotions about new technologies and incorporating values of stakeholders in decision making. In a way, different stakeholders could learn from the values and moral insight of each other instead of dismissing them as uninformed, irrational, or subjective. Despite the challenges in organizing it, a participatory approaches provide the means and methods both for citizens and stakeholders to ascertain their autonomy and self-determination, and enhances people's trust in procedural justice (Terwel et al., 2012).

5. Conclusions and directions for future research

In this chapter, we aimed at giving an overview of the current discussion on the ethical issues of AVs under two parts. In Section 3, we focused on the ethical settings of AV through its moral agency, application of different ethical theories to the decision making in critical situations, and the question of whether ethics setting should be mandatory or personal. In Section 4, we addressed some of the ethical challenges posed by the implementation of AV in the transport system.

It can be said that "doing the right thing" is quite difficult for humans and it is, of course, an even more complicated task for AVs. We can find proposals of ethical decision making for AVs in critical situations from all camps of philosophical theories. While each of them answers some questions, they raise others. Utilitarianism, which claims to balance right and wrong as they were physical magnitudes—numbers, probabilities, statistics—could lead to distortions. Deontological approach, on the contrary, hangs on the quite difficult burden of proof regarding the tenets, which are vulnerable to the charge of being biased, and hard to translate into algorithms suitable to govern artificial agents. Contractarians are not able to explain how to put "a veil of ignorance" on the eyes of single individuals and how could it be possible to calculate maximin in circumstances with unforeseen and uncountable variables. Theorists of randomness have similar issues, lacking grounds justifying a "neutral perspective." In fact, it is important to note that none of these moral theories was meant to be applied to the case of AVs by their founders. Although they provide a good starting point to feed our thinking, these proposals currently remain theoretical. Indeed, a lot of care is required when borrowing these ethical frameworks to tackle the challenges that are encountered with the development of new technologies. That is to say, research on the computational aspects and algorithmic calculations applying them are yet to be developed. For example, engineers favor remaining on one's lane to lane change because the uncertainty in predicting vehicle's lateral space is higher than that in longitudinal space (Davnall, 2020). This would mean a preference for brake rather than swerve at the low-level vehicle control, regardless of the high-level decision making function, from the developer's point of view. An ethics policy that would determine the eventual action of the vehicle, then, cannot afford ignoring this. Further research applying ethical frameworks to algorithms in order to test their feasibility and public acceptance could help to make decisions about which approach to lean toward, and to provide recommendations to regulators and policy makers.

The majority of articles reviewed focuses on the decisions of AV in critical, forced-choice situations. This was not a deliberate choice of the authors. Decisions in dilemma situations attract more attention, regardless of the likelihood of their actual occurrence and the soundness of arguments that animate public debate. To our knowledge, there are few publications elaborating on the mundane but ethically relevant situations (Goodall, 2019; Himmelreich, 2018). Goodall highlights four situations which are not associated with the popular ethical thinking but require a trade-off among conflicting objectives and an eventual risk distribution. These are following distance, brake strategies, lateral position within the lane, and permitting violations of the law by the AV. For instance, the way that the following distance is defined and how the margins are distributed between the vehicles in front of and behind the AV in our attempts to balance safety and efficiency will have impact on the risk allocation. Such short margins do not seem to matter at first. However, as Himmelreich puts it, large-scale, aggregate impact with the increasing number of AVs on the public roads will be substantial. Given that most of the ethical decisions to be made by AVs are likely to be in regular driving situations, there is a clear need for research in this area. Furthermore, ordinary situations are the ones that would require guidelines and policy making, rather than highly improbable and uncertain unavoidable accidents.

In Section 4, we tried to address some issues that necessitate ethical reflection with respect to the integration of the AV technology into the society and transport system. The issues we raised are neither exhaustive nor exclusive to the case of AV technology. Nonetheless, they require consideration as the transition to a disruptive technology of automated mobility is on the way. The emergence of non-conventional actors (e.g., Google) show the rapid evolution of the transport ecosystem with new innovations, partnerships, and business models. In such rapidly evolving and competitive system, policy makers should not fail to take into account ethical aspects of technology implementation, such as justice, autonomy, equity, and the democratic ideal of participation in the decision making, to name a few. One way to accommodate the right conditions for the development and testing of innovative solutions of automated mobility, while engaging people, is a living lab. In a report on the Future of road transport, Alonso Raposo et al. (2019) state that "*setting up a network of European living labs where new mobility solutions can be tested with the direct engagement of citizens can help both public and private entities to ensure that the new options will be financially sustainable while simultaneously contributing to improving the transport system*" (p. 107). A living lab could allow researchers to study many of the ethical challenges cited throughout this chapter. It could also allow analysis of the trade-offs among different ethical principles in transport decisions. Involving the citizens in the decision making process, providing them platforms to be directly heard could empower people, assuring them about the fairness of the decision making process and the protection and balance of public-private interests, thus enhancing public acceptance.

To conclude, automated vehicle technology is valuable to the extent that it improves the human condition. It is timely to scrutinize the ethical principles in the governance of AVs and the implications of AV for policy making decisions about its deployment in transport systems in a way enhancing the benefits for the society as a whole, to secure public acceptance.

Acknowledgment

This material is based on work supported by the STSM grant under the COST Action CA16222-42895 Wider Impacts of Autonomous and Connected Transport (WISE-ACT) for Ebru Dogan as a visiting researcher hosted by Federico Costantini at the University of Udine (IT) and the AVEthics project granted to Ebru Dogan (ANR-16-C22-008).

References

Alonso Raposo, M., Ciuffo, B., Ardente, F., Aurambout, J.-P., Baldini, G., Braun, R., Christidis, P., Christodoulou, A., Duboz, A., Felici, S., Ferragut, J., Georgakaki, A., Gkoumas, K., Grosso, M., Iglesias, M., Julea, A., Krause, J., Martens, B., Mathieux, F., Menzel, G., Mondello, S., Navajas Cawood, E., Pekár, F., Raileanu, I.-C., Scholz, H., Tamba, M., Tsakalidis, A., van Balen, M., Vandecasteele, I., 2019. The Future of Road Transport—Implications of Automated, Connected, Low-Carbon and Shared Mobility. EUR 29748 EN.

Anciaes, P.R., Thomopoulos, N., 2014. Ethical issues in transportation. In: Garrett, M. (Ed.), Encyclopedia of Transportation: Social Science and Policy. SAGE Publications, Thousand Oaks, California, USA, pp. 534–541.

Awad, E., Dsouza, S., Kim, R., Schulz, J., Henrich, J., Shariff, A., Bonnefon, J.-F., Rahwan, I., 2018. The moral machine experiment. Nature 563, 59–64. https://doi.org/10.1038/s41586-018-0637-6.

Bentham, J., 1988(1776). A Fragment on Government. Cambridge University Press, Cambridge.

Bergmann, L.T., Schlicht, L., Meixner, C., König, P., Pipa, G., Boshammer, S., Stephan, A., 2018. Autonomous vehicles require socio-political acceptance—an empirical and philosophical perspective on the problem of moral decision making. Front. Behav. Neurosci. 12, 31. https://doi.org/10.3389/fnbeh.2018.00031.

Bonnefon, J.-F., Shariff, A., Rahwan, I., 2016. The social dilemma of autonomous vehicles. Science 352, 1573–1576.

Brandão, M., 2018. Moral autonomy and equality of opportunity for algorithms in autonomous vehicles. In: Envisioning Robots in Society—Power, Politics, and Public Space: Proceedings of Robophilosophy 2018/TRANSOR 2018, Frontiers in Artificial Intelligence and Applications. Presented at the Robophilosophy 2018/TRANSOR 2018. IOS Press, Amsterdam, pp. 302–310. https://doi.org/10.3233/978-1-61499-931-7-302.

Contissa, G., Lagioia, F., Sartor, G., 2017. The ethical knob: ethically-customisable automated vehicles and the law. Artif. Intell. Law 25, 365–378. https://doi.org/10.1007/s10506-017-9211-z.

Davnall, R., 2020. Solving the single-vehicle self-driving car trolley problem using risk theory and vehicle dynamics. Sci. Eng. Ethics 26, 431–449. https://doi.org/10.1007/s11948-019-00102-6.

Declaration de Montreal IA Responsable, 2018. Partie 3: Rapport des resultats des ateliers de coconstruction de l'hiver (Declaration of Montreal Responsible AI, 2018. Part 3: Report of the Winter Coconstruction Workshops). https://docs.wixstatic.com/ugd/ebc3a3_fcdc3960bb9d482eb7967d7cc3530af7.pdf.

Dewitt, B., Fischhoff, B., Sahlin, N.-E., 2019. Moral machine' experiment is no basis for policymaking. Nature 567, 31. https://doi.org/10.1038/d41586-019-00766-x.

Epting, S., 2019. Automated vehicles and transportation justice. Philos. Technol. 32, 389–403. https://doi.org/10.1007/s13347-018-0307-5.

Etzioni, A., Etzioni, O., 2017. Incorporating ethics into artificial intelligence. J. Ethics 21, 403–418. https://doi.org/10.1007/s10892-017-9252-2.

European Group on Ethics in Science and New Technologies, 2018. Artificial Intelligence, Robotics and 'Autonomous' Systems. Publications Office of the European Union, Luxembourg, p. 2018.

Faulhaber, A.K., Dittmer, A., Blind, F., Wächter, M., Timm, S., Sütfeld, L.R., Stephan, A., Pipa, G., König, P., 2019. Human decisions in moral dilemmas are largely described by utilitarianism: virtual car driving study provides guidelines for autonomous driving vehicles. Sci. Eng. Ethics 25, 399–418. https://doi.org/10.1007/s11948-018-0020-x.

Foot, P., 1967. The Problem of Abortion and the Doctrine of Double Effect. Oxford Review 5, 5–15. reprinted in Steinbock B. and Norcross A., (Eds.), Killing and Letting Die, 2nd ed. New York: Fordham University Press, 1994, pp. 266–279; reprinted in Woodward, (Ed.), 143–155.

Gogoll, J., Müller, J.F., 2017. Autonomous cars: in favor of a mandatory ethics setting. Sci. Eng. Ethics 23, 681–700. https://doi.org/10.1007/s11948-016-9806-x.

Goodall, N.J., 2014. Ethical decision making during automated vehicle crashes. Transp. Res. Rec. 2424, 58–65.

Goodall, N.J., 2016. Can you program ethics into a self-driving car? IEEE Spectr. 53, 28–58.

Goodall, N.J., 2019. More than trolleys—plausible, ethically ambiguous scenarios likely to be encountered by automated vehicles. Transfers 9, 45–58. https://doi.org/10.3167/TRANS.2019.090204.

Greene, J., Rossi, F., Tasioulas, J., Venable, K.B., Williams, B., 2016. Embedding ethical principles in collective decision support systems. In: Thirtieth AAAI Conference on Artificial Intelligence, pp. 4147–4151.

Grinbaum, A., 2018. Chance as a value for artificial intelligence. J. Responsible Innov. 5, 353–360. https://doi.org/10.1080/23299460.2018.1495032.

Hevelke, A., Nida-Rümelin, J., 2015. Responsibility for crashes of autonomous vehicles: an ethical analysis. Sci. Eng. Ethics 21, 619–630. https://doi.org/10.1007/s11948-014-9565-5.

Himmelreich, J., 2018. Never mind the trolley: the ethics of autonomous vehicles in mundane situations. Ethical Theory Moral Pract. 21, 669–684. https://doi.org/10.1007/s10677-018-9896-4.

Kant, I., 1998(1785). Groundwork of the metaphysics of morals. M.J. Gregor, Trans. In: Introduction by Christine Korsgaard. Cambridge University Press, Cambridge.

Keeling, G., 2018. Legal necessity, pareto efficiency & justified killing in autonomous vehicle collisions. Ethical Theory Moral Pract. 21, 413–427. https://doi.org/10.1007/s10677-018-9887-5.

Leben, D., 2017. A Rawlsian algorithm for autonomous vehicles. Ethics Inf. Technol. 19, 107–115. https://doi.org/10.1007/s10676-017-9419-3.

Li, J., Zhao, X., Cho, M.-J., Ju, W., Malle, B.F., 2016. From trolley to autonomous vehicle: perceptions of responsibility and moral norms in traffic accidents with self-driving cars. In: Presented at the SAE 2016 World Congress and Exhibition. https://doi.org/10.4271/2016-01-0164.

Lin, P., 2014. Here's a Terrible Idea: Robot Cars With Adjustable Ethics Settings. Wired.

Loh, W., Loh Sombetzki, J., 2017. Autonomy and responsibility in hybrid systems: The example of autonomous cars | W. Loh. In: Lin, P., Abney, K., Jenkins, R. (Eds.), Robot Ethics 2.0: From Autonomous Cars to Artificial Intelligence. Oxford University Press, New York.

Luetge, C., 2017. The German ethics code for automated and connected driving. Philos. Technol. 30, 547–558. https://doi.org/10.1007/s13347-017-0284-0.

Milakis, D., van Arem, B., van Wee, B., 2017. Policy and society related implications of automated driving: a review of literature and directions for future research. J. Intell. Transp. Syst. 21, 324–348. https://doi.org/10.1080/15472450.2017.1291351.

Nyholm, S., 2017. Attributing agency to automated systems: reflections on human-robot collaborations and responsibility loci. Sci. Eng. Ethics 24, 1201–1219. https://doi.org/10.1007/s11948-017-9943-x.

Nyholm, S., 2018a. Attributing agency to automated systems: reflections on human–robot collaborations and responsibility-loci. Sci. Eng. Ethics 24, 1201–1219. https://doi.org/10.1007/s11948-017-9943-x.

Nyholm, S., 2018b. The ethics of crashes with self-driving cars: a roadmap, II. Philos. Compass 13, e12506. https://doi.org/10.1111/phc3.12506.

Nyholm, S., Smids, J., 2016. The ethics of accident-algorithms for self-driving cars: an applied trolley problem? Ethical Theory Moral Pract. 19, 1275–1289. https://doi.org/10.1007/s10677-016-9745-2.

Papa, E., Ferreira, A., 2018. Sustainable accessibility and the implementation of automated vehicles: identifying critical decisions. Urban Sci. 2, 5. https://doi.org/10.3390/urbansci2010005.

Rawls, J., 1971. A Theory of Justice. The Belknap, Cambridge.

Roeser, S., 2018. Risk, Technology, and Moral Emotions. Routledge.

Sandberg, A., Bradshaw-Martin, H., 2013. What do cars think of trolley problems: ethics for autonomous cars. In: Romportl, J., Ircing, P., Zackova, E., Polak, M., Schuster, R. (Eds.), Beyond AI: Artificial Golem Intelligence. Presented at the Beyond AI 2013, University of West Bohemia, Pilsen, Czech Republic.

Santoni de Sio, F., 2017. Killing by autonomous vehicles and the legal doctrine of necessity. Ethical Theory Moral Pract. 20, 411–429. https://doi.org/10.1007/s10677-017-9780-7.

Santoni de Sio, F., van den Hoven, J., 2018. Meaningful human control over autonomous systems: a philosophical account. Front. Robot. AI 5, 15. https://doi.org/10.3389/frobt.2018.00015.

Sinnott-Armstrong, W., 2019. Consequentialism. In: Zalta, E.N. (Ed.), The Stanford Encyclopedia of Philosophy. Metaphysics Research Lab, Stanford University.

Task Force on Ethical Aspects of Connected and Automated Driving, 2018. https://www.bmvi.de/SharedDocs/EN/publications/report-ethics-task-force-automated-driving.pdf?__blob=publicationFile.

Terwel, B.W., ter Mors, E., Daamen, D.D.L., 2012. It's not only about safety: beliefs and attitudes of 811 local residents regarding a CCS project in Barendrecht. Int. J. Greenhouse Gas Control 9, 41–51. https://doi.org/10.1016/j.ijggc.2012.02.017.

Thomson, J.J., 1985. The trolley problem. Yale Law J. 94, 1395–1415. https://doi.org/10.2307/796133.

Van Wee, B., Roeser, S., 2013. Ethical theories and the cost–benefit analysis-based ex ante evaluation of transport policies and plans. Trans. Rev. 33, 743–760. https://doi.org/10.1080/01441647.2013.854281.

Wintersberger, P., Prison, A.K., Riener, A., Hasirlioglu, S., 2017. The experience of ethics: evaluation of self harm risks in automated vehicles. In: IEEE Intelligent Vehicle Symposium. https://doi.org/10.1109/IVS.2017.7995749.

CHAPTER TEN

Governance cultures and sociotechnical imaginaries of self-driving vehicle technology: Comparative analysis of Finland, UK and Germany

Miloš N. Mladenović[a,*], Dominic Stead[b], Dimitris Milakis[c], Kate Pangbourne[d], Moshe Givoni[e,†]

[a]Aalto University, Espoo, Finland
[b]Delft University of Technology, Delft, The Netherlands
[c]Institute of Transport Research, German Aerospace Center (DLR), Berlin, Germany
[d]University of Leeds, Leeds, United Kingdom
[e]Tel Aviv University, Tel Aviv-Yafo, Israel
*Corresponding author: e-mail address: milos.mladenovic@aalto.fi

Contents

† Deceased

Advances in Transport Policy and Planning, Volume 5
ISSN 2543-0009
https://doi.org/10.1016/bs.atpp.2020.01.001

Abstract

As an emerging technology, the potential deployment of self-driving vehicles (SDVs) in cities is attributed with significant uncertainties and anticipated consequences requiring responsible governance of innovation processes. Despite a growing number of studies on policies and governance arrangements for managing the introduction of SDVs, there is a gap in understanding about country-specific governance strategies and approaches. This chapter addresses this gap by presenting a comparative analysis of SDV-related policy documents in Finland, UK, and Germany, three countries which are actively seeking to promote the introduction of SDVs and which have distinct administrative traditions. Our analytical framework is based on the set of premises about technology as a complex sociotechnical phenomenon, operationalized using governance cultures and sociotechnical imaginaries concepts. Our comparative policy document analysis focuses on the assumed roles for SDV technology, the identified domains and mechanisms of governance, and the assumed actors responsible for steering the development process. The results highlight similarities in pro-automation values across three different countries, while also uncovering important differences outside the domain of traditional transport policy instruments. In addition, the results identify different types of potential technological determinism, which could restrict opportunities for responsiveness and divergent visions of mobility futures in Europe. Concluding with a warning against further depolitization of technological development and a dominant focus on economic growth, we identify several necessary directions for further developing governance and experimentation processes.

Keywords: Automated vehicle, Smart mobility governance, Connected vehicles, Automated driving, Transport policy

1. Introduction

The landscape of urban mobility technologies is currently experiencing a period of significant change, with multiple emerging mobility technologies, which are by definition imbued with such features as uncertainty, prominent impact, and fast development (Rotolo et al., 2015). Focusing particularly on self-driving[a] vehicles (SDVs), there is a growing body of literature reflecting on the governance and policy implications in relation to multiple anticipated consequences (Blyth et al., 2016; Cohen and Cavoli, 2019; Fagnant and Kockelman, 2015; Faisal et al., 2019; Fraedrich et al., 2019; Guerra, 2016; Hopkins and Schwanen, 2018; Legacy et al., 2019; Milakis et al., 2017;

[a] Some other commonly used terms include automated and autonomous vehicles. The choice here was made based on the Aristotelian concept of *telos*, as end-purpose for the technological artifact, which in this case is assumed to be capacity to perform the act of driving (by) itself.

Porter et al., 2018; Stilgoe, 2018; Thomopoulos and Givoni, 2015). Starting from the fundamental governance rationales of efficiency, equity and ethics (Howlett, 2009; Lyons, 2018; Winfield and Jirotka, 2018), we observe that the domain of emerging mobility technologies such as SDVs faces a classic Collingridge double-bind dilemma.[b] This dilemma contrasts the early stage of development, when change is easy but there is uncertainty about consequences, with the later stages of technological maturity, associated with a lock-in when the technology has become societally embedded (Collingridge, 1980; Genus and Stirling, 2018). This dilemma is at the core of challenges for steering development of an emerging technology, highlighting the need for governing responsible innovation processes that would avoid different types of technological determinism (Wyatt, 2008).

While reflection about undesired consequences and responsible innovation is ongoing, there remains a gap in country-specific analysis of governance strategies (Milakis, 2019; Taeihagh and Lim, 2019). Addressing such gap is important for devising common and specific governance strategies across Europe, involving hybrid multi-actor networks. This research addresses this gap by comparatively reviewing national level SDV governance document for a set of three European countries: Finland, Germany and the UK. These countries have been selected as they are among the global leaders in SDV technology development and are actively developing related governance strategies. Moreover, each country represents a distinct administrative tradition of western democracy, namely Nordic, Rhinelandic, and "British Isles" (Loughlin et al., 2011), providing a useful dimension by which to compare and contrast. For achieving the above end, we form a novel framework for the analysis of technological innovation governance. The much-utilized Multi-Level Governance perspective often overlooks spatial variables (Pangbourne, 2010), and is more concerned with articulations between scale on the one hand, and the interplay of and the distribution of powers. Contrastingly, we draw theoretical constructs from both governance and technology studies to uncover additional political, cultural, historical and geographical factors, and consider their implications.

The chapter is divided into six sections. In Section 2, we set out our analytical framework, which synthesizes concepts of governance cultures and sociotechnical imaginaries, forming a technology-governance-culture triad.

[b] "attempting to control a technology is difficult ... because during its early stages, when it can be controlled, not enough can be known about its harmful social consequences to warrant controlling its development; but by the time these consequences are apparent, control has become costly and slow" (Collingridge, 1980).

We then list three research questions and describe how we apply this framework to our analysis of public documents on SDVs from our three case studies. In Sections 3–5, we systematically explore our three research questions relating to the assumed societal roles for SDVs, the identified domains and mechanisms of governance of SDV deployment, and the assumed actants[c] responsible for steering the development process. Section 6 concludes with a summary of analysis, discussion of potential for technological determinism, and a set of recommendations for further research through establishing epistemological parallels between technology studies and transport studies.

2. Methodology

2.1 Analytical framework

In order to develop our analytical framework, we first establish our understanding of SDV technology as a complex sociotechnical phenomenon (e.g., Mladenović, 2018, 2019). As a central premise of this perspective, technologies are understood not just as utilitarian artifacts, but as underpinned and shaped by dynamic interactions with human values and norms (Feenberg, 1999; Kroes and Verbeek, 2014; Kudina, 2019; Mladenovic et al., 2019; Verbeek, 2011). In fact, technologies mediate human activities and experiences, co-constructing decisions and moral standpoints. Understanding that we cannot treat technologies as merely objects and humans as subjects interacting with them has important implications for moral agency, as a hybrid affair of networked human beings and acting, networked, artifacts. In this way, we proceed by terming both humans and technologies as *actants* (Latour, 1992, 1996). Another important premise is that emerging technology has *interpretative flexibility*, where functioning of technology is the result and not the cause of it becoming a successful and acceptable artifact, often assessed through the lens of particular social groups (Pinch and Bijker, 1984).

Having grounded our analytical perspective on the understanding of emerging technology as a complex social-technical phenomenon, we identify two key concepts necessary for our analysis. First concept are *sociotechnical imaginaries*, as "imagined forms of social life and social order reflected in the

[c] Rather than the more common term, actor, which is reserved for humans and their organizations in this chapter, actant is a term introduced to overcome human-only connotations for action in technological innovation processes.

design and fulfillment of nation-specific scientific and/or technological projects" (Jasanoff, 2004; Jasanoff and Kim, 2015). This concept lies beneath intertwined processes of (national) identity construction and visions of technological innovation (Ryghaug and Toftaker, 2016). Such visions often include co-construction of hopes and fears among specific institutions and actors that exist in the midst of processes of technological emergence (Kaplan and Tripsas, 2008; Sturken et al., 2004). Clearly, sociotechnical imaginaries of one country will differ from that of another, due to the differences in cultural context in which they are embedded. Therefore, we can use this concept to inform our understanding of the institutionalized practices for testing and deploying knowledge claims in a society. Many knowledge claims are made about emerging technologies such as SDVs, which are highly complex innovations involving many different fields of knowledge and innovation. Such knowledge claims are associated with the ways in which the members of the given society imagine any given technology and its relationship to the social order. Thus, sociotechnical imaginaries will be used as one of the lenses for interpretation and comparison.

The second key concept for developing the analytical framework is that of *governance culture*, which underlines cultural meanings and values in relation to acceptable purposes and appropriate mechanisms of governance practices (Paulsson et al., 2017; Rogge and Reichardt, 2016; Stead, 2018). Here, we perceive that the governance of emerging technologies often faces an institutional void intertwined with distributed responsibility in hybrid networks of relevant institutions (Sclove, 1995; Wetmore, 2004). Following the ongoing discussion in the domain of technology ethics related to the responsibility gap for actions of learning automata, we recognize that responsibilities are formed during, often unstructured, negotiations between different groups of actants, such as designers, legislators, and users (Felt et al., 2017; Noorman, 2014; Schulzke, 2013; van de Poel, 2011). Furthermore, with the initial premise that SDV technology is a complex artifact, we recognize a potentially wider web of governance actants, beyond the human ones. In fact, technological development can be referred to as a "problem of many hands," where governments, transnational tech companies, individuals, and even technological devices themselves influence the redistribution of power and morality (Collingridge, 1980; Susskind, 2018; Winner, 1980). Therefore, our analytic framework has to provide a means of interpreting the wider cultural context in which these institutions are embedded, rather than solely focusing on the structure of institutional arrangements (Marsden and Reardon, 2017; Voß and Freeman, 2016).

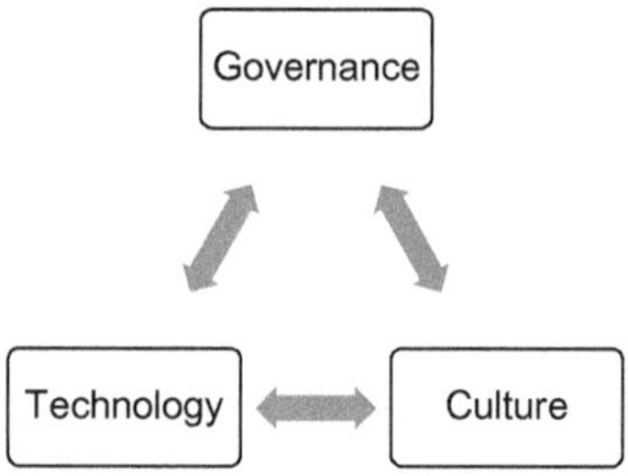

Fig. 1 Graphical representation of the technology-governance-culture triad.

Rather than reducing governance analysis to describing sets of bureaucratic institutions, the governance culture lens enables us to include a range of organizational mechanisms, operational assumptions, modes of thought, and consequential activities.

Combining the above concepts into a *technology-culture-governance triad* (Fig. 1) enables a deeper understanding of how emerging technologies are being framed, assessed and responded to in different national contexts. By synthesizing the concepts of governance cultures and sociotechnical imaginaries into a single framework, we are better able to analyze the discursive meanings of technology found in governance documents by setting them alongside broader (national) cultural assumptions. Thus, in addition to deepening the concept of emerging technology, we acknowledge rhetorical functions of governance (Mladenović, 2019; Pangbourne et al., 2019). Rhetoric is an important mechanism in the social construction of technology and challenges that technologies are supposed to address (Berkhout, 2006), and thus is crucial in the development of sociotechnical imaginaries.

2.2 Research questions and policy documents reviewed

In order to reveal the cultural interpretations of SDVs in Finnish, UK and German policies we ask three questions which are considered in turn in the next three sections of this chapter:

1. What are the assumed roles of SDV technology and its development process?
2. What are the identified domains and mechanisms of governance in relation to anticipated challenges and risks in SDV technological development process?
3. Who are the assumed actants responsible for the SDV technological development process?

Each of these questions is addressed through reviewing policy documents. Our data consists of a selection of national documents concerning transport and technological development policies in Finland, Germany and the UK. Several types of documents are reviewed, including strategies, policy statements, and governmental webpages. These span a period of 7 years, from 2013 to 2019, in order to try to identify the dominant discourse and governance culture that are embodied in the policy documents. A full list of the documents we sourced and examined is presented across Tables 1–3 (for Finland, UK and Germany respectively). In line with our analytical framework, we review these documents as political artifacts produced in a particular cultural context, which represent the stabilized agreements of negotiations among often-heterogeneous groups of people and organizations (Jasanoff and Kim, 2015). The analysis focuses on (a) explicit goals as expressions of sociotechnical imaginaries and (b) underlying assumptions and ideals expressed with specific terminology or visuals.

Table 1 Documents relevant to technological visions for transport in Finland and produced by governance actors, in chronological order of publication (accessed by the authors via source websites).

Year	Title	Source
2013	Toward a new transport policy: Intelligence in Transport and Wisdom in Mobility	Finnish Ministry of Transport and Communications
2014	Fair and Intelligent Transport	Finnish Ministry of Transport and Communications
2014	100 opportunities for Finland and the world: Radical Technology Inquirer (RTI) for anticipation/evaluation of technological breakthroughs	Committee for the Future, Parliament of Finland
2014	Innovation policy options for sustainability transitions in Finnish transport	Finnish Funding Agency for Technology and Innovation
2015	A Nordic Model for Human-centered Personal Data Management and Processing	Finnish Ministry of Transport and Communications
2017	Road Traffic Act	Finnish Ministry of Transport and Communications
2017	Finland's Age of Artificial Intelligence	Ministry of Economic Affairs and Employment

Continued

Table 1 Documents relevant to technological visions for transport in Finland and produced by governance actors, in chronological order of publication (accessed by the authors via source websites).—Cont'd

Year	Title	Source
2018	Act on Transport Service	Finnish Ministry of Transport and Communications
2018	Societal transformation 2018–37: 100 anticipated radical technologies, 20 regimes, case Finland	Committee for the Future, Parliament of Finland
2018	Work in the age of artificial intelligence	Ministry of Economic Affairs and Employment
2019	The impact of automated transport on the role, operations and costs of road operators and authorities in Finland	Finnish Transport and Communications Agency

Table 2 Documents relevant to technological visions for transport in the United Kingdom and produced by governance actors, in chronological order of publication (accessed by the authors via source websites).

Year	Title	Source
2015	The pathway to driverless cars: A code of practice for testing	Department for Transport
2016	Pathway to driverless cars: Proposals to support advanced driver assistance systems and automated vehicle technologies	The Department for Transport; Centre for Connected and Autonomous Vehicles
2016	Funding competition: connected and autonomous vehicles 2	Department for Business, Energy & Industrial Strategy
2017	Vehicle technology and aviation bill	UK Parliament
2017	New measures set out autonomous vehicle insurance and electric vehicle infrastructure	Centre for Connected and Autonomous Vehicles; Centre for Protection of National Infrastructure; Department for Transport
2017	The key principles of vehicle cyber security for connected and automated vehicles	Department for Transport

Table 2 Documents relevant to technological visions for transport in the United Kingdom and produced by governance actors, in chronological order of publication (accessed by the authors via source websites).—Cont'd

Year	Title	Source
2017	UK Testing Ecosystem for Connected and Autonomous Vehicles	Centre for Connected and Autonomous Vehicles
2017	Industrial strategy: The grand challenges	Department for Business, Energy & Industrial Strategy
2018	Automated and Electric Vehicles Act	UK Parliament
2018	The fundamental principles of automotive cyber security—Specification	Department for Transport; Centre for the Protection of National Infrastructure
2019	Code of Practice: Automated vehicle trialing	Department for Transport

Table 3 Documents relevant to technological visions for transport in Germany and produced by governance actors, in chronological order of publication (accessed by the authors via source websites).

Year	Title	Source
2015	Strategy for Automated and Connected Driving	Federal Ministry of Transport and Digital Infrastructure
2017	Road Traffic Act	Federal Ministry of Justice and Consumer Protection
2017	Report of the Ethics Commission on Automated and Connected Driving	Federal Ministry of Transport and Digital Infrastructure
2017	Data protection law recommendations of the Federal Commissioner for Data Protection and Freedom of Information for Automated and Connected Driving	Federal Ministry of Transport and Digital Infrastructure
2018	Report on the Implementation of the Automated and Connected Driving Strategy	Federal Ministry of Transport and Digital Infrastructure
2018	National Platform "Future of Mobility"	Federal Ministry of Transport and Digital Infrastructure; Federal Ministry of Economy

3. What are the presumed roles of SDV technology in society?

In analyzing the sociotechnical imaginaries for the role of SDV technology in society, we identified a set of common visions across all the three case countries, as well as some differences in focus and terminology. Across all the three countries, it is evident that SDVs are considered important for addressing significant national and global challenges around transport system efficiency, traffic safety, energy demand and sources in transport, and carbon neutrality. However, we found evidence that the societal role for SDV technology is not just imagined in relation to the transport system needs, but is shaped also by other assumptions about social needs and economic opportunities, as highlighted before by Stilgoe (2018).

Indeed, the central assumption present in all three countries is that innovation in the domain of SDV technology should contribute to the national economic growth, which is often equated with national identity characteristics such as prosperity and sense of pride. The arguments about economic growth also tend to be framed in some similar ways across Finland, the UK and Germany, as necessary responses to social imperatives. For example, the theme of the aging population is discursively related to challenging national demographic dependency ratio, directly related to the problems in economic productivity. It is also common for governance documents in all three countries to associate explicitly economic growth with competitiveness in the global labor and product market, not only between firms but also between nation states and regional blocks. Thus, governance imaginations center on narrating a global role for the specific nation in leading some aspect of the technological development of SDVs. We present examples over the next few paragraphs.

In Finland, the vision of economic development through technological innovation is shaped by long-term transition to knowledge economy and carving out a niche for specialization among large actors outside of EU, such as US or China. Thus, economic growth is portrayed as essential for national survival. In addition to challenges similar to UK and Germany (see below), Finnish documents mention several other challenges, such as lack of raw materials and dependence on foreign energy resources, late and under-utilized urbanization hand in hand with the loss of rural livelihood, and the need for large infrastructural investments for a relatively large area compared to population. Thus, SDV technology finds its role in the general shift of the Finnish nation's focus on being an information and knowledge economy, in contrast to its industrial past (Halme et al., 2014), and decoupling the prospect for economic growth from geographic factors. In particular, in the document "100 opportunities for Finland and the world," SDVs are listed among the 100 technologies that have the potential to develop into world-changing technology, and the value-networks developing SDV technology are already considered to be among the 20 most important value-networks for Finland's future. The significance of this role for SDV technology is pinpointed as arising from a specific synergy between innovation policy in the domains of digitalization, automation, and servitization,[d] exemplified with a focus on development of artificial intelligence (AI) application, and increasing citizen's digital literacy. Other significant national projects are also framed as supporting development of SDVs, such as development of 5G telecommunication technology and investments into know-how of building sensor components.

In contrast to Finland's imperative of "national survival," UK and German imaginaries of the role of SDVs in relation to economic growth are centered on perceived existing or intended global leadership in technological development. From the UK, we highlight this statement from its Industrial Strategy:

> We will become a world leader in shaping the future of mobility.
>
> ***(DBEIS, 2017, p. 48).***

A similar example about perceptions or aspirations for global technological leadership comes from the landing webpage of Germany's Strategy for Automated and Connected Driving:

> The motor car was invented in Germany. We have revolutionized it time and again. And today, we are still at the top of the international league table when it comes to innovations in the automotive sector. All the major innovations associated with the car - from the four-stroke engine to the anti-lock braking system - come from Germany.
>
> ***(FMTDI, 2015, no page).***

These two examples of the UK and German rhetoric exemplify important differences in the perceived nation's roles in being innovation leaders. UK governance documents see emerging opportunities from increased digitalization and intelligence in vehicles to attract foreign investment and develop high-skill, well-paying, jobs. On the other hand, the German vision for SDV

[d] Focus on providing services as oppose to products. In line with service economy concept.

technology is firmly based on its historically important contributions to the automotive industry, and reflects the continuing of strong partnerships between the industry and public sector.

Despite some similarities, there is a striking point of divergence between the UK and Germany in the assumed role for SDV technology. The UK policy documents highlight resilience and readiness of the industry, and links it to questions of national security. In the UK, an opportunity is perceived to use certain requirements of SDV technology to stimulate associated growth in the cybersecurity sector as well as to strengthen its citizens' responses to such threats. This latter point contrasts with Finland's focus on the digital literacy of citizens. The threat that the German industrial strategy centralizes is that of the climate crisis, and the vision of taking the global leading role in addressing that crisis. Finally, both UK and German governance documents base their arguments, for the important role to be played by investing in SDV technology as a key platform for economic growth, on the quality of their transportation, logistics, and telecommunication infrastructure. However, those arguments in the UK rhetoric are focused on the need for improving the failing infrastructure, while those in Germany are focused on infrastructure providing an excellent basis for technological testing.

4. What are the domains and mechanisms of governance?

4.1 Liability

Assumptions about underlying risks and adverse effects shape how different governance cultures perceive their domains and mechanisms of action. Overall, all three governance approaches have an underlying premise that risks are problems to be managed, without recognizing potentially unanticipated consequences (see also Taeihagh and Lim, 2019). One of the risks to be managed is the focus on liability in the case of traffic crashes, as a traditionally relevant question for the automotive industry. Here, it is interesting to note that the driver does not have a legal definition in the Finnish law, which refers to road user. Legally, the responsible user of the vehicle must be identifiable, but that person can legally have access to the vehicle via remote operation. Such cases of remote operation have been specifically included in the recent updates to Finnish legislation. In the UK, changes in the legislation have laid out a comprehensive list, clarifying the liability of insurers and SDV owners, ensuring that liability for accidents remains under the existing vehicle insurance scheme. In contrast, German legislative changes have gone one-step further, with the requirements that SDVs must have a black box recording during the entire journey to determine liability during collisions, and have doubled the maximum liability limits.

4.2 Public experiments

In addition to liability for accidents, a related domain of governance is emerging in all three countries—public experiments. Based on its current governance framework, Finland allows SDV trials on the entire road network. Several governance documents recognize the potentially challenging environmental conditions, such as winter and night, so encouragement of experimentation is seen a viable approach to managing technological risks. In addition, Finnish governance documents are mentioning the need for systematic classification of features for operational design domains (ODDs) as a response to anticipated impacts. Similarly, public trials in the UK have also been increasing. These trials are accompanied with the development of business plans and roadmaps for SDVs. In contrast with the legislation on accident liability, manufacturers are also protected under the Consumer Protection Act, if they demonstrate that vehicle was not defective at the time it was supplied, or that defect was detected only later, due to technological advancements. In addition, UK is the only country having recently proposed Code of Practice for public SDV experimentation. Thus, both Finland and UK seem to have opted for more experimental approach to governance, with a focus on informing and incentives as opposed to constraints and punishment-oriented legislation. German approach has focused on developing digital test beds on different road types (e.g., motorways, urban areas), for trials in real traffic situations. Similar to Finland and UK, this development approach has engaged actors from different sectors and levels, emphasizing the need for cooperation. In contrast to Finland and UK, German approach to testing has more explicitly been focusing on interoperability, exemplified with establishing a digital test bed together with France.

4.3 Data management

Hand in hand with experimentation, the question of data management in its widest sense has been identified as a domain in several governance documents. For example, even the Finnish Road Traffic Act, traditionally focused on transport legislation, has included that detailed location data on roads, signs, traffic lights and other control mechanisms should be available for SDVs operators to use. In general, the Finnish approach has focused on deregulation, opening public data sources, and providing supporting digital interfaces. Transport Service Law has played a particularly important role in this legislative change, influenced by the identified synergy between SDVs and development of working business models for the operation of the transport system (e.g., Mobility as a Service concept). Other governance documents have openly acknowledged that the Finnish ecosystem is missing prototype-level automotive hardware computing platforms and is lagging with industry investments. Thus, major focus remains of data "utilization," with assumption that "customers" will provide data on trip destination and origins, as this would be essential for traffic management mechanisms. The focus on data as synergetic with innovation incentives, domain of governance has been associated with financial mechanisms, such as adjustments in taxation and dedicated development strategies from the Finnish Funding Agency for Technology and Innovation. On the contrary, privacy and security issues are left aside, "to be solved," thus neglecting that data protection is not protection of personality, as exemplified with the quote below, from "The impact of automated transport on the role, operations and costs of road operators and authorities in Finland":

> It is assumed that for all automated vehicles the origin and destination are known, as this information is present in the vehicle when it commences the trip (the security and privacy issues have to be solved). Knowing the origin and destination is important to facilitate effective routing of the vehicles.
>
> ***(FTCA, p. 119).***

Slightly different from the Finnish understanding of the governance domain, the UK governance has explicitly focused on cybersecurity, recognizing challenges related to data theft and hacking. The guidelines recommend that manufacturers follow ISO standards, asking for personal information is "managed properly." For example, highlighted aspects include data storage and transmission, as well as ensuring that SDV user is able to delete "sensitive" data, although more specific definitions of "proper" management or "sensitive" data are not provided. In addition, as mentioned in relation to the role of SDV technology, UK governance underlines system design for resilience to attacks and having appropriate responses under failure. Thus, both Finnish and UK governance cultures neglect the importance of privacy as the important domain for public resistance, as has already proven decisive in the case of proposal for reforming road-pricing regulation in Finland to enable continuous driving monitoring. However, it is interesting to note that a governmental attempt from 2015 in Finland named "A Nordic Model for Human-centered Personal Data Management and Processing," or MyData in short, has fallen down in importance in the later governance documents. Developed as a form of data activism, MyData initiative assumed citizens and consumers being more active about their personal data, capable of controlling the gathering, sharing and analysis of personal data. Contrary to the dominant GDPR understanding, where data is considered as part of individual's personality, MyData treats personal data as a resource, which the individual can access, control, and benefit from. Ideologically provoking, this initiative is driven by "parallel development of digital rights, innovation and business growth," aiming to push for design of new services. Thus, as a form of data activism, MyData fails to address discrepancy between technological and social data activism (Lehtiniemi and Ruckenstein, 2019).

Contrary to the Finnish and UK approach, German governance culture has taken a more control-oriented approach regarding data access and processing. In addition, one distinct feature of German governance approach is the recognition that federated structure might spur innovation, but that consistency would require intervention on a federal level. Thus, federal cohesion is a secondary, but still an important governance mechanism. German data protection regulation is very similar to GDPR regarding the definition of personal data as any information with the slightest relation to an individual. Similar to GDPR, these regulations pertain to all data, and emphasize on complete transparency and drivers' full authority over the use of such data. As ethics has been central value of Germans national self-understanding and self-representation (Sperling, 2004), such emphasis is especially evident in its governance culture. In fact, Germany is the only EU country having formed a national Ethics Commission on SDVs, and provided 20 ethical guidelines for SDV development. Those guidelines are the first to suggest algorithms embedded in SDV technology as a necessary governance domain. For example, this document states that it is unethical for SDV algorithms to use any individual's data (e.g., age or gender) as discriminatory decision-making criteria during unavoidable accident scenarios. Moreover, these guidelines are underlying data protection with the notion of personal autonomy and informational self-determination, as important ethical concepts, largely missing from Finnish and UK governance rhetoric.

5. Who are the governance actants?

5.1 Non-humans

As highlighted in the previous section, one of the clearly recognized actants is the driver, or the road user in Finland, which can also be a remote operator. However, all the governance cultures in Finland, UK, and Germany do not recognize explicitly the role and power of non-human actants, taking a neutral stance to the meaning of technology. For example, an interesting change in the Finnish Road Traffic Act is replacing the continuous yellow lines on Finnish roads to white, as these are easier for machine vision detection. In this context, one could argue that technology has clearly acted on the governance actors, resulting in an unusual addition to the legislation that is otherwise not foreseen in such a document. Moreover, one can notice the importance of data as an actant, being at the center of major governance changes. For example, the Finnish Road Traffic Act asks for integrated detailed location data on road control devices, which could be used by SDV operators. Thus, the crucial point here is in neglecting the "missing masses," as Latour named artifacts whose power is not accounted for in innovation processes (Latour, 1992).

5.2 Experts

Aside from neglecting the power of technological actants, there is a dominant focus on particular expert-based roles in the transport, ICT, and economic sectors, and related practices of foresight and technological assessment in governance processes. Despite the fact that these three countries are considered leaders of the democratic Western world, such focus on narrow expertise can be central to non-democratic technological dogmatism, reducing societal reflexivity and inclusive deliberation. In particular, dogmatism persists due to the lack of process transparency, or in case of groups unable to exercise independent views of the technology, often being unduly optimistic and serving the particular needs of organizations by which their expertise is commissioned (Collingridge, 1992). Moreover, the challenge of dogmatism is highlighted even more if there is a tendency for domination of the field and risk estimation by a handful of experts.[e] Altogether, such expert-based practices do not only lack in process ethics, but could fail to deliver a careful balance between equity and efficiency, failing to establish high quality processes of responsible innovation.

In Finland, such tight network of human actors is spread across public, semi-public, and private organizations. In addition, there has been an ongoing division and restructuring of organizations in the transport sector. The Ministry is still the organization responsible for political and strategic

[e] Kehoe problem refers to "the leading scientific authority on environmental lead in the 1930s, whose findings came to determine an erroneous threshold limit for safe exposure to lead," as stated in Genus and Stirling (2018).

guidelines and legislation. However, recent changes have resulted in three other organizations. First, the Finnish Transport and Communications Agency, as responsible for transport licenses, competences, supervision, and safety. Second, the Finnish Transport Infrastructure Agency responsible for planning, developing, and maintaining road, rail, and maritime transport infrastructure, and on the coordination of transport and land-use. Third, the Traffic Management Finland Group, a state-owned company with a special mission to focus on traffic control tasks for road traffic, rail traffic, and maritime routes. In addition, there are also regional Centers for Economic Development, Transport and the Environment, and various other regional or municipal organizations, in close interaction with private sector. In fact, the Finnish governance documents explicitly recommend cooperation and dialogue between automotive industry, and national, regional, and local road operators and authorities. Similar networked governance roles of experts are visible in both UK and Germany. The UK was the first to set up a specific government department, the Centre for Connected and Autonomous Vehicles, followed later on by Germany with national platform "Future of Mobility," where one out of six working groups is "Digitization, Automated Driving and New Mobility Concepts." In addition, in all three countries, it is evident that assumed roles needed for governance of SDVs are not just in transport or ICT sector, but also in the economic sector, such as Department for Business, Energy & Industrial Strategy in the UK. However, the UK governance network was noticeably more focused on including security experts, such as those from the Centre for the Protection of National Infrastructure and National Cybersecurity Centre.

5.3 Citizens

Following the concept of *citoyen*[f] from the European tradition of French revolution, it is important to highlight that such a conception of an individual cannot be found in the existing governance imaginaries. In fact, words such as customer, consumer or user are more often used than the word citizen. The relation to such imagined "customer" is establishing a mediating or subordinate relation over citoyens. Several documents focus on a need to steer behavior toward consistency and predictability, arguing for familiarizing users with the rules. In addition, such "customer" is only expected to ask

[f] Envisioned as a citizen highly active in exercising her civil rights, while sharing the values of liberté, égalité, and fraternité, contrasted to the narrow interpretation of citizen in contemporary nation states.

for more functional service, but not for such aspects as social justice, exemplified with a quote below, from "The impact of automated transport on the role, operations and costs of road operators and authorities in Finland":

> The customer most likely wants a vehicle that can manage a large part of the journey by itself so that the vehicle occupants can utilise the travel to other uses than driving.
>
> ***(FTCA, p. 124).***

Surprisingly, despite the societal value of equality and legacy of social democracy, Finnish approach emphasizes that public sector organizations have to "show the public that they are actively involved in the development," which is supposed to increase trust and willingness to use new technologies, minimizing time for uptake. The recommendations continue with even suggesting joint communication campaigns with the industrial partners. Similarly, even German ethics commission does not take a usual stance as with some previous emerging technologies of accounting for citoyens in the governance network (Burri, 2015). Although social movements have historically played an important role in shaping discourses of technological innovation in Germany, the hypothetical individual of the ethical guidelines still relies on intervention of the state for ensuring her own personal autonomy. Altogether, governance roles for citizens are not envisioned as the one of equal partner in steering technological futures, but only as an actor that can potentially resist new technology. Consequently, in the German governance culture, issues oflegitimacy and trust have to be tackled through linear information exchange or digital education initiatives.

6. Discussion and conclusion

6.1 Summary discussion of findings

This chapter has analyzed the country-specific approaches to the governance of SDVs in Finland, Germany and the UK. In order to do so, policies for the automation of mobility have been reviewed in the light of the sociotechnical imaginaries and governance cultures. First, we compare assumed roles of SDV technology in three societies, second we relate governance efforts to representations of benefits and risks, and thirdly, we expose the assumed roles of responsible governance actors, including assumptions of state-society relations. The starting point for analysis is that sociotechnical imaginaries are simultaneously being enacted, constructed and reconstructed, each of which shape the form of political action. Returning to

Collingridge's dilemma for responsible innovation, we argue that the process of developing innovation governance is showing initial signs of reflection on unanticipated and undesired consequences, beyond the initial focal points, such as traffic safety and digital security.

The analysis of SDVs roles in all three countries highlights a strong relation to national economic growth, although with some differences in reasoning. While such economic growth for Finland might be a matter of long-term societal survival, UK and Germany are struggling to maintain a global image as leaders, while reconciling some additional values, such as security or environmental justice. Such aspects of national identity play a major role in shaping the assumptions about the role of SDV in the future. In understanding the governance relation to technological risks, all three countries focus on risk management approach, underlying that innovation requires both infrastructure and enabling regulation. In addition to the traditional transport governance domain of liability in case of accidents, all three countries are developing strategies for emerging domains of data and public experimentation. However, Germany has distinguished itself with the first set of ethical guidelines for SDV development, specifically including algorithms as the necessary domain of governance.

Despite this effort, no country recognizes the need for expanding the governance actant network to include citoyens as active entities in exercising their civil rights. On the contrary, the dominant framing of issues in relation to the constitution of expertise and the dissemination of knowledge leads to a re-stabilized notion of normativity through which technology is supposed to engage with other social institutions. The key findings that distinguish the three approaches are summarized in Table 4. Contrasting imaginaries do not mark rigid characteristics of the respective Finnish, UK or German political cultures. However, probing the tacit assumptions underlying governance documents through sociotechnical imaginaries has highlighted crucial aspects of SDV governance, discerning some distinct elements of how particular political cultures envision and respond to technological futures.

6.2 The treat of technological determinism for responsible innovation

Coming back to the initial point about fundamental governance rationales of efficiency, equity and ethics when faced with Collingridge's dilemma, the analysis points out an important set of questions for responsible innovation processes. The analysis points that expectations of benefits over risks are

Table 4 Summary of key findings from Finland, Germany and the UK according to the key research questions.

	Finland	UK	Germany
1. Roles of SDV technology in society	• Finding a global market niche • Digital society and knowledge economy agenda	• Industry resilience and competitiveness • National security	• Automotive leadership role • Climate action
2. Domains and mechanisms of governance	• Extensive public experimentation • Data utilization and transport services development • AI and digital literacy	• Liability and insurance • Public experimentation and business plans • Cybersecurity • Digital infrastructure	• Liability and ex post transparency • Public-private collaboration • Personal data privacy and algorithms • Federal cohesion
3. Governance actants in SDV development	• Artifacts decoupled from accountability • Tight network for expert-based foresight and assessment • Citizens as rule-following consumers	• Artifacts decoupled from accountability • New research and government organizations beyond transport sector • Citizens as resilient users	• Artifacts decoupled from accountability • New research and government organizations beyond transport sector • Citizens as subjects needing protection

highly weighted, bringing about asymmetry between hopes in future applications, hiding dissonance and conflict over desired futures. Thus, at the core of governance challenge is the understanding that technology is not a neutral and default-positive actant, and that technological development is irreducibly a political and value-driven choice rather than an instrumental facilitation of what is an inevitable (automated) future. In more details, the analysis indicates a threat of three different types of technological determinism, namely justificatory, methodological, and normative—which could be leading to potential technological myopia and somnambulism (Winner, 2014). Each of these types of technological determinism brings about a challenge for transparency, accountability, and responsiveness mechanisms in technological governance processes.

The above-identified aspects of national identities play a major role in shaping the assumed role of SDV technology in society, potentially leading to a version of justificatory technological determinism and techno-optimism. Justificatory determinism argument focuses on the point that specific technological change is necessary to achieve unquestionable benefits (Wyatt, 2008). Here, framing SDV technology through the lens of international competition is an important aspect that could have at least two challenges for responsiveness. First, as already highlighted by Collingridge, competition can actually serve to restrict the number of alternatives. Instead of sharpening reflexivity, a particular version of technology can become intrinsically embedded in the imaginaries, with the focus being on minimizing time to deployment as opposed to exploring alternatives. Second, responsiveness can be inhibited by potential fear from diseconomies of scale, increasing the cost per unit due to capital intensiveness and dependence on large-scale infrastructure, if decisions are subsequently found to be mistaken. Similarly, the investment in digital infrastructural layers is considered as an important factor as a potential challenge for automation. Thus, due to inherent uncertainty about future costs while under potential threat for increased cost, decision-making might prefer low sunk costs associated with incremental improvements of existing technological infrastructures as opposed to more different technological alternatives.

The findings indicate that all three governance approaches have an underlying premise that risks are problems to be managed, without recognizing potentially unanticipated consequences (see also Taeihagh and Lim, 2019). With such an approach, there is a potential threat of a second version of techno-determinism—methodological, which renders technology opaque, simplified, and with transferred assumptions from earlier technologies without questioning them (Wyatt, 2008). Such an example regarding SDV technology is transference of assumptions built into existing urban traffic control technology since the 19th century (Mladenovic et al., 2016). These unquestioned but transferred assumptions neglect the fact that technology is another actant in the web of responsibility, and not inanimate object, upon which human subjects act. The crucial stance here is not just in neglecting the "missing masses," as Latour named artifacts whose power is not accounted for in innovation processes (Latour, 1992). In fact, the crucial aspect is in consequent decoupling of technology from political accountability and intervention, which can be interpreted as a third category of technological determinism—normative (Wyatt, 2008).

From the findings, we can conclude that technological development is not based on the democratic enhancement of dialogue between state and society. Perhaps, an expectation might be that citoyens are lacking skills and knowledge to deliberate about advantages and disadvantages of this emerging technology. Thus, ideological zeitgeists of these three democratic societies in relation to SDV technology do not aspire to the very democratic ideals constituting their legal and moral foundations. Framing citizens as well-informed and willing consumers raises the question of potential loss of the notion of the commons in transport provision, if SDV development is largely intertwined with a commercialized overhaul of mobility markets. As previously identified by Lyons (2018) and Noy and Givoni (2018), there might also be a misunderstanding of relation between commercial and sustainability considerations related to technological development. In fact, European innovation processes could be overwhelmed by a large-scale commodification of the mobility commons, potentially erasing an important dividing line for moral limits of mobility markets. The resulting corruption of the nature of the transport good itself, and further transfer of existing monetary inequalities, as argued in general by Sandel (2012), could further push large groups of people to the position of subordinate dependents.

6.3 Further research and development needs

The use of technology studies concepts can help in opening new pathways for reconceptualizing SDV technology and associated governance processes. For example, reconceptualization of emerging automated mobility technologies will need to critically reflect on the ways SDV technology mediates human practices, experiences, and value frameworks (Mladenovic et al., 2019), or through heteromation, pointed out by Ekbia and Nardi (2017), as capital accumulation from extracting value through low-cost or free human labor redistributed in computer-mediated networks. In addition, further research should pay closer attention to trajectories of technological imaginaries across cultures and various segments of society, as they transform through heterogeneous cultural perceptions, experiences and identities. A particular focus should be paid to histories of success and failure in technological innovation, and their influence on shaping national identities and emotional relations to technological artifacts. Further analysis of the Finnish governance trajectory, as a society with reduced social hierarchy, could be enlightening new conceptualizations for collaboration in technological innovation processes.

As already recognized by Collingridge, governance of technological innovation is fundamentally about "muddling through" in the context of incumbent powers and vested interests. Similarly, current SDV technological development processes are largely depoliticized. If they are to be repoliticised, issues of interorganizational learning practices will be more challenging. Further studies of policy design should pay attention to dissonances between governance perspectives on the national, supranational, and subnational level. In particular, future studies should pay more attention to patenting regulation and regulatory structures for establishing ownership models that could balance monopolistic technological development processes. Moreover, transport studies can learn from the ongoing discussion in the domain of AI regulation, where strong levels of quality control are encouraged through robust data-sharing agreements, access rights for different stakeholders, and audits (Cath et al., 2018; Johal and Urban, 2017; Kerber and Frank, 2017). Some aspects of data collection, storage, sharing, ownership, liability, and pricing related to SDVs have already been identified (Brown et al., 2018). In the European context, the starting point for developing potential responses is the existing General Data Protection Regulation (GDPR) law on data protection and privacy. Further development of innovation indicators and public access to those would help in avoiding "gold plating" certain technological alternatives through financial subsidies or taxation allowances, in line with Collingridge's approach of incrementalism being more appropriate for generating and preserving technological alternatives in order to avoid unanticipated consequences arising once path dependence is too firmly established.

Finally, there is an urgent need to develop experimentation processes used for different stages and by different responsible actors, while reformulating procedures for openly collaborative technological development. In particular, it is necessary to have wider societal inclusion and empowerment of the missing "outsiders" (Van de Poel, 2000), as has already been identified before (Blyth et al., 2016; Cohen et al., 2018; Mladenović, 2019). More useful frameworks for enabling the practice of critical citizen engagement and participatory deliberation will be an essential component of such development (Flipse and Puylaert, 2018; Macnaghten and Chilvers, 2014; Mladenović, 2019; Mladenovic and McPherson, 2016). In developing such frameworks, we should not aim for creating artificial consensus over technological alternatives, but in exploring dissensus and perhaps inevitable conflict of societal values designed into SDV data structures and algorithms (Genus, 2006; Mladenović, 2019). In this strand of research, understanding how to reinforce accountabilities will inevitably lead to a larger question of how to govern by strengthening democracy itself. If these much-needed efforts are not taken seriously and technological development processes fail to reinforce accountability, we will potentially create conditions not just for loss of trust in technology or associated governing institutions, but also for legitimate moral preconditions for civil disobedience.

Acknowledgments

This chapter is dedicated to the memory of Moshe Givoni, a very dear friend and colleague who helped to develop the initial idea for this chapter during his sabbatical at Aalto University. Sadly, Moshe passed away before the chapter was finalized. This research received partial support from WISE-ACT COST Action (No. 16222), the Academy of Finland, through PROFI 4 initiative, as well as through the FINEST Twins Centre of Excellence.

References

Berkhout, F., 2006. Normative expectations in systems innovation. Tech. Anal. Strat. Manag. 18 (3–4), 299–311.

Blyth, P.L., Mladenovic, M.N., Nardi, B.A., Ekbia, H.R., Su, N.M., 2016. Expanding the design horizon for self-driving vehicles: distributing benefits and burdens. IEEE Technol. Soc. Mag. 35 (3), 44–49.

Brown, A., Rodriguez, G., Best, B., Hoang, K.T., Safford, H., Anderson, G., D'Agostino, M.C., 2018. Federal, State, and Local Governance of Automated Vehicles. Institute of Transportation Studies & Policy Institute for Energy, Environment and the Economy, University of California Davis.

Burri, R.V., 2015. Imaginaries of science and society: framing nanotechnology governance in Germany and the United States. In: Dreamscapes of Modernity: Sociotechnical Imaginaries and the Fabrication of Power. The University of Chicago Press, Chicago, pp. 233–253.

Cath, C., Wachter, S., Mittelstadt, B., Taddeo, M., Floridi, L., 2018. Artificial intelligence and the 'good society': the US, EU, and UK approach. Sci. Eng. Ethics 24 (2), 505–528.

Cohen, T., Cavoli, C., 2019. Automated vehicles: exploring possible consequences of government (non)intervention for congestion and accessibility. Transp. Rev. 39 (1), 129–151.
Cohen, T., Stilgoe, J., Cavoli, C., 2018. Reframing the governance of automotive automation: insights from UK stakeholder workshops. J. Responsible Innov. 5 (3), 257–279.
Collingridge, D., 1980. The Social Control of Technology. St. Martin's Press, New York.
Collingridge, D., 1992. The Management of Scale: Big Organizations, Big Decisions, Big Mistakes. Routledge.
DBEIS, 2017. Industrial Strategy. In: Department for Business, Energy & Industrial Strategy https://www.gov.uk/government/publications/industrial-strategy-building-a-britain-fit-for-the-future.
Ekbia, H.R., Nardi, B.A., 2017. Heteromation, and Other Stories of Computing and Capitalism. MIT Press.
Fagnant, D.J., Kockelman, K., 2015. Preparing a nation for autonomous vehicles: opportunities, barriers and policy recommendations. Transp. Res. A Policy Pract. 77, 167–181.
Faisal, A., Yigitcanlar, T., Kamruzzaman, M., Currie, G., 2019. Understanding autonomous vehicles: a systematic literature review on capability, impact, planning and policy. J. Transp. Land Use 12 (1), 45–72.
Feenberg, A., 1999. Questioning Technology. Routledge, London.
Felt, U., Fouché, R., Miller, C.A., Smith-Doerr, L. (Eds.), 2017. The Handbook of Science and Technology Studies. MIT Press.
Flipse, S.M., Puylaert, S., 2018. Organizing a collaborative development of technological design requirements using a constructive dialogue on value profiles: a case in automated vehicle development. Sci. Eng. Ethics 24 (1), 49–72.
FMTDI, 2015. Strategy for Automated and Connected Driving, German Federal Government. https://www.bmvi.de/SharedDocs/EN/publications/strategy-for-automated-and-connected-driving.pdf?__blob=publicationFile.
Fraedrich, E., Heinrichs, D., Bahamonde-Birke, F.J., Cyganski, R., 2019. Autonomous driving, the built environment and policy implications. Transp. Res. Part A Policy Pract. 122, 162–172.
Genus, A., 2006. Rethinking constructive technology assessment as democratic, reflective, discourse. Technol. Forecast. Soc. Chang. 73 (1), 13–26.
Genus, A., Stirling, A., 2018. Collingridge and the dilemma of control: towards responsible and accountable innovation. Res. Policy 47 (1), 61–69.
Guerra, E., 2016. Planning for cars that drive themselves: metropolitan planning organizations, regional transportation plans, and autonomous vehicles. J. Plan. Educ. Res. 36 (2), 210–224.
Halme, K., Lindy, I., Piirainen, K.A., Salminen, V., White, J., 2014. Finland as a Knowledge Economy 2.0: Lessons on Policies and Governance. The World Bank; Washington, DC. https://doi.org/10.1596/978-1-4648-0194-5.
Hopkins, D., Schwanen, T., 2018. Governing the race to automation. In: Marsden, G., Reardon, L. (Eds.), Governance of the Smart Mobility Transition. Emerald Publishing Limited, pp. 65–84.
Howlett, M., 2009. Governance modes, policy regimes and operational plans: a multi-level nested model of policy instrument choice and policy design. Pol. Sci. 42 (1), 73–89.
Jasanoff, S. (Ed.), 2004. States of Knowledge: The Co-Production of Science and the Social Order. Routledge.
Jasanoff, S., Kim, S.H. (Eds.), 2015. Dreamscapes of Modernity: Sociotechnical Imaginaries and the Fabrication of Power. University of Chicago Press.
Johal, S., Urban, M.C., 2017. Regulating Disruption. Mowat Centre for Policy Innovation, University of Toronto.
Kaplan, S., Tripsas, M., 2008. Thinking about technology: applying a cognitive lens to technical change. Res. Policy 37 (5), 790–805.

Kerber, W., Frank, J., 2017. Data Governance Regimes in the Digital Economy: The Example of Connected Cars. Available at SSRN 3064794.
Kroes, P., Verbeek, P.P. (Eds.), 2014. The Moral Status of Technical Artefacts (Vol. 17). Springer Science & Business Media.
Kudina, O., 2019. The Technological Mediation of Morality: Value Dynamism, and the Complex Interaction Between Ethics and Technology. Delft University of Technology.
Latour, B., 1992. Where are the missing masses? The sociology of a few mundane artefacts. In: Bijker, W., Law, J. (Eds.), Shaping Technology/Building Society: Studies in Socio-Technical Change. The MIT press, Cambridge, Massachusetss, pp. 225–258.
Latour, B., 1996. On actor-network theory: a few clarifications. Soziale welt 4, 369–381.
Legacy, C., Ashmore, D., Scheurer, J., Stone, J., Curtis, C., 2019. Planning the driverless city. Transp. Rev. 39 (1), 84–102.
Lehtiniemi, T., Ruckenstein, M., 2019. The social imaginaries of data activism. Big Data Soc. 6 (1), 1–12.
Loughlin, J., Hendriks, F., Lidström, A. (Eds.), 2011. Oxford Handbook of Local and Regional Democracy in Europe. Oxford University Press, Oxford.
Lyons, G., 2018. Getting smart about urban mobility–aligning the paradigms of smart and sustainable. Transp. Res. A Policy Pract. 115, 4–14.
Macnaghten, P., Chilvers, J., 2014. The future of science governance: publics, policies, practices. Eviron. Plann. C. Gov. Policy 32 (3), 530–548.
Marsden, G., Reardon, L., 2017. Questions of governance: rethinking the study of transportation policy. Transp. Res. A Policy Pract. 101, 238–251.
Milakis, D., 2019. Long-term implications of automated vehicles: an introduction. Transp. Rev. 39 (1), 1–8.
Milakis, D., Van Arem, B., Van Wee, B., 2017. Policy and society related implications of automated driving: a review of literature and directions for future research. J. Intell. Transp. Syst. 21 (4), 324–348.
Mladenović, M.N., 2018. Embracing the complexity and justice of mobilities automation? In: Blogged Environment. Alexandrine Press.
Mladenović, M.N., 2019. How should we drive self-driving vehicles? anticipation and collective imagination in planning mobility futures. In: Finger, M., Audouin, M. (Eds.), The Governance of Smart Transportation Systems. Springer, Cham, pp. 103–122.
Mladenovic, M.N., McPherson, T., 2016. Engineering social justice into traffic control for self-driving vehicles? Sci. Eng. Ethics 22 (4), 1131–1149.
Mladenovic, M.N., Abbas, M.M., Blyth, P.L., Kosonen, I., 2016, October. Intersecting our mobilities: path dependence from manually-operated semaphore to self-driving vehicles? In: In 2016 IEEE International Symposium on Technology and Society (ISTAS). IEEE, pp. 1–6.
Mladenovic, M.N., Lehtinen, S., Soh, E., Martens, K., 2019. Emerging urban mobility technologies through the lens of everyday urban aesthetics: case of self-driving vehicle. Essays Philos. 21 (2), 1–25.
Noorman, M., 2014. Responsibility practices and unmanned military technologies. Sci. Eng. Ethics 20 (3), 809–826.
Noy, K., Givoni, M., 2018. Is 'smart mobility' sustainable? Examining the views and beliefs of transport's technological entrepreneurs. Sustainability 10 (2), 422.
Pangbourne, K., 2010. The Changing Geography of Scottish Transport Governance. PhD Thesis, University of Aberdeen.
Pangbourne, K., Mladenović, M.N., Stead, D., Milakis, D., 2019. Questioning mobility as a service: unanticipated implications for society and governance. Transp. Res. A Policy Pract. in press.
Paulsson, A., Hylander, J., Hrelja, R., 2017. One for all, or all for oneself? Governance cultures in regional public transport planning. Eur. Plan. Stud. 25 (12), 2293–2308.

Pinch, T.J., Bijker, W.E., 1984. The social construction of facts and artefacts: or how the sociology of science and the sociology of technology might benefit each other. Soc. Stud. Sci. 14 (3), 399–441.
Porter, L., Stone, J., Legacy, C., Curtis, C., Harris, J., Fishman, E., Kent, J., Marsden, G., Reardon, L., Stilgoe, J., 2018. The autonomous vehicle revolution: implications for planning/the driverless city?/autonomous vehicles—a planner's response/autonomous vehicles: opportunities, challenges and the need for government action/three signs autonomous vehicles will not lead to less car ownership and less car use in car dependent cities—a case study of sydney, australia/planning for autonomous vehicles? Questions of purpose, place and pace/ensuring good governance: the role of planners in the development of autonomous vehicles. Plan. Theory Pract. 19 (5), 753–778.
Rogge, K.S., Reichardt, K., 2016. Policy mixes for sustainability transitions: an extended concept and framework for analysis. Res. Policy 45 (8), 1620–1635.
Rotolo, D., Hicks, D., Martin, B.R., 2015. What is an emerging technology? Res. Policy 44 (10), 1827–1843.
Ryghaug, M., Toftaker, M., 2016. Creating transitions to electric road transport in Norway: the role of user imaginaries. Energy Res. Soc. Sci. 17, 119–126.
Sandel, M.J., 2012. What Money can't Buy: The Moral Limits of Markets. Macmillan.
Schulzke, M., 2013. Autonomous weapons and distributed responsibility. Philos. Technol. 26 (2), 203–219.
Sclove, R., 1995. Democracy and Technology. Guilford Press.
Sperling, S., 2004. Managing potential selves: stem cells, immigrants, and German identity. Sci. Public Policy 31 (2), 139–149.
Stead, D., 2018. Policy preferences and the diversity of instrument choice for mitigating climate change impacts in the transport sector. J. Environ. Plan. Manag. 61 (14), 2445–2467.
Stilgoe, J., 2018. Machine learning, social learning and the governance of self-driving cars. Soc. Stud. Sci. 48 (1), 25–56.
Sturken, M., Thomas, D., Ball-Rokeach, S. (Eds.), 2004. Technological Visions: The Hopes and Fears that Shape New Technologies. Temple University Press.
Susskind, J., 2018. Future Politics: Living Together in a World Transformed by Tech. Oxford University Press.
Taeihagh, A., Lim, H.S.M., 2019. Governing autonomous vehicles: emerging responses for safety, liability, privacy, cybersecurity, and industry risks. Transp. Rev. 39 (1), 103–128.
Thomopoulos, N., Givoni, M., 2015. The autonomous car—a blessing or a curse for the future of low carbon mobility? An exploration of likely vs. desirable outcomes. Eur. J. Futures Res. 3 (1), 14.
Van De Poel, I., 2000. On the role of outsiders in technical development. Tech. Anal. Strat. Manag. 12 (3), 383–397.
Van de Poel, I., 2011. The relation between forward-looking and backward-looking responsibility. In: Vincent, N.A., van de Poel, I., van den Hoven, J. (Eds.), Moral Responsibility: Beyond free will and determinism. the. Springer, Netherlands, pp. 37–52.
Verbeek, P.P., 2011. Moralizing Technology: Understanding and Designing the Morality of Things. University of Chicago Press.
Voß, J.P., Freeman, R. (Eds.), 2016. Knowing Governance: The Epistemic Construction of Political Order. Springer.
Wetmore, J.M., 2004. Redefining risks and redistributing responsibilities: building networks to increase automobile safety. Sci. Technol. Hum. Values 29 (3), 377–405.
Winfield, A.F., Jirotka, M., 2018. Ethical governance is essential to building trust in robotics and artificial intelligence systems. Philos. Trans. R. Soc. A Math. Phys. Eng. Sci. 376 (2133), 20180085.

Winner, L., 1980. Do artifacts have politics? Daedalus 109, 121–136.
Winner, L., 2014. Technologies as forms of life. In: R. Sandler, (Ed.), Ethics and Emerging Technologies. Palgrave Macmillan, London, pp. 48–60.
Wyatt, S., 2008. Technological determinism is dead; Long live technological determinism. In: Hackett, E.J., Amsterdamska, O., Lynch, M.E., Wajcman, J. (Eds.), Handbook of Science and Technology Studies. MIT press, pp. 165–180.

CHAPTER ELEVEN

Wider implications of autonomous vessels for the maritime industry: Mapping the unprecedented challenges

Hadi Ghaderi*
Department of Business Technology and Entrepreneurship, Swinburne Business School, Swinburne University of Technology, Hawthorn, VIC, Australia
*Corresponding author: e-mail address: hghaderi@swin.edu.au

Contents

Abstract

With the advent of computers, sensor technologies and advanced data analytics, unmanned shipping is not just a concept for maritime researchers, but it has become a serious debate for the international maritime community. Early studies have revealed promising economic and environmental benefits for the users of autonomous vessels which potentially results in lower operational costs and higher safety levels. Furthermore, many researchers believe that with the current technology, it is achievable to develop and run unmanned ships capable of meeting safety and operational standards. However, future implications of unmanned vessels for the maritime industry are diverse, difficult to measure and unknown to some extent. The maritime industry is a complex industrial sector encompassing various players involved in transport, logistics, regulatory, engineering, finance and insurance activities which are vertically and

Advances in Transport Policy and Planning, Volume 5
ISSN 2543-0009
https://doi.org/10.1016/bs.atpp.2020.05.002

horizontally intertwined. Therefore, introducing autonomous vessels will not only transform the way vessels are operated across international waters, but also comes with major ramifications for all players involved in providing an end-to-end freight transport solutions. Given this gap, this chapter's objective is to explore the policy implications of autonomous ships for the maritime industry. Our exploration identifies new cost implications and asset management challenges, examines the likely impacts of embracing autonomous ships on port and shipbuilding sectors, and also, provides an industry maturity framework and debates the potential impacts of unmanned vessels on different shipping markets.

Keywords: Autonomous ship, Autonomous vessel, Connected freight, Unmanned shipping, USV

1. Introduction

Technology often provides the prospective of improving the productivity of transportation systems, but the shipping sector in general appears to have embraced little of the advancing technology to improve their service offerings. In this context, several researchers claim that the maritime industry is considered as a brick-and-mortar sector when compared with other transport modes in terms of adoption and implementation of technology (Österman and Hult, 2016; Suárez-Alemán, 2016). However, as the result of fierce competition, the shipping industry is embarking on a journey of digital transformation.

As the result of embracing advanced manufacturing techniques, the industry is experiencing major improvements in the design and manufacturing of vessels, particularly around efficient hull design (Peri et al., 2001), integrated bridge management systems (IBMS) (Freire, 2004; Sauer et al., 2002), engine performance and enhanced ship-to-shore/ship-to-ship communication (Giannopoulos, 2004). However, ship management and operations is considered as a human-centered business with a major focus on maximizing financial benefits through cost reduction (Ghaderi, 2019). Gains achieved through such productivity improvements are limited in scale and scope and do not necessarily lead to transformative and sustainable competitive advantages.

In the age of computers, sensor technologies and advanced data analytics, unmanned shipping is no longer merely a concept for maritime researchers (Batalden et al., 2017; Perera, 2018); rather, it has become a serious debate for the international maritime community. Fuelled by rising interest from the major shipping companies for a speedy adoption, the level of capital invest in development of such systems has grown exponentially.

In this context, early studies have revealed promising economic and environmental benefits for the users of autonomous vessels which may potentially result in lower operational costs and improved navigational safety (Kretschmann et al., 2017; Porathe et al., 2013; Rødseth and Burmeister, 2012). However, the future implications of unmanned vessels for the maritime industry are diverse, difficult to measure and unknown to some extent. Thus, wrong interpretation of such implications could potentially bring huge ramifications to a smooth transition toward their extensive use in the global supply chains.

In particular, the maritime sector is a complex industrial sector encompassing players involved in transport, logistics, regulatory, engineering, information technology, finance and insurance activities, with many vertically and horizontally intertwined. Given this inherent complexity, the introduction of unmanned ships will have a radical impact on how the industry is currently running (Baldauf et al., 2018), and such implications are important to be examined in a systematic approach.

Knowing the existing gap, the motivations for preparing this book chapter are aligned with mapping the long-term implications of unmanned ships for the maritime industry. Furthermore, we believe the literature on the policy and managerial facets of autonomous shipping is rare and fragmented. Thus, this research aims to establish the grounds for future investigations by identifying areas of importance with strong relevance for the maritime industry and its diverse range of stakeholders.

To achieve the objectives of this chapter and present a comprehensive industry-based analysis, Section 2 provides a brief overview of *E*-Navigation and its role in introducing the concept of autonomous maritime systems. A summary of the major projects involved in design, assessment and development of unmanned shipping across the world is presented in Section 3. Section 4 provides a series of new discussions on the cost and asset management implications associated with the implementation of unmanned vessels. Section 5 discusses the issues around shipbuilding, maintenance and repair of autonomous vessels and its potential effects on existing and future ship operators. The impacts of unmanned shipping on the port sector are explored in Section 6, while Section 7 presents an industry maturity process with a summary of potential impacts which unmanned vessels will have for various shipping markets. Finally, conclusions and recommendations for future research are drawn in Section 8.

2. E-Navigation: A paradigm for adopting unmanned shipping

Autonomous vehicles are already in the state of commercialization for land-based transport systems (Milakis et al., 2017) with several examples in using autonomous vehicles for freight delivery including Uber's Otto self-driving vehicle and Amazon's Prime Air delivery drone. In another instance, 20% of train runs were being undertaken autonomously by the Australian Rio Tinto mining company. However, when observing the developments occurring in other transport modes, relatively, shipping has failed to embrace the opportunities arising from the implementation of automation. Interestingly, the use of unmanned navigation at sea is not a new exercise and such applications have been in practice for many years, namely as Autonomous Underwater Vehicles (AUV) for purposes such as vessel inspection, military, piping, resource exploration, and search and rescue (SAR) operations in deep waters.

In the last three decades, automation has been playing a more apparent role in operations of seagoing vessels, particularly by implementation of unattended and IBMS (Perera and Soares, 2015, 2017). Perhaps, the advancements in AUV technology, coupled with wider use of sensors and automated decision support systems (DSS), have been the major catalysts toward development of what we are observing today as platforms for commercial Unmanned Surface Vehicles (USV). The combination of growing demand for ship automation, rapid technological advancements impacting vessel operations and increasing pressure for safer navigational practices is creating a need for wider use of computers in ship navigation and operations, or what is generally framed as E-Navigation.

The concept of e-Navigation commended by the International Maritime Organization (IMO) in 2006 with the aim to develop a comprehensive strategy to assist the shipping industry and other stakeholders responsible for the safety of shipping with advanced tools. Effective incorporation of such tools and techniques is essential for responsive and accurate decision making to reduce navigational errors and keep the operations and communications of vessels more reliable and more accommodating by user. Since the advancements in navigational technology are diverse and lack in standardization, the need for a clear strategy was vital to reduce the complexity and enhance systems compatibility in the future. Given this gap, IMO (2007) defined E-Navigation as:

"the harmonized collection, integration, exchange, presentation and analysis of marine information on board and ashore by electronic means to enhance berth to berth navigation and related services for safety and security at sea and protection of the marine environment."

The intention of E-Navigation strategy was to improve the safety and security of conventional vessels through the enhanced utilization and management of data and enhanced exchange and communication of information between ships and shore (Vanem et al., 2015). However, it has since gone beyond this scope and been playing a key role in supporting a better vision for the future of autonomous shipping.

As part of these developments, in December 2018 IMO's Maritime Safety Committee (MSC) accomplished its 100th session, with progress in a regulatory scoping exercise on maritime autonomous surface ships (MASS). For the purpose of this exercise, MASS is defined as "a ship which, to a varying degree, can operate independently of human interaction." The process was mainly aimed at assessing how IMO instruments may apply to ships with varying degrees of autonomy, as well as examining the safety, security and environmental fitness of autonomous navigation in relation to existing IMO frameworks (IMO, 2018). As the result of this process, IMO identified four levels of ship autonomy:

1. Ship with automated processes and decision support: Seafarers are on board to operate and control shipboard systems and functions.
2. Remotely controlled ship with seafarers on board: The ship is controlled and operated from another location.
3. Remotely controlled ship without seafarers on board: The ship is controlled and operated from another location. There are no seafarers on board.
4. Fully autonomous ship: The operating system of the ship is able to make decisions and determine actions by itself.

Although such characterization of autonomous shipping is subject to change in relation to advancements in navigational technology which impacts the basic concepts of ship operations, they are useful to provide a general framework for governance and operations of vessels in future. To further facilitate the future operation of autonomous vessels, in, 2019 IMO will progress with assessing some of the existing regulatory instruments such as those related safety (SOLAS), collision regulations (COLREG), loading and stability, training (STCW, STCW-F), SAR, Tonnage Convention, Safe Containers (CSC) and special trade passenger ship instruments (SPACE STP, STP) (IMO, 2018).

3. Recent developments in autonomous maritime systems

Progress in the development and trial of commercial unmanned ships commenced in the late 2000s by demonstrating numerous opportunities and sizeable support for its use in the not-too-distant future (Hogg and Ghosh, 2016). Two major factors have been driving the recent developments in this space. First, it is important to acknowledge the challenges associated with the training, recruitment and retention of maritime workforce have become increasingly diverse and complex. There is much evidence showing that ship operating costs are on the rise over the last decade, with crew costs considered the main contributing factor. Crewing involves numerous direct and indirect cost components such as wage, superannuation, training, traveling, supplies and insurance premiums, with many of these elements remaining relevant in vessels with advanced automation (Wu and Winchester, 2005). Based on the ship's flag state and shipping company's policies, the costs could increase up to half of overall operating costs (Stopford, 2009). As the shipping markets become more competitive and price-oriented, many companies have started to reduce their operating costs through optimization of crew management, which generally translates into additional workload (Alderton, 2004; Nguyen et al., 2014; Tai, 2016). And yet, while ship navigation technology is advancing, the number of incidents and accidents in waterways is on the rise. A myriad of reasons have been identified including congested water ways, larger ships with less maneuverability, pressure from cargo owners and ports for punctual service and most importantly, human factors due to smaller crew structure, more stress, and job dissatisfaction (Akyuz et al., 2016; Nguyen et al., 2014; Porathe et al., 2014). In this context, autonomous shipping brings a unique value proposition for addressing the majority of these challenges by promising safer operations free of human error at significantly lower crew costs (Ghaderi, 2019; Kretschmann et al., 2017). To achieve a reference point for the status of development in autonomous maritime systems, the remainder of this section summarizes the major projects associated with the assessment and commercial development of autonomous maritime technologies across the globe.

In recent years, the global maritime industry has been taking substantial steps toward developing the necessary technologies and regulatory frameworks for adoption of USV. With growing environmental concerns, congested waterways and difficulties in securing skilled seafarers, the level of investment from both public and private sectors has substantially increased (IMO, 2018; Xiao et al., 2019).

In this context, the European Union (EU) faces several challenges for sustainable shipping, including growing freight volumes, environmental restriction and shortage of skilled workforce (van Leeuwen, 2015). To overcome such difficulties, several projects have been developing across EU countries in partnership with other international players to address the technical, operational and regulatory aspects of autonomous shipping. Perhaps one the first and most instrumental projects is MUNIN (Maritime Unmanned Navigation through Intelligence in Networks). MUNIN was a platform to develop a technically feasible model for the design and operation of an autonomous bulk carrier, which also provided deep insights on the economic and legal practicability of such systems. The MUNIN platform suggests that unmanned shipping can contribute to more sustainable maritime supply chains within Europe through reduced operational costs, lower environmental impacts and also attracting a skilled workforce (Kretschmann et al., 2015; Rødseth and Burmeister, 2015).

In a similar initiative, Rolls-Royce (Rolls-Royce, 2014) has embarked on a journey of ship intelligence titled Advanced Autonomous Waterborne Application (AAWA) with the aim to understand the existing state of technical, safety, regulatory and financial facets of remote and unmanned shipping The project aimed to inform the technical features and design specification for a proof of concept model by the end of 2017 and a fully commercial remote controlled vessel by the end 2020.

DNV GL (the accredited registrar and classification society) also perceived the enormous benefits of unmanned shipping technologies by building an autonomous ship concept with no human on board (ReVolt) for coastal and short sea shipping (SSS) within local waters. ReVolt is a 60-m-long autonomous containership which is fully powered by battery. The vessel will travel at a speed of 6 knots with a capacity of 100 20-foot equivalent (TEU) and a range of 100 Nautical miles (NM) (DNV GL, 2014). Similar to DNV GL's concept, Kongsberg, the ship simulator manufacturer has commenced a project with Yara to design and build the world's first unmanned electric merchant ship. The ship which is called "YARA Birkeland" is expected to start its first journey in 2020, shipping fertilizer between Yara's production facilities within Norwegian waters. It is expected that Yara will reduce 40,000 diesel-powered truck trips every year. In another project, a consortium of industry and research organizations led by MOL Shipping Line is aiming to develop advanced navigational support systems for autonomous oceangoing vessels. In particular, the project is not only looking to develop the necessary technology for an unmanned vessel, but also paving the way to develop the relevant infrastructure and societal implications of implementing such a system (MOL, 2017).

It is clear that R&D activity in the space of autonomous shipping has grown exponentially in the last 5 years, with several projects receiving strong engagement from major players in shipping and governments. Furthermore, as the applications of Artificial Intelligence (AI) and Deep Learning (DL) are becoming more accessible, a number of start-ups have been founded, looking at retrofitting existing vessels with fully and semi-automated tools to assist shipping operations with more intelligent tools. This may become an extremely attractive market for owners of conventional vessels to upgrade their assets with more intelligent tools and automation, which will potentially reduce the human error and minimize the need for a seagoing workforce. Such solutions may not provide a full autonomy capability, but it will assist safer navigation through advanced decision support systems. Table 1 the main projects involved in the development of unmanned shipping with a focus on the origin, type and organizations involved.

Beside those projects with a focus on designing and developing all-inclusive unmanned vessels, a growing number of studies have undertaken more specialized aims. This includes SINTEF's Hull-to-Hull (H2H) for safe navigation of autonomous vessels in close proximity of other vessels and objects, and an initiative by Samsung and Amazon Web Services for building a platform which enables the self-piloting of container vessels with different aspects of design, construction and operations of autonomous ships.

As part of reviewing the developments in the design and construction of autonomous shipping technologies, a number of trends are evident. Kongsberg is observed as a key catalyzer in many of the projects. This indicates that the technologies used for ship simulation and training are being adopted for the navigation and operations of autonomous vessels. Furthermore, it seems that the current slate of projects focus on small-scale cargo vessels (100–200 TEU) suitable for coastal domestic shipping, mainly because it's more convenient to seek permission locally for a single flag vessel. Electrically powered vessels are those that commence operations first, mainly because of ease of operations and maneuverability compared to conventional engines. What's more, the involvement of shipping lines in design and development of unmanned ships is becoming more evident

Table 1 Summary of autonomous shipping projects.[a]

Project	Type	Country	Organization(s)
YARA Birkeland	Fully Autonomous Bulk Carrier	Norway	Yara and Kongsberg
Hrönn	Offshore utility vessel	Norway	Automated Ships Ltd., Kongsberg and BOURBON
RAmora	Autonomous Fireboat	Norway and Canada	Robert Allan Ltd. And Kongsberg
MUNIN	Unmanned Ship Research Platform	Multiple European	European Union and multiple partners
Massterly	Autonomous Shipping Company	Norway	Wilhelmsen and Kongsberg
ReVolt	Autonomous container vessel (100 TEU)	Norway	DNV GL supported by Transnova
AAWA	Intelligent Ship	UK	Rolls-Royce
UCSDA	Unmanned cargo vessel	China	HNA, CCSm ABS and CSSC
MOL	Intelligent Awareness System	Japan	MOL and Rolls-Royce
Retrofitting systems			
NVIDIA GPUs	AI-based autonomous navigation (Start-up)	US	Shone Automation and CMA-CGM
SM200/300/400	Remote control navigation (Start-up)	US	Sea Machines

[a]The projects summarized in this table were collected from various media and company websites at the time of preparing this research. Such information are subject to change.

(e.g., MOL, CMA CGM, Wilhelmsen), which again demonstrates the commercial attractiveness of this concept to operators. It is also important to acknowledge a complete autonomous approach, in which all decisions are performed without the involvement of humans, seems not a practical option in a close future (Ghaderi, 2019). Knowing the regulatory and operational limitations, remotely operated navigation through a control center is the likely option for autonomous maritime transport in the next decade. To support this statement, the above-illustrated examples of MUNIN, Rolls-Royce, ReVolt and YARA Birkeland are distance-supervised using a Shore-based Control Center (SCC). Finally, there seems to be an interest from cargo owners/producers to invest in the development and implementation of autonomous shipping (e.g., Yara Birkeland). Perhaps, the saving achieved through enhanced management and optimization of supply chains by engaging autonomous ships for transportation of large quantity of cargo is a major motive behind this involvement.

4. Cost implications and challenges for asset management

One of the preliminary discussions in the topic of autonomous maritime transport is around understanding the commercial viability and economic fitness of vessels into existing and future supply chains (Kretschmann et al., 2017). Systematic research on modeling the vessel costs is extremely limited, and to date, there is no internationally recognized standard for the classification of costs. While there are similarities in the cost structures, several differences exist between the running costs of conventional and autonomous vessels, which are essential to recognize and assess for many reasons.

In the context of autonomous shipping, literature is still at its developing stages with an emerging number of studies starting to explore the viability of unmanned shipping from economic and financial perspectives. With no doubt, MUNIN project has been an instrumental research platform in addressing a wide range of issues that will revolutionize the landscape of the shipping industry in the presence of unmanned vessels (Rødseth and Burmeister, 2015; Rødseth et al., 2014). The preliminary results of MUNIN have been a key catalyst to understand the economic implications, technical, environmental impacts and regulatory requirements for autonomous maritime systems. In particular, MUNIN's Quantitative Assessment is perhaps the most consistent and inclusive assessment on understanding the economic and financial aspects of running unmanned vessels (Kretschmann et al., 2015). This study focuses on the economic feasibility of their proposed unmanned vessel by developing a shipping cash-flow model and incorporating several microeconomic factors such as operational expenses, voyage cost and necessary capitals. The study compares the expected present value of an autonomous bulk carrier with a conventional ship, resulting in an addition of up to 7 million US dollar savings over a lifespan of 25 years. Compared to the reference manned vessel, MUNIN claims the main savings are associated with the removal of crew and enhanced fuel efficiency, while additional expenses arise with higher capitals and port-based support services (Kretschmann et al., 2017). With more optimistic outcomes, ReVolt project from DNV GL Group estimates an annual savings of more than USD 1 million for their unmanned vessel prototype. With increasing cargo capacity achieved through the removal of crew facilities and lower operating and maintenance expenses, it is estimated that ReVolt will save up to USD 34 million over a lifespan of 30 years (DNV GL, 2014).

Similarly, using a cargo-based cost-benefit analysis with varying voyage speed and demand levels, Ghaderi (2019) explored the financial implications and savings of employing autonomous vessels in SSS markets through a Continuously Unmanned Ship (CUS) running by a SCC. Ghaderi (2019) identifies a number of factors which are influential on such savings such as trip length, level of cargo utilizations, cargo type and indirect costs associated with running the SCC. Furthermore, demand volatility was considered a key success factor for adoption of autonomous ships in SSS and coastal markets. For example, comparing with human-operated vessels, financial gains are greater when demand uncertainty exists. Moreover, the results of the study take into consideration the speed limitations of unmanned vessels as part of a shipping network.

Despite the limited status of literature, a number of key complex challenges are evident. First, due to safety and technical restrictions, it is expected that the first generations of autonomous ships sail at a lower speed (e.g., ReVolt 6 knots and Yara 8 knots). Such reduction in speed results in significantly longer voyage time and lower productivity in terms of annual cargo-handling volumes (Ghaderi, 2019). Most container ships are designed to sail at 22–24 knots (Ronen, 2011) with a slow steaming speed around 18–20 (Rodrigue et al., 2013). In the case of lower speed, the shipping company is required to deploy additional vessels and provide more frequent services to deliver the same service levels. However, deployment of additional vessels may only address the challenge of longer lead time in SSS and adding a vessel to the operating fleet to meet the same demand level may not be a financially attractive option. On the other hand, in deep sea shipping, actual sailing time is a major portion of total fleet availability, and thus, more frequent service will not deliver the same service level and lead-times.

Second, with the removal of crew, two major tasks will be transferred to the shore. As the first generation of unmanned vessels are managed through a human-operated center at shore, the cost of operating such systems are potentially diverse and significant, ranging from variable crew salaries, to capital and to fixed facility costs. Furthermore, with the absence of on-board crew, a port-based crew is required to undertake the cargo handling and on-going maintenance activities during the time that the vessel is in port. Although the technical characteristics of unmanned vessels and shore-based centers are highly influential in determining the characteristics of such services, this will remain a key factor in determining the full economic costs of using autonomous maritime systems. It is also essential to acknowledge that the existing economic and financial assessments are constructed based on a series of assumptions (Kretschmann et al., 2015), with several uncertainties around the full technical, operational and regulatory requirements of employing unmanned vessels.

5. Shipbuilding, repair and maintenance

Many researchers believe that with the existing technology, development and operations of unmanned ships is feasible (Burmeister et al., 2014b; Perera and Soares, 2015). However, there exist several challenges and unknown areas for large-scale construction and maintenance of such vessels which could potentially disrupt the shipbuilding industry in a number ways.

Milner (1971) states that in industries such as shipbuilding, innovation is not so simply observable given that developments in different modules and sub-systems can be overshadowed by the total product. In other words, innovation is distributed over many different components and timespans. Advancements in technology are now driving several innovations in the shipbuilding industry and it is fair to say that over the last decade shipbuilding has effectively embraced a diverse range of technologies to address the issues arising from mounting fuel costs, environmental impacts, crew efficiency and navigational safety. Some of these technologies include 3D printing for spare parts, robotics, fuel and pollution efficient marine engines, electric propulsion and IBMS. However, many of these advancements are claimed as incremental improvements while some are leading to more transformative innovations such as the development of fully autonomous vessels.

Research platforms and concepts such as MUNIN, Yara Birkeland, ReVolt and Rolls-Royce have revealed fundamental differences in the design and technical specifications of autonomous ships, which will have important ramifications on how commercial vessels are constructed in future (Rødseth and Burmeister, 2015). With the transition of decision making from ship to shore and responsibilities from man to machine, enhanced coordination and exchange of data on ships and on shore is required to sustain the necessary safety standards for the operation of autonomous vessels (IMO, 2007).

Such level of safe autonomy is not achievable without development of advanced sensors, data analytics and other ICT systems (Burmeister et al., 2014a). The systems to operate a vessel's engine, propulsion, ballast tank and other machinery for extended periods without any on-site human involvement must be highly reliable and advanced (Höyhtyä et al., 2017; Im et al., 2018). Most importantly, development of the SCC capable of continuously monitoring and commanding the vessel through the real-time exchange of information is a key technological challenge when considering the accessibility of internet in oceans. Furthermore, there is a gray area on whose responsibility it is to develop and maintain the SCC, the shipbuilder or technology supplier.

From the perspective of technology availability, a number of likely scenarios exist on how the existing shipyards will access and adopt advanced equipment and specializations into their existing manufacturing processes. The pursuit of constructing autonomous vessels is expensive and brings challenges between acquisition of cutting-edge technology and the associated costs. Therefore, if demand for autonomous ships arise, the survival of many shipbuilders depends on how efficiently they acquire the necessary skills and knowledge to satisfy their customers. In addition, it is likely that many players will not be able to react to the challenges relating to manufacturing and maintenance of highly automated vessels and supporting systems, which may lead to extensive closure of many facilities.

On the other hand, the shipbuilding industry has demonstrated strong capabilities in establishing successful supplier networks and proactive outsourcing practices (Caniëls et al., 2016). External factors such as globalization and greater demand for specialization have been strong catalysts to increased outsourcing. This in turn has been enabling shipyards to focus on cost reduction and offer more purpose-built ships to the market. Over time, shipyards have increasingly become system integrators while suppliers have become responsible for the majority of technology development and manufacturing of advanced systems (Held, 2010). For instance, due the complexity involved in the production of marine propulsion engines, a handful of players have addressed the majority of market demand (e.g., Hyundai Heavy Industries, Rolls-Royce and Wärtsilä). Therefore, in a future with autonomous shipping, shipyards will not necessarily be isolated, but will be positioned within a complex network of suppliers who can provide the necessary services and products for construction of autonomous vessels. However, even with this degree of outsourcing, certain skills are required for a smooth transition toward a position in which shipbuilders become competent in constructing autonomous ships.

As discussed in Section 2, as part of developments toward autonomous shipping, a new market is shaping, in which technology-based companies are beginning to retrofit existing conventional vessels with autonomous technologies. Shone Automation, a San Francisco-based start-up has partnered with CMA CGM to assist on-board crews to detect and predict the movement of other vessels through AI, advanced analytics and data captured from sensors installed on the vessel. Such technologies will assist piloting and provide an anti-collision alert system. Similarly, Sea Machines is a start-up based in Boston providing commercial autonomous systems, which can be installed on-board of existing seagoing vessels, or can be included as a package in new build vessels enabling remote and autonomous operations.

In addition to the considerations of new build, there will be additional limitations and requirements for maintenance and repair of autonomous ships. The repair and maintenance operations of a vessel can be loosely categorized into "regular" or "periodic." The regular maintenance largely includes replacing parts and lubricating the moving parts. It is most likely that the majority of regular maintenance work will be transferred to a shore-based crew during port stays. What's more, it is expected that the simplified ship design and potentially electric propulsion systems will drastically reduce the lubricating oil consumption (e.g., ReVolt). However, the periodic maintenance of autonomous vessels comes with some fresh complexity. Periodic maintenance generally consists of dry docking and surveys (Granot, 2016). Dry docking work is diverse, ranging from the repair of engine rooms, decks, automations and electrical systems. Depending on the size and deadweight tonnage (DWT), type and physical characteristics of a vessel, dry docking and other periodic maintenance services are offered by a wide range of supplier across the globe, with many close to major international shipping routes. Unmanned vessels would encompass advanced and complex systems to ensure their safe and reliable operation; as such, compatible repair and maintenance technology is not likely to be readily available at all dry docking suppliers in the short term. This perhaps will require new models of partnership between shipbuilders, dry docks and suppliers of autonomous technologies to jointly perform the maintenance and repair activities, which may add more expenses to the full acquisition costs.

One of the main motivations behind the development of unmanned shipping is to improve safety standards by reducing the incidents resulted from human and machine errors. To achieve such targets, enhanced maintenance arrangements are required to remove the risk of incidents caused by systems failures (e.g., oil leakage) when vessels are unattended. With the absence of crew to undertake regular maintenance during the voyage and extra complexity associated with the on-board autonomous systems, it is expected that the cost and time required to perform the periodic maintenance of unmanned vessels will be lengthier compared to conventional vessels. Furthermore, it is likely that maintenance of unmanned vessels requires highly specialized skills (such as software updates) and systems which may not be readily available by a ship maintenance provider in proximity. As a result, a vessel may need to travel extensively to receive the essential services from a properly equipped provider, which is not necessarily close to the typical operational zone of the vessel. While the cost and availability of such services remain a concerning area for early adopters, extended maintenance work with limited accessibility could also bring new challenges in terms of vessel availability and mobility. Therefore, such repair and maintenance difficulties in running an autonomous vessel may eventually deteriorate the attractiveness of autonomous shipping for players with operational diversity.

6. Autonomous vessel and impacts on the port sector

While there is an growing amount of research on various aspects of autonomous vessels, research on their long-term implications for the port sector is extremely limited. Thus, this section aims to recognize the challenges facing ports in preparing for unmanned vessels in the future and explore the potential opportunities to gain from servicing them.

While autonomous transport at sea is still at the R&D stage, progress in port automation is decades in advance. However, most of these advancements are observed in cargo-handling operations, while the accommodation of vessels entering/exiting harbor is still performed from a very human-centered approach. Perhaps one of the major technical challenges for ports in servicing autonomous vessels will be around safe navigation, berthing and maneuvering. R&D platforms such as MUNIN (Rødseth et al., 2014) have expressed the need for an On-board Control Team (OCT) which is responsible for taking control of the vessel for its arrival to port, and similarly, in the final leg from port for autonomous control point. Therefore, it is expected that ports will take a critical part in the future by providing such services as supported by advanced on-shore ICT.

However, to assess the readiness of ports in addressing their future role in such operational environments, it is relevant to examine their progress in adoption of remote pilotage practices. Although these are two separate issues, they tackle a same problem, which is safe accommodation of vessels around the port operational zone. Hadley (1999, p. 3) defines remote pilotage as "an act of pilotage carried out in a designated area by a pilot licensed for that area from a position other than on board the vessel concerned…." Unfortunately, to date, remote pilotage has not been adopted by the global port sector (PWC, 2012) and very little technological and regulatory progress has been made in this area over the past. Brooks et al. (2016) indicate that barriers to adoption of remote pilotage are not necessarily purely technological; that is, managerial and cultural factors could also hinder the adoption of such technologies by ports. While some technical challenges exist in terms of systems compatibility, with the existing technology it is feasible to implement remote pilotage systems as part of ports' navigational practices (Bruno and Lützhöft, 2009). Given the lessons from the adoption of remote pilotage, to prepare ports for safe and efficient accommodation of autonomous vessels, a more collaborative culture will be required between ports, shipping companies, maritime agencies and those involved in advancement of autonomous shipping technologies.

On the other hand, with the absence of crew on board, ports will be required to provide a wider range of services to ships. As discussed in earlier sections, a port-based crew is required to undertake a range of activities previously performed by the on-board crew. In particular, regular maintenance is an area in which ports are expected to actively participate and facilitate. This can potentially lead to the opening of new repair and maintenance businesses within the port area for servicing autonomous vessels (British Ports Association, 2018). Similarly, most cargo-handling operations such as cleaning, stability assessments, ballast arrangements, stowing and other safety procedures that currently performed by the on-board personnel are instead expected to be offered by a port-based crew. While it is expected that a number of tasks will potentially be removed as the result of simplified ship design and automation, the need for a port-based crew is still inevitable.

The arrival of autonomous vessels comes with some other operational challenges for ports in terms of productivity. The fact that a number of maintenance and cargo-handling tasks which were previously performed during the voyage will be undertaken at ports by an on-shore crew, will open new challenges in terms of ship average turnaround time (ATT). Adding the required time for regular maintenance and other relevant activities to the ATT will significantly increase berth occupancy and asset occupation. Accordingly, increased berth occupancy per vessel is translated into a fewer number of vessels serviced by the port, congestion, and potentially lower infrastructure and asset productivity for both the shipping company and port operator. Such implications are significant, underestimated and possibly deteriorating the attractiveness of autonomous shipping for many ports.

Taking everything into account, the opportunities for the port sector can be observed in terms of job creation in new services such as maintenance, repair, cargo handling, increased SSS activity across inland and territorial waters, and potentially higher port dues and other commercial arrangements. Furthermore, enhanced automation and communication will provide an opportunity for ports to play a more integral role in both domestic and international supply chains. Traditionally in SSS markets, the vessel is employed based on the cargo type and requirements for smooth accommodation at ports (Becker et al., 2004). Such tendency hinders many ship operators from providing a more cost-effective service to a wider range of customers (Saldanha and Gray, 2002), and thus, deteriorates supply chain performance and standardization.

Although opportunities arising from the arrival of autonomous vessels are diverse and numerous for ports across the world, a chief concern surrounds the readiness of ports to embrace and benefit from such advancements. Certainly, ports need to address these issues in regards to investment in ICT infrastructure, advanced communication systems and re-skilling the human resource for servicing autonomous vessels. In this context, regional and smaller ports are more likely to be the one to accommodate the first generation of autonomous vessels in early days. Thus, a new level of investment and leadership is needed to transform the brick-and-mortar business models synonymous with smaller ports into more technologically adoptable ones. Such development will be exponentially beneficial to ports in terms of trade gateways created through extra revenue, while furthermore promising wider economic benefits for their hosting region (Koliousis et al., 2019).

7. Technology adoption, maturity lookout and impacts on market structure

Growing seaborne trade, shrinking profit margins and challenges in recruitment and retention of a seagoing workforce are key contributing factors to the growth in demand for autonomous maritime systems. According to a recent market report, the size of the autonomous shipping market is projected to grow from USD 6.1 billion in 2018 to USD 13.8 billion by 2030, at a Compound Annual Growth Rate (CAGR) of 7% (Markets and Markets, 2019). However, this growth is highly dependent on many factors, particularly the degree of technology adoption by shipping companies and wider market actors. This section serves two purposes. First, it presents a maturity process for the maritime industry relating to the adoption of autonomous vessels. Second, it discusses the likely scenarios which autonomous shipping may bring along for the wider maritime transport market and how the introduction of such technologies could potentially disrupt the current market structure and competition forms in different sub-markets.

7.1 Industry maturity process

Despite the diverse benefits that autonomous technologies promise to its stakeholders, it is important to acknowledge any technological change has the ability to disrupt and/or transform the way organizations conduct business and operate in markets. The transformative effects of technology are diverse, ranging from developing competitive advantage at a firm level to structural changes in the way an industrial sector delivers products and services to its clients.

As discussed in the earlier sections, the deployment of autonomous vessels will not only transform the way vessels are operated and voyaged in waterways, but also comes with major implications for all players involved in providing end-to-end freight transport solutions and such changes may transform the ways goods are distributed globally. In the long term, such adjustments may eventually revolutionize the landscape of the entire maritime industry, and thus, establishing a roadmap which outlines the maturity process can be highly useful for making investment, policy and regulatory decisions (Van Looy et al., 2012).

The importance of maturity models is widely acknowledged in many fields, resulting in a diverse range of models for characterizing the progress of organizations toward achieving a goal (Van Looy et al., 2012). While the majority of these methods are intended to characterize the process maturity at firm level, a framework which could hypothetically outline a maturity roadmap for the maritime industry in the presence of autonomous vessels is highly valuable.

To achieve this, a two-dimensional approach has been applied here to represent the maturity process of the sector. The first dimension denotes the levels of autonomy, which is largely associated with technology advancement. The second dimension is linked to adoption and the effects that those advancements will have on wider sector dynamics such as ports, shipbuilding and freight management practices. As a result, five key stages of maturity have been identified in Fig. 1, representing the likely developments in the maritime industry over time.

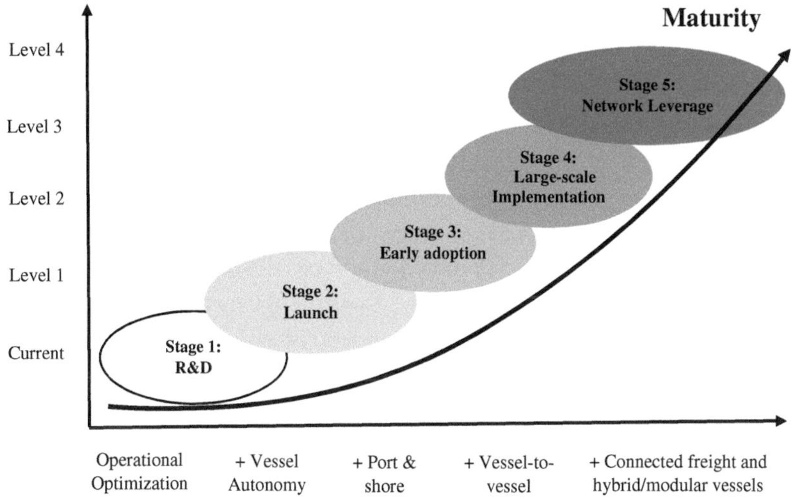

Fig. 1 Industry maturity process framework for adoption of autonomous ships.

Stage 1 is associated with development and testing of autonomous maritime systems, with small-scale trials under controlled environments occurring around the world by different system developers (e.g., Kongsberg). Furthermore, as part of this development, several policy and regulatory implications have been identified by IMO and other local and international maritime-related authorities. Stage 2 denotes the situation in which the first commercial trials will happen within local waters where permission is not required from international maritime authorities. The early adoption of autonomous ships will occur in Stage 3 where a limited number of operators will employ autonomous vessels for short voyages and simplified operations. Depending on the maturity of maritime safety regulations for autonomous vessels, such operations could potentially extend into international waters. Furthermore, the role of ports in facilitating the smooth operations of unmanned ships will be more pronounced at this stage, particularly in safe accommodation of vessels into harbors and providing support services such as maintenance and cargo handling. Stage 4 describes the scenario where large-scale adoption of autonomous vessels by the wider maritime community takes place. At this stage, the technology for an autonomous maritime system is sufficiently advanced and reliable to address the safety and operational requirements demanded by its users. With this level of technology maturity, the focus will shift toward reducing the capital cost of building autonomous vessels and identifying value adding options. Finally, a full level of autonomy will be reached in Stage 5 in which the ship is able to undertake decisions and perform actions by itself. Given the advancement in cargo-handling technology and Internet of Things (IoT), it is expected that the physical characteristics of vessels will provide more flexibility for cargo-handling operations and diversification. Such developments could be accompanied by other concepts such as connected freight and modular ships in which customers would have more influence on the design of their shipping service. With such level of technological capability and hybrid operations, network capacity could be leveraged and new concepts like Shipping-as-a-Service (SaaS) may emerge in which provision of cargo transportation solutions is more focused on the needs of shippers instead of availability, type and capability of vessels. Such innovations provide the opportunity to radically improve the way shippers select shipping services, reduce freight costs, and boost supply chain capacity while addressing the increasing demand for just-in-time (JIT) shipping practices.

7.2 Technology adoption and impacts on market structure: A market-based analysis

The deployment of unmanned vessels will bring another set of strategic challenges for shipping companies, particularly in terms of fleet productivity and asset utilization, with diverse network effects on operators depending on their fleet type and size. Knowing the progressive nature of autonomous shipping adoption into the industry, it is expected that in some stages the global fleet will consist of mixed vessels ranging from fully autonomous, remotely controlled and conventional human-operated ships. Besides the safety incompatibility, such mixed traffics will bring new industry challenges in terms of productivity and asset optimization.

It is common for shipping companies to deploy a fleet of homogeneous vessels to standardize operational procedures and reduce maintenance costs (Karlaftis et al., 2009; Reinhardt et al., 2016). Furthermore, in many cases a fleet consists of vessels with different ages, lease and finance conditions, which comes with long-term commitments for the shipping company and owners. Given such complexity, a small to medium-sized shipping company would not have the flexibility to either invest in an entire fleet of newly built autonomous vessels or even simply incorporate a single autonomous vessel into an existing human-operated fleet. Thus, technology transfer and adoption will remain a key challenge for many operators in the short to mid-run. Furthermore, a fully autonomous vessel wherein humans are absent and all decisions are made by computers is likely to be a long-term vision. This means vessels will require a SCC for remote operations in Levels 2 and 3 of autonomy. Depending on the vessel specification and geographical dispersion of the operations, the capital costs associated with the establishment and integration of such a system is significant (Kretschmann et al., 2015), which may further hinder the adoption of autonomous ships by many small and medium-sized operators.

Such adoption barriers could bring new implications in terms of market entry and concentration. In particular, since the capital cost for the control center will be subsidized into a higher number of vessels, larger shipping companies with standard operations and homogenous fleet types have more incentive to replace their conventional ships with a fleet of autonomous vessels. Furthermore, as autonomous ships are highly technologically advanced, a large portion of the cost for new build vessels are associated with R&D as well as the customization of cutting-edge systems and technologies fitting to the company's unique operational environment. Accordingly, if the size of a shipping company is large enough to order several new build vessels, the acquisition cost per vessel will be significantly subsidized. The combination of these factors results in a significantly lower total cost of ownership (TCO) for a business with large operations. However, once autonomous maritime systems advance to Level 4 in which the operating system of the vessel makes decisions independently of a remote control center and technology becomes more readily available, the costs of acquisition and running an autonomous vessel lowers.

The level of technology adoption and its impacts on the market structure must also be investigated from the perspective of individual shipping submarkets. To achieve a better understanding of how each sub-market could possibly respond to these technological advancements, we characterize the degree of adoptability from the perspectives of economic incentives, regulatory barriers and operational compatibility. Although shipping markets can be investigated from many different aspects, for the purpose of this analysis, geographical dispersion of operations and core service offerings are considered.

In the freight space, coastal shipping is a complex and operationally diverse market. Traditionally, SSS operators deploy a vessel based on the nature of commodity (Becker et al., 2004). However, with the greater use of containerization, SSS has embraced standardization to a larger extent. Given the low degree of economies of scale and scope in many SSS origin-destination routes, there exist many single vessel operators who provide their service to a diverse range of customers with vessels capable of handling general cargo. Therefore, despite the lower regulatory obstacles for adoption of unmanned ships in SSS markets, the economic benefits and operational compatibility are not promising enough for a speedy adoption.

The characteristics of costing in deep-sea shipping are completely different to short-distance operations. Compared to SSS, the cost of manpower is relatively lower in deep-sea when considering the total costs of running a vessel. Such utilization is achieved through longer origin-destination routes which results in higher crew utilization and larger volumes of cargo shipped by vessel over a longer period of time. However, this does not mean the speed of adoption is similar for every operator.

In the bulk and general cargo markets, there is a large number of single-vessel operators offering their cargo capacity on a charter or less long-term contract basis to a wide range of shippers with dissimilar demand characteristics. Therefore, similar to SSS markets, unless simplified autonomous shipping technology such as retrofitting solutions become easy-to-install and commercially viable, incentives for adoption are minimal for small operators. On the other hand, the speed of adoption would be much higher for larger deep-sea operators with multiple (semi) homogenous vessels as the result of greater savings in acquisition and running the fleet. However, due to the geographical dispersion of operations and absence of globally accepted regulatory frameworks, shipping companies that service international ports using autonomous vessels may face legal and administrative difficulties. Furthermore, the market space for specialized cargo leaves very limited opportunity for embracing autonomous systems in a near future as seafarers play a wide range of roles in terms of cargo handling and the operation of specialized ships.

In the passenger sector, autonomous technologies can massively contribute to short-distance ferry services where vessels travel in less disruptive, more routine and operationally simple conditions. In particular, autonomous vessels promise lower human errors and higher safety levels (Burmeister et al., 2014b), which is a priority for congested and narrow waterways where public transport is offered. However, the use of autonomous navigation in long-haul passenger services, such as cruises, may not be an option so long as the on-board role of crew is intertwined with several other non-seafaring activities such as servicing passengers. The activities of cruise ship crew may furthermore continuously evolve based on several operational and service-level dynamics. Table 2 provides a summary on the degree of adoption by different shipping markets.

Although the information provided in Table 2 is not definite and comes with several assumptions, such analysis is beneficial to establish an understanding of the likely scenarios in terms of changes in market structure and competition in the presence of autonomous ships.

Table 2 Adoption of autonomous technology by different shipping markets.

	Freight					Passenger	
	SSS small fleet	**SSS large fleet**	**Deep-sea /charter**	**Deep-sea /linear**	**Specialized cargo**	**Ferry**	**Cruise**
Economic incentives	Low	High	Low	Medium	Low	High	Low
Regulatory barriers	Low	Medium	High	High	High	Low	High
Operational compatibility	Low	High	Low	High	Low	High	Low

8. Conclusion

In recent years, the global maritime industry has embarked on an intensive journey of digital transformation. Associated with this has been the extensive embracement of ship automation, and more recently, the technological developments linked to the design and development of unmanned vessels. The benefits of autonomous navigation are diverse and the appetite of the maritime industry to seize the opportunities driven by such technology is extremely high.

However, any technological advancements have the potential to introduce significant productivity benefits, or conversely, create systematic interruptions for the wider market actors. Similarly, while the future role of autonomous ships pertain to the transport of goods, such technological advancement will have vertical and horizontal effects on other supply chain players, such as ports, shipbuilding, insurance, etc. These implications must be recognized and examined to fully embrace the benefits of autonomous technologies in the near future. Perhaps a key outcome of this chapter is seen in examination of the full costs of adopting autonomous vessels into maritime supply chains. While the existing research promises economic and financial benefits, such savings are mainly assessed from the perspective of shipping companies. In other words, some cost elements may transfer to upstream and/or downstream actors in the supply chain, which are important to be fully measured.

The complexity of autonomous vessel systems opens numerous avenues for future research. Similar to the use of autonomous vehicles in road transport, the need for governance frameworks to facilitate safe navigation of autonomous vessels is an essential and crucial step. This is principally imperative in the early stages of adoption where mixed traffics of conventional, autonomous or remotely controlled vessels exist simultaneously. Another important area for further investigation is observed around the connectivity and data governance of future ships. A smooth and safe transition toward adoption of autonomous vessels relies on robust internet connectivity, which is free of cyber-attacks and malfunctions. Thus, the question remains open on how such services will be readily available in the middle of oceans, and how secure and reliable it would be accessed by autonomous ships. Finally, this study recommends that future studies explore the long-term impacts of autonomous vessels on the maritime workforce market. This is an imperative issue as the removal of crew from vessels will abandon a substantial number of seagoing workforce jobless, but at the same time create demand for new skills. Therefore, strategic workforce planning and development will become an inevitable need to supply the required human resources capable of constructing, maintaining and operating autonomous vessels in the future.

References

Akyuz, E., Celik, M., Cebi, S., 2016. A phase of comprehensive research to determine marine-specific EPC values in human error assessment and reduction technique. Saf. Sci. 87, 63–75.

Alderton, T., 2004. The Global Seafarer: Living and Working Conditions in a Globalized Industry. International Labour Organization Geneva, Switzerland.

Baldauf, M., Kitada, M., Mehdi, R., Dalaklis, D., 2018. E-Navigation, digitalization and unmanned ships: challenges for future maritime education and training. In: 12th Annual International Technology, Education and Development Conference (INTED), Barcelona.

Batalden, B.-M., Leikanger, P., Wide, P., 2017. Towards autonomous maritime operations. In: 2017 IEEE International Conference on Computational Intelligence and Virtual Environments for Measurement Systems and Applications (CIVEMSA). IEEE, pp. 1–6.

Becker, J., Burgess, A., Henstra, D., 2004. Short Sea Shipping Policy From a Community Perspective. European Transport Conference, Strasbourg, France.

British Ports Association, 2018. Automation of Ships in Ports and Harbours. Setfords, London, UK.

Brooks, B., Coltman, T., Yang, M., 2016. Technological innovation in the maritime industry: the case of remote pilotage and enhanced navigational assistance. J. Navig. 69 (4), 777–793.

Bruno, K., Lützhöft, M., 2009. Shore-based pilotage: pilot or autopilot? Piloting as a control problem. J. Navig. 62 (3), 427–437.

Burmeister, H.-C., Bruhn, W., Rødseth, Ø.J., Porathe, T., 2014a. Autonomous unmanned merchant vessel and its contribution towards the e-navigation implementation: the MUNIN perspective. Int. J. e-Navig. Marit. Econ. 1, 1–13.

Burmeister, H.-C., Bruhn, W.C., Rødseth, Ø.J., Porathe, T., 2014b. Can unmanned ships improve navigational safety? In: Proceedings of the Transport Research Arena, TRA 2014, 14–17 April 2014, Paris.
Caniëls, M.C.J., Cleophas, E., Semeijn, J., 2016. Implementing green supply chain practices: an empirical investigation in the shipbuilding industry. Marit. Policy Manag. 43 (8), 1005–1020.
DNV GL, 2014. The ReVolt: a new inspirational ship concept. https://www.dnvgl.com/technology-innovation/revolt/index.html.
Freire, P.E.M., 2004. An Investigation into the Design of an Unmanned Ship. University College London.
Ghaderi, H., 2019. Autonomous technologies in short sea shipping: trends, feasibility and implications. Transp. Rev. 39 (1), 152–173.
Giannopoulos, G.A., 2004. The application of information and communication technologies in transport. Eur. J. Oper. Res. 152 (2), 302–320.
Granot, A., 2016. Autonomous Cargo Vessels: Analysis for a Future Operations Model. Erasmus University Rotterdam.
Hadley, M., 1999. Issues in remote pilotage. J. Navig. 52 (1), 1–10.
Held, T., 2010. Supplier integration as an improvement driver—an analysis of some recent approaches in the shipbuilding industry. In: Engelhardt-Nowitzki, c., Nowitzki, O., Zsifkovits, H. (Eds.), Supply Chain Network Management: Gestaltungskonzepte und Stand der praktischen Anwendung. Gabler, Wiesbaden.
Hogg, T., Ghosh, S., 2016. Autonomous merchant vessels: examination of factors that impact the effective implementation of unmanned ships. Aust. J. Marit. Ocean Aff. 8 (3), 206–222.
Höyhtyä, M., Huusko, J., Kiviranta, M., Solberg, K., Rokka, J., 2017. Connectivity for autonomous ships: architecture, use cases, and research challenges. In: 2017 International Conference on Information and Communication Technology Convergence (ICTC), 18–20 Oct. 2017, pp. 345–350.
Im, I., Shin, D., Jeong, J., 2018. Components for smart autonomous ship architecture based on intelligent information technology. Prog. Comput. Sci. 134, 91–98.
IMO, 2007. Strategy Fot the Development and Implementation of E-Navigation. International Maritime Organisation, London, UK.
IMO, 2018. Maritime Safety Committee (MSC), 100th Session—Regulatory Scoping Exercise on Maritime Autonomous Surface Ships (MASS). International Maritime Organisation, London, UK.
Karlaftis, M.G., Kepaptsoglou, K., Sambracos, E., 2009. Containership routing with time deadlines and simultaneous deliveries and pick-ups. Transport Res. E-Log. 45 (1), 210–221.
Koliousis, I.G., Papadimitriou, S., Riza, E., Stavroulakis, P.J., Tsioumas, V., 2019. Strategic correlations for maritime clusters. Transp. Res. A Policy Pract. 120, 43–57.
Kretschmann, L., Rødseth, Ø., Sage Fuller, B., Noble, H., Horahan, J., McDowell, H., 2015. MUNIN Deliverable 9.3: Quantitative Assessment. MUNIN Project/Europen Commission, Brussels, Belgium.
Kretschmann, L., Burmeister, H.-C., Jahn, C., 2017. Analyzing the economic benefit of unmanned autonomous ships: an exploratory cost-comparison between an autonomous and a conventional bulk carrier. Res. Transp. Bus. Manag. 25, 76–86.
Markets and Markets, 2019. Autonomous Ships Market by Autonomy (Fully Autonomous, Remote Operations, Partial Automation), Ship Type (Commercial, Defense), End Use (Linefit, Retrofit), Solution (Systems, Software, Structures), and Region—Global Forecast to 2030. Markets and Markets, Pune, India.
Milakis, D., van Arem, B., van Wee, B., 2017. Policy and society related implications of automated driving: a review of literature and directions for future research. J. Intell. Transp. Syst. 21 (4), 324–348.

Milner, C.G., 1971. Innovation in shipbuilding. R D Manag. 2 (1), 41–53.

MOL, 2017. MOL Launches R & D on Autonomous Ocean Transport System [Online]. Available: m http://www.mol.co.jp/en/pr/2017/17031.html.

Nguyen, T.T., Ghaderi, H., Caesar, L.D., Cahoon, S., 2014. Current challenges in the recruitment and retention of seafarers: an industry perspective from Vietnam. Asian J. Shipp. Logist. 30 (2), 217–242.

Österman, C., Hult, C., 2016. Administrative burdens and over-exertion in Swedish short sea shipping. Marit. Policy Manag. 43 (5), 569–579.

Perera, L.P., 2018. Autonomous ship navigation under deep learning and the challenges in COLREGs. In: ASME 2018 37th International Conference on Ocean, Offshore and Arctic Engineering. American Society of Mechanical Engineers. V11BT12A005-V11BT12A005.

Perera, L.P., Soares, C.G., 2015. Collision risk detection and quantification in ship navigation with integrated bridge systems. Ocean Eng. 109, 344–354.

Perera, L.P., Soares, C.G., 2017. Weather routing and safe ship handling in the future of shipping. Ocean Eng. 130, 684–695.

Peri, D., Rossetti, M., Campana, E.F., 2001. Design optimization of ship hulls via CFD techniques. J. Ship Res. 45 (2), 140–149.

Porathe, T., Burmeister, H.-C., Rødseth, Ø.J., 2013. Maritime unmanned navigation through intelligence in networks: The MUNIN Project. In: 12th International Conference on Computer and IT Applications in the Maritime Industries, COMPIT'13, Cortona, 15–17 April 2013.

Porathe, T., Prison, J., Man, Y., 2014. Situation awareness in remote control centres for unmanned ships. In: Human Factors in Ship Design & Operation. London, UK.

PWC, 2012. Study of Pilotage Exemption Certificates. PWC.

Reinhardt, L.B., Plum, C.E.M., Pisinger, D., Sigurd, M.M., Vial, G.T.P., 2016. The liner shipping berth scheduling problem with transit times. Transport Res. E-Log. 86, 116–128.

Rodrigue, J.-P., Comtois, C., Slack, B., 2013. The Geography of Transport Systems. Routledge, New York, NY.

Rødseth, Ø.J., Burmeister, H.-C., 2012. Developments toward the unmanned ship. In: Proceedings of International Symposium Information on Ships–ISIS, pp. 30–31.

Rødseth, Ø., Burmeister, H.-C., 2015. MUNIN Deliverable 10.2 New Ship Designs for Autonomous Vessels. MUNIN Project/Europen Commission.

Rødseth, Ø.J., Tjora, Å., Baltzersen, P., 2014. MUNIN Deliverable D4.5: Architecture Specification. MUNIN Project/Europen Commission. http://www.unmanned-ship.org/munin/wp-content/uploads/2014/02/d4-5-architecture-v11.pdf.

Rolls-Royce, 2014. Remote and Autonomous Ships—the Next Steps. Rolls-Royce. https://www.rolls-royce.com/~/media/Files/R/Rolls-Royce/documents/%20customers/marine/ship-intel/rr-ship-intel-aawa-8pg.pdf.

Ronen, D., 2011. The effect of oil price on containership speed and fleet size. J. Oper. Res. Soc. 62 (1), 211–216.

Saldanha, J., Gray, R., 2002. The potential for British coastal shipping in a multimodal chain. Marit. Policy Manag. 29 (1), 77–92.

Sauer, J., Wastell, D.G., Hockey, G.R.J., Crawshaw, C.M., Ishak, M., Downing, J.C., 2002. Effects of display design on performance in a simulated ship navigation environment. Ergonomics 45 (5), 329–347.

Stopford, M., 2009. Maritime Economics 3e. Routledge, New York, NY.

Suárez-Alemán, A., 2016. Short sea shipping in today's Europe: a critical review of maritime transport policy. Marit. Econ. Logist. 18 (3), 331–351.

Tai, S.K., 2016. Review of the development of seafarers in Hong Kong. Marit. Bus. Rev. 1 (2), 149–162.

van Leeuwen, J., 2015. The regionalization of maritime governance: towards a polycentric governance system for sustainable shipping in the European Union. Ocean Coast. Manag. 117, 23–31.
Van Looy, A., De Backer, M., Poels, G., 2012. Towards a Decision Tool for Choosing a Business Process Maturity Model. Springer, Berlin Heidelberg, pp. 78–87.
Vanem, E., Yarmolenka, D., Korody, G., 2015. Ship port pre-arrival reporting and ship survey status as eMar services. In: Ehlers, S., Asbjornslett, B.E., Rodseth, O.J., Berg, T.E. (Eds.), Maritime-Port Technology and Development. CRC Press, pp. 227–236.
Wu, B., Winchester, N., 2005. Crew study of seafarers: a methodological approach to the global labour market for seafarers. Mar. Policy 29 (4), 323–330.
Xiao, Z., Fu, X., Zhang, L., Zhang, W., Agarwal, M., Goh, R.S.M., 2019. MarineMAS: a multi-agent framework to aid design, modelling, and evaluation of autonomous shipping systems. J. Int. Marit. Saf. Environ. Aff. Shipp. 2 (2), 43–57.

CHAPTER TWELVE

The potential for automation to transform urban deliveries: Drivers, barriers and policy priorities

Daniela Paddeu*, Graham Parkhurst
University of the West of England, Bristol, United Kingdom
*Corresponding author: e-mail address: daniela.paddeu@uwe.ac.uk

Contents

Abstract

Urban freight transport is crucial to ensuring the economic vitality of a city. However, significant negative "externalities" arise from freight flows in urban areas. Current solutions to reduce the impact of freight transport in urban areas aim at

Advances in Transport Policy and Planning, Volume 5
ISSN 2543-0009
https://doi.org/10.1016/bs.atpp.2020.01.003

reducing the number of vehicles (e.g., introducing traffic regulations and restrictions, or providing for transhipment to lower-environmental impact vehicles at an Urban Consolidation Centre), or to reduce the polluting emissions of the delivery fleet (e.g., use of electric vans, electric scooters, cargo-bikes). However, the future might offer very different additional options. Hence, the chapter explores developments in automation (i.e., autonomous surface and aerial delivery vehicles), such as might achieve sustainability benefits through replacing or integrating with current delivery systems, including providing the "last mile," in urban areas. Specifically, the chapter presents a review of current and future developments in automated urban freight transport systems and the results of a series of stakeholder engagement workshops on future solutions for urban freight. The chapter demonstrates that, despite the potential importance of automation for improving the efficiency and competitiveness of the urban freight sector, research evidence gaps exist related to the identification of competitive advantages for these new technologies, micro and macro-economic benefits, and the costs of those developments. It is also considered that, while there may be potential for automation in the urban delivery sector to enhance welfare, particularly in terms of quality-of-life-factors, significant practical and policy barriers remain.

Keywords: Urban deliveries, Automation, Freight, Connected autonomous vehicles, Unmanned aerial vehicles, Drones, Delivery bots, Last-mile deliveries

1. Introduction

Despite its important role for economic growth, freight transport is responsible for traffic congestion and air pollution, which generally impose significant costs on society through impacts on public health, transport safety, and the environment (Korzhenevych et al., 2014). The impact of last-mile deliveries is particularly significant, due to the high density of activities and people in urban areas, and growing e-commerce, which is responsible for a high number of commercial vehicle movements in city centers (Iwan et al., 2016). According to Angelovska (2018), the UK leads Europe for its adoption of e-commerce: 86% of the UK population that has internet access makes online purchases. Other European countries with a percentage higher than 80% are all in the western half of the continent, including Sweden, Denmark, Germany, Luxembourg, Netherlands, and Switzerland. On the other hand, e-commerce is less popular in Montenegro (18%), Northern Macedonia (20%), Romania (23%), Bulgaria (27%) and Turkey (32%). In the United Kingdom, e-customers spent on average £1600 in 2017, while "millennials" make 54% of their purchases online, and it is predicted that, by 2040, 95% of purchases will be facilitated by e-commerce (KOL Limited, 2018). E-commerce generates a high number of deliveries, usually not optimized in terms of load factor, which is a key contributor to the negative social, economic and environmental conditions in urban areas.

According to Gevaers et al. (2014), last-mile deliveries can be considered the worst-performing part of the supply chain, due to high costs, low efficiency, and high impact on the environment. As a response, a number of innovative solutions, such as automated freight vehicles, drones, and 3D printing, are under development. These show some potential to reduce urban congestion and air pollution, while at the same time improving transport system safety (Paddeu et al., 2019). However, these new technologies, and the policy and governance frameworks to support them, still need further testing and development, and for this reason are subject to focused academic and practice research and development. Hence, the present chapter offers an overview of the main new technologies under development which might shape the future of urban freight, with an analysis of drivers and barriers to their implementation.

The remainder of the paper is organized as follows: Section 2 presents the methodology used to carry out the literature review; Section 3 presents the key emerging concepts identified, which include considerations about automated vehicles and driverless pods (Section 3.1), unmanned aerial vehicles for urban deliveries (Section 3.2), and other automated options for urban freight (Section 3.3); Section 4 introduces the stakeholders that are involved in the urban freight system and considers how their role profiles might change in the future; Section 5 shows factors that can enable or prevent the adoption of new technologies and automation and considers how the innovative solutions could be integrated with existing ones. The chapter concludes with Section 6 providing insights into policy implications and a research and policy agenda to guide the future implementation of automation in the urban freight sector.

2. Methodology

The review was carried out through an online search on terms related to "freight," "city logistics," "new technologies," "automation" and "ITS." Documents identified included scientific papers, reviews, empirical studies, and technical reports. In addition to online searching, posts were made to email lists of expert academics to encourage them to suggest documents, for example, items not easily identified through online searching. The review was to be international in scope. Papers were included in the review according to the following two-step process:

Step 1—Filtering. Works identified through the search were scored against two criteria: "A. Relevance to the topic," with A ranging from 0 (no relevance) to 3 (high relevance); works accepted for $A>=2$; and "B. Transferability of results," with $B=1$ if the work is likely transferable, $B=0$ otherwise; works accepted for $B=1$.

Step 2—Ranking. Sources passing the initial filter were scored against two further criteria: "C. Impact of the work," with C ranging from 0 (no citations) to 4 (>20 citations); and "D. Type of source," with D ranging from 0 (blogs and forum) to 4 (review).

The review findings were strengthened by the results of a series of Stakeholder Engagement Workshops carried out in January–March 2019 in Bristol (UK) within the project "Innovative and Collaborative Solutions to shape Freight Transport Systems of the Future: a Co-design Process." The project responded to the challenge that multiple stakeholders are involved in the urban freight system. They have different needs and expectations, all of which should be considered within the policy process. For this reason, studying stakeholders' behavior is of high importance within policymaking, as a poor understanding of their needs might result in unintended or undesirable consequences, such as higher external costs then predicted, or lower transport system efficiency than expected (Stathopoulos et al., 2012).

To this end, 10 key stakeholders, including supply chain managers and logistics operators, managers of a major shopping area, transport planners and consultants, and policy makers, participated in two workshops in Bristol. Subsequently, a group of six citizens took part in a workshop facilitated within the "Bristol Forum," a 1-day citizen-engagement event considering a range of research topics.

Both professional and citizen participants of the three workshops were asked to share their ideas about automated systems and new technologies for urban deliveries, considering implications on society, economy, environment, and the overall transport system. They were also asked to "co-design the urban freight system of the future," including identifying innovative solutions and potential drivers and barriers to their implementation. Qualitative analysis of the results was undertaken to understand the different perspectives.

3. Emerging concepts for higher-technology urban freight systems

This section presents an overview of the main new technologies that have been developed in recent years to enhance urban freight systems.

3.1 Autonomous vehicles and driverless pods

Automated Vehicles (AVs) or Driverless Vehicles (DVs) can be used for road freight transport on the long haul or to deliver goods within urban environments, e.g., last mile (Priemus et al., 2005). AV trucks are expected to be more expensive than AV cars; however, their uptake might be more rapid, as acceptance and adoption are expected to be higher (Guerra, 2015). Several authors acknowledged the potential benefits due to AV trucks. However, the literature offers few investigations of AVs for last-mile deliveries, as the majority of the studies consider AV trucks on the long haul or other modes of transport, e.g., rail freight, shipping (Paddeu et al., 2019) and are therefore beyond the scope of this chapter.

A noteworthy conceptual application of AVs for urban freight transport has been developed within the European project FURBOT (Freight Urban RoBOTic vehicle), which proposes a delivery vehicle that integrates a mobile robot, a van, and a forklift. The vehicle is not fully automated; rather, it is equipped with a driver assistance system for emergency issues, parking assistance, and speed control (FURBOT, 2014). The use of specific loading/unloading bays would avoid conflicts with other road users and reduce congestion.

Alessandrini et al.'s (2015) response to the opportunity is to suggest the adaptation of the Cargo Hopper System developed in Utrecht to a light duty automated transport vehicle (Fig. 1). This would consist of an electric automated (driverless) driving module connected to a set of cargo modules that can be used to deliver goods from an urban consolidation center to a number of destination points. The overall system would seek to reduce congestion and polluting emissions, while reducing operating costs and improving overall efficiency.

Another remarkable application is the use of electric autonomous robots, such as the small six-wheeled autonomous pods developed by Starship Technology (STARSHIP, 2018) (Fig. 2). Seven European countries and the United States have been involved in testing this technology.

Fig. 1 Representation of the automated multi-trailer vehicle for last mile deliveries. *Source: Alessandrini, A., Campagna, A., Delle Site, P., Filippi, F. and Persia, L., 2015. Automated vehicles and the rethinking of mobility and cities. Transp. Res. Proc. 5, 145–160, fig. 6. doi: doi.org/10.1016/j.trpro.2015.01.002. Under a Creative Commons license CC-BY-NC-ND.*

Fig. 2 Starship technologies delivery robot. *Source: Potter, S., 2019. A Group of the 'Starship' Robot Delivery Vehicles a Kingston Shopping Centre, Milton Keynes. Awaiting a Call to Make a Home Delivery. The Closest Vehicle Has Been Temporarily Decorated for Valentine's Day. Available at: https://commons.wikimedia.org/wiki/File:Starships_at_Kingston_15.2.19.jpg (Accessed: 05/11/2019). Under a Creative Commons license CC-BY-SA-4.0.*

The autonomous robot drives itself from the origin to the destination, using a path algorithm to find the quickest and safest path, traveling at an average of 6.5 km/h speed (up to a maximum 16 km/h) and, controversially, sharing the pavement with pedestrians. The AV robot is equipped with a set of micro-cameras connected to a control center where a human operator can constantly monitor the pods and provide support in case of incidents. Security is also guaranteed through an audible alarm that is activated in case of unauthorized access to the load for malicious purposes (e.g., stealing the goods).

The system offers an on-demand service, which could drastically reduce the number of failed deliveries, suggesting that indirect positive effects on traffic congestion, polluting emissions and operational costs for logistics operators might follow.

However, there is concern about public acceptance, due to pavement sharing, and, in many countries, this is not merely a matter of preference but related to regulations, as these vehicles are not allowed to circulate on the roadway or footway, because they might reduce the accessibility for pedestrians with mobility and visual impairments (Paddeu et al., 2019). Furthermore, the results of the stakeholder engagement workshops showed resistance also among professionals to the sharing of public space with AVs or AV robots. They did not raise any objections to AVs circulating at night, when traffic is light, but they did not want to see them in public spaces during times with very high flows of vehicles or pedestrians.

Commercial viability is also not proven: Kunze (2016) argued that delivery costs might actually increase due to the low compatibility of tools/ equipment at the destination points and to safety and security issues due to human backup being remote rather than proximate.

In summary, overall, the literature provides only limited consideration of the advantages and disadvantages of surface AVs for urban freight, and there is still a large uncertainty in terms of technological development and regulatory change such that would enable or promote full adoption and implementation of AVs for deliveries on roads and in public spaces (Neuweiler and Riedel, 2017).

3.2 Unmanned aerial vehicles for urban deliveries

The idea of adopting Unmanned Aerial Vehicles (UAVs—commonly known as "drones") to deliver goods has generated significant interest among logistics companies. The use of UAVs to date has been highest profile for military purposes, but the technology has also seen application in the civilian context for emergency deliveries (e.g., medical products and equipment) in areas with limited accessibility, due to poor infrastructure, low population density, or rurality (DHL, 2014). However, their full application to last-mile deliveries remains limited due to their small cargo capacity, which would imply the use of 15–16 drones to replace one van (Paddeu et al., 2019). Nevertheless, there might be a significant economic advantage, because a delivery might cost six times less compared with the same consignment being moved by a traditional van (D'Andrea, 2014).

Nonetheless, despite the high advantages of being highly penetrating in places with poor accessibility and high competitiveness in terms of costs, there are several major issues that might prevent the adoption and application of drones to last-mile deliveries. Paramount among these are safety and security (D'Andrea, 2014; Kunze, 2016; Whitlock, 2014): drones might be involved in aerial collisions or malfunctions and could crash into people or property. They might also be hacked for malicious use or for the theft of personal information. Furthermore, current models at least are associated with acoustic pollution (electric fan "buzzing" by the multiple rotors) and might have a negative ecological impact on birdlife. On the other hand, they are expected to be better than vans in terms of CO_2 emissions, even though the best-case scenario would be a mixed delivery system based on integration with vans, so that drones provide only for the very last-mile (Goodchild and Toy, 2018). However, their current energetic inefficiency (Kunze, 2016) and the existence of regulations preventing them from circulating freely in the air, are other major constraints to their full deployment in the short-to-medium period (Paddeu et al., 2019).

Even if there are limitations on drones providing last-mile deliveries, though, they can be a very useful resource within warehouses: they have been widely used in the United States to assist or replace human beings. Results show that the adoption of drones can reduce operational costs and avoid human errors almost completely with the inventory (Jackson, 2017). According to Argon Consulting, 100 humans can be replaced by only two drones that are able to deal with the same workload over a given period and with better-quality performance. However, as now subject to systematic analysis by a range of commentators (Office for National Statistics, 2019), automation might have an overall negative effect on employment, as roles requiring low levels of skill might be almost completely replaced by drones, due to the evident operational benefits.

Within the stakeholder engagement workshops, most of the stakeholders involved did not like the idea of "having the sky full of noisy drones" and thought UAVs should be used only in cases of emergency (e.g., urgent medical supplies). They had a generally negative perception of drones, and were concerned about privacy and security issues, overall considering the disadvantages expected to arise from their application in urban areas being much higher than the real advantages (e.g., fast delivery).

3.3 Other automated options for urban freight

Another option for avoiding urban road freight movements is 3D printing, which in effect combines "virtual" delivery with local automated production. The process of 3D printing allows the user to 3D print a product by him/herself, using a specific material or materials, by means of software that transmits the design instructions to the 3D printer. Hence it is contrasted with the examples shown in the previous sections, in that rather than being a delivery solution, 3D-printing avoids the need for transport, as users "fulfill" their own products locally (Mckinnon, 2016).

3D-printing has recently become a commercial proposition, with the market worth estimated at $5.2 billion in 2015 (Keeney, 2016). By 2020 that figure was expected to reach $15.8 billion, and subsequently grow to $23.9 billion in 2022, and $35.6 billion in 2024 (McCue, 2019).

There are several advantages with the use of 3D printing. From a customer perspective, products can be highly customizable and the lead-time can be drastically reduced. From an overall urban freight system perspective, the reduced demand for goods movement (Taniguchi and Thompson, 2014) would arise from a reduction of the overall kilometers traveled across the whole supply chain (both upstream and downstream, including last-mile deliveries). This would have a related positive impact on congestion, polluting emissions and noise (Paddeu et al., 2019).

However, if 3D printing looks promising from these perspectives, several issues limit its actual applicability. First of these is market needs: the available 3D printers are not able to produce sophisticated and varied products, so 3D printers cannot deal with many market requirements at the moment. Second is cost: more complex 3D printers have very high costs (both capital and operational) and are generally not affordable by private households. The stakeholders involved in the workshops in Bristol also highlighted the issue of the supply of printer raw materials: even though the need for transport of products would be reduced or avoided, the receiver would still need filament to be delivered. The view was expressed that it would be preferable to buy a finished product rather than 3D print it, as it was suspected that the quality would not be as high as from a commercial production line, and that the printing process might take a long time, and perhaps require the user to be available during the printing, e.g., to refill printer consumables. These shortcomings suggest a mode of deployment based around commercially-offered or shared-ownership facilities at the neighborhood level (Kunze, 2016), following the business model that used to apply to photographic

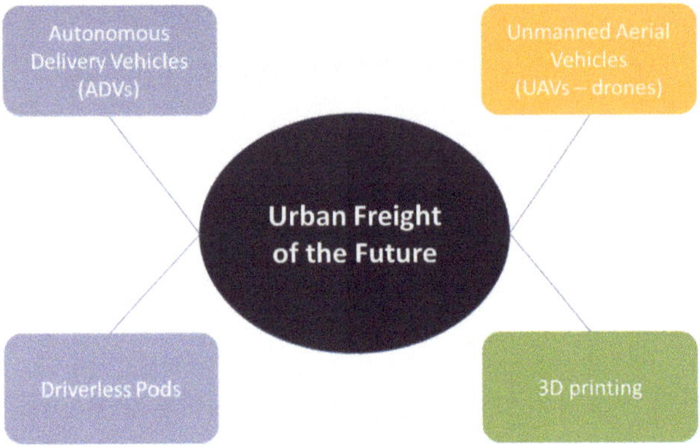

Fig. 3 Main technologies potentially available in the future for urban freight systems.

celluloid film processing, or photocopying, prior to the rise of digital media and low-cost personal printer-copiers.

Fig. 3 presents the main technologies that are expected to be available in the future for urban freight solutions.

3.4 Main gaps

The literature review identified that there are several knowledge and evidence gaps, mainly related to the identification of real competitive advantages for the new technologies, affirmation of the presence of micro and macro-economic benefits, and the costs of the new technologies. Considering the high uncertainty of technological development in general, it is not easy to clearly predict costs and benefits, and so to understand whether these new technologies could represent a competitive advantage for companies in a new or changing market. Furthermore, the different solutions might have different applications, with investment and operating costs that might vary significantly, depending on the technology. Unfortunately, there are not many applications in the real world to have a clear understanding of their costs, in order to be able to evaluate costs and benefits and define or validate newly-proposed business models. However, due to the wider potential benefits related to the new technologies, a likely feature of the corresponding business models is that they would be innovative private-public partnership (Shladover, 2017), with local, national, or European authorities financially supporting companies and universities to develop and test new solutions. However, more evidence is needed to encourage policy makers to design new policies to foster innovation in urban freight.

The literature review identified several works dealing with the estimation of cost savings due to reduced fuel consumption as a result of AV adoption (Bakermans, 2016). However, fuel only represents about 20% of overall logistics costs (Paddeu et al., 2019), so it is essential to consider other costs as well. Appraising AVs more generally, Wadud (2017) argued that the benefits due to AVs would indeed be higher than the costs, but his considerations are based on a multi-scenario analysis (e.g., optimistic, baseline, pessimistic), with estimates that would significantly vary between each other (by 25–60%). The inability to provide an accurate estimation of costs and benefits might lead to misinterpretation and under/overestimation of impacts, which might significantly undermine the basis of any evaluation with a view to their adoption. In general, the literature does not provide or suggest an appropriate methodology to evaluate impacts of automated urban freight systems in terms of noxious emissions, noise and congestion (Kunze, 2016).

Furthermore, the new business models might imply the involvement of new stakeholders in the urban freight system. Due to the high importance of city stakeholders in the design of new solutions for urban deliveries, the next section provides an insight of how current stakeholder profiles could potentially change and what kind of new stakeholders might access the urban freight system.

4. Evolution of stakeholders roles in the urban freight system of the future

The core, most frequently involved stakeholders in the urban freight subsector are carriers, truck/van drivers, receivers, policy makers, and citizens. However, this profile of core stakeholders might assume a very different shape in the urban freight system of the future, and new stakeholders might arise due to new market needs. The following subsections consider the changed roles of stakeholders that will potentially co-exist in possible future scenarios for urban freight.

4.1 The carrier

The carrier is the stakeholder responsible for moving goods for a specific client, to an agreed schedule and costs (Paddeu et al., 2019). Carriers of the future could potentially use automated trucks and vans or pods to make deliveries in urban areas. According to Bakermans (2016), carriers have a positive attitude with respect to new technologies, as they acknowledge these will save fuel and improve safety. However, a high level of automation in the future would probably require carriers to collaborate with other competitors, especially if they decide to use platooning options (e.g., as there might be connectivity issues if the AVs are not from the same manufacturer), or to join a network within the block-chain. This would add complexity to the overall system and might increase the risk of delays and inefficiencies, which carriers would need to manage and avoid.

4.2 The driver

Under current regulations, a driver is required to operate the vehicle from origin to destination, according to time and cost constraints. In the future, drivers might become operatives doing little or no driving, but continuing to provide administrative tasks (Bakermans, 2016), represent the carrier, provide security for the goods and confirm successful consignment. In the meantime, during the transition period toward higher automation, operatives will likely be asked to use driver-assistance tools or other new technologies to improve the efficiency of the overall transport service. Their willingness to use automation will have an impact on the speed with which AVs will be accepted in the market. This might be influenced by current views, particularly by drivers themselves (but not only), about the impact of AVs on the availability of and nature of driving roles. According to Neuweiler and Riedel (2017), some drivers show a positive attitude toward AVs, especially if they are assumed to be connected to other vehicles, to the infrastructure, or platooned.

4.3 Receivers

In the traditional model of supply to individual consumer households, receivers are usually undertaking commercial retailing activities from store premises and are the destination points of the whole supply chain for traditional commerce (and this is a key distinction with e-commerce, in which other destinations, such us private homes, workplaces, and public-access collection points become the "receivers"). Under this model, receivers place orders and wait for the products to be delivered to the store, with consumers carrying products themselves from the point-of-sale to home. Sometimes receivers can set the delivery time or at least some constraints, depending on the policy of the carrier. Receiver sensitivity to delivery options strongly depends on the type of products. Indeed, they represent the most complicated stakeholders in the urban freight system, as it is quite difficult to design and implement freight policies to influence receivers' behavior (Stathopoulos et al., 2012).

Receivers of the future might be asked to interact with driverless pods or vans using human-machine interfaces. Grosman (2017) argues that the number of stores will reduce, or at least the proportion of trade conducted via traditional shops is reducing due to the increasing growth of e-commerce. However, Savills Commercial Research in their report on the impact of e-commerce on local physical retailing highlight that, despite the challenges to the retail sector from e-commerce, physical stores remain the preferred option for many sectors (e.g., food and grocery—9% of sales online by 2022; health and beauty—expected to stay under 12%). Also, "click and collect" options (from a store) currently accounts for 10.5% of non-store sales, and it is expected to have an annual growth of 9.3% through to 2022, underlying the importance of the presence of physical stores. Nonetheless, stores might evolve into interconnected places where customers may still purchase in a traditional way, but can also attend a themed event, or enjoy an interactive experience using new technologies, so the retail premises are no longer just "stores" of stock, but also points of sale with fulfillment occurring direct to the purchaser's residence. Moreover, the customer service staff who currently act as the receiving agent during a physical consignment to a store might in any case be replaced by robots who assist customers, as currently 67% of consumers prefer self-service options (Grosman, 2017).

4.4 The systems provider

The systems provider is a new type of stakeholder, who will be responsible for the manufacturing, provision, and servicing of automated freight equipment, including "mechatronics," sensors, data-processing hardware, communications hardware for connectivity and the firmware and software that operates and connects the hardware. This category includes developers, manufacturers and providers of automated, connected and electric systems, and may also involve systems for sharing assets. They will have a critical role in supporting the integrated operation of the system, make the difference in terms of efficiency benefits being achieved, including reduction of costs.

4.5 The policymaker

Policymakers stimulate and oversee the design and implementation of new policies and regulations to foster the adoption of new technologies in the freight sector, in line with objectives which, in a democratic context, are typically set or influenced by national and local politicians (e.g., improved air quality, reduced traffic congestion, improved quality of life in urban areas).

For example, considering the promised social benefits due to the adoption of new technologies, and subject to clear evidence of the positive impact on environment and society being provided, policymakers should provide a regulatory scheme to clarify under what operating conditions AV delivery vehicles could circulate in public spaces and on roads.

4.6 Citizens

Local citizen stakeholders, in the context of urban freight, are constituted both by residents of the city in question, as well as those who visit; whether for shopping, education, tourism or work. They are responsible for attracting freight flows in urban areas (e.g., shopping at the shop or e-commerce), and at the same time susceptible to the negative externalities due to urban freight (e.g., increased congestion and pollution, reduced safety). Technological change has also been influencing consumer behavior and customer expectations. For examples, customers can now access product information and purchasing channels at any time with online shopping, while in the past they could visit shops only during opening times. It is also argued that consumers have shown increasing expectations in terms of enjoying a high-value shopping experience (Deloitte, 2018). In this context, automation and machine learning could allow "upskilled" customer engagement staff to deliver innovative tasks, providing a high-quality experience to customers, with a positive impact on productivity and time saving (Deloitte, 2018).

Moreover, in the future, customers might be expected, or have the option, to interact with AV vans or drones in collecting their own purchases, or to share the public space with AV robots. They represent key stakeholders in the urban freight system, and in the uptake of new technologies, as public acceptance and adoption has been widely recognized as a key factor (Paddeu et al., 2019). More specifically, a number of subfactors have been identified as influencing public acceptance and adoption of new technologies, including trust (Carter and Bélanger, 2005; Choi and Ji, 2015; Gefen et al., 2003; Körber et al., 2018; Lee and Moray, 1992; Lee and See, 2004; McKnight et al., 2002; Merritt and Ilgen, 2008; Parasuraman et al., 2008; Pavlou, 2003; Shariff et al., 2017; Siebert et al., 2013), perceived usefulness and safety (Zhang et al., 2019), and social norms (Lee and See, 2004). However, most of the published works focus on automation and new technologies for passengers. More research is needed to understand public perception of new technologies for future urban deliveries.

Fig. 4 summarizes the main stakeholders involved in the urban freight system of the future.

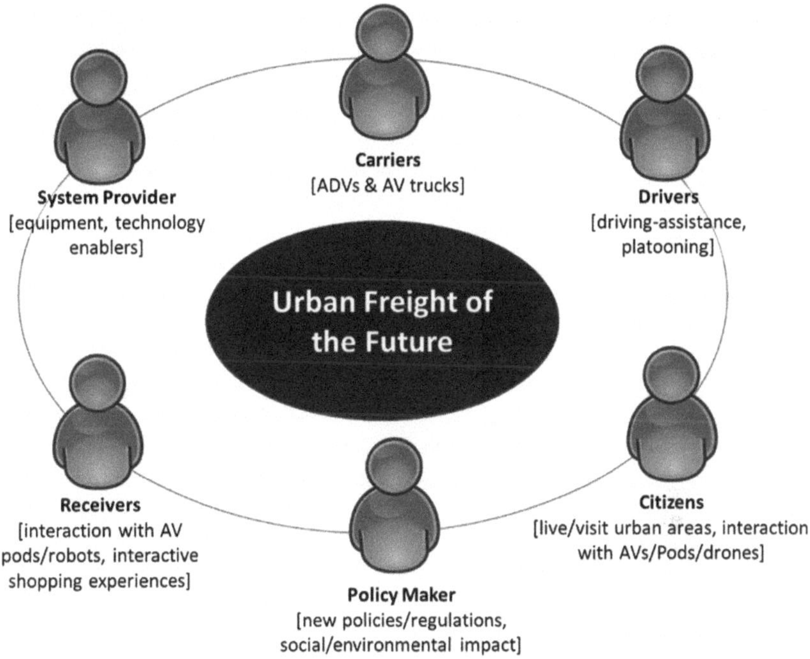

Fig. 4 Main Stakeholders involved in the Urban Freight system of the future.

5. Factors enabling and preventing the adoption of new technologies for urban freight transport

5.1 Enablers

The analysis of the literature review provides some interesting considerations and insights on potential factors that might support or inhibit the implementation of automation in the urban freight sector. In terms of enablers, from a logistics sector perspective, according to Keeney (2017), automation is expected to reduce operating costs in the urban environment. This is due to the combination of electric propulsion, improved driving performance (with a related reduced fuel consumption), and a reduction in personnel costs (i.e., ultimately there might not be the need for a human driver, or perhaps a human presence for loading, security or administrative purposes at all). However, such propositions depend upon future scenarios which draw upon a range of assumptions and hypotheses, which in part are supported by theoretical underpinnings. However, the design of feasible and financially sustainable business models should be based on real and specific evidence of cost reduction, which should be provided through trials and real-world experiments. Given the financial costs and other risks associated with trials and experiments, however, the need for public financial support and public-private relationships to facilitate trials, due to the mutual advantages (e.g., reduced operational costs and reduced environmental impacts), emerge as important.

Another important enabling factor is the use of Information and Communication Technologies (ICTs) to enable and foster data-sharing among different stakeholders across the supply chain, with the aim of improving the overall performance of the chain, including the last mile. The use of ICTs would support inter-modality and city logistics operations (Giannopoulos, 2009), and would foster connectivity for vehicle-to-vehicle and vehicle-to-infrastructure communication with AVs and drones. This can also be related to the concept of the block-chain, which would automatically regulate all the information (and the related physical) flows over the supply chain, improving efficiency of the urban freight system in terms of costs, times, quality, and environmental impact.

5.2 Barriers

Despite the potential benefits due to automation and other new technologies in the urban freight environment, certain barriers could prevent their adoption for urban deliveries. Without a doubt, the lack of specific supporting policies and regulations is a major barrier to their adoption. For example, a specific regulatory framework would be necessary to ensure safety, security, and address responsibility in case of accidents. Such frameworks are only now emerging for vehicle automation in urban areas, but with an emphasis on passenger mobility or freight operations on highways (e.g., International Transport Forum, 2015). Support from the public sector is also needed for the procurement of equipped-roadway infrastructures, necessary to enable CAVs to circulate and communicate under a full implementation of system-managed automation.

Another important barrier is the extent of technological development for AVs and drones. At the moment there is not enough evidence about safety and reliability of high-level (Levels 4 and 5) AVs in the real world (Ginsburg and Uygur, 2017). This implies overall perceived safety concerns that might prevent large-scale adoption in the near future. Opposition from drivers, who are worried about losing their role, is also a major barrier due to the influence they could have in the transition period from lower to higher levels of automation.

Furthermore, the lack of economies of scale might be a major issue, as automation might have a competitive disadvantage in respect to the more traditional urban freight solutions, at least in short run, when overcoming the inertia of established solutions. For example, the high unit costs of 3D printing make it uncompetitive against traditional batch production.

Finally, a major barrier is the lack of collaboration between logistics operators, who are usually not willing to share data on new technologies and operating practices. Policymakers might play a key role in addressing this constraint, as they might support a "fair collaboration" scheme to encourage the logistics sector to work together, pool resources, and share best practice. This would drive behavior change with a related positive impact on the urban freight system.

Fig. 5 summarizes the main drivers and barriers to the implementation of new technologies for the urban freight system of the future.

5.3 Integration of new technologies with existing urban freight solutions

One approach to overcoming the barriers due to inertia in the existing arrangements is to consider how synergies can be achieved by combining automation and other new technologies with existing advanced urban freight solutions, such as urban consolidation centers. Urban freight Consolidation Centres (UCCs) are city logistics solutions designed to mitigate the negative impacts of urban goods distribution (Paddeu, 2017). However, despite a number of benefits arising from UCC adoption (e.g., reduced congestion, pollution and collisions, combined with improved

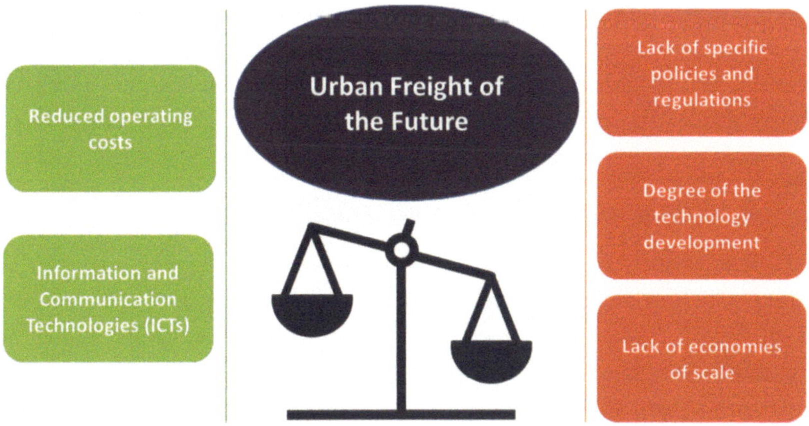

Fig. 5 Factors enabling and impeding the adoption of new technologies for the Urban Freight system of the future.

logistics efficiency), significant issues accrue from their financial un-sustainability, due to the high costs of investment and operations. For this reason, after the "pump-priming" period when public funding is provided to foster its implementation ends, UCCs tend to cease operation (Paddeu, 2017). However, where they can enable cost reductions and efficiency improvements, new technologies might represent a means of improving the successful implementation of UCCs and enabling their longevity. Conversely, the integration of AVs, drones and 3D printing into the UCC might also render the performance of those elements more viable, hence creating synergetic benefits for the overall urban freight system. For example, polluting emissions due to last-mile deliveries could be reduced thanks to electric automated vehicles operating from urban consolidation centers which are optimized for the urban duty cycle and avoiding the need for the electric drive-train to be able to achieve highway-level performance. Driver cost reductions, safety improvements, and reduced delivery bay allocation are also achievable with this system. Local consolidation centers could also host pooled (and varied) 3D printers offering the "nearby" fulfillment of 3D-print-on-demand products, creating economies of scale and offering a level of service not achievable with "on-site" facilities.

Another interesting solution might be the integration of automated delivery systems with the parcel locker or automated delivery station concept, which has been recognized having high potential demand for e-customers (de Oliveira et al., 2017). Online shoppers would collect their own parcels by walking to an automated delivery station and accessing their allocated delivery slot at any time of the day (24/7) using a digital pickup code. According to Orenstein et al. (2019), the use of automated service points would reduce the delivery costs arising from failed deliveries. Such stations might host parcels from different logistics operators and carriers within a shared-station environment, and might be located in a public or private space (e.g., gas stations, parking, shopping center, rail station, etc.).

6. Policy implications and conclusions

The chapter has sought to provide an insight into automated urban freight solutions and an analysis of their potential impact on the future of urban freight. In general, it can be expected that new technologies are promoted according to the extent that they are identified as having a positive impact on at least one of the economy, environment, or society, while not having any serious disbenefits for any of these. In the case of AV technology, claims are made about its benefits for the logistics market and the overall transport system, in terms of safety, reduced congestion, fuel consumption and costs, and increased efficiency and flexibility.

It is also important to note that the new technologies are emerging in a context that is itself evolving. For example, with the rise of e-commerce and deliveries to the home there might be a reduction in personal mobility but at the same time a corresponding increase in (un-optimized) freight trips in urban areas. For this reason, the integration of innovative solutions with existing practices for passengers and freight might have a doubly-positive effect. The overall mobility system could be optimized, with a reduction in inefficiencies (e.g., low occupancy of vehicles) and of overall mobility costs. This might be achieved with shared mobility systems: solutions that require passengers and freight to share the same vehicle in order to maximize the load factor and reduce the number of vehicles in urban areas. At the same time, existing solutions (e.g., urban consolidation center) could benefit from new technologies and automation, as these could improve efficiency and reduce costs with a resulting optimized urban freight system.

However, most of the arguments at this stage are based on logical argument rather than evidence, with consequent uncertainties about whether these benefits will in fact materialize. Given the broad potential benefits combined with uncertain development paths, policymakers are reaffirmed as having an essential role in fostering and managing the introduction of automated freight systems where they bring clear benefits, while at the same time ensuring equity in economic and social terms. Five specific priorities can be identified for policy makers:

(1) *To engage citizens and other "user group" stakeholders in urban revisioning.* In the industrialized democracies at least, a revolutionized urban freight delivery system will only be accepted if it is customized to its users' needs and expectations. Here, it will be fundamental to openly debate the nature of the opportunities: while the intrusion of small electric delivery "bots" might not be welcome to citizens observing the current urban status quo, they might become highly acceptable if part of a policy package of wider-area exclusion of private vehicles, such as in environmental zones to manage air pollution, which then result in far more space for walking, cycling and street activities, with passenger and freight shuttles providing for essential vehicle trips.

(2) *To establish the extent to which relatively high and low technology solutions are appropriate, alone or in combination.* Among the possible solutions are shared passenger/freight local collective services (buses, taxis) which might be automated, but alongside these there also relatively low-technology, low environmental-impact solutions, such as crowd-shipping and e-cargo-bikes. The right combination of such innovations would allow the optimization of the vehicle load during off-peak hours, for example, in order to reduce congestion and air pollution. However, orthodox transport planning generally emphasizes separating freight and passenger flows, and often in practice prioritizes individual, not collective, solutions. The disciplines influencing urban and transport systems would therefore need to be encouraged to evolve in ethos, to embrace shared solutions for the mobility of passengers and freight.

(3) *To develop the regulatory canvas.* Where high-technology solutions are supported, they will require interventions to design and provide specific infrastructures and regulations, e.g., to allow AVs and pods/robots to circulate in public spaces. Specific regulations would be needed to allow drones to fly in the public airspace, due to the high risks in terms of safety and security. Policy makers should develop a strategic plan to steer the adoption of new technologies in the freight sector, which is mostly privately managed and operated, through providing a specific regulatory framework to integrate new technologies with the more traditional ones, whether that prove to be a transition period or permanent "cohabitation."

(4) *To understand how the economic niche of urban freight deliveries fit in with wider emerging socioeconomic change.* Automation is not just a transport and logistics-sector trend; there is a wider socioeconomic context, and in particular great uncertainty about the role of human work as a productive force in the economy, and through remuneration, as a driver of consumption. According to Lawrence et al. (2017), automation will re-shape the labor market as a whole, although freight transport and storage are the sectors that will be most affected by automation. This identifies automation as a major influence on future socio-economic inequalities, as employees may find themselves out of work, or required to acquire new knowledge and skills, with those less-well educated generally being more likely to be affected by the rise of automated systems. On this basis, in countries such as India it has already been argued that highly automated vehicles are inappropriate for its development path (Das Gupta, 2017). In the highly industrialized states, in the absence of a new "social contract," a significant "backlash" could in fact occur. However, emerging high-technology solutions might drive the establishment of new businesses and new business models that would be adapted to the market conditions. Such development might underpin the emergence of new jobs. Policy makers need to be informed about the real prospects for the extent and scope of the future labor market, support education and training to enable people to develop new skills for the emerging working opportunities, but also prepare for more fundamental shifts in socioeconomic relations if paid work opportunities do indeed become scarce.

(5) *To promote responsible innovation and knowledge-sharing.* Underpinning the previous four priorities is a need for to fill significant knowledge gaps with high quality evidence placed clearly in the public domain. Policymakers should invest in research to develop quantitative and qualitative studies into the impact of new technologies on urban freight. They should cautiously consider the actual potential benefits of new technologies for sustainable urban freight in a holistic sense, by means of funding for innovative trials and pilot projects, to be subject to careful monitoring and evaluation, and the commissioning of objective and realistic assessments of risk to ensure technological change is accompanied by further enhancements in public security and safety.

Acknowledgments

Collation and collection of the data and information drawn upon for the present chapter was supported from two sources. The authors would like to thank the UK Government Office for Science for funding the evidence review "New Technology and Automation in Freight Transport and Handling Systems" (Paddeu et al., 2019) and the UWE Bristol Vice Chancellor's Early Career Researcher Fund for supporting the "Innovative and Collaborative Solutions to shape Freight Transport Systems of the Future: a Co-design Process" project. The authors benefitted from membership of the European Commission-funded Cost Action (CA16222) "Wider Impacts and Scenario Evaluation of Autonomous and Connected Transport" network in developing the paper. The authors also express thanks to the participants of the workshops for their time and insights.

References

Alessandrini, A., Campagna, A., Delle Site, P., Filippi, F., Persia, L., 2015. Automated vehicles and the rethinking of mobility and cities. Transp. Res. Proc. 5, 145–160.

Angelovska, N., 2018. Europe's Leading and Lagging Countries in E-Commerce. Forbes, 11/10/2018. Available at: https://www.forbes.com/sites/ninaangelovska/2018/10/11/europes-leading-and-lagging-countries-in-ecommerce/#626199c36c77. [Accessed: June 2019].

Bakermans, B.A., 2016. Truck Platooning: Enablers, Barriers, Potential and Impacts. Master's thesis, TU Delft [online]. Available at: https://repository.tudelft.nl/islandora/object/uuid%3A3e4e265b-b84c-474b-85b9-9840a5c85464. [June, 2019].

Carter, L., Bélanger, F., 2005. The utilization of e-government services: citizen trust, innovation and acceptance factors. Inf. Syst. J. 15, 5–25.

Choi, J.K., Ji, Y.G., 2015. Investigating the importance of trust on adopting an autonomous vehicle. Int. J. Hum. Comput. Interact. 31 (10), 692–702.

D'Andrea, R., 2014. Can drones deliver? IEEE Trans. Autom. Sci. Eng. 11, 647–648.

Das Gupta, M., 2017. Won't Allow Driverless Cars That Take Away Jobs: Nitin Gadkari. Hindustan Times. July 25, 2017. https://www.hindustantimes.com/india-news/won-t-allow-driverless-cars-that-take-away-jobs-says-union-minister-nitin-gadkari/story-JCDjBMoDQ4yzXrWv3ltxsK.html. (Accessed 24 June 2019).

de Oliveira, L.K., Morganti, E., Dablanc, L., de Oliveira, R.L.M., 2017. Analysis of the potential demand of automated delivery stations for e-commerce deliveries in Belo Horizonte, Brazil. Res. Transp. Econ. 65, 34–43.

Deloitte, 2018. The Deloitte Consumer Review. Digital Predictions 2018. March 2018. Available at: https://www2.deloitte.com/content/dam/Deloitte/uk/Documents/consumer-business/deloitte-uk-consumer-review-digital-predictions-2018.pdf [Accessed: June 2019].

DHL, 2014. Logistics Trend Radar: Delivering Insight Today. Creating Value Tomorrow. DHL Customer Solutions & Innovation, Troisdorf, Germany.

FURBOT, 2014. FURBOT Project Brochure [Online]. Available at: http://www.furbot.eu/Pdf%20docs/Brochure%20FURBOT.pdf. [Accessed: May, 2019].

Gefen, D., Karahanna, E., Straub, D.W., 2003. Trust and TAM in online shopping: an integrated model. MIS Q. 27, 51–90.

Gevaers, R., Van de Voorde, E., Vanelslander, T., 2014. Cost modelling and simulation of last-mile characteristics in an innovative B2C supply chain environment with implications on urban areas and cities. Procedia Soc. Behav. Sci. 125, 398–411.

Giannopoulos, G.A., 2009. Towards a European ITS for freight transport and logistics: results of current EU funded research and prospects for the future. Eur. Transp. Res. Rev. 1 (4), 147–161.

Ginsburg, R., Uygur, A.R., 2017. Changing Technology in Transportation: Automated Vehicles in Freight. Report for Illinois Department of Transportation [online]. Available at: https://utc.uic.edu/wp-content/uploads/Automated-Vehicles-inFreight__Final-Report-08312017.pdf. [Accessed: December 2017].

Goodchild, A., Toy, J., 2018. Delivery by drone: an evaluation of unmanned aerial vehicle technology in reducing CO_2 emissions in the delivery service industry. Transp. Res. Part D Transp. Environ. 61, 58–67.

Grosman, L., 2017. The Future of Retail: How We'll Be Shopping in 10 Years. Forbes (June, 20, 2017). Available at: https://www.forbes.com/sites/forbescommunicationscouncil/2017/06/20/the-future-of-retail-how-well-be-shopping-in-10-years/. [Accessed: June, 2019].

Guerra, E., 2015. Planning for cars that drive themselves: Metropolitan planning organizations, regional transportation plans, and autonomous vehicles. J. Plan. Educ. Res. 36, 1–15. https://doi.org/10.1177/0739456X15613591.

International Transport Forum, 2015. Automated and Autonomous Driving: Regulation under Uncertainty. International Transport Forum (ITF), Paris. Available at: https://www.itf-oecd.org/sites/default/files/docs/15cpb_autonomousdriving.pdf. [Accessed November 2019].

Iwan, S., Kijewska, K., Lemke, J., 2016. Analysis of parcel lockers' efficiency as the last mile delivery solution—the results of the research in Poland. Transp. Res. Proc. 12, 644–655.

Jackson, T., 2017. The Flying Drones That Can Scan Packages Night and Day. BBC News. 27 October [online]. Available at: http://www.bbc.co.uk/news/business-41737300 [January 2018].

Keeney, T., 2016. 3D Printing: A Disruptive Innovation in its Infancy. ARK Invest. Available at: https://research.ark-invest.com/3d-printing-white-paper. [Accessed: May, 2019].

Keeney, T., 2017. Autonomous Electric Trucks Could Disrupt Rail and Transform Logistics. ASK Invest. Available at: https://ark-invest.com/research/autonomous-trucks. [Accessed: June, 2019].

KOL Limited, 2018. UK Ecommerce Growth Trends 2018. Available at: http://www.instantshift.com/2018/05/09/uk-ecommerce-growth-trends-2018-infographic/. [Accessed: June 2019].

Körber, M., Baseler, E., Bengler, K., 2018. Introduction matters: manipulating trust in automation and reliance in automated driving. Appl. Ergon. 66, 18–31.

Korzhenevych, A., Dehnen, N., Bröcker, J., Holtkamp, M., Meier, H., Gibson, G., Cox, V., 2014. Update of the Handbook on External Costs of Transport. European Commission DG MOVE.

Kunze, O., 2016. Replicators, ground drones and crowd logistics a vision of urban logistics in the year 2030. Transp. Res. Proc. 19, 286–299.

Lawrence, M., Roberts, C., King, L., 2017. Managing Automation: Employment, Inequality and Ethics in the Digital Age. Institute for Public Policy Research, London.

Lee, J., Moray, N., 1992. Trust, control strategies and allocation of function in human-machine systems. Ergonomics 35 (10), 1243–1270. https://doi.org/10.1080/00140139208967392.

Lee, J.D., See, K.A., 2004. Trust in automation: designing for appropriate reliance. Hum. Factors 46 (1), 50–80.

McCue, T.J., 2019. Significant 3D Printing Forecast Surges to $35.6 Billion. Forbes, March, 27, 2019. Available at: https://www.forbes.com/sites/tjmccue/2019/03/27/wohlers-report-2019-forecasts-35-6-billion-in-3d-printing-industry-growth-by-2024/#3123cce27d8a. [Accessed: June 2019].

Mckinnon, A.C., 2016. The possible impact of 3D printing and drones on last-mile logistics: an exploratory study. Built Environ. 2 (4), 617–629.

McKnight, D.H., Choudhury, V., Kacmar, C., 2002. The impact of initial consumer trust on intentions to transact with a web site: a trust building model. J. Strateg. Inf. Syst. 11 (3–4), 297–323.

Merritt, S.M., Ilgen, D.R., 2008. Not all trust is created equal: dispositional and history-based trust in human-automation interactions. Hum. Factors 50 (2), 194–210.

Neuweiler, L., Riedel, P.V., 2017. Autonomous Driving in the Logistics Industry: A Multi-Perspective View on Self-driving Trucks, Changes in Competitive Advantages and Their Implications. Jönköping University International Business School.

Office for National Statistics, 2019. The Probability of Automation in England: 2011 and 2017. Accessed 24/06/2019: https://www.ons.gov.uk/employmentandlabourmarket/peopleinwork/employmentandemployeetypes/articles/theprobabilityofautomationinengland/2011and2017.

Orenstein, I., Raviv, T., Sadan, E., 2019. Flexible parcel delivery to automated parcel lockers: models, solution methods and analysis. EURO J. Transp. Logist. 8 (5), 683–711.

Paddeu, D., 2017. The Bristol-Bath freight consolidation centre: analysis of impacts from the perspective of its users. Case Stud. Transp. Policy 5 (3), 483–491.

Paddeu, D., Calvert, T., Clark, B., Parkhurst, G., 2019. New Technology and Automation in Freight Transport and Handling Systems. Available at: https://assets.publishing.service.gov.uk/government/uploads/system/uploads/attachment_data/file/781295/automation_in_freight.pdf. [Accessed: June, 2019].

Parasuraman, R., Sheridan, T.B., Wickens, C.D., 2008. Situation awareness, mental workload, and trust in automation: viable, empirically supported cognitive engineering constructs. J. Cogn. Eng. Decis. Mak. 2, 140–160.

Pavlou, P.A., 2003. Consumer acceptance of electronic commerce: integrating trust and risk with the technology acceptance model. Int. J. Electron. Commer. 7, 101–134.

Priemus, H., Nijkamp, P., Konings, J.W., 2005. The Future of Automated Freight Transport: Concepts, Design and Implementation. Edward Elgar. ISBN 1845422392, 9781845422394.

Shariff, A., Bonnefon, J.F., Rahwan, I., 2017. Psychological roadblocks to the adoption of self-driving vehicles. Nat. Hum. Behav. 1 (10), 694.
Shladover, S., 2017. Connected and automated vehicle policy development for California. Policy Briefs 2017 (03), 1–17.
Siebert, F.W., Oehl, M., Höger, R., Pfister, H.-R., 2013. Discomfort in automated driving: the disco-scale. In: Stephanidis, C. (Ed.), Communications in Computer and Information Science. HCI International 2013—Posters' Extended Abstracts: International Conference. In: vol. 374. Springer, Berlin, pp. 337–341. https://doi.org/10.1007/978-3-642-39476-8_69.
STARSHIP, 2018. Press [online]. Available at: https://www.starship.xyz/news/.
Stathopoulos, A., Valeri, E., Marcucci, E., 2012. Stakeholder reactions to urban freight policy innovation. J. Transp. Geogr. 22, 34–45.
Taniguchi, E., Thompson, R.G. (Eds.), 2014. City Logistics: mapping the Future. CRC Press.
Wadud, Z., 2017. Fully automated vehicles: a cost of ownership analysis to inform early adoption. Transp. Res. A Policy Pract. 101, 163–176.
Whitlock, C., 2014. When drones fall from the sky. Washington Post. 20 June [online]. Available at: http://www.washingtonpost.com/sf/investigative/2014/06/20/when-drones-fall-fromthe-sky/?utm_term=.f46983fad8a7. [January 2018].
Zhang, T., Tao, D., Qu, X., Zhang, X., Lin, R., Zhang, W., 2019. The roles of initial trust and perceived risk in public's acceptance of automated vehicles. Transp. Res. Part C Emerg. Technol. 98, 207–220.

Further reading

Flämig, H., 2016. Autonomous vehicles and autonomous driving in freight transport. In: Maurer, M., Gerdes, J.C., Lenz, B., Winner, H. (Eds.), Autonomous Driving. Springer, Berlin and Heidelberg, pp. 365–385.
Savills Commercial Research, 2018. Retail Revolutions. Exploring the Impact of E-Commerce on Local Physical Retailing. Retail 2018. Available at: https://pdf.euro.savills.co.uk/uk/commercial-retail-uk/retail-revolutions-ecommerce-and-local-physical-retailing.pdf. [Accessed: June 2019].
Society of Automotive Engineers International (SAE), 2014. Taxonomy and Definitions for Terms Related to On-Road Motor Vehicle Automated Driving Systems J3016_201401. Available at: https://www.sae.org/standards/content/j3016_201401/. [Accessed: May, 2019].

CHAPTER THIRTEEN

Overall synthesis and conclusions

Bert van Wee[a,*], Dimitris Milakis[b], Nikolas Thomopoulos[c]
[a]Faculty of Technology, Policy and Management, Delft University of Technology, Delft, The Netherlands
[b]Institute of Transport Research, German Aerospace Center (DLR), Berlin, Germany
[c]Department of Tourism and Transport, School of Hospitality and Tourism Management, University of Surrey, Guildford, United Kingdom
*Corresponding author: e-mail address: g.p.vanwee@tudelft.nl

Contents

Abstract

This chapter first systematically summarizes the most important findings and policy implications of each of the chapters included in this book volume. Next it synthesizes the overall findings and policy implications, and discusses future avenues for policy making and research. A first conclusion is that the chapters make clear that the ranges in policy relevant implications of AVs, within the scope of each chapter/topic, are still relatively broad. Secondly we conclude that research that is conceptually rich is more valuable for policy making. Thirdly we hypothesize that context matters for the uptake, impacts, and specific system design characteristics of real world AV implementation. Fourth we conclude that research on the global south has been limited so far. Fifth we argue that AVs, shared vehicles and electric vehicles (EVs) might stimulate each other in a positive way, in all directions. Finally we conclude that AVs will have wider societal implications, such as in the area of land use, accessibility, social exclusion, governmental expenditures, the labor market, and the environment. The more indirect the effects of AVs are, the more difficult they are to understand. For policy making a first conclusion is that the issues of ethics, cyber security and data protection deserve way more attention than they currently get. We also conclude that future motorway network extensions might not be no-regret anymore, because of possible congestion reductions due to AVs, but also because of decreasing marginal values of time. Finally we argue that countries that introduce AVs later than other countries can learn a lot from the real world experiences elsewhere.

Keywords: Autonomous vehicles, Synthesis, Policy, Summary

Advances in Transport Policy and Planning, Volume 5
ISSN 2543-0009
https://doi.org/10.1016/bs.atpp.2020.06.001

1. Introduction

This chapter first systematically summarizes the most important findings and policy implications of each of the chapters "Factors affecting traffic flow efficiency implications of connected and autonomous vehicles: A review and policy recommendations" by Narayanan et al.; "Automated bus systems in Europe: A systematic review of passenger experience and road user interaction" by Heikoop et al.; "Cyber security and its impact on CAV safety: Overview, policy needs and challenges" by Katrakazas et al.; "Cybersecurity certification and auditing of automotive industry" by Mateo Sanguino et al.; "The wider use of autonomous vehicles in non-commuting journeys" by Kimber et al.; "Policy implications of the potential carbon dioxide (CO_2) emission and energy impacts of highly automated vehicles" by Annema; "Potential health and well-being implications of autonomous vehicles" by Singleton et al.; "Data protection in a GDPR era: An international comparison of implications for autonomous vehicles" by Costantini et al.; "Ethical issues concerning automated vehicles and their implications for transport" by Dogan et al.; "Governance cultures and sociotechnical imaginaries of self-driving vehicle technology: Comparative analysis of Finland, UK and Germany" by Mladenović et al.; "Wider implications of autonomous vessels for the maritime industry: Mapping the unprecedented challenges" by Ghaderi; "The potential for automation to transform urban deliveries: Drivers, barriers and policy priorities" by Paddeu and Parkhurst. Next it synthesizes the overall findings and policy implications, and discusses future avenues for policy making and research. Table 1 gives an overview of the results and policy implications per chapter.

Table 1 shows that most chapters are based on systematic non-country specific literature reviews. In addition, all chapters do not only have clear conclusions, they also discuss policy implications. When we started the initiative to edit this book, we were a bit uncertain about the viability of all chapters we would like to include. Despite the fact that the attention paid to AVs started booming only about a decade ago (see, for example, the reference list of Milakis et al. (2017) or of the chapters in this book), we are very glad we now can conclude that the authors were able to review the literature on so many different aspects, and write a chapter that survived the review process.

Table 1 Overview of the results and policy implications per chapter.

Chapter	Topic	Review method	Country	Conclusions	Policy implications
Short-term implications of AVs					
1	Traffic flow efficiency	Systematic review of academic literature	Non-Specific	Four categories of factors influencing traffic flow are identified: (i) Vehicle characteristics, (ii) Travel behavior, (iii) Network characteristics and (iv) Policies. The expected impacts of AVs on the roadway capacity are found to be not at all unanimous, not only because of different assumptions with respect to these factors, but also because of differences in modeling conditions	Policy makers should enact laws to ensure connectivity between AVs to experience significant benefits, integrate CAVs with public transport to avoid mode shifts, incentivize ridesharing to reduce network load, develop suitable parking management policies to avoid empty relocations and introduce congestion pricing to curb induced demand
2	Humans-automated bus systems interaction	Systematic review of academic literature	Non-Specific	Public acceptance of automated bus systems is generally positive. People appear to have a high level of trust in the automated bus system. Questionnaires are the most used means of method for conducting experiments in relation to user acceptance or satisfaction. An important gap in literature is the lack of objective measures used for the assessment of human interaction with automated bus systems	AVs are not prepared and will not respond appropriately when other road users deviate from the formal rules. The general wait-and-see attitude of planners need to change into a more proactive approach from public planners and authorities when deploying AVs such as automated bus systems are implemented in real-life traffic
3	Cybersecurity and safety	Systematic review of academic literature	Non-Specific	Current solutions are solely concerned either with collisions and casualties or with the prevention of cyber-attacks with regards to both hardware and software issues. Thus, there is still not a reported strong correlation between cyber security breaches and the potential decrease in road safety levels	The evolution of an international collaborative directory linking cybersecurity liabilities with passenger and traffic safety concerns is suggested. A lot more AV miles need to be self-driven until such an international agreement is reached

Continued

Table 1 Overview of the results and policy implications per chapter.—cont'd

Chapter	Topic	Review method	Country	Conclusions	Policy implications
4	Cybersecurity Certification and Auditing	Systematic review of academic literature	Non-Specific	The risk of adding automation to vehicles has not been properly understood by car manufacturers in the past and it is a serious problem just as the insecure vehicular connectivity is being addressed nowadays. Most cars use components that are based on old hardware and software developed years ago and with basic flaws inherent to design, so errors and vulnerabilities are transferred to these new generation of vehicles	Cybercrime as a Service (CaaS) could generate millions in losses to the automotive industry, justifying new approaches of cybersecurity applied to the automobile industry, which must be flexible and adaptive along the production chain and the lifetime of CAVs. A collaborative approach in the automotive industry may be required to overcome the investments in time, money and broader organizational changes
5	Non-commuting journeys	PRISMA	Non-Specific	Public interest in AVs for leisure might exceed that for commuting while sharing might be less likely for AVs non-commuting journeys. Some non-commuting journeys will require a lower level of automation. Non-commuting journeys by AVs could involve spatial impacts	Increased policy attention to non-commuting journeys in the AVs context including Global South is required. Policy and regulation should focus on preserving equity, privacy and safety for shared AVs serving leisure travel and promoting infrastructure changes needed as a response to the spatio-temporal patterns of leisure activities
Long-term implications of AVs					
6	Carbon dioxide (CO2) emissions and energy	Review of academic literature	Non-Specific	The net energy and CO_2 emission balance for AVs seems, at its best, to be neutral, but is probably negative. However, the potentially accelerating role of AVs in relation to the uptake of electric vehicles could have the biggest impact on the CO_2 emissions per kilometer driven, but this accelerating role in the uptake of electric technology remains uncertain	Policies promoting alternative vehicle propulsion systems other than fossil fuel technologies seem most effective at the moment. Additional measures such as energy taxes, AV maximum speed limits as well as policies to curb the growth of VKTs could put in place to ensure further energy and emissions related benefits as soon as the adoption of electric AVs progresses

Table 1 Overview of the results and policy implications per chapter.—cont'd

Chapter	Topic	Review method	Country	Conclusions	Policy implications
7	Health and well-being	Deductive approach	Non-Specific	AVs are likely to have overall positive impacts on some health and well-being aspects (safety, travel satisfaction, access to activities) and overall negative impacts on others (physical activity), while effects are more uncertain for other topics (urban built environments, air and noise pollution). An evolving systems approach to explore the multitude of potential impacts of AVs on health and well-being is proposed	Policy measures should try to limit the possible negative effects of AVs on health and well-being, such as reduced physically-active travel (e.g., through improved infrastructure for cyclists and pedestrians) and increased vehicle-distances traveled (e.g., focusing on provisions for active travel rather than placing high hopes on shared AVs which may also be associated with increased distances traveled) and urban sprawl (e.g., through compact and mixed-use neighborhoods)
8	Data protection	Mapping review of legal frameworks and regulations, experts survey	Austria, Brazil, Greece, Italy, New Zealand, Slovakia and Switzerland	Data management and protection of AV data is still at a nascent stage	Collaboration among stakeholders and countries (e.g., development of "regulatory sandboxes"). Regulatory attention to (a) the capability to "re-identify" originally anonymous data through AI or Big Data, (b) the legal status of such artificial agents
9	Ethics	Review of academic literature and policy reports	Non-Specific	Most research focuses on the decisions of AV in critical, forced-choice situations. Philosophical theories (e.g., consequentialism and utilitarianism, deontology, contractarianism and randomness theory) provide some answers but they raise others questions as well	Ordinary situations(e.g., following distance, brake strategies, lateral position within the lane, permitting violations)would require more guidelines and policy making, rather than highly improbable and uncertain unavoidable accidents. Policy makers should take into account ethical aspects of technology implementation, such as justice, autonomy, equity, and the democratic ideal of participation in the decision making about integration of the AV technology into the society

Continued

Table 1 Overview of the results and policy implications per chapter.—cont'd

Chapter	Topic	Review method	Country	Conclusions	Policy implications
10	Governance of AVs	Policy documents review	Finland, UK, and Germany	All three countries (Finland, UK, and Germany) think that AVs should contribute to the national economic growth. The UK and German positions AVs in the context of global leadership in technological development. Governance do not see citizens as equal partners in steering technological futures, but only as an actor that can potentially resist new technology. Consequently technological development is not based on the democratic enhancement of dialogue between state and society	The governance challenge centers around the understanding that technology is not a neutral and default-positive actant, and thus technological development is irreducibly a political and value-driven choice rather than an instrumental facilitation of what is an inevitable (automated) future. Three different types of technological determinism are identified: justificatory, methodological, and normative. Each of these types of technological determinism bring about a challenge for transparency, accountability, and responsiveness mechanisms in technological governance processes
Implications of AVs for the maritime and freight industry					
11	Maritime industry	Review of academic literature and overview of key maritime projects	Non-Specific	Autonomous ships will have vertical and horizontal effects on other supply chain players, such as ports, shipbuilding, and insurance. Existing research promises economic and financial benefits for shipping companies, yet some cost elements may transfer to upstream and/or downstream actors in the supply chain	There is a need to focus on the co-ordination of regulations and standards internationally, while supporting workforce training to develop new skills in demand. All stakeholders need to be taken into account when evaluating deployment of autonomous vessels, safeguarding that appropriate mechanisms exist to compensate losers through the gains of winners

Table 1 Overview of the results and policy implications per chapter.—cont'd

Chapter	Topic	Review method	Country	Conclusions	Policy implications
12	Urban deliveries	International overview of technologies, review of key stakeholders role, stakeholders workshops	Non-Specific	Despite the potential importance of automation for improving the efficiency and competitiveness of the urban freight sector, research evidence gaps exist related to the identification of competitive advantages for these new technologies, micro and macro-economic benefits, and the costs of those developments. Concerns related to introduction of automation technologies in urban freight also include low co-ordination levels among stakeholders, low load factors, short term cost increases, employment implications and urban planning issues such as sharing of public space, as well as privacy, safety and security	Policymakers should promote introduction of automated freight systems where they bring clear benefits, while at the same time ensuring equity in economic and social terms. Five specific priorities can be identified for policy makers: (1)To engage citizens and other "user group" stakeholders in urban revisioning, (2) To establish the extent to which relatively high and low technology solutions are appropriate, individually or in combination, (3) To develop the regulatory canvas, (4) To understand how the economic niche of urban freight deliveries fits in with wider emerging socioeconomic change, and (5) To promote responsible innovation and knowledge-sharing

2. Overall synthesis and conclusions

Looking at the conclusions and policy implications of Table 1 a few general lessons can be learned. Starting with the research findings, the chapters make clear that the ranges in policy relevant implications of AVs, within the scope of each chapter / topic, are still relatively broad. A first reason for the wide range is the differences in the scope and demarcation of the studies reviewed. Take the impact of AVs on CO_2 emissions and road capacity as examples: it really matters if studies only include the impact of AVs on speed and distances between vehicles, or also include induced demand and changes in mode choice (from public transport and active modes to AVs).But even if the scope and demarcation is equal, estimates on impacts vary a lot, which is understandable because AVs at SAE levels 4 and 5 are not on the roads yet, so researchers cannot measure real world impacts, and have to rely on other methodologies to derive estimates. Research that is conceptually rich is more valuable for policy making. With "conceptually rich" we mean that it includes more relevant (clusters of) variables, and both direct and indirect relationships between (clusters of) variables. Policy makers need to be well informed about expected effects, including all factors and relationships influencing these effects. Future research aiming to estimate societally and policy relevant impacts of AVs therefore, preferably includes all dominant factors and interrelationships. Secondly, we hypothesize that context matters for the uptake, impacts, and specific system design characteristics of real world AV implementation. Take, for example, the more anti—government sentiments in the USA compared to most European countries. This could influence the support of the public for *cooperative* AV systems—such support probably is higher in European countries than in the USA. Another example: income levels influence the willingness to pay for travel time savings (e.g., Lam and Small, 2001) and probably also the willingness to pay for AVs: people with higher incomes are probably not only willing to pay more for travel time savings but also for AVs. So, in countries with lower incomes fewer people could be willing to pay for AVs. Such important concerns only started being addressed in 2019 via, e.g., the WISE-ACT multinational survey about AV user preferences and similar activities worldwide are essential to inform policy makers. The impacts of context factors on the design characteristics, implication options, and societally relevant effects therefore are a next promising research topic that deserves more attention. Third, and as a special case of topic 2, the chapters show that the focus in research on the global south has been limited so far. Especially because of the importance of context conclusions that hold for the global North do not necessarily apply for the global south (Thomopoulos and Nikitas, 2019).

Extending the scope from AVs only to their position in the transport system, there is an increasing awareness that AVs, shared vehicles and electric vehicles (EVs) might stimulate each other in a positive way, in all directions, as conceptualized in Fig. 1, at least as far as cars are concerned (e.g., Webb, 2019). Below we limit the discussion on these interactions to cars. Sharing can include both sharing cars as well as sharing rides. In the following discussion, we limit ourselves to sharing cars (or other small vehicles, like minibuses). AVs will make sharing vehicles more attractive and vice versa because AVs will likely be more expensive than conventional

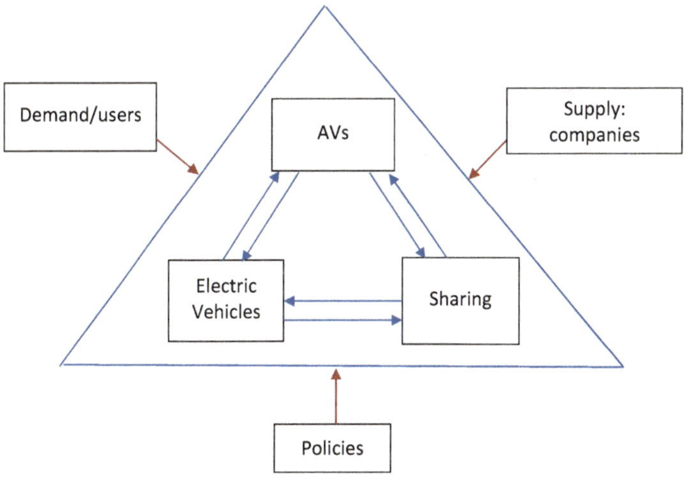

Fig. 1 Interactions between AVs, electric vehicles and sharing.

cars, and sharing reduces the (fixed) costs. And the combination of AVs and sharing will increase the market share of electric vehicles because people can use shared electric AVs for most of their trips at a lower cost because of the lower operation costs of such vehicles (Annema, 2020) and use internal combustion engine vehicles for only those trips for which the range limitations of EVs are problematic. EVs might stimulate sharing, at least as long as purchase costs of EVs (especially with a long range) are higher, again because sharing can decrease the fixed costs of cars. The links between AVs and EVs are a bit less obvious, but it could be that the status of cars becomes less important if people cannot drive their car anymore, so that for people who think AVs provide a lower status than a conventional car, that negative aspect of EVs might reduce. And vice versa: if people own an EV providing them less status, the barrier of being driven in an AV, and drive oneself might be reduced. In addition, speeding becomes impossible, while driving cycles and energy recovery is optimized in case of AVs (Annema, 2020), so the strong range penalty for EVs is diminished. Fig. 1 also makes clear that the way AVs, EVs, and sharing interact, depends on policies (fiscal incentives, infrastructure provision, regulations for vehicle types), on activities of companies (developing AVs, EVs, and sharing services) and on users/consumers who buy or share and use vehicles. Many research challenges relate to the complex relationships as conceptualized in Fig. 1.

Extending the scope to beyond the transport system, it is clear that AVs will have wider societal implications, such as in the area of land use, accessibility, social exclusion, governmental expenditures, the labor market, and the environment. The more indirect the effects of AVs are, the more difficult they are to understand. This because the impacts on the transport system need to be understood first, and these are already uncertain, and next the wider impacts need to be understood, adding more uncertainty. Yet, understanding the wider impacts of AVs on society is extremely relevant for policy making.

We now continue this chapter by focusing on policy making. Policy makers can guide the transport related developments and also these wider developments to some extent so that they work out in a societal desirable way. Although we cannot precisely predict which policies each government agency should implement in each geographical context and when, we briefly reflect subsequently on some of the roles of policy.

First, we argue that "wait and see" can be a good strategy for some possible implications of AVs, but not for all. We now reflect on what policy makers could or even should do in the short term (the coming few years), the medium term (up to 10 years) and the long term (>10 years). In the short term, the issues of cyber security and data protection deserve way more attention than they currently get, in case of cyber security at least of the automotive industry, probably also of public bodies, in case of data protection of public and next private bodies. Also ethical issues, particularly those focusing on ordinary situations, deserve attention before the (large scale) introduction of level 4 and 5 vehicles. Next, involving citizens in shaping the future of AVs deserves more attention than it currently gets, since this is the core of the demand side (Fig. 1). Regardless of the topic, for reasons of efficiency and avoiding border issues, interstate or international collaboration with respect to policy making is to be preferred in many cases. Regarding the global maritime industry, international public bodies should by default take the lead in the process of future automation because vessels travel between countries and world regions, thus highlighting the need for even intercontinental policy making collaboration.

Extending the time horizon a bit further, say the next decade, an important lesson is that in developed countries with more or less complete motorway networks, future motorway network extensions might not be no-regret anymore. Many regions and countries face a diminishing population growth, if not: a decline in population. Car ownership levels seem to be not very far from saturation. If there are no (major) missing links, future extensions of motorways mainly aim to reduce congestion. But if car ownership does not increase substantially, and if more people can avoid the rush hours because they can work online as widely proven during the COVID-19 restrictions, the costs of motorway extensions may exceed the benefits. AVs could further strengthen this process, first of all because they may reduce congestion levels (despite induced demand) and secondly they will reduce peoples' willingness to pay for travel time reductions (Zhong et al., 2020) because of the possibilities for other categories of time use in AVs.

On the longer term, it is important to realize that the introduction of SAE level 4 and 5 vehicles will not happen at the same moment in time across the world and the transition to AVs will vary widely. So, countries that introduce AVs later than other countries can learn a lot from the real world experiences elsewhere. We expect research and business interest on the many effects of AVs to boom after their widespread real world introduction. Respecting the differences in context as addressed above, we do think that many lessons can be learned, in many areas, such as the process of decision making, acceptance and acceptability, the pros and cons of design alternatives, the societally relevant implications of AVs (accessibility, safety, security, the environment, land use, impacts on other modes), and the evaluation of policy alternatives (including all relevant effects, but also fairness issues). So, learning from real world experiences it is both a very important topic for research as well as for policy making and AV trials pave the way in this respect.

We conclude that it is still unclear how autonomous vehicles will shape the future of transport systems, and what the policy relevant effects of AVs will be. But it is clear that the role of AVs in the vehicle fleets will have many policy relevant implications, some of which did not receive a lot of attention by policy makers yet. On the other hand, policy makers can also influence the uptake of AV. With this book, we review the AV literature on a wide range of topics. We hope it provides a source of inspiration for researchers, policy makers, and planners.

References

Annema, J.A., 2020. Policy implications of the potential carbon dioxide (CO2) emission and energy impacts of highly automated vehicles. In: Milakis, D., Thomopoulos, N., van Wee, B. (Eds.), Policy Implications of Autonomous Vehicles. Elsevier, The Netherlands, pp. 149–162.

Lam, T.C., Small, K.A., 2001. The value of time and reliability: measurement from a value pricing experiment. Transport. Res. E-Log. 37 (2–3), 231–251.

Milakis, D., van Arem, B., van Wee, B., 2017. Policy and society related implications of automated driving: a review of literature and directions for future research. J. Intell. Transp. Syst. 21 (4), 324–348.

Thomopoulos, N., Nikitas, A., 2019. Smart urban mobility futures, editorial. Int. J. Automot. Technol. Manag. 19 (1/2), 1–9.

Webb, J., 2019. The future of transport: literature review and overview. Econ. Anal. Policy 61, 1–6.

Zhong, H., Li, W., Burris, M.W., Talebpour, A., Sinha, K.C., 2020. Will autonomous vehicles change auto commuters' value of travel time? Transp. Res. Part D: Transp. Environ. 83, 102303.

Kolibri 360 GmbH
Ferdinand-Jühlke-Straße 7
99095 Erfurt, Deutschland
produktsicherheit@kolibri360.de